WOMEN *of* SUFISM

May the Stories of this book
be a Source of Strength
& Inspiration
& May we Stand together
In light

Azadeh
Spring 2021

OTHER BOOKS BY CAMILLE ADAMS HELMINSKI

Rumi Daylight, A Daybook of Spiritual Guidance
MEVLANA JALALUDDIN RUMI
Selected and translated by Camille and Kabir Helminski, 1990

Jewels of Remembrance: A Daybook of Spiritual Guidance
MEVLANA JALALUDDIN RUMI
Selected and translated by Camille and Kabir Helminski, 1996

Awakened Dreams
AHMET HILMI
Translated by Refik Algan and Camille Helminski, 1993

Happiness without Death, Desert Hymns
ASSAD ALI
Translated by Camille and Kabir Helminski and
Dr. Ibrahim Al-Shihabi, 1991

Mevlevi Ayins
Translated by Refik Algan and Camille Helminski, 1997

The Light of Dawn: A Daybook of Verses from the Holy Qur'an
Selected and rendered by Camille Adams Helminski, 1998

The Mevlevi Wird: The Prayers Recited Daily by Mevlevi Dervishes
Translation Offered by Camille Helminski, with assistance from
Cuneyt Eroglu, Mahmoud Mostafa, and Amer Latif, 2000

WOMEN *of* SUFISM

A Hidden Treasure

WRITINGS AND STORIES OF
MYSTIC POETS, SCHOLARS & SAINTS

SELECTED & INTRODUCED BY
Camille Adams Helminski

SHAMBHALA *Boulder* 2003

Shambhala Publications, Inc.
4720 Walnut Street
Boulder, Colorado 80301
www.shambhala.com

14 13 12 11 10 9 8 7

Printed in the United States of America

♾ This edition is printed on acid-free paper that meets the American National Standards Institute z39.48 Standard.
♻ Shambhala Publications makes every effort to print on recycled paper. For more information please visit www.shambhala.com.
Shambhala Publications is distributed worldwide by Penguin Random House, Inc., and its subsidiaries.

Chapter heading ornaments courtesy of Gulben Efe
Designed by Lora Zorian

LIBRARY OF CONGRESS CATALOGING-IN-PUBLICATION DATA
Women of Sufism: a hidden treasure/selected and edited by Camille Adams Helminski
p. cm.
Includes bibliographical references.
ISBN 978-1-57062-967-9
1. Sufis—Biography. 2. Muslim women—Biography.
I. Helminski, Camille Adams, 1951–
BP189.4 .W66 2003
297.4'092'2—dc21
2002008067

DEDICATED

To my sisters in spirit and in blood,
Marian and Anne, my mother, Mimi,
and the mothers, sisters, and friends
who preceded us and those who accompany us,
to my Godmothers, Carolyn Fox and Dolly Ann Tyler
and her daughter Connie,
to my daughter, Carolyn Grace;
and my nieces, Mira and Usha,
to my Goddaughter Alex and her sisters Tyler and Ashley,
and the many daughters and friends who will follow us,
to those mentioned here and those who remain nameless
who carried the Light of Divine Presence
and will continue to carry it,
to those who stand witness at the Threshold of both worlds
that in the end are One
in acknowledgment of the infinitude of sustenance that comes
from our Most Generous and Gracious Sustainer.

Whenever Zachariah visited her in the sanctuary,
he found her provided with food. He would ask,
"O Mary, from where did this come to you?"
She would answer: "It is from God;
see how God grants sustenance to whom He/She wills,
beyond all reckoning."

—Qur'an, Surah 'Imran 3:37

Contents

Preface

*I was a Hidden Treasure and I loved to be known,
so I created the two worlds in order that My treasoure
of lovingkindness and generosity might be known.*

—Hadith Qudsi

Many years ago, the impulse arose to gather material about women who have followed the Way of Sufism, the mystical heart of Islam. Being a woman on the Sufi Path myself, I had become aware of how little was available either in current example or in historical notation about women who had matured in this Way. The search began, to understand more myself, and to discover stories of women that could be shared. Since that first impulse, eighteen years ago now, much has unfolded. Manuscripts once thought lost, such as as-Sulami's biography of Sufi women, have resurfaced and in recent years new research has also been made available. The pile in my study of references, stories, and writings of experience of women on this Way has grown over the years, until now the moment of birthing of this book has arrived with the gracious help of Our Most Generous Sustainer, and of many women and men for whose efforts in sharing these stories and excerpts I am most grateful. Due to space limitations it was not possible to include all that might be included; this volume is just a small offering in respect of all those strong women of Spirit of the Sufi Path who have come before us and all those who continue with us and all those who will, with God's grace, follow after us. May God forgive me for whatever mistakes I have made in this humble attempt.

The selections have been ordered in a roughly chronological manner but also thematically. The first section relates the stories of three women who might be referred to as the first "Sufi" women—Khadija, Fatima, and 'A'isha—all luminous women of the family circle of the Prophet Muhammad, may peace and blessings be with them all. The second section relates the stories of some of the Sufi women of the early centuries of Islam when the world of Sufism flourished mainly in what we now refer to as the Middle East and adjacent regions. The third section relates the stories, knowledge, and experience of women in Sufism throughout the remaining centuries up to this present moment, from many regions of the world where Sufism has spread, representing many of the predominant Sufi orders that have developed. Our aim has been to share the vast and varied treasure of women's experience and contribution in the world of Sufism, this treasure that has been for so long relatively hidden. And in the sharing, it was my hope also to open to the understanding of the reader the essential perspectives, principles, and practices of the Way that is Sufism. As it is recited repeatedly in all moments of life, *Bismillah ar-Rahman ar-Rahim*, we begin in the Name of God.

When referring to God in the text, in some cases I have used both the feminine pronoun and the masculine so that those reading this book may be reminded that within the universe and understanding of the Qur'an, the sacred text of Islam, God is without gender. I also occasionally use both in reference to the human being as well, so that we may be reminded that humanity and its evolving experience is, naturally, inclusive of both genders. Truly, Our Sustainer is beyond anything by which we may seek to define Him/Her (Surah as-Saffat 37:180). The Qur'an is one of the few Holy Books with which I am familiar that speaks directly to both "men who have faith" and "women who have faith" in numerous passages. In fact, the number of times that "men" and "women" are mentioned is equal. It is understood that in God's sight, men and women are equal; what matters is not gender, wealth, or power, but that we bring to our Sustainer a sound heart (Surah ash-Shu'ara' 26:89) when we return to Our Source. It is these who shall find themselves abiding in the Garden, now and eternally . . . a Garden underneath which rivers flow, and where everywhere one is met with the greeting, "Peace" (Surah Ya Sin 36:58).

Numerous foreign terms appear in the text; most are italicized. Some of these terms as well as proper names have been rendered with different spellings by the different authors included. This variation has to do with the difficulty of conveying Arabic and Persian letters into English. As much as possible, transliteration has been simplified and regularized, but one may still encounter variations such as *zhikr/zikr/dhikr* (remembrance of God).

It is becoming strongly clear that there will continue to be more and more stories of women of Spirit on the Sufi Way to share as women in the current era rediscover more and more their rightful role as equal partners on the spiritual path as well as in the world of daily human duties. We will look forward to witnessing the continued reflecting of the Divine Light in all the ways and being through which it may be granted by our Most Gracious Sustainer. May the stars of this universe shine ever more and more brightly.

God is the Light of the heavens and the earth.
The parable of His/Her light is,
as it were, that of a niche containing a lamp;
the lamp is enclosed in glass, the glass like a radiant star;
lit from a blessed tree—an olive-tree
that is neither of the east nor of the west—
the oil of which would almost give light
even though fire had not touched it: light upon light!
God guides to His/Her Light the one who wills to be guided;
and God offers parables to human beings,
since God has full knowledge of all things.

—Surah an-Nur 24:35

ACKNOWLEDGMENTS

All thanks be to God,
the Infinitely Compassionate and Most Merciful.

Many thanks are due to Mary, mother, daughter,
and her son, Jesus, both signs of God,
and to our mother, Eve, and her husband, Adam,
to Khadija and Muhammad,
their daughter Fatima and her husband, 'Ali,
peace and blessings upon them,
and all the prophets and messengers of the One,
and the many friends who reflect the Light,
to Dr. Refik Algan,
to Metin Bobaroglu, to Hoca Cahit Goskan,
to Suleyman Hayati Dede and Fahrunnisa Hanim,
to Avidye Ana and Turgut Baba,
to Şefik Can Efendi and Sabahat Hanim,
to Dr. Asad Ali, to Llewellyn Vaughan-Lee,
to Mahmoud Mostafa, to Hakan Talu,
and to Michael Wolfe for their helpful suggestions
and brotherly support of this project
and to Michael's wife, our sweet friend Cathy;
to my mother, Mimi, and my father, Lee,
my sisters Marian and Anne,
to my spirited daughter, Carolyn Grace,
my best childhood friends, Connie and Trudy,
my dear mother-in-law, Mary, her husband, Ed,
and their son, my husband, Kabir,
and my dear sons, Matthew and Shams;
to Dr. Celalettin Çelebi and his wife, Guzide Hanim,
and their son, Faruk Hemdem Çelebi,
to women of Threshold and Sufism in the world today,
to Nuket Kardam for her steady assistance with translation,
to Marjorie Wolfe for her cheerful help with permissions,
to the gracious staff of Shambhala Publications,
especially my editors, Kendra Crossen Burroughs and Emily Bower,
to Hamida Battla, such a generous soul,
and to my dear friend Elizabeth Hin.

Thanks also to Lora Zorian for her painstaking and loving care of the design of this book,

And to all the dear sisters of Spirit who have supported the unfolding of this work with their being and who have contributed to these pages—too numerous to name here—please know that deep gratitude flows out to you.

INTRODUCTION

Women and Sufism

SINCE THE BEGINNING of consciousness, human beings, both female and male, have walked the path of return, of recognition and reunion with the Source of Being. Though in this world of duality we may find ourselves in different forms, ultimately, within Truth, there is no male or female, only Being. Within the Sufi traditions, the recognition of this truth has made possible the spiritual maturation of women in a way that has not always been possible in the West.

From the earliest days onward, women have played an important role in the development of Sufism, which is classically understood to have begun with the Prophet Muhammad. Muhammad brought a message of integration of spirit and matter, of essence and everyday life, of recognition of the feminine as well as the masculine. Though cultural manifestations have layered over some of the original purity of intention, the words of the Qur'an convey the equality of women and men before the eyes of God. At a time when the goddess-worshiping Arabian tribes were still quite barbaric, even burying infant girls alive because male offspring were preferred, this new voice of the Abrahamic tradition attempted to reestablish the recognition of the Unity of Being. It tried to address the imbalances that had arisen, advising respect and honor for the feminine as well as for the graciousness and harmony of nature.

In the early years of this new revelation, Muhammad's beloved wife Khadija filled a role of great importance. It was she who sustained, strengthened, and supported him against his own doubt and bewilderment. She stood beside him in the midst of extreme difficulty and anguish and helped carry the light of the new faith. It was to Muhammad's and

❧ "Women and Sufism," by Camille Adams Helminski, originally appeared in *Gnosis* magazine (www.gnosismagazine.com), no. 30 (Winter 1994). Reprinted by permission.

Khadija's daughter, Fatima, that the deeper mystical understanding of Islam was first conveyed, and indeed she is often recognized as the first Muslim mystic. Her marriage with the close friend and cousin of Muhammad, 'Ali, bound this new manifestation of mysticism into this world, and the seeds of their union began to blossom.

As the mystical side of Islam developed, it was a woman, Rabi'a al-'Adawiyya (717–801 C.E.), who first clearly expressed the relationship with the Divine in the language we have come to recognize as particularly Sufic, by referring to God as the Beloved. Rab'i'a was the first human being to speak of the realities of Sufism with a clear language that anyone could understand. Though she experienced many difficulties in her early years, Rabi'a's starting point was neither fear of hell, nor desire for paradise, but only love. Her method was love for God because "God is God; for this I love God . . . not because of any gifts, but for Itself." Her aim was to melt her being in God. According to her, one could find God by turning within oneself. As Muhammad said, "He who knows himself knows his Lord." It is love that carries and sustains us through this process. The door of Sufism will finally open only with Love, because—though knowledge may be important and can assist in our discrimination along the way and may help us to reach the threshold—it is ultimately through Love that we are brought into unity of Being.

Throughout the centuries, women as well as men have continued to carry the Light of this Love. For many reasons, in many places, the women have been less visible than the men, less verbal, less demonstrative in society at large, but nevertheless active participants. Within some Sufi circles that developed over the centuries, women were integrated with men in ceremonies; in other orders women gathered in their own circles of remembrance and worshiped apart from men. Some women devoted themselves to Spirit ascetically, apart from society, as Rabi'a did; others chose the role of benefactress and fostered circles of worship and study. Many of the great masters with whom we are familiar had teachers, students, and spiritual friends who were women and who greatly influenced their thought and being. And wives and mothers gave support to their family members while continuing their own journey toward union with the Beloved.

Ibn 'Arabi, the great Islamic metaphysician (1165–1240 C.E.), tells in his writings of time spent with two elderly women mystics who had a profound influence on him: Shams of Marchena, one of the "sighing ones," and Fatima of Cordova. About Fatima, with whom he spent a great deal of time, he says:

> I served as a disciple one of the lovers of God, a gnostic, a lady of Seville called Fatimah bint Ibn al-Muthanna of Cordova. I served her for several years, she being over ninety-five years of age. . . . She used to play on the tambourine and show great pleasure in it. When I spoke to her about it she answered, "I take joy in Him Who has turned to me and made me one of His Friends (Saints), using me for His own purposes. Who am I that He should choose me among mankind? He is jealous of me for, whenever I turn to something other than He in heedlessness [*ghaflah*, the opposite of remembrance, *dhikr*, and thus a lapse from true awareness into illusion], He sends me some affliction concerning that thing." . . . With my own hands I built for her a hut of reeds as high as she, in which she lived until she died. She used to say to me, "I am your spiritual mother and the light of your earthly mother." When my mother came to visit her, Fatimah said to her, "O light, this is my son and he is your father, so treat him filially and dislike him not."[1]

When Bayazid Bestami (d. 874), another well-known master, was asked who his master was, he said it was an old woman whom he had met in the desert. This woman had called him a vain tyrant and showed him why: by requiring a lion to carry a sack of flour, he was oppressing a creature God himself had left unburdened, and by wanting recognition for such miracles, he was showing his vanity. Her words gave him spiritual guidance for some time.

Another woman for whom Bestami had great regard was Fatima of Nishapur (d. 838), of whom he said, "There was no station [on the Way] about which I told her that she had not already undergone."[2] Someone once asked the great Egyptian Sufi master Dhu an-Nun al-Misri, "Who, in your opinion, is the highest among the Sufis?" He replied, "A lady in Mecca, called Fatemah Nishapuri [Fatima of Nishapur], whose discourse displayed a profound apprehension of the inner meanings of the Qur'an which were astounding." Further pressed to comment on Fatima, he added, "She is of the saints of God, and my teacher."[3] She once counseled him, "In all your actions, watch that you act with sincerity and in opposition to your lower self (*nafs*)."[4] She also said, "Whoever doesn't have God in his consciousness is erring and in delusion, whatever language he speaks,

1. Ibn al-'Arabi, *Sufis of Andalusia*, pp. 25–26.
2. Dr. Javad Nurbakhsh, *Sufi Women*, p. 162.
3. Ibid.
4. Ibid.

whatever company he keeps. Yet, whoever holds God's company never speaks except with sincerity and assiduously adheres to a humble reserve and earnest devotion in his conduct."[5]

The wife of the ninth-century Sufi al-Hakim at-Tirmidhi was a mystic in her own right. She used to dream for her husband as well as for herself. Khidr—the immortal prophet who mysteriously appears in order to assist a devoted servant of God—would appear to her in her dreams. One night Khidr told her to tell her husband to guard the purity of his house. Concerned that perhaps Khidr was referring to the lack of cleanliness that sometimes occurred because of their young children, she questioned Khidr in her dream. Khidr responded by pointing to his tongue: she was to tell her husband to be mindful of the purity of his speech.

Among the women who followed the Way of Love and Truth, there were some who rejoiced, and some who continuously wept. Sha'wana, a Persian, was one of those who wept. Men and women gathered around her to hear her songs and melodious discourses. She used to say, "The eyes which are prevented from beholding the Beloved, and yet are desirous of looking upon Him, cannot be fit for that Vision without weeping."[6] She was not only "blinded by tears of penitence, but dazzled by the radiant glory of the Beloved."[7] During her life she experienced intimate closeness with the Friend, or God. This profoundly influenced her devout husband and son (who became a saint himself). Sha'wana became one of the best-known teachers and guides of her time.

One of those who rejoiced was Fedha, who was also a married woman. She taught that "joy of heart should be happiness based on what we inwardly sense; therefore we should always strive to rejoice within our heart, till everyone around us also rejoices."[8]

For the most part, the words of such saintly women from centuries past come from traditional accounts of their comments or from poems that developed around their words, rather than from writings of their own. Though the Qur'an strongly encourages the pursuit of knowledge and education for women as well as men, women sometimes received fewer opportunities than men in similar circumstances. I will not be attempting here to address the evolving role of women in exoteric Islam, as it is varied and complex. We must recognize, though, that women in general around the world have often faced prejudicial treatment because of their gender.

5. Ibid.
6. Margaret Smith, *Rabi'a the Mystic and Her Fellow-Saints in Islam*, p. 146.
7. Ibid, p. 148.
8. Nurbakhsh, *Sufi Women*, p. 165.

Within Islamic society as well as within our own, difficult treatment of women has occurred—in some cases obvious, in some cases insidious. Though local cultural overlays and male-dominated jurisprudence may have increased restrictions on women in various areas, the Qur'an basically enjoins mutual respect and valuation of the human being regardless of sex or social situation. Within Sufism, this more essential Qur'anic attitude has prevailed.

The cultures in which Sufism was practiced tended to convey more material orally than in written form, and women in particular may have had less of a tendency to write, preferring instead to simply live their experience. Nevertheless, there were women who wrote of their mystical experience in songs, in journals, and in critical exposition. As Western scholarship brings more of these works into translation, more of the story of Sufism is becoming accessible to us.

As this story unfolds, we are discovering the work and lives of many Sufi sisters. Among these was Fatima, or Jahanara, the favorite daughter of Shah Jahan (1592–1666), the Mughal emperor of India. Fatima wrote an account of her initiation entitled *Risila-i Sahibiyya,* which is known as a beautiful and erudite exposition of the flowering of Sufism within her heart.

'A'isha of Damascus, one of the well-known mystics of the fifteenth century, wrote a famous commentary of Khwaja 'Abdallah Ansari's *Stations on the Way* (*Manazel as-sa'erin*) entitled *Veiled Hints within the Stations of the Saints* (*Al-esharat al-khafiys fi'l-manazel al-auliya'*).[9] Bibi Hayati Kermani belonged to a family immersed in the Sufi tradition. Her brother was a *shaykh* (spiritual guide) of the Nimutallahi order, and she became the wife of the master of the order. After her marriage, she composed a *divan* (collection of poems) that revealed her integration of both the outer and inner knowledge of Sufism.

Among the Bektashis, an order in which women have always been integrated together with men in ceremonies, many women have continued the tradition of composing sacred songs (*ilahis*). In 1987, a songbook, *Gul deste* (Rose Bouquet) was published in Turkey, bringing together sacred hymns written by women and men within the Bektashi tradition from the nineteenth century to the present day. Several of those songs of Spirit are included in this volume.

Sufi women around the world today continue to teach and to share their experience personally as well as in written form. In the Sudan, for instance, there continue to be *shaykhas* who are particularly adept in the healing arts.

9. Ibid., p. 147.

In the Middle East, women continue to mature in many Sufi orders. In Turkey in particular, the teachings are transmitted through women as well as men—perhaps even more so now than in the past, for with the advent of the Turkish Republic under the leadership of Attaturk in 1925, the Sufi orders were banned and Sufi practice was driven into private homes, where women were more easily able to participate. One luminous lady, Samiha Ayverdi, carried the Rifa'i tradition in Istanbul until her recent death; Zeynep Hatun of Ankara continues to inspire people in Turkey and abroad with her poems and songs.

In central Turkey, the mother of a friend of ours one day heard someone knocking and answered her door. A man stood at her threshold with a message. He had come to ask her to lead a Naqshbandi women's circle. He explained that his *shaykh*, who lived quite a distance away, had seen her in a dream, and had sent him to the place that had been indicated. When our friend's mother protested that she did not know his *shaykh* and felt inadequate for such a responsibility, the man replied, "Do not worry. Our *shaykh* has seen your purity. He says that whenever you have a question, you should hold that question in your heart, and in your dreams he will bring you the answer." Thus began her apprenticeship.

Sufi schools spread from the Middle East to Europe long ago, and new waves continue to arrive. Irina Tweedie, the author of the memoir *Daughter of Fire,* recently conveyed an Indian branch of the Naqshbandi line back to her native England. Her work is being continued through the Golden Sufi Center in California. This is one of the many branches of Sufism that are beginning to take root in America.

A popular strain of Sufism that has been very welcoming of women in the United States is the Chishti order, which was first brought to America by Hazrat Inayat Khan. Of the many women involved, Murshida Vera Corda is perhaps the most well-known spokesperson. Her work with children in particular has been a great inspiration to many parents.

One branch of Sufism that has become better known in the West in recent years is the Mevlevi. Within this tradition founded upon the example of Mevlana Jalaluddin Rumi (1207–1273), women have always been deeply respected, honored, and invited to participate in all aspects of the spiritual path. There have often been Mevlevi *shaykhas* who have guided both women and men. Mevlana himself had many female disciples, and women were also encouraged to participate in *sema*, the musical whirling ceremony of the Mevlevis. (Women usually had their own *semas*, but sometimes performed *semas* together with men.) One of Mevlana's chief disciples was Fakhr an-Nisa, known as the Rabi'a of her age. In recent years, for various reasons of renovation and road rerouting, it was decided to reconstruct her tomb. As Shaykh Suleyman Hayati Dede was then the acting spiritual head of the Mevlevi order, he was asked to be present when she was exhumed. He told of how, when her body was uncovered, it was totally intact and emitted a fragrance of roses.

Of course such women have always existed and have brought much light into our world; one might ask how anyone could question otherwise. Unfortunately, in many parts of the world in many eras, in various spiritual traditions, this has been questioned. Within Sufism, however, though practical manifestation may differ according to brother/sisterhood, women have always been respected as equals on the spiritual path. Everyone, regardless of gender, is expected to establish his or her own direct connection with the Divine.

Within Sufism, the language of the Beloved[10] and the recognition of the feminine helps to balance some of the old cultural stereotypes that were sometimes used in expository writing and which the Western media have chosen to highlight. Jalaluddin Rumi often speaks beautifully of the feminine and presents woman as the most perfect example of God's creative power on earth. As he says in his *Mathnawi*, "Woman is a ray of God. She is not just the earthly beloved: she is creative, not created."

It is precisely this creative ability and the coincident capacity for relationship and love that suit women so well for the Sufi way of opening to relationship with the Divine. As we come to recognize the magnificence of the Benevolent Source of Life, we can come to see ourselves in harmony with that Source. In the Qur'an, each *surah* (chapter) of the revelation begins with *Bismillah ar-Rahman ar-Rahim,* which means "In the Name of God, the Infinitely Compassionate, the Infinitely Merciful." *Rahman* indicates the fundamental beneficence and compassion inherent in the divine nature; *Rahim*, the particular mercy that manifests. Both words come from the same root, which is the word for "womb." God's mercy and benevolence are always emphasized as being greater than God's wrath; the encompassing generosity and nurturance of the Divine are the milieu in which we live.

As women, we come from the womb and carry the womb. We give birth from the womb and can find ourselves born into the womb of Being. Mary, the mother of Jesus, is very much revered in Sufism and Islam as an example of one who continually took refuge with the Divine and opened to receive divine inspiration within the womb of her being. Women have a great capacity for patience, for nurturing, for love. A contemporary male Sufi teacher once described an ideal guide as one who is like a mother—

10. Within Sufism, God is referred to as the true "Beloved" of the human being. The path of Sufism is profoundly relational. As the literature of the path developed, feminine beauty and graces became metaphors for the attraction of the Divine.

who is always there for her child, not demanding, though willing to instruct and set limits, but also ready to stay up all night or rise at any hour to nurse a suffering child.

Sufism recognizes that committed relationship and family are not contrary to the flowering of spirituality, but rather wonderful vessels for spiritual ripening. Committed partnership, children, and wider family are great blessings, containing the inspiration, the breathing in, of the Divine. As we deepen our capacity for relationship and fidelity in the human sphere, we also increase our capacity for relationship with the Divine.

Women and men need to stand together in the Light. Especially in our own time, the way is opening for greater recognition of equal partnership. We have much to learn from each other, and male and female need to recognize each other so that we can come to balance within ourselves as well as create balance outwardly in the world. The masculine attributes of strength and determination also belong to women; the feminine attributes of receptivity and beauty also belong to men. As we look to see the Divine in each other, encouraging each other to rise to the fullness of his or her own divine nature, we push against our own limitations until those limits dissolve and a gift unfolds. As we learn to witness the miracle of creation, a time comes when *Wheresoever you look, there is the Face of God; everything is perishing except the One Face* (Surah Baqarah 2:115).

Whether we choose celibacy or committed partnership, whether we are female or male, the same work remains of polishing the mirror of the heart, of being in remembrance moment by moment, breath by breath. Each moment, we reaffirm the inner marriage until there is no longer lover or Beloved but only Unity of Being. Little by little, we die to that which we thought we were. We are dissolved into Love, and we become love, God willing.

As Rabi'a says,

> In love, nothing exists between breast and Breast.
> Speech is born out of longing,
> true description from the real taste.
> The one who tastes, knows;
> the one who explains, lies.
> How can you describe the true form of Something
> in whose Presence you are blotted out?
> And in whose Being you still exist?
> And Who lives as a sign for your journey?[11]

11. Charles Upton, *Doorkeeper of the Heart*, p. 36.

WOMEN *of* SUFISM

In the Heart of the Prophet

A NEW TIME OPENED with the Prophecy of Muhammad, may peace and blessings be upon him. The rights of women and the enslaved, the weak and the tribally defenseless, were recognized. The Qur'an brought redress of rights for all and called humankind to new and deeper respect for nature and for each other, male and female, while remembering and worshiping the One Sustainer who created all that is. This revelation opened into the predominantly pagan atmosphere of seventh-century tribal Arabia, where the birth of a boy brought honor to a family while infant girls were frequently buried alive. An *ayat*, or "sign," as the verses of the Qur'an are called, was voiced to terminate this practice.[1] There are many verses in the Qur'an which speak to both "women who are faithful and men who are faithful." All but one of the *surahs* (chapters) of the Qur'an begin with the verse *Bismillah ar-Rahman ar-Rahim,* "In the Name of God, the Infinitely Compassionate, the Infinitely Merciful." *Ar-Rahman* and *ar-Rahim* are both derivatives of the root *rhm,* which refers to the word "womb," emphasizing the beneficent encompassing nature of the Divine Sustainer.

Several women are mentioned specifically in the Qur'an. Among them, Mary, the mother of Jesus, is mentioned more than any other. One *surah* bears her name in Arabic: Maryam. Together with Surah 'Imran, this *surah* relates some of the story of this purest of women who was so intimately devoted to her Sustainer, who became the mother of Jesus, the "Word of God." Mary is also honored in many other verses of the Qur'an, as are the

1. See Surah 81, Takwir, and also such verses as Surah al-A'raf 6:140.

natural mother and the adoptive mother of Moses. Another *surah,* Nisaa (Women), begins with this *ayat*:

O humankind!
Reverence your Educator
who created you from a single soul,
created likewise its mate,
and from these two spread countless men and women—
reverence God, through Whom you demand your mutual rights,
and (reverence) the wombs (that bore you):
for indeed, Allah is watching over you.

–SURAH AN-NISAA 4:1

When we return to the record of the early days of the Islamic community, it is clear that women were respected and participated equally with men in the development and sustaining of the newly emerging spiritual community. A new sense of justice was conveyed, and by the words of the Qur'an, women were given the right to witness in legal cases centuries before any women in Europe had such rights, long before the United States even existed. Also through the revelation of the Qur'an, women received the acknowledged right to own property of their own and to share distinctly in inheritance. In a world where previously they had most often been treated as chattel, they were now, by the Qur'an, granted specific rights of marriage and divorce. Though addressing all, both men and women, a Hadith Qudsi[2] also states, "Of all things permitted, that which is most displeasing to God is divorce." Kindness in relationship and mutual consideration are enjoined:

Among the signs of God is this: that He/She created you from dust,
and then, see how you become human beings ranging far and wide!
And among His/Her Signs is this: that He/She created for you mates
from among yourselves
that you may dwell in tranquillity with them,
and He/She engenders love and compassion between you;
truly in that are signs for those who reflect.

—SURAH AR-RUM 30:21

2. A "Hadith Qudsi" is a saying of the Prophet Muhammad that was spoken as though God were speaking. These sayings of the Prophet stand out from the record of other statements of his that were from his own individual personage. They are closer in tone and import to the revelation of the Qur'an.

Education for all was also encouraged. Muhammad said, "Seek knowledge even unto China." It was due to such injunctions that throughout the centuries, women as well as men traveled great distances to be with those of deeper knowledge. However, due to centuries of cultural social overlays and mainly male jurisprudence, the rights of women in many Islamic countries have been eroded. Thanks be to God, in recent years, some of the imbalance is beginning to be redressed once again.

Among other things, it is beginning to be remembered that in the early days of the Prophet, women actively participated in all aspects of the community. Women helped to build the first mosque in Medina and worshiped there alongside men: the men stood in rows to one side, and across an aisle the women stood shoulder to shoulder in mirrored lines. Some communities today are beginning to restore this original form of prayer that began in the Prophet's Mosque in Medina. There is a beautiful story of how Muhammad would sometimes take his granddaughter Umayma, the daughter of his eldest daughter, Zaynab, into the mosque with him and put her on his shoulders while he prayed. When the moments for prostration arrived, he would set her down beside him and then put her back on his shoulders when he rose again to standing witness in the ritual prayer.[3]

In the early days of the Muslim community, there were women who made the call to prayer, and there were also women who led the ritual prayer, not only for women but also for men. In particular, Umm Waraqa bint Abdallah, who was trained by Muhammad himself, acted as the prayer leader for her whole tribe. She also was one of those who "handed down the Qur'an before it was put in final written form."[4] It was the wives of the Prophet Muhammad who conveyed many of the *hadith*, the recounting of his words and behavior, after his death. And it was a woman, his daughter Fatima, who is looked to as the fountainhead of his descendants and the first to manifest the mystical aspects of Islam.

Following here are accounts of three of the most outstanding and most beloved women of the early Islamic community—Khadija, Fatima, and 'A'isha—whose living example continues to inspire and encourage. They each shared deeply with others of the Spirit that nourished and sustained them. Because the original impulse of Sufism is classically understood to have opened with the example of Muhammad and the revelation of the Qur'an, even though these women lived before anyone used the term "Sufi," we might consider them to be foremost among the first Sufi women.

3. Muhammad Saeed Sidiqqi, *The Blessed Women of Islam*, p. 103.
4. Wiebke Walther, *Women in Islam*, p. 111.

KHADIJA

KHADIJA BINT KHUWAYLID (c. 554–619 C.E.) was known in the community of Mecca[1] as at-Tahira, "the pure one." A woman of great integrity, intelligence, and spiritual depth, she became the wife of Muhammad, peace and blessings be upon them both, before the responsibility of Prophethood came to him. Before marrying Muhammad, she had been widowed, and had developed and been conducting her own business in caravan trade. She was forty years old, when, being aware of Muhammad's sincere trustworthiness and skillfulness, she hired him to oversee one of her caravans. At the time, Muhammad was twenty-five and of meager financial means. When her caravan returned from a very successful trading venture under his charge, through her cousin Khadija proposed marriage to Muhammad. At first Muhammad was hesitant to believe such a match was possible for someone of his financial state and limited tribal status—he had been orphaned at an early age and taken under the wing of his uncle.[2] However, he was of the noble tribe of the Bani Hashem, who held the honorable responsibility of providing water to the pilgrims visiting the Kaaba.

Muhammad accepted Khadija's offer, and a very happy marriage unfolded. More independent now that he was supported by Khadija's love as well as her wealth, Muhammad would often retire to a nearby cave to meditate and pray for long periods. It was here, during the month of Ramadan in 610 C.E., that at the age of forty he received the first revelation of the

1. Mecca is the locale where Muhammad was raised. It is here that the Kaaba is located, the temple that was dedicated to the one God by Abraham and originally, it is said, built by Adam; it was later cleansed and rededicated by Muhammad. Mecca is in Saudi Arabia near the Red Sea and is the direction toward which all Muslims turn in prayer five times a day.

2. The Prophet was born after the death of his father, 'Abdullah ("servant of the One God"). When he was six, his mother, Amina, died, and he became the ward of his grandfather, 'Abdul Muttalib. When he was nine, his grandfather also died, and he was taken in by his father's brother, Abu Talib. Abu Talib loved the Prophet dearly and often took him with him on his trading journeys; his wife, Fatima, gave Muhammad a mother's love. He grew into manhood alongside their sons, including the young 'Ali.

Qur'an.[3] Overwhelmed and concerned that perhaps he was losing his mind, he rushed home to Khadija and told her to cover him with a blanket. She held him close and reassured him that a man such as he did not suddenly go crazy but that indeed what had taken place was a tremendous spiritual experience. She went to her cousin Waraqa, a Christian who was well versed in Jewish and Christian prophecy, and he confirmed for her that indeed Muhammad must be the messenger whose coming was referred to in the Jewish and Christian scriptures and that this must be the opening of his Prophethood. Khadija was the first to have faith in his mission as a prophet who had come to renew the message of monotheism of the whole Abrahamic tradition, coming both to the peoples of Arabia and *as a mercy to all the worlds.*[4]

Through the early years of prophecy, Khadija valiantly stood by Muhammad when many in the community were against him. Even though she and her family were eventually ostracized and forced to endure great hardship, she never wavered in her support of Muhammad and his mission. She was his constant companion and confidante, and welcomed and helped to support all who joined with them in the newly awakening faith.

After years of deprivation due to the intensity of the boycott against the emerging Muslim community, Khadija died at the age of sixty-five, in 619 C.E., just before permission came for the *hijrah*.[5] She and Muhammad had lived contentedly together for twenty-five years. Together they had had two sons, Qasim and 'Abd Allah, who both died in infancy, and four daughters, Zaynab, Ruqqaya, Umm Kulthum, and Fatima, who were the only children of the Prophet to live past infancy. Khadija raised them all with a strong sense of Spirit and reliance upon their Sustainer. She was known for her purity, her wisdom, her generosity, and her kindness. Khadija was buried in the al-Mala' cemetery in Mecca.

Even after remarrying, Muhammad long mourned his devoted wife. "Khadija had been for the Holy Prophet more than a wife. She had placed all her wealth, which was considerable, at his disposal. She had given him love. She was the first person to be converted to Islam, and had been a pil-

3. Surah 96, Iqra (al-Alaq): *"Recite, in the Name of your Sustainer who created. . . ."*

4. Surah al-Anbiyaa 21:107.

5. *Hijrah*, the emigration in 622 C.E. of the beleaguered new Muslim community from Mecca 260 miles north to the settlement of Yathrib, subsequently known as Medina, where they were received by Arab and affiliated Jewish tribes who were looking to Muhammad to help them establish peace among their warring factions. This year of the emigration is the year 0 in the Muslim lunar calendar; thus, for example, the year 2003 C.E. (common era) is the same year as 1425 A.H. (A.H. = anno Hegirae, in the year of the Hijrah.)

lar of strength for the Holy Prophet as well as the Muslims."[6] When his later wife, 'A'isha, questioned him about the extent to which he continued to remember and miss her, he said, "She embraced Islam when people disbelieved me, and she helped me in her person and her wealth when there was none else to lend me a helping hand. I had children only from her."[7]

6. *Alim*: see "Khadija."

7. *Musnad Ahmad* 6:117, 118.

FATIMA

FATIMA (c. 608–633 C.E.), may God preserve her secret, was called the "resplendent one" (az-Zuhra) because of her luminous face, which seemed to radiate light.[1] It is said that when she stood for prayer, the *mihrab*[2] would reflect the light of her countenance. She was also called al-Batul ("the virgin" or "the devoted one") because of her asceticism. She spent a great deal of her time in prayer and worship, in recitation of the Qur'an, in fasting, and in service to the growing Muslim community. The youngest daughter of Khadija and Muhammad, she was born just around the time of the opening of his prophethood, and so she grew up under the dynamic influence of the new message that was being conveyed.

As his youngest child, she would often accompany Muhammad as he moved about the Meccan community, handling the family errands, praying at the Kaaba, or visiting Muslim friends and families, continually speaking of the new faith. During these early years of Islam, she witnessed countless episodes of persecution and would staunchly defend her father and care for him. Some years later, after the death of her mother, when she was the only one of his own children still living at home with him, witnessing his sorrow, this loving concern for her father intensified and so earned her the title Umm Abi-ha ("the mother of her father"). Some also refer to this title as being indicative of the fact that his familial line was carried forward through her.

1. *Alim*: see "Fatima." It is interesting to note that one of the most important appearances of the Virgin Mary in recent times is "Our Lady of Fatima." Mary appeared to three young children in Portugal in 1917, near the small village of Fatima, named after the Prophet Muhammad's daughter, and was subsequently witnessed there by tens of thousands of people. Since that event, numerous Christians worldwide address the Virgin Mary in prayer as "Our Lady of Fatima," further interweaving the strands of the Abrahamic faiths.

2. The *mihrab* is the prayer niche, which indicates the direction of prayer. It is also the word for "sanctuary"; see Surah al-'Imran 3:37.

Fatima's fine manners and gentle speech were part of her lovely and endearing personality. She was especially kind to poor and indigent folk and would often give all the food she had to those in need even if she herself remained hungry. She had no craving for the ornaments of this world nor for the luxury and comforts of life.[3]

After enduring extreme hardship during the Meccan boycott, two years after the community emigrated to Medina, and three years after the death of her beloved mother, at the age of approximately sixteen, Fatima married 'Ali ibn Abu Talib (the son of Muhammad's dear uncle Abu Talib), who had been living with the family since the death of his father some years earlier and who had been among the first to become a Muslim. 'Ali was known for his courage, virtue, and piety. He and Fatima soon had a hut of their own near the Prophet in Medina. Two sons were born to them, Hasan and Husain, and two daughters, Umm-i-Kulthum and Zaynab. A third child of theirs, a son, Muhsin, died in infancy. The line of the family of the Prophet traces itself through Fatima, Hasan and Husain, and their children.

The marriage of Fatima and 'Ali, although inspired by the Angel Gabriel,[4] also, like many marriages, had its vicissitudes. One day when Fatima and 'Ali were at odds with each other, Muhammad came to visit them. It is said that he lay down between them and had each of them place a hand on his belly. He told them to breathe with him and to remain together in that position until peace came to both of them. Sometime later he left their hut, smiling broadly. A companion who witnessed the difference in his countenance from when he had entered questioned him as to why he was now smiling. He responded that he was now smiling because the two people most beloved by him were now at peace.[5]

Fatima's life with 'Ali was as simple and frugal as it had been in her father's household. To relieve their extreme poverty, 'Ali, when he was not called to battle to defend their faith, worked as a drawer and carrier of water and she as a grinder of grain. One day Fatima told 'Ali, "I have ground grain until my hands are blistered."

"And I've drawn water until my chest is aching," said 'Ali. He suggested

3. *Alim*: see "Fatima."

4. See H. A. Rose and John P. Brown, *The Darvishes*, pp. 397–400.

5. See Muhammad Ibn Sa'd, *The Women of Madina*, p. 18.

to her that she ask her father, whose power and influence had grown since coming to Medina, to give her a servant.

Reluctantly, she did go to the Prophet, but when he inquired what had brought her to him, she could only respond, "I came to give you greetings of peace," and could not bring herself to ask for what she had intended.

When she returned home, she told 'Ali she had been ashamed to ask, so they went together to the Prophet and asked him for assistance, but the Prophet felt that others were in greater need, especially the Ahl as-Suffah, the "People of the Bench."[6]

> 'Ali and Fatimah returned home somewhat dejected, but then that night, after they had gone to bed, they heard the voice of the Prophet asking permission to enter. Welcoming him, they both rose to their feet, but he told them: "Stay where you are," and sat down beside them. "Shall I not tell you of something better than that which you asked of me?" he asked and when they said yes, he said: "Words which Jibril [Gabriel] taught me, that you should say: 'Subhaan Allah—Glory be to God' ten times after every Prayer, and ten times 'Al hamdu lillah—Praise be to God,' and ten times 'Allahu Akbar—God is Great.' And that when you go to bed you should say them thirty-three times each." 'Ali used to say in later years: "I have never once failed to say them since the Messenger of God taught them to us."[7]

It was often to the "word of God" that they turned for nourishment and well-being.

It is said that Fatima greatly resembled her father and that her ways of sitting and standing and speaking were quite similar.

6. These were impoverished Muslims who lodged on a bench at the entryway to the mosque in Medina. They were devoted servants of God, purifying their hearts of all but Him. Many among them learned the Qur'an by heart. Some refer to these early faqirs (in addition to the Prophet's family) as the first "Sufis," referring to the *suffa*, the bench, upon which they stayed and where they engaged in *muhhabat* ("affectionate conversation," especially with the Prophet). The Prophet was known to have said, "Poverty (*faqr*) is my pride." A dervish often refers to himself/herself as a *faqir*, a poor one, dependent upon God alone.

Some refer to *safa*, "purity," or *suf*, "wool" (indicative of the coarse clothing of the early Sufis), as the origin of the word "Sufi." Though there is much debate about the origin and definition of the word "Sufi," all would agree that the focus of the Sufi is the purification of the heart/mind which empties the heart/mind of all but God, making possible the reunion with one's Lord while still in life; as Muhammad, peace and blessings upon him, has been reported to have said: "Die before death." (C.A.H.)

7. *Alim*: see "Fatima." See also Ibn Sa'd, *The Women of Madina*, pp. 17–18. "Ali is also reported to have said: 'The Prophet of God has taught me a thousand doors of knowledge, each of which has opened to me a thousand others'" (Rose and Brown, *The Darvishes*, p. 432). ('Ali is sometimes referred to as the "gate" to the "city of knowledge" that is Muhammad.)

She inherited from Muhammad a persuasive eloquence that was rooted in wisdom. When she spoke, people would often be moved to tears. She had the ability and the sincerity to stir the emotions, move people to tears and fill their hearts with praise and gratitude to God for His grace and His inestimable bounties.[8]

'A'isha, the later wife of the Prophet, said of her: "I have not seen any one of God's creation resemble the Messenger of God more in speech, conversation, and manner of sitting than Fatimah, may God be pleased with her. When the Prophet saw her approaching, he would welcome her, stand up and kiss her, take her by the hand and sit her down in the place where he was sitting." She would do the same when the Prophet came to her. She would stand up and welcome him with joy and kiss him.[9]

The Prophet had a special love for Fatima. He once said: "Whoever pleases Fatima has indeed pleased God and whoever has caused her to be angry has indeed angered God. Fatima is a part of me. Whatever pleases her pleases me and whatever angers her angers me, and whoever injures her injures me." When he went on a journey the last person of whom he took leave was Fatima, and when he returned from the journey the first person he would see was Fatima. [10]

Fatima is regarded by some Sufis and theologians as the first spiritual head (*qutb*) of the Sufi fellowship.[11] The Prophet extolled her as one of the four most exemplary women in history along with Mary, mother of Jesus; her own mother, Khadija; and the wife of Pharoah, who rescued and raised Moses. These four women are considered the four holiest women of Islam.

One day while the Prophet was ill, he whispered something to Fatima and she cried, and then he whispered again in her ear and she smiled. After the Prophet's death, 'A'isha asked her what Muhammad had whispered to her. She answered that at first he had told her of his impending death, but then he had told her that she would be among the first to join him in paradise.

It was Fatima who eloquently delivered her father's eulogy. She deeply mourned the death of the Holy Prophet and is later reported to have said:

8. *Alim*: see "Fatima."

9. Ibid.

10. Ibid.

11. I. Goldziher, *Muhammedanische Studien* 2 (Halle, 1989), p. 300.

"It is not surprising that whoever catches the fragrance of Muhammad's tomb will never know another perfume. Destiny injured me with a bereavement so sorrowful, and so dark, that if it had fallen on the days they would have been turned into eternal nights."[12]

Then, six months after the death of her beloved father, after a prolonged illness, she arose one morning smiling and called for a mat to be placed in the open courtyard of their home. She asked her companion, Salma, for assistance in washing and perfuming herself, and then with her face turned toward the heavens, she asked for her husband, 'Ali.

> He was taken aback when he saw her lying in the middle of the courtyard and asked her what was wrong. She smiled and said: "I have an appointment today with the Messenger of God." 'Ali cried, and she tried to console him. She told him to look after their sons, al-Hasan (age seven) and al-Husayn (age six), and advised that she should be buried without ceremony. She gazed upwards again, then closed her eyes and surrendered her soul to the Mighty Creator.[13]

She was twenty-nine years old when she passed from this world in 633 C.E.

'Ali used to visit the grave of Fatima frequently, and used to write verses to express his grief. On one occasion he wrote:

> O thou grave, to thee I resort for paying homage to thee.
> O thou, the repository of my beloved, thou answer me not.
> O thou beloved tomb, what ails thee—
> Thou respondeth not to my supplications.
> Art thou, out of humor, Because of the love that I bear thee?[14]

Though there is a sepulcher referred to as Fatima's tomb near the Prophet's tomb in Medina, she most probably rests in al-Baqi cemetery on the outskirts of Medina, and it was probably here that often 'Ali would go for solace.

12. *Alim*: see "Fatima."

13. Ibid.

14. Ibid.

‘A’ISHA

‘A’ISHA (c. 612–678 C.E.) was the daughter of the Prophet Muhammad’s closest friend, Abu Bakr. She was betrothed to the Prophet at an early age[1] after the death of his dear wife Khadija. Gabriel appeared to Muhammad in a dream, carrying to him a bundle wrapped in red silk, saying, “This is your wife.” Muhammad later told ‘A’isha, “When I uncovered the face, I discovered it was you, so I said, ‘If this is from Allah, it will be done.’ ”[2] ‘A’isha had previously been betrothed to another, but that family had not accepted Islam. They decided they would rather not have one who was a member of the beleaguered Muslim community marry into their family. So, she was instead betrothed to Muhammad. This lightened his heart after the long “year of sorrow” in which he had lost both his beloved wife, Khadija, and his devoted uncle, Abu Talib.

Meanwhile, at the encouragement of friends, Muhammad married the widowed Sawdah who was a kind and supportive companion and helped him to raise his daughters. It was not until several years later, after the *hijrah,* that the marriage between ‘A’isha and Muhammad took place and she went to live with Muhammad in a little hut in what had become his family compound adjacent to the first mosque in Medina. Their hut was just adjacent to the hut of Fatima and ‘Ali and opened into the common courtyard shared with the community mosque.

‘A’isha was the only wife of Muhammad who had not been previously married. During the years that followed the *hijrah*, Muhammad married nine women in the process of consolidating tribal loyalties and providing for the widows of Muslim men who died defending their faith. At the time of Muhammad, polygamy was commonly practiced indiscriminately as though women were mere property to be owned and exchanged at a man’s

1. It was customary for girls to be betrothed at an early age and to marry shortly after the onset of menses.

2. Al-Bukhari (*hadith*).

whim; however the revelation of the Qur'an enjoined new respect for women and their rights, and Muhammad was careful to provide each of his wives with a hut of her own, and to treat each with equal respect.

A verse of the Qur'an was revealed then limiting to four the general number of wives possible for a man, but stating that even this condition was allowable only if such a man were able to treat them all equally:

> *If you fear that you may not act with equity in regard to orphans, marry such women as are good for you, two or three or four—but if you fear that you may not be fair, then one (only) or what your right hands possess;*[3] *that will be more suitable to prevent you from doing injustice....*
>
> —SURAH AN-NISAA 4:3

As Wiebke Walther points out in her book *Women in Islam*, "modern Muslims often interpret this verse as essentially an exhortation in favor of monogamy, since at another point the Qur'an states that a man who is married to several wives at the same time cannot be equally just to all of them—Qur'an 4:128–129."[4] Secret relationships outside of marriage were of course prohibited. Truthful, committed connections with equality and tenderness between partners were encouraged. "It is to be emphasized that ... the Qur'an and the greater part of the traditions (sayings of the Prophet) define these relations [between husband and wife in marriage] as based on love."[5]

> *And among His Signs is this:*
> *that He created for you*[6] *mates from among yourselves*
> *that you may dwell in tranquillity with them,*
> *and He engenders love and compassion between you;*
> *truly in that are signs for those who reflect.*
>
> —SURAH AR-RUM 30:20

3. As in most countries of the world, slavery also was practiced in the Arabian region until recently. "Since the mid-nineteenth century, starting with the more progressive Islamic countries, decrees were issued for the restrictions of slavery" (Walther, *Women in Islam*, pp. 68–69). Though the Qur'an acknowledged the practice, it enjoined the freeing of slaves as one of the most meritorious acts. Meanwhile, any slave was to be treated in the same way as other members of the family: clothed in similar clothing and eating of the same food at the same table. Any child born of a legal relationship with a slave had exactly the same status as children of free wives. (See Walther, *Women in Islam*, p. 68.)

4. Walther, *Women in Islam*, p. 57. Today, polygamy is outlawed in a number of Muslim countries. In any case, for the sake of equity and harmony, it is important for the husband first to ask permission of his wife before taking a second wife. A woman also has the right to specify monogamy in her marriage contract, as did the great-granddaughter of the Prophet Muhammad, Amina.

5. Ibid., p. 59.

6. "You" is in the plural here.

Several verses of the Qur'an speak of the creation of "man and his mate" from a single soul: *It is He who created you from a single soul and likewise his mate of like nature, in order that he might dwell with her (in love)* (Surah al-A'raf 7:189).[7] The first couple in Prophecy, Adam and Eve, are pointed to as exemplary of the original harmonious "one to one" relationship intended for us as human beings: *O Adam, dwell thou and thy wife, in the Garden* . . . (Surah al-Baqarah 2:35).[8] The Qur'an indicates that it is intended that husband and wife be a "garment" of comfort for each other (Surah al-Baqarah 2:187).

A moment did arise when Muhammad's dear friend and son-in-law, 'Ali, considered taking a second wife, but Muhammad, knowing that it would cause distress to Fatima, asked him to either refrain from doing so or divorce her. 'Ali relinquished the idea and did not remarry until some time after Fatima's death. It is clear from the historical records that Muhammad's own situation of polygamy was not an easy one.

In Islam it is said, "Marriage is half the faith." In close relationship, the sharp edges of our nafs (ego-soul) can be little by little smoothed. There is in marriage much to be learned. Even so was the case for 'A'isha. Growing up as the wife of the Prophet, she learned a great deal from Muhammad's example and shared intimately with him the journey of soul.

> Aisha is said to have laid down the fundamental rules of Arab-Islamic ethics. She is said to have affirmed that noble qualities of character were: "honesty of speech, reliability, truthfulness and steadfastness in misfortune, the provision of protection for friend and neighbor, and readiness to give aid in the ups and downs of life, to feed the needy, to treat slaves with kindness and to revere one's parents."[9]

> Aisha reported that the Messenger of God said: "Certainly the most perfect of the faithful in faith is one who is the best of them in conduct, and is the most affable of them to his/her family."[10]

> Muhammad was known for his kindness and consideration of all and many traditions have been reported by Aisha to this effect. In his own home, the Prophet repaired sandals, sewed [by] himself, gave

7. See also Qur'an 4:1, 39:6. It may be pointed out that grammatically, as the word *nafs* is feminine, the verse actually says, ". . . created from a single soul and likewise her mate." For a further discussion of the feminine gender of the *nafs*, see Sachiko Murata's selections, pp. 177–85 below.

8. For a further discussion of these issues one might refer to *Status of Women in Islam* by Qamaruddin Khan.

9. Walther, *Women in Islam*, p. 106.

10. *Mishkat-ul-Masabih*, vol. 1, p. 213.

fodder to his camel used for carrying water, swept the house, ate with the servant and kneaded dough with him, and carried his [own] goods from the market, a job which he allowed nobody else to do for him.[11]

It was often when Muhammad was with 'A'isha that revelation would come to him. She never hesitated to ask him questions or discuss with him the meaning of the revelation or of his own actions. From an early age she had been present during innumerable conversations between Muhammad and her parents regarding the revelation and the needs of the emerging community. Her mental acumen enabled her to easily learn the evolving Qur'an by heart and to memorize additional revelations as they came.

After Khadija, 'A'isha was Muhammad's favorite wife. When he became ill he was grateful that he was allowed by his other wives to stay in her hut, and he remained for many hours at a time resting with his head in her lap. It was thus that he died.

Two years after the passing of the Prophet, 'A'isha's father, who had become the caliph, or leader, of the developing Islamic state after the Prophet's passing, also died in her arms. It is related that she was the one who delivered his eulogy "in moving words of resounding rhymed prose."[12] He was buried beside Muhammad under the floor of her room. The companion 'Umar became the next caliph. When he was dying he asked that he, too, might be buried with Muhammad and Abu Bakr under the floor of her room. Though she felt somewhat shy of this, she agreed. However, after that she curtained off that portion of the room and would not enter there without first enwrapping herself with her veil. Before Muhammad's death, she had had a dream of three moons setting in her room; now they had indeed all come to rest.

'Uthman followed 'Umar as caliph but a few years later was murdered during the still-stormy years that followed Muhammad's passing. After some debate, 'Ali then assumed the position of caliph. 'A'isha was concerned that 'Ali was not actively bringing the murderers of 'Uthman to justice. Two of the early companions of the Prophet, Talhah and az-Zubayr, the husbands of her sisters, gathered forces against 'Ali and persuaded 'A'isha to join them. She journeyed on camel-back to participate in the battle. When the army was passing a certain town, the barking of a dog reminded her of something the Prophet had said to her in caution, years

11. *On the Obligation of Migrating*, by the Shehu, p. 152; cited in Beverly B. Mack and Jean Boyd, *One Woman's Jihad*, p. 10.

12. Walther, *Women in Islam*, p. 106.

earlier. She began to doubt the rightfulness of their endeavor and wanted to turn back, but her companions persuaded her to continue. A terrible battle ensued in which thousands of lives were lost, including those of her brothers-in-law. When her side was completely defeated, her own brother, Muhammad, who had been on the side of 'Ali, was the one to help her off the back of her camel. She was given safe passage back to Medina.

In Medina, she resumed residence in the hut where she had lived with her husband. One half of the hut was now taken up with the three graves—those of the Prophet Muhammad; her father, the beloved companion and second caliph, Abu Bakr; and the companion and third caliph, 'Umar. She lived in the other half of the hut. In her little room she would receive visitors from many regions who came to her to learn and understand the Qur'an and the sayings and ways of the Prophet. She is reported to have conveyed over two thousand sayings (*hadith*) of his. She was also well versed in medicine, history, and poetry. This small room became her classroom where she taught young boys and girls, and women and men of the community. One was considered very blessed to have been able to study with 'A'isha. Though she had no children of her own, she adopted a number of young people, whom she carefully instructed and through whom many of the traditions of the faith were conveyed. She made the annual pilgrimage (*hajj*) to Mecca every year and would pitch a tent there in order to be able to receive those who came to study with her during that time of annual gathering of the extended Muslim community.

Throughout her lifetime she continued to live in the style of utter simplicity that she had experienced together with Muhammad as his wife. As they had often had little to eat and drink—no more than a few dates and water—she never learned to cook. In later life, she continued to fast often, and when the stipend allotted to her by the government treasury was brought to her, she would often distribute it to those in need the same day, keeping back nothing for herself. She also continued throughout her life to immerse herself in prayer, adding to the five daily ritual prayers the extra early morning prayer (*dhuha*, after sunrise) and the extra night prayer (*tahajjud*), which she had so often observed together with Muhammad. Often in the night they had stood for hours in prayer, tears cascading down their cheeks as they worshiped their Sustainer. Sometimes when 'A'isha tired, she would sleep, and Muhammad would continue to pray. Their hut was quite small, so when she would lie down, it would often happen that she would be lying down right in front of him as he prayed, and when he would bow in prostration, she would tuck up her feet to make space for his forehead and hands.

Though 'A'isha lived many years after the rebellion against 'Ali, she continued until her death to regret her part in it. When at age sixty-five she was dying, one of those who had been a close friend for many years came to visit her. She was hesitant to hear his praise of her, saying she wished she were but a stone or a clod and had never behaved as she had. When he suggested that there yet remained space beside Muhammad and her father and 'Umar for one more grave where she might be buried, she reproached him, saying, "Would you have me undo all my repentance?" She insisted on being buried at night in the communal cemetery, al-Baqi, on the outskirts of Medina. Even though the funeral was held at night, thousands came out to honor her passing, out of love and respect for this "Mother of the Faithful."

Early Sufi Women

THE BIOGRAPHIES OF MUSLIM SAINTS, such as those composed by Abu Nu'aym,[1] Fariduddin Attar,[2] Ibn al-Jawzi,[3] Jami,[4] and Ibn Khallikan,[5] al-Munawi[6] and many others, are full of the mention of women Sufis, their saintly lives, their good deeds, and their miracles.[7] Jami (d. 1492 C.E.) concluded his Persian work *Nafahat al-uns* (The Breaths of Intimacy) with an appendix consisting of accounts of remarkable Sufi women. The biographical histories written by as-Sulami (d. 1021 C.E.), which documented the existence of numerous female saints and women of remarkable capacity, were often quoted in some of these later works. This section of Sulami's original manuscript, *Dhikr an-niswa al-muta 'abbidat as sufiyyat*, was lost until quite recently, and it is now thanks to the excellent work of Rkia Cornell,[8] a contemporary Sufi woman, that we have available an English translation of as-Sulami's biographies of early Sufi women as a primary source. Other excellent scholarship has also been accomplished in this field by

1. *Hilyat al-awliya* (Adornment of the Saints).

2. *Tadkhirat al-awliya* (Memoirs of the Saints).

3. *Sifat as-safwa* (The Nature of the Elect).

4. *Nafahat al-uns* (The Breaths of Intimacy).

5. *Wafayat al-a'yan*.

6. *Al-kawakib ad-durriya fi tarajim as-sada as-sufiya*. For a French translation of the biographical information on female Sufis of this text, see Nelly and Laroussi Amri, *Les Femmes soufies où la passion de Dieu* (1992).

7. See Margaret Smith, *Rabi'a the Mystic and Her Fellow-Saints in Islam*, p. 3

8. Rkia Cornell is currently teaching at University of Arkansas and continuing her research on Sufi women. Her *Early Sufi Women* is an excellent sourcebook for documentation of women's participation in the early years of Sufism.

women like Margaret Smith and Wiebke Walther, as well as by men. Continually more information is being unveiled.

Most accounts include mention of Rabi'a al-'Adawiyya (also known as Rabi'a of Basra), acknowledging her as the first proponent of the Sufi approach toward God as the Beloved. As Margaret Smith witnesses in her book *Rabi'a the Mystic and Her Fellow-Saints in Islam*, "The high position attained by the women Sufis is attested further by the fact that the Sufis themselves give to a woman [Rabi'a al-'Adawiyya] the first place among the earliest Islamic mystics and have chosen her to be the representative of the first development of mysticism in Islam."[9] Rkia Cornell also notes that "rather than being validated by Sufi men, as-Sulami's Sufi women just as often validate their male colleagues by educating them in Sufi doctrine and practices."[10] After the death of the Prophet Muhammad and the first four caliphs who followed him, the spiritual authority he initiated became fragmented. These early Sufis sought to clarify and deepen that interior spiritual connection that they saw as the essence of Islam.[11]

Maryam of Basra, a companion and disciple of Rabi'a who served her, was, like Rabi'a, one who focused on the centrality of divine love. She, also, used to lecture on the subject of love (*muhabbah*),[12] and as-Sulami reports that whenever she would listen to discourses on the doctrine of love she would go into ecstasy. As-Sulami relates that Maryam said, "I have never been preoccupied with my sustenance, nor have I exhausted myself in seeking it from the day when I heard the statement of God the glorious and Mighty, 'For in heaven is your sustenance, as is that which you are promised.' [Qur'an 61:22]."[13]

9. Smith, *Rabi'a the Mystic and Her Fellow-Saints in Islam*, p. 3.

10. Cornell, *Early Sufi Women*, p. 46.

11. "It could at least be said that the first community as a whole was open to mysticism as it could never be once certain barriers of exotericism had crystallized. . . . If the night of the Revelation is *better than a thousand months,* it is so because *the Angels and the Spirit descend therein*; [Surah 97:3–4] and this penetration of the natural by the supernatural, which may be said to continue throughout the mission of the Messenger, is bound to bring certain possibilities within the reach of those who would not normally attain to them. A multitude of souls can be endowed, through the impact of miracles, with a degree of certainty which in other ages is the prerogative only of mystics in the fullest sense; . . . [allowing] for a more general attainment of what was soon to become the distinguishing mark of the Sufis alone, namely *Ihsan* (the beautiful)—that thou shouldst worship God as if thou sawest Him, and if thou seest Him not, yet He seeth thee." (Martin Lings, *What Is Sufism?*, p. 103)

12. On *muhabbah* (affection), see note 17 in the selection on Fatima, page 8.

13. Lings, *What is Sufism?*, p. 84; this illustrates the doctrine of *tawwakul*, "leaving all initiative to God," trusting in God for sustenance and support.

Among the many spiritual luminaries in Basra in the eighth and ninth centuries was also Hafsa bint Sirin, sister of Muhammad ibn Sirin (d. 729 C.E.), one of the earliest masters of dream interpretation. He used to refer people to his sister for commentaries on the Qur'an. Their saintly mother raised them both with great care. "Once someone visited Imam Ibn Sirin in the presence of his mother and remarked about his outstanding respect for her. When the man left, he asked, 'Is Muhammad not feeling well?' Someone replied, 'He is well, but he reveres his mother so much that he nearly melts away in her presence.'"[14] Hafsa was herself a specialist in the ways of asceticism and scrupulousness, and would manifest exemplary signs and miracles. It is related that she used to light her lamp at night and then would rise to pray through the night; sometimes the lamp would cease burning, but her home would remain illuminated until dawn.[15] During these early centuries of the Islamic community, many spiritual luminaries inhabited Basra and Baghdad (in what is now Iraq), Damascus (Syria), Cairo and northern Egypt, and Nishapur and greater Khorasan. Interchange between these spiritual centers was greatly facilitated by the frequent passage of trading caravans. The wise often sought out the company of the wise.

Umm 'Abdallah, the wife of Abu 'Abdallah as-Sijzi, who lived in the late 800s of the common era was known to have said, "Being in the company of one's spiritual brethren in this world is the consolation for being in the abode of materiality." Her husband was one of the great shaykhs of Khorasan and a master of Sufi chivalry (*futuwwah*).[16] He described this code of Sufi conduct: "It means accepting the excuses of humankind and your own shortcomings; seeing their perfection and your imperfections; and having compassion for all creatures, in their goodness and evil. The perfection of *futuwwa* is that you not busy yourself with humankind at the expense of God, the Glorious and Mighty."[17] 'A'isha of Merv, the wife of Ahmad ibn as-Sari, was heard to have said, "Whenever one of the practitioners of Sufi chivalry (*fityan*) from anywhere seeks me out, I sense the light of his intention in my inner soul until that person arrives. If I am successful in serving that person and fulfilling his or her needs, that light becomes fully mine, but if I cut short my service, the light goes out."[18]

14. Muhammad M. Al-Akili, *Ibn Seerin's Dictionary of Dreams*, pp. x–xi.

15. Cornell, *Early Sufi Women*, p. 122.

16. *Futuwwah* is the ethical code of conduct known as Sufi chivalry. It is based on the example of the Prophet Muhammad.

17. Cornell, *Early Sufi Women*, p. 200.

18. Ibid., p. 196.

Al-Qushayri (986–1021 C.E.), a student of as-Sulami of Nishapur who wrote the *Tabaqat as-sufiyya*, (Generations of the Sufis) was another radiant light among the early Sufis[19] who also was well aware of the spiritual gifts of many Sufi women, as his own wife, Kadbanu Fatima, was a woman of great scholarly achievement and inner development. She was the daughter of his teacher, Abu 'Ali ad-Daqqaq, a Sufi master of the lineage of Junayd of Baghdad, and was known for her piety and capacity for transmitting the Prophetic traditions.[20] "The pattern of erudition persisted into the third generation and included female as well as male descendants of the great master. The Qushayris became in fact one of the four principal Shafi'i families of Nishapur, and administered a *madrasa* [religious school] that bore their name."[21]

Al-Qushayri tells the story of an anonymous wise woman who catalyzed repentance—a turning to God—in a man "afflicted" with high social status:

> 'Ali b. 'Isa, the vizier, rode in a great procession, and strangers began asking, "Who is this? Who is this?" A woman who was standing by the side of the road inquired, "How long will you say, 'Who is this? Who is this?' This is a servant who has fallen from God's protection. So He has afflicted him in the way that you see." When 'Ali b. 'Isa heard her, he returned to his house, resigned from the vizierate, went to Mecca, and never left it again.[22]

Among the early Sufi women, Umm Ahmad bint 'Aisha was one of those who remained secluded in worship. For fifty years she remained within her home and was well known for her advanced spiritual state. As-Sulami reports that she said, "Knowledge (*'ilm*) is the life of humanity, spiritual practice (*'amal*) is its conveyance, and intellect (*'aql*) is its ornament, and gnosis (*ma'rifa*) is its illumination and insight."[23]

19. As Dr. Barbara von Schlegell writes in her translator's note to al Qushayri's *Principles of Sufism (Risala)*: "A manual on how to proceed on the Sufi path, the *Risala*'s section on states and stations also provides a picture of individuals and groups of Sufis before the rise of formal Sufi institutions (6–7th/12–13th centuries). . . . Al-Qushayri describes the stations [of spiritual attainment, *maqamahs*] as being the result of the seeker's effort. The states [*ahwal*], on the other hand, come to the heart without any intention on the part of the recipient. "The states are given [by God], the stations are earned."

20. Annemarie Schimmel, *Mystical Dimensions of Islam*, p. 427.

21. Al-Qushayri, *Principles of Sufism*, trans. B. von Schlegell, pp. viii–ix. Imam al-Shafi'i was one of the four founders of major schools of Islamic jurisprudence (see note 2 in the Lady Nafisa selection, page 56).

22. Al-Qushayri, *Principles of Sufism*, p. 11.

23. Cornell, *Early Sufi Women*, p. 218.

The famous Egyptian Sufi, Dhu an-Nun al-Misri (d. 861 C.E.) relates his encounter with an anonymous woman who conveys to him the attributes of a Sufi:

> Dhu an-Nun said: I saw a woman on the coast of Syria and asked her, "Where are you coming from (may God have mercy on you)?" She replied: "From a people who 'are moved to rise from their beds at night [calling on their Lord in fear and hope].'"[24] Then I asked: "And where are you going?" She said: "To 'men whom neither worldly commerce nor striving after gain can divert from the remembrance of God.'"[25] "Describe them for me," I said. And she recited:
>
> A people who have staked their aspirations on God,
> And whose ambitions aspire to nothing else.
>
> The goal of this folk is their Lord and Master,
> Oh what a noble goal is theirs, for the One beyond
> compare!
>
> They do not compete for the world and its honors,
> Whether it be for food, luxury, or children.
>
> Nor for fine and costly clothes,
> Nor for ease and comfort that is found in towns.
>
> Instead they hasten toward the promise of an exalted
> station,
> Knowing that each step brings them closer to the farthest
> horizon.[26]
>
> They are the hostages of washes and gullies,
> And you will find them on mountain-tops.

By concluding one of the most important chapters of his book with this poem, al-Kalabadhi[27] reveals his high regard for its anonymous author's understanding of Sufism. Dhu an-Nun, who created the Sufi

23. Cornell, *Early Sufi Women*, p. 218.

24. Surah as-Sajda 32:16.

25. Surah an-Nur 24:37.

26. Reflective of the verse of the Qur'an: And We will show them Our signs on the farthest horizon and within themselves until they know that this is the Truth (Surah al-Fussilat 41:53).

27. Al-Kalabadhi (d. 990 C.E.) wrote the important *Kitab al ta 'arruf li madhhab ahl al tassawuf* (Introduction to the Methodology of the Sufis). The chapter referred to is the chapter on the meaning of the word "Sufi."

> doctrine of spiritual states (*awhal*) and stations (*maqamat*), is reminded by this woman that the essence of Sufism is not to be found in paranormal states but in spiritual practice, an idea that mirrors al-Kalabadhi's own view of Sufism as a "Way of proceeding" or methodology (*madhhab*). True Sufis are Muslims [those who are surrendered] whose hearts vibrate with the spirituality of the Qur'an. They "rise from their beds at night," devoted to the remembrance of God. They "stake their ambitions on God" and aspire to nothing else. Their goal is God alone.[28]

There were those who wept out of continual longing for God and recognition of their own shortcomings; there were those ecstatic ones who were continually enraptured by God's Presence. And there were many who might have responded as Habiba 'Adawiyya did. It is told that often when she would be immersed in devotion, she would go up onto her roof and pray:

> God! All the stars have set and all eyes are shut in sleep. Kings have shut their gates, yet Your portal is still open. Every friend has sought seclusion with his sweetheart; I stand alone before Your Face.[29]

28. This anecdote and explanatory paragraph are excerpted from Rkia Cornell, *Early Sufi Women*, pp. 15–16. For further explanation of states and stations, see note 19.

29. Dr. Javad Nurbakhsh, *Sufi Women*, p. 119

A DOORKEEPER OF THE HEART

RABI'A AL-'ADAWIYYA (eighth century), a major saint of Islam and one of the central figures in Sufi tradition, was born (according to one reckoning) in 717 C.E. and died in 801. "Stories about her and poems attributed to her have come down to us through many Sufi writers, including Attar, her major biographer, and al-Ghazali[1]—the central pole where Sufi lore and orthodox Islam meet."[2] "In a time characterized by so marked a diminishing of the sense of values, it was her vocation—we might almost say mission for such was her greatness—to incarnate at the highest level, that is the domain of the Spirit, the putting of first things first—God before Paradise, the Absolute before the relative."[3]

> Attar states that if Rabi'a were not present at the assembly of Hasan of Basra,[4] he left the assembly at once. The same writer relates that Hasan said about his relationship with Rabi'a, "I passed one whole night and day with Rabi'a speaking of the Way and the Truth, and it never passed through my mind that I was a man nor did it occur to her that she was a woman, and at the end when I looked at her, I saw myself a bankrupt [i.e., spiritually worth nothing], and Rabi'a as truly sincere."[5]

1. Al-Ghazali more than anyone else may be said to have prepared the way for the general acceptance of Sufism. "His longest and best-known work, *The Revival of the Science of Religion* [*Ihya' `ulum al-din*], was written as a means of reminding the whole community of the mystical bias which had characterized the Islam of the Prophet and his Companions." Martin Lings, *What Is Sufism?*, p. 111.

2. Charles Upton, *Doorkeeper of the Heart*, p. 7.

3. Lings, *What Is Sufism?*, p. 106

4. [Hasan of Basra was one of the most famous early Muslim ascetics.] Though born in Basra, he had sat as a young man at the feet of 'Ali in Medina. Many of the later Sufi orders trace their lineage through him back through 'Ali to Muhammad. "His mother was a *mawlat* and servant of the Prophet Mohammad's wife Umm Salama." Cornell, *Early Sufi Women*, p. 122.

5. Smith, *Rabi'a the Mystic and Her Fellow-Saints in Islam*, p. 14.

There are many tales of interactions between Hasan of Basra and Rabi'a, including stories of his proposal of marriage to her, which she declined. "Most of the stories about Rabi'a are 'legendary'—meaning that they don't correspond to the Western sense of factual history because they seem more symbolic than factual in intent—as if the actual events of people's lives can't be just as 'symbolic' as any invented romance. So here are seven legends of Rabi'a—which, if 'character is fate,' are true as any date carved in stone:"[6]

[1]

On the night Rabi'a was born, there was no cloth to wrap her in, and no oil for the lamps. Her mother asked her father to borrow oil from a neighbor, but he refused because he was under a vow never to ask for anything from anyone but God.

Then he fell asleep, and the Prophet Muhammad appeared to him in a dream: "Don't worry," he said, "the daughter just born to you will be a great saint; 70,000 of my followers will venerate her. Tomorrow you are to write a letter to the Amir, reminding him that he is in the habit of praying to me a hundred prayers every night, and four hundred on Friday. Say that since he missed last Friday, he has to make up for it by giving you four hundred dinars."

Rabi'a's father wrote and sent the letter—and when the Amir received it he gave this command: "Give two thousand dinars to the sage who has written this, telling him that I would willingly grant him an audience, except that it would be an insult to him: I'll travel to his house instead, and rub my beard on his threshold."

And the father named his daughter "Rabi'a," which means "the fourth."

[2]

After death and poverty had scattered Rabi'a's family, she was approached by a slave-trader; she tried to run, but slipped and sprained her wrist. When she knew her freedom was lost, she cried: "O God! I am an orphan, and am about to become a slave; on top of that, my wrist

6. This quotation and the following biographical anecdotes about Rabi'a are excerpted from Charles Upton, *Doorkeeper of the Heart* (Putney, Vt.: Threshold Books, 1988), pp. 8–12. Reprinted by permission of Threshold Books.

is broken. But that's not what I care about; the thing I have to know is: are You satisfied with me?"

Immediately a Voice answered her: "Don't worry—on the Day of Resurrection your rank will be so high that even the closest companions of God will envy you."

Then Rabi'a submitted to the Will of God, and became a slave.

[3]

In her life as a slave, Rabi'a found time for her worship of God by doing without sleep. She fasted and prayed. One night her master awoke, looked down from the window of his house into the courtyard, and saw Rabi'a in prayer. As he was watching her he was amazed to see a lamp appear above her head, suspended in mid-air; the light from this miraculous lamp lit up the whole house. Terrified and astonished, he went back to bed, and sat wondering until dawn.

Then he called Rabi'a to him, confessed what he had seen, and gave her freedom, with the option of staying on with him if she wanted to. She asked permission to leave and it was granted; so she went out of the house, and out of that city, and into the desert to pray.

A number of stories about Rabi'a have to do with her pilgrimage to Mecca to see the Kaaba. She never quite seemed to be able to get there—ultimately the Kaaba had to come to her instead (which seems to be a sort of reversal of the Muhammed-and-the-mountain story). Her difficulties in completing the pilgrimage seem to symbolize both the struggles of the mystic path and her own difficulty in coming to terms with the conventional Islamic community; and the Kaaba's coming to her may also point to the truth that the last (as well as the first) step on that path is taken not by the mystic, but by God Himself.

[4]

On pilgrimage to Mecca, Rabi'a went into the desert leading an ass to carry her baggage; but the ass died. Others in the caravan offered to help her but she refused; instead she prayed to God, " Is this how a great King treats a weak, helpless woman He has invited to visit His House?" Immediately the ass came back to life, stood up, and Rabi'a continued on her journey.

[5]

It took Ibrahim Ibn Adham fourteen years to reach the Kaaba in pilgrimage, because he said long prayers at every shrine along the way—but when he got there, there was no Kaaba to be seen. "What is this?" he asked to himself. "Have I gone blind?"

"No," a Voice said, "you can't see the Kaaba because it has gone out to meet a woman." Burning with jealousy, Ibrahim ran toward the outskirts of Mecca till he ran into Rabi'a, who was just arriving. He turned around, and saw the Kaaba back in its usual place. Then he turned to Rabi'a.

"What's this craziness you've brought into the world, woman?" he demanded.

"It's not I who am the author of craziness," she replied, "but you. You were crazy enough to take fourteen years to get to the Kaaba with your ritual prayer, while I, with my inner prayer, am here already."

[6]

Once upon a time several different men wanted to marry Rabi'a, including Abd al-Wahid Ibn Zayd, Hasan of Basra, the Amir of Basra himself, and even the provincial governor. This was her answer to the Amir:

"I'm not interested, really, in 'possessing all you own,' nor in 'making you my slave,' nor in having my attention distracted from God even for a split second."

And she told the governor:

"Control yourself. Don't let others control you. Instead, better share your inheritance with them, and suffer like they do the common suffering of the time. As for you: remember the day of your death. As for me: whatever bride-price you come up with, understand that the Lord I worship can double it.

"So goodbye."

Several of Rabi'a's poems have to do with her habit of keeping all-night vigils. In line with Islamic tradition, she practiced the ancient technique of combating spiritual sleep by avoiding physical sleep—of sitting up on the roof all night, while the lights are out and the consensus of the day is asleep, watching the Universe turn. There's even a story that, after an accusing dream, Rabi'a never slept again as long as she lived.[7]

[7]

Once upon a time Rabi'a fasted, prayed and stayed awake for seven days and nights. Then somebody brought her a bowl of food. Rabi'a accepted it, and went to find a lamp—but when she came back with the lamp she saw that a cat had knocked over the bowl. "So I'll drink water instead," she said to herself, and went to find the water-jug, but by the time she came back with it, the lamp had gone out. "Then I'll drink my water in the dark," she said—but then, without warning, the jug fell out of her hands, and broke into a thousand pieces. At that point she cried out, loud, loud, almost loud enough to set the whole house on fire. "God! God!" she cried, "What are You trying to do to me?"

"Be careful," a Voice answered, "if you really want Me to, I'll fill your heart with all the pleasures of this world, and empty it of all your care for Me. You want something and I want something, and these desires cannot be mixed."

After this, Rabi'a gave up all worldly hope.

"For the sake of sharpening, with the barb of paradox, her demonstration of the right of the Absolute, Rabi'a sacrifices every other point of view."[8] As it is told, "Sufyan Thawri often came to Rabi'a with questions, and also requesting her advice and prayers. One day Sufyan asked her, 'What is the best thing by which the servant seeks nearness to God Most High?' She said, 'That God knows that the servant loves nothing in this world or the next except God.' "[9]

7. "Knowing the feats of the Hindu and Tibetan yogis I can't call this impossible—but I suspect that what this story refers to is an unbroken stream of consciousness through the waking state, the dream state, and deep sleep—which may, in fact, come to the same thing." Upton, *Doorkeeper of the Heart*, p. 11.

8. Lings, *What Is Sufism?*, p. 97.

9. Carl W. Ernst, *Teachings of Sufism*, p. 183.

Rabi'a al-Adawiyya

I am fully qualified to work as a doorkeeper, and for this reason:
What is inside me, I don't let out:
What is outside me, I don't let in.
If someone comes in, he goes right out again.
He has nothing to do with me at all.
I am a Doorkeeper of the Heart, not a lump of wet clay.[10]

Serving-girl: "It's Spring, Rabi'a. Why not come outside,
And look at all the beauty God has made!"
Rabi'a: "Why not come inside instead, serving-girl
And see the One who made it all
Naked, without veil."[11]

The true knower looks for a heart that comes from God alone.
As soon as it is given to him, he gives it back again
So that God can hold it hidden in His Mystery,
Safe from the tampering of human hands.[12]

MIRACLE STORY:

One day Hasan of Basra saw Rabi'a down by the riverside.

He came up to her, spread his prayer-rug on the surface of the water, and said: "Come sit with me and pray."

"Do you really have to sell yourself in the market of this world to the consumers of the next?" said Rabi'a. Then she unrolled her own prayer-rug in thin air, and sat on it:

"What you did any fish can do, Hasan, and what I did any fly can do. Our real work is far beyond the work of fish and flies."[13]

The majority of these anecdotes and sayings of Rabi'a are excerpted (except as otherwise noted) from *Doorkeeper of the Heart* by Charles Upton (Putney, Vt.: Threshold Books, 1988). Reprinted by permission of Threshold Books.

10. Upton, *Doorkeeper of the Heart*, p. 21.

11. Ibid.

12. Ibid., p. 27.

13. Ibid., p. 30.

MIRACLE STORY:

One day Rabi'a and her serving-girl were getting ready to break a fast of several days. The serving-girl needed an onion and was about to go next door and borrow one, but Rabi'a said: "Forty years ago I vowed never to ask for anything from anyone but God—we can do without onions."

Just then a bird flew over, and dropped an onion into Rabi'a's frying pan, peeled and ready to fry.

"Interesting but not convincing," she said. "Am I supposed to believe that God is an onion-vender? I mean, really."

That day they fried their bread without onions.[14]

A leading scholar of Basra visited Rabi'a on her sick-bed. Sitting beside her pillow, he reviled the world.

"You love the world very dearly," Rabi'a commented. "If you did not love the world, you would not make mention of it so much. It is always the purchaser who disparages the wares. If you were done with the world, you would not mention it either for good or evil. As it is, you keep mentioning it because, as the proverb says, whoever loves a thing mentions it frequently."[15]

I love God: I have no time left
In which to hate the devil.[16]

I carry a torch in one hand
And a bucket of water in the other:
With these things I am going to set fire to Heaven
And put out the flames of Hell
So that voyagers to God can rip the veils
And see the real goal.[17]

14. Ibid., p. 31.

15. A. J. Arberry, *Muslim Saints and Mystics*, p. 51.

16. Upton, *Doorkeeper of the Heart*, p. 41.

17. Ibid., p. 43.

"Rabiʻa—Rabiʻa—how did you climb so high?"
"I did it by saying:
'Let me hide in You
From everything that distracts me from You,
From everything that comes in my way
When I want to run to You.' "[18]

"What miracles have you done, if any, Rabiʻa?"
"If I were to admit to a miracle
I'd be worried it might bring in money—
So my answer is: not one!"[19]

DREAM FABLE:

After an all-night vigil, I prayed to God at dawn, and slept.

In my dream I saw a tree: green, bright, vast, of indescribable beauty; and on this tree were three kinds of fruit, such as I had never seen among all the fruits of this world. They shone like the breasts of maidens, red, white, and yellow; they shone like globes and living suns in the green hollows of the tree. I marveled at them, and asked: "Whose tree is this?"

A voice replied, "This is your tree, sprung from the seed of your prayers." Then I began to walk around it, and as I did so I counted eighteen fruits the color of gold, lying on the ground beneath it.

I said, "It would be better if these fruits hadn't fallen, but were still on the Tree."

And the voice answered, "They would be there still except for the fact that while you were praying you kept worrying: 'Did I remember to add the yeast to the dough?' And so they fell, and there they lie."[20]

O God, Another Night is passing away,
Another Day is rising—

18. Ibid., p. 46.

19. Ibid.

20. Ibid., p. 50.

Tell me that I have spent the Night well so I can be at peace,
Or that I have wasted it, so I can mourn for what is lost.
I swear that ever since the first day You brought me back to life,
The day You became my Friend,
I have not slept—
And even if You drive me from your door,
I swear again that we will never be separated.
Because You are alive in my heart.[21]

O God, Whenever I listen to the voice of anything
    You have made—
The rustling of the trees
The trickling of water
The cries of birds
The flickering of shadow
The roar of the wind
The song of the thunder, I hear it saying:
"God is One!
Nothing can be compared with God!"[22]

My joy—
My Hunger—
My Shelter—
My Friend—
My Food for the journey—
My journey's End—
You are my breath,
My hope,
My companion,
My craving,
My abundant wealth.
Without You—my Life, my Love—
I would never have wandered across these endless countries.
You have poured out so much grace for me,

21. Ibid., p. 51.

22. Ibid., p. 48.

Done me so many favors, given me so many gifts—
I look everywhere for Your love—
Then suddenly I am filled with it.
O Captain of my Heart,
Radiant Eye of Yearning in my breast,
I will never be free from You
As long as I live.
Be satisfied with me, Love,
And I am satisfied.[23]

23. Ibid., p. 47. Rabi'a's "single-minded devotion to her Sustainer reminds one of the ecstatic devotion of some later Christian mystical sisters, some medieval Christian women saints such as Catherine of Genova, who said, 'I do not want what comes from thee, but I want thee alone, O sweet love!' And Juliana of Norwich's similar statements quoted in William Ralph Inge, *Christian Mysticism*, p. 209." Annemarie Schimmel, *As through a Veil: Mystical Poetry in Islam*, p. 218, n. 28.

SUFI WOMEN OF SYRIA

HALIMA OF DAMASCUS (mid-ninth century) was a descendant of the Prophet. She dwelled in Syria and was the teacher of Rabi'a of Syria. Rabi'a, the wife of Ahmad ibn Abi al-Hawari, once visited Halima and has related the following story:

> When I entered, Halima was reading from the Qu'ran. She addressed me saying, "Rabi'a, I have heard that your husband desires another wife besides you."
>
> "Yes," I affirmed.
>
> With all his intelligence, how can he allow his heart to become distracted from God with two wives? Have you not heard the interpretation of the Qu'ranic verse But for one who comes towards God with pure heart . . . ? [36: 88–89]
>
> "No," I admitted.
>
> "Its meaning," she said "is that you should attend to God, the Exalted, and not have anything other than Him in your heart!"
>
> As I left Halima, I was so deeply moved by her words that I rocked back and forth as I walked in a kind of trance, but felt embarrassed at my condition—that passersby might think me drunk.

RABI'A BINT ISMAIL—or Rabi'a of Syria, as she was also called, was one of the great women of Syria who used her wealth to support her husband, the renowned Sufi teacher Ahmad ibn Abi al-Hawari, and his companions. She was herself a renowned teacher of both women and men, and her husband often acknowledged her superiority in spiritual matters. He recounts

❧ The selection regarding Halima of Damascus is from *Sufi Women* by Dr. Javad Nurbakhsh (New York: Khaniqahi-Nimatullahi Publications, 1990), p. 120. It is a translation of an excerpt from *Nafahat al-uns* (Breaths of Intimacy), a history of Sufi mystics by the great Sufi poet Jami. Reprinted by permission of Khaniqahi-Nimatullahi Publications.

how one day he called to her but received no response; an hour later she told him, "My heart was so filled with the joy of God that I could not answer you."[1] He further relates:

> Once when I was engaged in performing the prayers of the night vigil, I remarked to Rabi'a that I never saw anyone remain so concentratedly awake as she. Rabi'a replied, "God be glorified! Do not speak like this. I am called, I arise."[2]

This Rabi'a rests in Jerusalem on the Mount of Olives, next to the tomb of the Christian saint Pelagia of Antioch.

LUBABA [al-Muta 'Abbida, or Lubāba the Devotee, who is noted as being a native of Syria (and also of Jerusalem)], was a specialist in the ways of gnosis (*ma'rifa*) and self-denial (*mujahadat*).

Abū Ja'far Muḥammad ibn Aḥmad b. Sa'īd ar-Rāzi reported from al-'Abbās ibn Hamza through Aḥmad ibn Abī al-Ḥawārī that Muḥammad ibn Rawḥ related:[3] Lubāba the Worshipper said: "I am ashamed lest God see me preoccupied with other than Him."

Lubāba also said: "The more I observe self-denial, the more comfortable I become with its practice. Thus, when I get tired from human encounter, I find intimacy in the remembrance of God. And when human discourse tires me, I take my rest in dedication to the worship of God and fulfilling His service."[4]

A man said to her: "This is the question:[5] I want to perform the pilgrimage to Mecca, so what invocation should I make during this period?" She

❧ The selection regarding Lubāba is excerpted from *Early Sufi Women* by Rkia Cornell (Louisville, Ky.: Fons Vitae, 1999), pp. 82 and 124. This and all the following selections from *Sufi Women* are reprinted by permission of Fons Vitae.

1. Ibid., p. 81.

2. Ibid.

3. It is traditional to note carefully the chain of conveyance of sayings, as for centuries the transmission was oral, and the relating of the chain of authority (*isnad*) was the manner of documentation of veracity.

4. Lubāba here reminds us of Surah ar-Ra'd 13:28: He guides to Himself all who turn to Him—those who have faith and whose hearts find satisfaction in the remembrance of God—Truly in the remembrance of God, hearts find rest. (C.A.H.)

5. This question is posed in the form of a *mas'ala*, or query on a point of Islamic law. Several of the women discussed in this work [i.e., *Early Sufi Women* by Rkia Cornell], such as Lubāba al-Muta 'Abbida and Rabi'a al-'Adawiyya, are depicted by as-Sulami as specialists in the field of *fiqh al-'ibadat*, the study of legal doctrines pertaining to worship. Although such issues would seldom come up in court, they were highly important to the spiritual life of the community.

said, "Ask God Most High for two things: that He will be pleased with you, so that He will make you attain the station of those who find their satisfaction in Him, and that He will magnify your reputation among His friends (*awliyā'*)."[6]

Lubāba was a specialist in the ways of scrupulousness (*wara'*) and reclusiveness (*nusuk*). Ahmad ['Abdallah] ibn Muhammad of Antioch reported from Ahmad ibn Abī al-Ḥawārī that Aḥmad ibn Muḥammad related: Lubāba said, "I am ashamed lest God see me preoccupied with other than Him after having known Him."

He also related that she said: "Knowledge of God bequeaths love for Him; love for Him bequeaths longing for Him; longing for Him bequeaths intimacy with Him; and intimacy with Him bequeaths constancy in serving Him and conforming to His laws."

FATIMA OF DAMASCUS was unique in her age. She used to rebuke the Sufi shaykhs. I heard 'Alī ibn Aḥmad of Tarsus say, "When Abū al-Ḥasan al-Mālikī entered Damascus, he lectured at the Umayyad mosque of Damascus and spoke well. Fāṭima attended his session and said to him, 'O Abū al-Ḥasan! You spoke very eloquently, and you have perfected the art of rhetoric. Have you perfected the art of silence?' Abū al-Ḥasan became silent, and did not utter a word after that."

❧ The selection regarding Fatima of Damascus is excerpted from *Early Sufi Women* by Rkia Cornell, p. 204.

6. *Wali* (pl. *awliya'*) as used in the Qur'an means "manager," "guardian," "protector," or "intercessor." In Sufi discourse it also means "intimate" or "friend," as in *waliAllah*, "friend of God." This latter term is often translated in English to mean a Muslim "saint" who is Allah's "friend" and is thus able to protect or intercede for others as Allah's deputy or vicegerent.

THOSE WHO WEEP

SHA'WANA (eighth century C.E.), a Persian woman known for her devotion to God and her beautiful voice, lived in Obollah (or al-Ubulla) on the Tigris. She was one of the early Sufi women who, though married and gifted with a son, continuously devoted her life to remembrance of her Sustainer. She was so impressed with her own limitations in regard to God and her longing for union with her Creator that she would continually weep. Still, in the midst of her weeping, she would conduct gatherings of lovers of God. Ascetics, pious men and women, as well as renowned mystics used to attend these sessions. Sha'wana would say, "Can an eye be separated from its Beloved and yearn to be united with Him without weeping? This isn't just!"[1]

She is one of the female mystics who are mentioned frequently in the anthologies of saints composed throughout the history of Sufism. Al-Ghazali relates one of her prayers:

> O my God, how great is my desire to meet with Thee and how great is my hope of Thy reward. Thou art gracious, there is no disappointment from Thee, the Hope of all who hope; there is no frustration with Thee, Thou Desire of all who yearn. O my God, if I am unworthy of Thee and my works do not bring me near to Thee, yet my weakness has made confession of my sins, and if Thou dost forgive—Who has more power (to forgive) than Thyself, and if Thou dost punish—Who is more just to perform it than Thyself? O my Lord, my tears have flowed for my soul in looking upon her, but there remains for her the beauty of looking upon Thee, and woe be to my soul if she rejoices not therein. O my God, let not faith fail me all the days of my life, nor cut off from me Thy benevolence after my death. I have hoped that He whose goodness has followed me all the days of my life will be near me

1. Cornell, *Early Sufi Women*, p. 106.

> with His pardon at the hour of death. O my Lord, how should I despair of the Vision of Thyself after my death, when Thou hast bestowed upon me nought but good in my life-time? O God, if my sins have made me afraid, verily my love towards Thee has protected me (or brought me near to Thee). O my Lord, if it were not for the sins I have committed, I would not have feared Thy chastisement, and if I had not known Thy grace, I should not have hoped for Thy reward.[2]

According to an anthology of biographies of the saints, *Safinat al-awliya'* by Dara Shikoh, the brother of Jahanara,[3] Sha'wana died in 792.

GHUFAYRA AL-'ABIDA (Ghufayra the Worshiper, d. 718 C.E.) of the Basra region was a predecessor of Sha'wana who was also one of those who wept in love and awe of God.

> It is said that she wept until she became blind. According to Ibrahim ibn al-Junayd who reported from Muhammad ibn al-Husayn [al-Burjulani] that Yahya ibn Bistam related that a man said to Ghufayra, "How devastating is blindness!" To which she replied: "Being veiled from God is worse. And the blindness of the heart from understanding the intent of God's commands is even greater!"[4]

> Sha'wana may certainly claim a place among the mystics as well as among the ascetics, for her prayers show plainly that she followed the way of Love, like Rabi'a, and that her eyes were not only blinded by tears of penitence but dazzled by the radiant glory of the Beloved, and that what she looked for after this life was the Vision of her Lord in His perfect Beauty. Her prayer shows also that in her life she was in conscious communion with her Friend, feeling herself to be in His personal presence, a relationship to which the Sufis of the earliest ascetic school hardly dared to aspire.
>
> It was undoubtedly the recognition that she was possessed of the mystic gnosis, and truly walked with God, that made her an acknowledged teacher and spiritual guide to the Sufis of her day.[5]

2. Smith, *Rabi'a the Mystic and Her Fellow-Saints in Islam*, p. 147.

3. See the chapter "A Princess of Piety" on pages 128–32 below.

4. Cornell, *Early Sufi Women*, p. 96.

5. Smith, *Rabi'a the Mystic and Her Fellow-Saints in Islam*, p. 148.

Tears of Devotion

It is related that when [Sha'wana would be] afflicted by spiritual desolation, her performance of prayers and devotions was inhibited. Once [when she fell asleep during one such period], someone in a dream recited these verses to her:

Spill tears if you have grief
As tears of grief provide relief
Strive to be straight
Try to be upright upon the Path
To fast and heave sighs of burning grief
For the way of those acquiescent to God
Is to live with sighs and burning grief.

Rising up, she resumed her devotion, weeping and humming the verses to herself. Other woman wept with her.

They say that when she became old, Fodhayl Ebn 'Iyadh came to see her and asked her to pray for him. She replied, "Is there anything between you and God that makes you think He would answer?" At that he cried out and fainted.[6]

Moadh Ebn Fazi relates, "Sha'wana cried so much that we thought she would go blind. When I mentioned this to her, she said, 'By God, it is better for me to go blind in this world because of tears, than in that world because of fire.' "

Malek Ebn Dhaigham related how a certain man from Oballah used to visit his father, Abu Kathir, describing Sha'wana's condition and continual weeping. Upon being asked for more details, he replied: "Should I explain how she weeps night and day without any break?"

Malek replied, "No, tell me how she begins to weep."

He said, "When she hears any mention of God, tears begin to flow from within her like a rain."

Malek asked, "Do the tears come mainly from the corner of the eye near the nose or from the corner near the temple?"

He replied, "Her tears are so abundant that I cannot say from where

This selection is excerpted from *Sufi Women* by Dr. Javad Nurbaksh, pp. 138–44. Reprinted by permission of Khaniqahi Nimatullahi Publications.

6. The above sections are from Jami, *Nafabit al-uns*.

they flow. I can only say that when the Name of God is mentioned, her eyes become like four shining stars." Abu Kathir began to weep and said, "Her fear of God derives from the fact that the whole of her heart is on fire. They say that the amount a person weeps depends on the amount of fire in the heart."

Malek Ebn Zaygham relates that one day, his father went with Manbudh and Abu Homan to visit her in Oballah. Manbudh greeted her and told her he was the son of her brother. She replied, "Greetings to a nephew whom I have never before seen, but whom I love. By God, I would like to visit your father, but I do not, because I fear I might prevent him from worship. Serving God is much more necessary than that he should talk with Sha'wana. Who is she but a destitute and disobedient woman?" Then she began to weep and kept on weeping until they left.

Qorashi said, "I went with a friend to Oballah. We asked Sha'wana's permission to visit with her. After admitting us into a poor cottage in which destitution was visible everywhere, my friend said to Sha'wana, 'O, if you only could have more compassion on yourself and lessen your crying, in the long run it would be better for you in obtaining the object of your desire.'"

Sha'wana broke out crying again, and confessed, "I swear by God, I would like to cry until no tears are left. Such a shower of blood then I would weep, that no drop of blood would remain in any part of my body."

"My friend," cites Qorashi, "only reiterated his former request to Sha'wana, yet her eyes turned back in their sockets and wept blood until she swooned and fell, whereupon we rose and left, leaving her as she was."

On the word of Rub Ebn Salama, a certain Mohammad quotes Modher as saying, "I never saw anyone weep as much as Sha'wana, nor did I ever hear a voice similar to hers, scorching the hearts of those fearful of God. She would continually lament, 'O dead one, O dead son, O dead brother!'"

"I asked Abu 'Omar Dharir," recounted Mohammad, "if he had ever encountered Sha'wana." "Yes," he admitted, "I have often frequented her gatherings, but she was so drowned in weeping that I could never fathom her sermons."

"Do you remember anything at all of what she said?"

"I can recall nothing," he said, "of her words, except the following declaration, 'Whosoever is present here and can weep, should do so, and if not, should pity the tears of others. For whoever cries here, does so from awareness of the full extent to which his lower soul (*nafs*) has crossed and confounded him, and understanding how his passions have made him a transgressor!' "

Of the verses of spiritual requiem that Sha'wana would sing for her lady companions, the following are recorded:

> To remain forever in the world you love
> is an ambition beyond reach;
> Remember the date-palm that still stands
> after the gardener's demise.

Sha'wana would often come to visit Hasan Ebn Yahya Qorashi. He recounts, "She cried and stimulated others to tears as well. She would lament and cry out the following verse:

> Secure he stands,
> the proud man
> upon his own,
> within his home;
> yet all this complacent peace shall pass—
> indeed a day is near—
> all the same it all shall change
> to fright and fear.

—EBN JAWZI, *Sefat as-safwat*

Sha'wana went one year with her spouse on a pilgrimage. As they completed their circumambulation of the Black Stone,[7] he exclaimed to his wife, "I so thirst for God's love that my tongue has left me."

"Diverse pains," Sha'wana answered, "have diverse remedies. The remedy for the lovers of God is His Grace" (Ebn Jawzi, *Salwat al-abzan*). Sha'wana has further said, "Lord, You know that one who thirsts for Your love can never be sated."

One of Sha'wana's devoted disciples stated that from the instant she laid eyes upon her, by way of the saint's charismatic blessing, never again

7. The Black Stone is the sacred stone set into the corner of the Kaaba. It is told that this stone fell from Paradise at the time of the expulsion of Adam and Eve. It was brought to the region of Mecca by the angel Gabriel, where it was then used by the Prophet Adam in the first temple to God. Later, it was rebuilt into the then-ruined temple by the Prophet Abraham and later, when the Kaaba was being reconstructed once again, was repositioned by the Prophet Muhammad, may peace and blessings be with them all. Traditionally during the rites of the annual pilgrimage to Mecca, one kisses the Black Stone with each circumambulation of the Kaaba. (C.A.H.)

did she feel inclined to pursue the world and never again did she feel contempt for a fellow Muslim.[8]

It is related that God gave Sha'wana a son whom she raised with the best possible education. On reaching maturity, he begged his mother to allow him to dedicate his life to God. "It would be improper to direct you toward kings and nobles, O son," his mother replied. "Better that you keep the company of literary people and persons of good character. What's more, O son, you have not even tasted youth; you lack all conception of the demands which will be made of you and which will seem intolerable."

Her son held his silence. One day he set out for the mountains to chop wood and gather it for his mother. Reaching the middle slope of the mountain, he descended from his horse and engaged in his work, arranging each group of logs in a separate bundle. Upon finishing his work, he went to look for his horse to fasten the bundles on its back. In the meantime, however, a wild lion had attacked and broken the neck of his horse. The lion stood nearby. When Sha'wana's son saw what had happened, he extended his arm and laid his hand on the beast's neck. Then he said, "In the same way that you have afflicted my horse, O rapacious beast, I shall, by God, burden you with this load of wood." Placing the firewood on the lion's back and the bit in his mouth, he led the animal to the gate of his mother's cottage and knocked on her door.

"Who is there?" she demanded.

"Your son is here," he answered, "begging for the mercy of God who is the Provider to all His devotees."

Opening the door, she beheld the firewood, bound to the back of the lion. "What is all this?" she inquired. As her son related the tale, his mother inwardly rejoiced, knowing that God had bestowed special grace upon him and had accepted him as a devotee.

"Now son," Sha'wana replied, "you are worthy to [serve]. Go! I dedicate and entrust you to God." So she bade her son farewell, praying for his journey.[9]

8. Sha'rani, *Tabaqjt al-kobra,* vol. 1, p. 51.

9. Nabahani, *Jame' Karamat al-auliya'.*

THE ENRAPTURED ONES

DHAKKARA [the Invoker, ninth century], was one of the enraptured worshipers of God (*al-'ābidāt al-wālihāt*). Abū Ḥafṣ 'Umar ibn Masrūr, the ascetic from Baghdad, reported from Aḥmad ibn al-Ḥusayn b. Muḥammad b. Sahl al-Wā'iẓ (the Preacher) through Muḥammad (i.e., ibn Ja'far) through Ibrāhim ibn al-Junayd through Muḥammad ibn al-Husayn [al-Burjulānī] that 'Abbās al-Iskāf (the Shoemaker) related: A madwoman (*majnuna*)[1] called Dhakkara used to live among us. One holiday she saw me holding a piece of *fālūdaj* [a Persian sweet made of starch, honey, and water] in my hand. "What do you have?" she asked. "*Fālūdaj*," I replied. She said: "I am embarrassed to be regarded disapprovingly by God Most High. Shall I explain to you how to make real *fālūdaj* so that you may go home and make it if you are able to do so?" "Certainly," I said.

She said: "Take the sugar of the divine gift, the starch of purity, the water of modesty, the butter of self-awareness, and the saffron of recompense, and strain them in the sieves of fear and hope. Then place under the mixture a tripod of sorrow, hang the sauce-pots of grief, seal it with the lid of contemplation, light beneath it the fire of sighs, and spread it out over caution until it is touched by the fragrant breeze of the night-vigil. When you take a bite of it, you will become one of the wise and will be liberated from vain fantasies. It will bring you near to people's hearts, the ploys of the clever will become distasteful to you, you will be protected from 'the evil of the Whisperer, who withdraws' [Surah an-Nas 114:4], and the Houris will wait on you in Paradise with goblets of heavenly wine."

The selections regarding Dhakkara and Fatima al-Barda'iyya are excerpted from *Early Sufi Women* by Rkia Cornell, pp. 182 and 150.

1. *Majnun(a)*, mad with love of God.

Then she recited the following verse:

> The lover's aspirations wander in the angelic realm,
> The outer heart complains but the inner heart is mute!

FATIMA [al-Barda'iyya, tenth century] used to live in Ardabīl [a city in the 'Abbasid province of Adharbayjan, in Iran]. She was one of the female gnostics who speak words of ecstasy (*al-mutakallimāt bi-ash-shaṭḥ*).

I heard Abū al-Ḥasan as-Salāmi say: A shaykh asked Fāṭima al-Barda'iyya about the statement of the Prophet (may God bless and preserve him) relating [a saying] from his Lord: "I am the Companion of the one who remembers Me." After he had argued with her about the meaning of the tradition for some time, she said: "No. Complete remembrance of God means that you witness yourself being remembered by the One you are remembering, while maintaining constant remembrance of Him. Therefore, your remembrance is annihilated in remembrance of Him, whereas His remembrance of you persists beyond place and time."

SUFI WOMEN OF NISHAPUR

NISHAPUR WAS ONE OF THE THRIVING CENTERS of culture and learning during the ninth, tenth, and eleventh centuries C.E. Formerly one of the most important cities of the Islamic world, it is located in the region of Khorasan, in what is now eastern Iran. As-Sulami, the early biographer, was born there, and many Sufis journeyed there to study with the wise ones who congregated in Nishapur. It was one of the early centers of the Melamatiyya order.

'A'ISHA (tenth century), of all the children of Abū 'Uthmān [al-Ḥīrī], was the most ascetic and scrupulous. She was the best among them in her spiritual state and in conforming to the requirements of the moment.[1] She was also known for her prayers being answered.

I heard her daughter, Umm Aḥmad bint 'Å'isha,[2] say: My mother said to me: "Oh daughter, do not take pleasure in that which perishes, and do not anguish over that which vanishes. Rather, take pleasure in God, and be anxious about falling out of God's favor."

I also heard her say: My mother said to me: "Commit yourself to good conduct *(adab)* both outwardly and inwardly; for whenever one transgresses the bounds of conduct outwardly, he is punished outwardly, and whenever one transgresses the bounds of conduct inwardly, he is punished inwardly."

The selections regarding the Sufi Women of Nishapur are excerpted from *Early Sufi Women* by Rkia Cornell, pp. 184 ('Å'isha), 142 and 144 (Fāṭima), 206 (Fuṭayma), and 226–28 (al-Wahaṭiyya).

1. As-Sulamī's student al-Qushayri (fl. 438/1046) defined "the moment" *(al-waqt)* as follows: "The Sufi is 'the son of his moment.' In other words, he is only concerned with what concerns him in his present state, firmly maintaining what is required from him at the present moment."

2. See page 13 above and Cornell, *Early Sufi Women*, p. 218.

[As-Sulamī] said: 'Ā'isha said: "When one feels lonely in his solitude, this is because of his lack of intimacy with his Lord."

She also said: "He who shows contempt for God's slaves shows his lack of knowledge of the Master. For he who loves the Craftsman glorifies the Craftsman's handiwork."

She died in the year 346/957–58.

FATIMA [ninth century] was a woman from one of the oldest families of Khurasan. She was one of the greatest female gnostics. Abū Yazīd al-Bisṭāmī[3] praised her and Dhū an-Nūn [al-Misri][4] sought her advice on doctrinal matters. She used to spend time devoted to worship in Mecca. Possibly she also went to Jerusalem and then returned to Mecca. There was no other woman like her in her time.

It is related that she once sent Dhū an-Nūn a gift. Dhū an-Nūn sent it back to her and said: "Accepting the gifts of Sufi women is a sign of humiliation and weakness." Fāṭima replied: "There is no Sufi in this world more lowly than one who doubts another's motives."[5]

Abū Yazīd al-Bisṭāmī said: "In all of my life, I have only seen one true man and one true woman. The woman was Fāṭima of Nishapur. There was no station (on the way) about which I spoke with her, but that she had already experienced it herself."

Dhū an-Nūn said to her when they were together in Jerusalem: "Advise

3. Abū Yazīd (or Bāyazīd) Tayfūr ibn 'Isā b. Surūshan al-Bisṭāmī (d. 261/875 or 264/877–78) was the grandson of a convert from Zoroastrianism and the son of one of the notables of Bistam in northern Iran. Al-Junayd said about him: "Bāyazīd holds the same rank among us as Gabriel does among the angels." Al-Hujwirī calls him one of the "Ten Imams of Sufism." He was a master of the station of love *(mahabba)* and a founder of the *malāmatiyya*, or "path of blame." He was also known for his ecstatic utterances *(shātahāt)*. He was an ascetic for over thirty years, but later abandoned this discipline, saying: "Those who are most veiled from God are three: First is the ascetic who is veiled by his asceticism, second is the worshipper who is veiled by his devotion, and third is the scholar who is veiled by his knowledge." See as-Sulami, *Tabaqat as-sufiyya* 67–74. . . .

4. Abū al-Fayḍ Dhū an-Nūn Thawbān ibn Ibrāhim al-Miṣrī (d. 246/861) was of Nubus descent and was from the town of Akhmim (ancient Panopolis) in Egypt, about 350 miles south of Cairo. Like Abū Yazīd al-Bisṭāmī, he followed the path of blame. . . . He is reputed to be one of the first to discuss the doctrine of spiritual states *(ahwahl)* and spiritual stations *(maqamat)* in Sufism. He is said to have recited the following verses on his death-bed: "O Ultimate Goal of all lovers, grant me a favored place among Your visitors! For I care not for bygones, so long as You are my only Companion in the two abodes!" See as-Sulamī, *Tabaqāt aṣ-ṣūfiyya*, 15–26. . . .

5. Literally, "investigates the cause." This means that the person who rejects such a gift is needlessly suspicious or lacking in thankfulness, as in the English expression, "One who looks a gift horse in the mouth."

me." So she said to him: "Make truthfulness obligatory and mortify yourself in your actions and your words. God Most High has said: And when a matter is resolved, it would be best for them if they were true to God [Qur'an, Muḥammad 47:21]."

Ahmad ibn Muhammad ibn Miqsam reported with certification[6] (*ijāzatan*) from Abū Muḥammad al-Ḥusayn ibn 'Alī b. Khalaf from Ibn Malūl (a very aged shaykh who met Dhū an-Nūn al-Miṣrī), who related: I asked [Dhū an-Nūn], "Who is the most excellent person you have ever seen?" To which he replied, "I have never seen anyone more excellent than a woman I saw in Mecca who is called Fāṭima of Nishapur. She used to discourse wonderfully on matters pertaining to the meaning of the Qu'ran."

I asked Dhū an-Nūn about her and he said: "She is a saint from among the friends of God, the Glorious and Mighty. She is also my teacher (*ustādhī*)."

[Dhū an-Nūn said]: "I heard her say: 'When God ignores a person, he will wander aimlessly in every city square and will prattle constantly with every tongue. When God does not ignore a person, He silences him except for the truth and compels him to hold Him in reverence and sincerity.'"

[Dhū an-Nūn] said: Fāṭima of Nishapur said: "Today, the person who speaks the truth and the person who is aware of God finds himself in a wave-tossed sea. He calls upon his Lord with the prayer of the drowning man and asks his Lord to be saved and rescued."

Fāṭima said: "One who acts for the sake of God while desiring to witness Him is a gnostic (*'ārif*), whereas one who acts in the hope that God will notice him is the sincere believer (*mukhliṣ*)."

Fāṭima (may God have mercy on her) died in Mecca in the year 223/838 while on her way to perform the lesser pilgrimage (*'umra*).

FUTAYMA [ninth century], the wife of Hamdun al-Qassar,[7] attained a high rank in her spiritual state and was very highly regarded.

It was reported that Fuṭayma said: "The ethical rules of the Sufi in his

6. An *ijaza* is a written certificate given by a teacher of oral traditions (*riwāya*) to his or her pupil. This certificate entitles the pupil to transmit the traditions that are stipulated in the *ijaza* to his or her own students.

7. Abū Salih Hamdun ibn Aḥmad b. 'Ammara al-Qassar (d. 271/884) introduced the *malāmatiyya* to Nishapur. He was an expert in both theology and jurisprudence and followed the legal school of Sufyan ath-Thawri. He was asked to preach to the people of Nishapur but refused, saying: "My heart is still attached to the world, so my words will make no impression on the hearts of others. To speak unprofitable words is to despise theology and deride the sacred Law. Speech is permissible to him alone whose silence is injurious to religion, and whose speaking would remove the injury."

relationship with others include: When a person seeks him he accepts him; when a person is away from him he does not forget about him; when a person associates with him he shapes his conduct; and when a person refuses to associate with him he will not force him to be his companion."

Fuṭayma was asked about the sage (*al-ʿāqil*). She said: "The sage is one who revives your heart when you sit with him."

Fuṭayma also said: "When a person truly knows himself, his only characteristic is servitude (*ʿubūdiyya*),[8] and he takes pride in nothing but his Master."

Fuṭayma also said: "The fulfillment of the heart is in rejection of the world and the destruction of the heart is in reliance on humankind."

Fuṭayma also said: "When one reflects on the bestowal of God's bounties upon him, maintaining his gratitude for them should preoccupy that person from everything else."

AL-WAHATIYYA [Umm al-Fadl, tenth century] was unique in her age in her speech, her knowledge, and in her spiritual state. She was a companion of most of the spiritual masters in her time, and at the end of her life she joined Shaykh Abū ʿAbdallāh ibn Khafīf [in Shiraz]. She visited Nishapur and met there [as-Sulamī's maternal grandfather] Abū ʿAmr ibn Nujayd and [Abū al-Qasim] an-Naṣrābādhī. The shaykh and imam Abū Sahl Muḥammad ibn Sulaymān (may God have mercy on him) used to attend her teaching sessions and listen to her lessons, as did a group of Sufi shaykhs, such as Abū al-Qāsim ar-Rāzi, Muḥammad al-Farrāʾ, ʿAbdallāh al-Muʿallim [the Teacher], and others from their generation.

I [as-Sulamī] heard al-Wahaṭiyya say: "Beware not to be occupied with seeking peace of mind, assuming that you are pursuing knowledge; for the one who seeks knowledge is one who acts on it. Acting on one's knowledge is not in the amount of fasting, almsgiving, and praying that one does. Rather, acting on one's knowledge is in sincerely dedicating one's actions to God with correct intention and the awareness that God Most High is observing him, even if he is not observant toward his Lord and witnessing Him at all times."

I heard her say: "Among the requirements of the actualized Sufi is not

8. Literally, the Arabic word *ʿubūdiyya* means "slavery." It describes the state of being a slave (*ʿabd*) of God. When used by the Sufis, it may also refer to service, as when the virtues of pious behavior are seen as one's service to the Lord. In the value system of the premodern Islamic world, the relationships between master and slave, master and servant, and master and disciple were often culturally intertwined.

to beg, not to aggrandize oneself through anything, not to reject a windfall when it is not from a doubtful source, and not to put off one time for another or for any time at all."

I heard her say: "The master of reality (*ṣāḥib ḥaqīqa*) does not return to temporary spiritual states (*aḥwāl*) after attaining realization (*taḥaqquq*); rather, all of the states occur through his agency."

I heard her say: "The reality of love (*maḥabba*) is that the lover is mute before all but his Beloved and deaf to all but His speech, for the Prophet (may God bless and preserve him) has said: 'Your love for a thing makes you blind and deaf.'"

I heard a trustworthy person relate about al-Wahaṭiyya: I asked her to define Sufism and she said: "Sufism means rejecting all worldly means of support (*naqḍ al-asbāb*) and ending all worldly attachments (*qaṭʿ al-ʿalāʾiq*)."

GOING HOME

I ONCE MET A MAIDEN IN THE DESERT, related Abu Mohammad Morta'ash, and had the following conversation with her:

"O lady, where do you hail from?" I asked.

"From my homeland."

"Where are you going?" I asked.

"To my home."

"Where are your provisions?" I inquired.

"That One who has summoned me forth grants my provisions because I have trusted in Him."

"Don't you have any water?" I asked.

"Only those who fear thirst take water along," she said.

"Have you no mount to ride upon?' I asked. "The journey is long."

"On the contrary," she responded. "Instead of one mount I have four, yet you are veiled and cannot perceive them. My first mount is that of contentment, upon which I sit whenever God's Providence besets me. Next, when adversity arrives, I ride upon the mount of patience and exercise forbearance. Thirdly, when I am favored by Divine Grace, I sit upon the mount of gratitude and praise God. Lastly, whenever I am blessed by God's Love, I mount the steed of yearning." Or she may have said, "When I am granted the grace of devoted obedience to God, I mount the steed of sincerity."

Turning heavenwards, the maiden lamented, "O Lord, your Love has consumed my soul, driven me from house and home and made me an aimless wanderer."

I saw that the maiden was crying and asked why she wept. "Yearning pulls me," she answered. "The Friend is absent. My heart is love-crazy and

This selection is excerpted from *Sufi Women* by Dr. Javad Nurbakhsh, pp. 232–34. Its source is *Ferdaws al-morshediya*. Reprinted by permission of Khaniqahi Nimatullahi Publications.

indifferent to itself. Since such is my state, how can there be any comfort or peace of heart for me?"

"What is the true way to the Transcendent?" I finally inquired.

"To seek for the Beloved through the heart upon the scales of the Invisible World."

SUFI SISTERS

ZUBDA AND MUDGHA [Essence and Embryo, ninth century] lived in Baghdad and were both known for their states of scrupulousness and asceticism.

Aḥmad ibn Ḥanbal[1] said: "If one wants to know how far he is from the ways of the scrupulous, he should visit the sisters of Bishr al-Hafi.[2] He should listen to their counsel and observe their ways."

Zubda, the sister of Bishr, said: "The heaviest thing for the slave is sinfulness, and the lightest is repentance.[3] So why does one not relinquish that which is heavy for that which is light?"

Mudgha, the sister of Bishr, said to a client (*mawlā*) of her family who visited her: "How strange it is that you are not guided toward God, and are not seeking the way to Him!"

This selection is excerpted from *Early Sufi Women* by Rkia Cornell, pp. 192 (Zubda and Mudgha) and 194 ('Abda and Amina).

1. Aḥmad ibn Ḥanbal (d. 241/855) was a traditionist and jurist who is credited with founding the Ḥanbalī school of jurisprudence. He advocated a strict interpretation of the Qur'ān and Sunna and was opposed to many aspects of Sufi doctrine. However, he associated with a number of Sufis, including Bishr al-Hāfī, whose asceticism and scrupulousness he admired. See Smith, *An Early Mystic*, 80–81. . . .

2. Abu Nasr Bishr ibn al-Harith al-Hafi [the Barefoot] (d. 226/840 or 227/841–42) was born in Merv and lived a life of celibacy and asceticism in Baghdad. He was a student of Yūsuf ibn Asbāṭ (d. 199/814–15), followed the legal school of Sufyān ath-Thawrī (d. 161/777–78), and had an ambiguous relationship with Aḥmad ibn Ḥanbal. Abū Ṭālib al-Makkī mentions that Bishr was a specialist in jurisprudence and that Ibn Hanbal would refer questions about Sufi practice to him and his sisters. Although he is not specifically identified as such, Bishr may also be considered one of the founders of the *malāmatiyya*, the path of blame. He said that the Sufi should count it good fortune to be neglected by the public and have his true state concealed from them; for when people contend for superiority, it means ruin. The unusual names of his sisters follow the *mālamatī* pattern.

3. For an excellent discussion of repentance as well as other basic principles of Sufism, see *Principles of Sufism* by al-Qushayri, translated by B. von Schlegell.

'ABDA AND AMINA [Servant and Faith, ninth century, of the region of Damascus] attained an exalted level of intellect (*'aql*) and religious observance (*dīn*).

'Abda, the sister of Abū Sulaymān [ad-Dārānī],[4] said: "Asceticism bequeaths peacefulness in the heart, and generosity of spirit in respect to one's wealth."

'Abda also said: "The intelligent person (*'āqil*) is one who protects the interests of his brothers, not one who follows his brothers' desires."

Aḥmad ibn Abū al-Ḥawārī related that Abū Sulaymān [ad-Dārānī] said: I heard my sister Amina say: "The Sufis (*fuqarā*) are all dead, except for the one whom God revives through the glory of satisfaction with his portion in life (*qana'a*) and contentment (*riḍā*) in his poverty (*faqr*)."[5]

4. Abū Sulaymān ad-Dārānī (d. 215/830) lived for a time in Basra, but spent the latter part of his life in the village of Dūrāyā, near Damascus. He was influential in establishing the Sufi doctrine of hope (*rajā'*) and fear (*khawf*), linking the fear of God to self-discipline (*mujāhada*) and hope with the contemplation of God (*mushahada*). He was the spiritual master of Aḥmad ibn Abī al-Ḥawārī.

5. In the context of early Sufism, poverty (*faqr*) meant both poverty in the material sense and emptiness for God's presence. It is important not to Christianize this concept by thinking only of the spiritual meaning of poverty in the Gospels, nor to anachronistically refer to the later Sufi meaning of the concept, which downplayed the idea of material poverty. The majority of as-Sulamī's Sufi women were extreme ascetics by the standards of later generations. It was felt that their spiritual poverty was both reinforced and proven by their material austerities.

BE THERE FOR GOD, TODAY

'UNAYZA OF BAGHDAD [tenth century] served Abu Muhammad al-Jarīrī.[1] She was one of the wittiest female Sufis and was full of spirit. She experienced great spiritual states.

I heard one of our companions say: I said to 'Unayza: "Advise me." She said: "Be there for God, today, as you want Him to be there for you tomorrow."

Someone else reported to me that she said: "One who loves God never tires of His service. On the contrary, he or she takes pleasure in it."

It was also reported that she said: "The gnostic (*'ārif*) is neither one who describes God nor one who passes on information about Him."[2]

It was also reported that she said: "Knowledge of God (*'ilm*) bequeaths awe, whereas gnosis (*ma'rifa*) bequeaths reverence."

She said: "Human forms are the mines of servitude."

❧ The selection regarding 'Unayza of Baghdad is excerpted from *Early Sufi Women* by Rkia Cornell, p. 248.

1. There is some question about the exact name of Abū Muhammad al-Jariri (d. 311/923–24). He was one of the foremost disciples of al-Junayd and succeeded al-Junayd after the latter's death. Like his shaykh, he was learned in the Law as well as in theology and Sufi doctrine.

2. The meaning of this statement is that the true knower of God is neither a theologian, who defines God through His attributes, nor a purveyor of traditions, who merely passes on information about God. True knowledge of God goes beyond mere description.

A JEWEL OF KNOWLEDGE

LADY NAFISA (ninth century), who was known as "the jewel of knowledge" and "the mother of the helpless," was the great-granddaughter of Hasan, son of Lady Fatima and Imam 'Ali. She was born in Mecca in the year 760 C.E. and brought up in Medina. Her life was the expression of good works and immersion in the worship of God.

Her tomb, like that of many of the *ahl al-bayt* (family of the house, of Muhammad), continues to be a place of pilgrimage and prayer where many receive blessings. The shrine of her great-aunt, Sayyida Zaynab, is another shrine of one of the women of the early *ahl al-bayt* where many find spiritual nourishment and healing. Both Muslims and Christians, men and women, visit Lady Nafisa's sanctuary, especially in the evenings.

Sayyida Nafisa was particularly known for the ability to heal eye ailments.[1] The Egyptian government, not blind to her healing influence, established a hospital specifically for the healing of eye diseases in the neighborhood of her tomb in Cairo. The sanctuary area around her tomb includes a mosque, a library, and a number of Sufi cells. It is considered a great blessing to be buried near her.

Waters of Blessing

[Nafisa] married Ishaq, son of the Imam Jafar al-Sadiq, and bore him two children, al-Qasim and Umm Kulthum. After her marriage, [they] went to Egypt with her cousin Sakina al-Madfuna, and settled down to live not far from the Khalifa's palace in Cairo. Like the other ascetics of Islam,

❧ This selection (except for bracketed sections credited as noted) is excerpted from *Rabi'a the Mystic and Her Fellow-Saints in Islam*, by Margaret Smith (Cambridge: Cambridge University Press, 1928), pp. 147–50. Reprinted with the permission of Cambridge University Press.

1. True vision, *basirah*, clear-sightedness both outwardly and inwardly, is one of the gifts of God to the faithful. See also Rabia Terri Harris's essay "Reflections on Retreat," pages 161–168 below. (C.A.H.)

she used to fast all day and spend the night in prayer.

She was reputed to know the Qur'an and the commentaries by heart and was so versed in religious knowledge that even her great contemporary, the Imam al-Shafi'i,[2] used to come and listen to her discourses and enter into discussions with her; the degree of his respect for the scholarship of this saintly woman and for her sanctity also, may be judged from the fact that he used to pray with her the special prayers for Ramadan.[3]

[Whenever Al-Shafi'i would fall ill, he would send word with a messenger to Nafisa asking for her prayers, and as soon as the messenger would return to Al-Shafi'i he would find him recovered from his ailment. When he came down with his fatal illness, he again sent the messenger to Nafisa, but this time she told the messenger to go back and tell Al-Shafi'i that "God has blessed him with the pleasure of seeing His Noble Face." When the messenger returned to the imam he asked the messenger what happened, and when he relayed the words of Lady Nafisa, Al-Shafi'i knew his time had come to make his final preparations. He made his last will and testament, asking that Lady Nafisa perform the funeral prayers for him when he died. When the imam died, his body had to be brought to her house because she was so weak due to her constant fasting and worship that she could not leave her house to go to him to perform the prayer. . . . She prayed extensively for him and offered the eulogy: "May God have mercy on Al-Shafi'i because he performed his ablutions in the most beautiful way." She said this because she understood that ablution[4] is the key

2. Al-Shafi'i was one of the four great Sunni Muslim jurists. Lady Nafisa had studied in her youth with one of the other great jurists, Malik ibn Anas. The four major schools of legal thought in Islam are the Shafi'i, Maliki, Hanbali, and Hanifi. The Ja'fari school of law, upon which the Shi'ite Muslims base their practice, follows the interpretation of Imam Ja'far as-Sadiq (the sixth Imam descended from 'Ali), Lady Nafisa's father-in-law. Lady Nafisa was one of the many early Sufi women who were well versed in the principles of law (based on the Qur'an and the *hadith*). Her opinion on rightful ways of action and being was sought by many notables of her time, as was her illuminative presence. (C.A.H.)

3. Ramadan is the annual lunar month of fasting for Muslims. Observation of this month of fasting is one of the pillars of Islam and is understood to bring great blessing in many ways. From first light of day until sunset, Muslims refrain from eating and drinking, as well as sexual intercourse. They also are especially during this month to refrain from gossip and to carefully watch their speech so that no ill words might be spoken. During this month special prayers are recited, and families and friends gather frequently in intensified remembrance and worship of God. (C.A.H.)

4. Ablution is the ritual washing that precedes all prayer. Certain conditions nullify the ablution, and one must renew it. As one cleans the body, one is simultaneously with intention clearing the inner capacities as well and renewing one's connection with one's Sustainer. The faithful strive as much as possible to always be in a state of ablution so that they might also rightfully be continuously in prayer and ever ready for the meeting with their Lord. As one never knows when the moment of death may arrive, one wishes always to be as clear as possible, outwardly and inwardly prepared for that meeting. (C.A.H.)

to prayer and that whoever excels in ablution excels in the other works of the Way.][5]

[Lady Nafisa's niece, Zaynab, was asked about her aunt's sustenance. She said, "She used to eat once every three nights. She would hang a small basket in front of her place of prayer; whatever she needed she would find in that basket. I used to find in it things I would never imagine finding there, and I never knew where they came from. This amazed me and I asked my aunt about it. She told me, 'O Zaynab, whoever sets things right with God, the whole universe is theirs.'"][6]

[During the time of Lady Nafisa, there was an old, poor widow with four daughters who made their living by weaving cloth and then selling it. One day, the old woman was on her way to the market with their weaving when a bird swooped down and snatched the sack in which she was carrying it. The woman was so distressed that she fainted. When she regained consciousness, she reflected, "What shall I do? How will I provide for my family?" and she began to weep. People gathered around her and when they heard what had happened, they took her to Lady Nafisa. Nafisa listened to her story and then began to pray for her, saying, "O my God, You are exalted in ability, and You are the Compelling Sovereign. Relieve your servants from their sorrows. They are Your creation and Your dependents and You have ability over all things." Then she said to the widow, "Stay here a while, and know that God has power over all things." The old woman sat down, full of concern for her children's plight.

[After a while a group of people came to the house asking for Lady Nafisa. When they entered her presence they told her, "An amazing thing happened to us. We were traveling by ship and when we approached your coast, our vessel was damaged and water began filling our ship. We tried to plug the hole but could not, and we thought we would drown. Then suddenly a bird swooped down from the sky and dropped a sack on us. We found in it woven cloth which we used to plug the hole enough to be able to reach safety by God's will. And we are here to give 500 dinars as a gift of our gratitude for our safety." When Nafisa heard this, she burst into tears and said, "My God, my Master, my Friend! How merciful You are! How gentle you are with Your servants!"

[She then called the old widow near to her and asked her how much she would have expected to receive in exchange for her goods at the market. The woman told her she had hoped to earn 25 dirhems; Nafisa handed her

5. This portion of the selection is from Sheikh Taha Abdul Rauf Saad and Hasan Muhammad Ali Saad, *Al sayyidah nafisat al ilm karimat al daariya*, translated by Mahmoud Mostafa, p. 33.

6. Ibid., pp. 31–32.

the 500 dinars (a much greater amount). The woman took the money home to her daughters and related to them what had taken place. They all returned to Lady Nafisa and devoted their lives in her service.][7]

[Lady Nafisa] was famed throughout Egypt and wherever she went her reputation followed her, and she gained the full approbation of all, both individuals and the people generally, who revered her for her good works,[8] her frequent pilgrimages,[9] her lengthy fasts, and her nights spent in prayer. She died in Cairo in the month of Ramadan, in the year A.H. 208 [824 C.E.].

One of her biographers [Munawi] relates that when she was at the point of death, and, as usual, fasting, those with her tried to compel her to break her fast, but she refused, saying, "This would seem a strange thing to me. For thirty years I have been asking God that I should meet with Him when I was fasting, and shall I break my fast now? This shall not be." Then she repeated the Surah al-An'am and when she reached the part where God said, "For them is an abode of peace with their Lord" [6:127] she passed away.

The same writer [Munawi] tells us that during her lifetime she had dug her grave with her own hands and had descended into it and prayed and there repeated the whole Qur'an six thousand times. When Nafisa died, the people assembled from all the villages and towns in the neighbourhood and lighted candles that night and the sound of the wailing for the dead was heard from every house in Cairo, and they prayed over her body, while many bore witness that they had seen none like her. Then she was buried in the grave that she had dug in her own house. Up to the time of the writer [Munawi], and even to the present time, her shrine has been a place of pilgrimage for travelers from afar. Her husband, indeed, wished to convey her body to Medina, for burial in the sacred city, but the people of Cairo begged that she should be buried among them.

Many miracles, showing her charity towards others, were attributed to Nafisa. The story is told of how one year the Nile failed to rise in flood at the usual time and the people were in great distress. They were afraid that for lack of water for their crops they would perish from famine, and in this extremity they came to the saint, appealing for her help. She gave them her veil and bade them cast it into the river, and when they had done so, immediately the river rose in an unusually high flood and the people were saved.

7. Ibid., pp. 32–33.

8. "When people complained to her about the Egyptian governor of that time, she is said to have stood in his path and handed him a note in which she accused him of tyranny and called on him to be more just." (Wiebke Walther, *Women in Islam*, p. 110.)

9. She is reported to have made thirty pilgrimages. (C.A.H.) See Wiebke Walther, *Women in Islam*, p. 110.

HIDDEN WAYS

UMM 'ABDALLAH (tenth century) is one of the few early Sufi women whose journey through dreams has been documented. It is through the journals of her husband, translated by Sara Sviri, that we have access to her story. The following reflections regarding her life are excerpted from Sara Sviri's book, *The Taste of Hidden Things.*

Sara Sviri, Ph.D., studied Arabic and Islamic Studies at the Hebrew University of Jerusalem, where she later taught in the Department of Arabic and Islamic Studies. She currently holds the Catherine Lewis Lectureship in medieval studies at University College, London, and also teaches at Oxford, where she now lives. Sara has written numerous articles on Sufism and other topics from a Sufi perspective, including depth psychology, dreams, and Jewish mysticism. She has lectured on Sufism extensively in Europe and the United States, as well as in Israel. In her work, published in various compilations and journals, she has focused on the formation and characteristics of the early mystical schools of Islam, with special interest in the Malamati movement of Nishapur and in the mystical psychology of al-Ḥakim at-Tirmidhi. For many years she has herself worked in the Naqshbandi line of Sufism under the direct light of Irina Tweedie.

Her book portrays Sufism as a living tradition in which insights into the stations of the heart play an important role. As she says in her preface, "It has been my wish to share with the reader the conviction that now as centuries ago, the mystical path carves its hidden routes within the hearts of men and women who, at certain moments in their lives, awake to an insatiable hunger, to an irreconcilable nostalgia for something which they cannot clearly define, and which is nevertheless powerful enough, when this awakening becomes an inner commitment, to shape their destiny."

Dream Lessons

The art of dreaming and dream interpretation has always been part of the Sufi tradition. According to medieval theories, dreams, as well as visions, which appear during mystical states, are explained as symbolic representations of transcendental, spiritual realities. These realities, or meanings (*ma'ānī*—close to the Platonic ideas), are archetypal; they belong to a realm of incorporeal entities, a realm which lies beyond the grasp of ordinary, corporeal sense perception. This realm is named "the World of the Imagination" (*'ālam al-mithāl*). When one is dreaming, the formless archetypes appear in front of the mind's eye in recognizable forms and images. This process in which meanings become images is facilitated through the activity of a special faculty, the imaginative faculty (*al-khayāl*).[1]

Mystics and philosophers have maintained that imagination, as one of the functions of the psyche, operates in the twilight zone between the world dominated by the senses and the world dominated by transcendent reality. By clothing the transcendent and the formless in images, imagination bridges these two worlds. Its ability to function in this way increases in states in which sense perception is withdrawn and the psychic energy is directed inward rather than outward, that is to say, in sleep, in voluntary "active imagining," in meditation, and in mystical states. By producing such images, imagination acts for the dreamer as a revealer of things to come; it points to, or prophesies, future events which lie dormant in the realm of the spirit. . . .

Whatever the theoretic, epistemological aspect of dreaming, the literary evidence shows the great attention with which dreams have been listened to in the Sufi tradition. Some of the earliest evidence comes from the further reaches of the Islamic world. There, in Tirmidh, a town on the shores of the Oxus river (the Amu Daria) in the border zone of Afghanistan, Tadzikistan, and Turkestan, a ninth century seeker went in search of inner knowledge. Abū 'Abdallāh Muhammad ibn 'Alī al-Ḥakīm

❧ This selection is excerpted from *The Taste of Hidden Things: Images on the Sufi Path* by Sara Sviri (Inverness, Calif.: Golden Sufi Center Publishing, 1997), pp. 54, 61–76. Reprinted by permission of the Golden Sufi Center.

1. Henri Corbin, who studied imagination in Islamic mystical philosophy, writes: "This imagination does not construct something unreal, but unveils the hidden reality"; see his *Spiritual Body and Celestial Earth*, p. 12. See also Corbin, *Creative Imagination in the Sufism of Ibn 'Arabi*, "Introduction," pp. 6ff.

at-Tirmidhī has left a personal document which describes his search, a document which is, to the best of my knowledge, the first autobiography written, or at least preserved, in Sufi literature, and probably also in Muslim literature at large.[2]

In the Sufi tradition at-Tirmidhī's name has become associated with the doctrine, fundamental to his teaching, concerning the *awliyā'*, the friends of God, the holy ones of Islam.[3] According to this doctrine, one of the routes by which God communicates with His elect is through dreams. This is based on the understanding of a Qur'anic verse which reads:

> Surely God's friends—no fear shall be with them, neither shall they sorrow . . . for them is good tidings (*bushrā*) in the present life and in the world to come. [10:62–4]

"Good tidings," at-Tirmidhī writes in his *The Way of the Friends of God* (*Sīrat al-awliyā'*), "is a veridical dream. . . . The dream of the faithful is God's word spoken to him and her in their sleep."[4]

In his autobiography, which is entitled *The Beginning of the Matter* (*Buduww sha'n*) al-îakim at-Tirmidhī describes the key events in his life, dreams, mystical experiences and also—and this is unique—his extraordinarily clear relationship with his wife. Since at-Tirmidhī does not disclose her name, I shall refer to her simply as Umm 'Abdallāh (the mother of 'Abdallāh), in the same way that he was called Abū 'Abdallāh (the father of 'Abdallāh); it has always been a custom in the orient to refer to parents by the name of their child.

The inner link between at-Tirmidhī and his wife was so strong that she used to dream teaching dreams for him. In fact, most of the dreams recorded in his autobiography are his wife's dreams for him. However, the dreams also make it clear that she is not just a mediumistic messenger for him. The dreams reflect her own inner development. Significantly, at-Tirmidhī's record ends with Umm 'Abdallāh's own deeply moving mystical experiences, and the understanding thereof, which were given to her alone.

In other words, this autobiography is a document which describes the inner journey, through dreams and experiences, of a mystical couple,

2. See al-Hakim at-Tirmidhī, *Buduww sha'n*, pp. 315–43. See also Radtke, "*Tirmiḍiana Minora*," pp. 242–98.

3. See al-Hujwiri, *Kashf al-Mahjub*, pp. 210ff. See also Chodkiewicz, *Seal of the Saints*, pp. 27–32.

4. See Radtke (ed.), *Sīrat al-awliyā'*, pp. 66–67 (Arabic text; trans. SS).

united in marriage as well as in the spiritual quest; whose inner and outer lives are closely knit together.[5] In this respect, I think, it is not only a rare document, but also a rare and precious human experience.

In his autobiography, at-Tirmidhī tells how for years, after his initial spiritual awakening which took place during a pilgrimage to the Ka'ba, he kept searching on his own, with no teacher, and without companions. He writes:

> The love of solitude came into my heart. I would go out into the wilderness and wander about in the ruins and graveyards around my quarter. This was my practice, and I kept it diligently. I was looking for true companions who would support me in this, but it was difficult for me to find any. So I took refuge in ruins and in solitary places.
>
> One day, while in this state, I saw, as if in a dream, the Messenger of God, peace be upon him. He entered the great mosque of our town and I followed him closely, step by step. He walked until he entered the *maqṣūra* (the section reserved for dignitaries) and I followed him, almost cleaving to his back, stepping upon his very footsteps. . . . Then he climbed up the pulpit, and so did I. Each step that he climbed, I climbed behind him. When he reached the uppermost step he sat down and I sat down at his feet, on the step beneath him, my right side facing his face, my face facing the gates which lead to the market, and my left facing the people (in the mosque). I woke up in this position.

This is the first auspicious dream which at-Tirmidhī records. He does not find it necessary to interpret the dream. Its symbolic meaning is, to him, apparent. Traditionally, seeing the Prophet in a dream is understood as a true, real event and must be taken at face value and not interpreted away.[6]

At a certain point in at-Tirmidhī's spiritual journey, his wife starts having dreams which contain clear messages for him. This is a phenomenon for which I don't see a parallel in Sufi literature. It is made clear that Umm 'Abdallāh herself becomes involved in the transformative process initiated through the dreams, and is told that she and her husband are on the same rung. Tirmidhī writes that, while he was going through a period of great

5. For a dream of Ibn Arabi's wife, Maryam, recorded by her husband, see Ralph Austin, *Sufis of Andalusia*, pp. 22–23.

6. For the *hadīth* "He who sees me in a dream sees [really] me, for Satan cannot embody me" (*man ra'ānī fī 'l-manām faqad ra' ānī fa-inna 'sh-shayṭān lā yastaṭī'u an yatamaththala bī*), see al-Ḥakim at-Tirmidhī, *Nawādir al-uṣūl*, p. 116.

hardships, being harassed and persecuted by certain religious and political groups, his wife said to him:

> I saw in a dream, as if standing in mid-air, outside the house on the path, an image of an old man, curly-haired, wearing white clothes, on his feet sandals, and he was calling to me from the air (in the vision I was standing in front of him):
>
> "Where is your husband?"
>
> I said, "He has gone out."
>
> He said, "Tell him: The prince commands you to act justly." and he disappeared.

This is clearly a teaching dream. In spite of the persecution he encounters, at-Tirmidhī's position among his companions has become that of a spiritual guide. He tells how people of his hometown started gathering in front of his door beseeching him "to sit in front of them" (*al-quʿūd lahum*). This is the Sufi expression for becoming a guide to other wayfarers on the Path. In the Sufi tradition this is one of the most difficult stages on the Path. Many a Sheikh, so the tradition tells us, has forfeited his or her spiritual attainments because the position of leadership has inflated his or her ego. "Sitting in front of people" is considered a great test, and can never be practiced without an *ijāza* (permission from one's superiors). At-Tirmidhī, however, does not have a spiritual teacher in the flesh. His authorization, or license to teach (*ijāza*), comes by means of dream messages. Through the dreams of his wife, he is being prepared for the role of a master. The old man, white-haired, clad in white, is the archetypal description of Khiḍr, the teacher of Divine Knowledge who comes to those appointed seekers who do not have a flesh-and-blood guide.

A similar figure appears also in Umm ʿAbdallāh's second dream. Al-Ḥakim at-Tirmidhī writes:

> Now my wife kept dreaming about me, dream after dream, always at dawn. It was as if she, or the dreams, were messengers for me. There was no need for interpretation, because their meaning was clear. This was one of her dreams:
>
> > I saw a big pool in a place unknown to me. The water in the pool was as pure as spring water. On the surface of the pool there appeared bunches of grapes, clear white grapes. I and my two sisters were sitting by the pool, picking up grapes from these bunches and eating them, while our legs were dangling upon the surface of the

water, not immersed in the water, only touching it.

I said to my youngest sister: "Here we are, as you see, eating from these grapes, but who has given them to us?" and lo, a man came towards us, curly-haired, wearing a white turban on his head, his hair loose behind his turban, his clothes white.

He said to me: "Who is the owner of a pool such as this and of such grapes as these?" Then he took me by the hand, raised me, and said to me at a distance from my sisters, "Tell Muḥammad ibn 'Alī to read this verse: *We shall set up just scales on the day of Resurrection (so that no man shall be wronged in the least)* [Qur'an 21:47]. On these scales neither flour is weighed, nor bread, but the speech of this will be weighed," and he pointed to his tongue, "and it will be weighed with this and these," and he pointed to his hands and legs. "You do not know that excess of speech is as intoxicating as the drinking of wine."

I said, "Please, would you tell me who you are?"

He said, "I am one of the angels; we roam the earth, and our abode is in Jerusalem."

Then I saw in his right hand [a bunch] of young green myrtle [branches], and in his other hand two branches of fragrant herbs. While he was talking to me he was holding them in his hands. Then he said: "We roam the earth and we call on the worshippers. We place these fragrant herbs on the hearts of the worshippers (*aṣ-ṣādiqūn*), so that by them they could carry out acts of worship. And this myrtle we place upon the hearts of the just (*aṣ-ṣāddīqūn*) and those who possess certitude (*yaqīn*), so that by them they can discern what is just. These herbs in summer look like this. But the myrtle is ever green; it never changes, neither in summer nor in winter. Tell Muḥammad ibn 'Alī: is it not your wish that you could have these two?" and he pointed to the myrtle and the herbs.

Then he said: "God can raise the piety of the pious to such a stage that they will need no piety; yet He had commanded them to have piety. So that they should [come to] know it, tell him, 'Purify your house!' "

I said: "I have small children, and I cannot make my house completely pure."

He said: "I do not mean of urine. What I mean is this . . ." —and he pointed to his tongue.

I said: "And why don't you tell him so yourself?"

He said: . . . "[What he does] is neither a grave sin nor a minor sin.

In the eyes of people it is a minor sin, but for him this is a grave one; why should he commit it?"

Then he moved the hand which was holding the myrtle and said: "Because this is [as yet] remote from him."

Then he plucked out of the bunch which he was holding some of the myrtle branches and handed them to me. I said: "Shall I keep it for myself or shall I give it to him?"

He laughed, and his teeth shone like pearls. He said: "This is for you. And as for these which I am holding, I myself shall take them to him. This is between the two of you, because you are both together at the same place. Tell him, this is my last counsel to him. Peace be with you!"

Then he added: "May God bestow on you, O sisters, 'green gardens' [joy and fruitfulness], not because of your fasts and prayers, but because of the purity of your hearts. . . ."

I said to him: "Why don't you say it in front of my sisters?"

He said: "They are not like you and they are not your equal."

Then he said: "Peace be with you," and went away.

I woke up.

As in the previous dreams, here too one is struck by the allusions to ancient traditions, teachings, and archetypal images: the pool of clear water, the bunches of grapes, the messenger clad in white. The myrtle, a central image in Umm 'Abdallāh's dream, is an ancient symbol for the just, the righteous, the *ṣiddīq* (and in the Jewish tradition: the *zaddīq*), the "evergreen" man, symbolic of Khiḍr and for the ever-living, ever-fresh, teaching. In the Biblical book of Zachariah (1:8–11), the prophet is shown a vision which is in many ways reminiscent of Umm 'Abdallāh's dream images:

> I saw by night and behold a man riding upon a red horse, and he stood among the myrtle trees that were in the bottom. . . . Then I said, "O, my lord, what are these?"
>
> And the angel that talked with me said unto me: "I will show you what these be."
>
> And the man that stood among the myrtle trees answered and said: "These are they whom thy Lord has sent to walk to and fro through the earth." And they answered the Angel of the Lord that stood among the myrtle trees, and said, "We have walked to and fro through the earth, and behold, all the earth sitteth still, and is at rest."

The Arabic for myrtle—*ās*—derives from a linguistic root which denotes "healing." In the East, myrtle has been known for millennia to possess healing qualities. For certain religious groups it had special holy connotations. Umm 'Abdallāh's dream alludes, through the symbolism of herbs and myrtle, to two levels of spiritual healing or instruction: the level of ordinary good worshippers (*aṣ-ṣādiqūn*), who are symbolized by the fragrant herbs, and the level of the just (*aṣ-ṣiddīqūn*). The latter, who in at-Tirmidhī's teaching are synonymous with "the friends of God," are symbolized by the myrtle. Both types of worshippers are sincere—as is indicated by the linguistic root *ṣ-d-q*, common to their respective designations. Nevertheless, they represent a hierarchical distinction between those who worship God externally and those who worship God both externally and internally. The nature of the worship of the first group is not altogether firm; it's rather fickle, since the herbs which symbolize them "in summer . . . are like this," namely, withered, "and in winter . . . are green." As for the *ṣiddīqūn*, the mystics, "those who have attained certitude," they are symbolized by the evergreen myrtle which never withers, neither in winter nor in summer.

The hierarchy which distinguishes the *ṣadiqun* from the *ṣiddīqūn* is one of the main themes in at-Tirmidhī's vast literary corpus. A clear relationship exists, therefore, between his, or his wife's, dream experiences and the development of his mystical teaching. Thus the dream indicates a process of inner integration, whereby the symbolic messages become truly directive and instructive. The dream brings good tidings also for Umm 'Abdallāh. She is distinguished from her sisters and is told in unambiguous terms that she and her husband "are together in the same place," and she, too, is given a branch of myrtle. Thus through the dream both wife and husband have become prepared for the next phase of their spiritual journey.

The next stage is inaugurated by a dream in which Umm 'Abdallāh is shown the process of spiritual transformation which is going to take place in her husband and in the world around him through his teaching. The dream points to her own deep involvement in this process: she becomes, or pledges to become, the custodian and protector of her husband's work. Without her his mission cannot be complete. Here is the dream:

> [In her dream] she was in the open hall of our house . . . There were several couches there, upholstered with brocade. One of the couches stood next to the family mosque. She said:
>
> I saw a tree growing by the side of this couch, facing the mosque. It grew up to a man's height, and it looked very dry, like a withered

piece of wood. It had branches, similar to a palm tree, but the branches were all dry, like wooden pegs or filings. Now from the bottom of the trunk new branches emerged, about five or six, and they were all green and moist. When these branches reached the middle of the dry tree it started stretching and extending upwards to about three times a man's height, and so did the branches, too. Then from amidst the branches there appeared bunches of grapes. I heard myself saying: "This tree is mine! No one from here to the other end of the world has a tree like this!"

I came closer to the tree and I heard a voice coming from around it, although I could see no one there. I looked at the trunk and I saw that it had grown out of a rock, a big rock. By the side of this rock I saw another big rock which had a hollow, like a pool. From the trunk of the tree a brook emerged and its waters, which were pure, flowed into the hollow of the rock and gathered there.

Again I heard a voice calling me from the bottom of the tree: "Can you make a pledge to protect this tree so that no hand would touch it? Then this tree is yours. Its roots have stood in sand and soil; many hands have touched it, and its fruit became worthless, then rotted and dried up. But now we have placed a rock around it, and we have nominated a bird over it, to watch over the fruit of this tree. Look!"

I looked, and I saw a green bird, the size of a pigeon. It perched on one of the branches, not on the green moist ones that grew from the bottom of the trunk, but on a dry branch. . . . The bird hopped upwards, climbing from branch to branch; whenever it perched on a dry branch, which looked like a dry peg, it became green and moist, and bunches of grapes hung down from it. The voice said: "If you protect this tree faithfully the bird will reach the top of the tree and the whole tree will become green; otherwise the bird will stay here, in the middle."

I said, "I will, indeed, I will protect it!" But there was no-one to be seen.

The bird flew to the top of the tree, branch after branch, and the whole tree became green. When it reached the top of the tree I exclaimed with amazement: "*Lā ilāha illā 'llāh!* (There is no god but God). Where are all the people? Can't they see the tree and come nearer?"

And the bird answered from the top of the tree: "*Lā ilāha illā 'llāh!*"

I wanted to pick up a tender grape from the tree, but a voice said to me: "No! Not until it has ripened!" And I woke up.

This dream carries a prophetic message for both husband and wife. Its images, as those of the previous dream, are ancient and archetypal. Discourse on the meaning of tree, rock, brook, the bunches of grapes (again), and the green bird could take up many pages. But Abū 'Abdallāh is content to let the dream speak for itself. The magical transformation of the withered tree which takes place in front of Umm 'Abdallāh's eyes, the clear, authoritative messages which are conveyed to her through a hidden messenger, the green bird—a touch of Khiḍr?—which calls out the formula of faith and surrender from the top of the tree—all these images carry a lucid numinosity that touches the reader as it touched the dreamer. For her, who has a complete and utter faith in her husband's mission and destiny, the dream speaks with prophetic truth. She understands and accepts her role in his mission with enthusiasm and joy. Though the time is not yet ripe, the tree is destined to grow to immense dimensions and be protected by the "angelic" bird which is nominated upon it.

. . . Information about Sufi women does not exist in abundance. We are fortunate to have access to this unique record which tells us about this loyal, sincere, prophetic woman, whose dreams have been carefully and lovingly recorded by her husband. This unnamed woman from Central Asia, more than eleven hundred years ago, became awakened, through her deep empathy with her husband's destiny, to her own inner quest. Alongside her dreams for him, at-Tirmidhī's autobiography records Umm 'Abdallāh's own spiritual ripening through dreams. In one of these dreams she sees herself and her husband sleeping together in the same bed. The Prophet Muḥammad comes and lies down with them.

In another dream, one of the last dreams in the document, and one which—the record says—is meant for her alone, she sees the Prophet enter their house. She wants to kiss his feet, but he does not allow it.

> "He gave me his hand," she told her husband, "and I kissed it. I did not know what to ask of him. One of my eyes had been badly inflamed, so I said: 'Messenger of God, one of my eyes has been infected by inflammation.'
>
> "He said: 'In this case, cover it with your hand and say: *Lā ilāha illā 'llāh*, the One without partner, His is the kingdom and His is the praise, He revives and He kills, He holds the good in His hand, He is the omnipotent One.'
>
> "I woke up, and since then, whenever anything befalls me I repeat these words and the obstacle is removed."

The final passages of at-Tirmidhī's autobiography record Umm 'Abdallāh 's own mystical experiences. He writes:

> After these dreams she felt an urge to search for Truth herself. The first experience that she had, which confirmed the veracity of her dreams, was this: While she was sitting one day in the garden, five or six days after she had seen this last dream, the following phrases descended upon her heart:
>
> "The Light and Guide of all things! You are He whose Light pierces the darkness!"
>
> She said: "I felt as if something penetrated my chest, circled my heart, and enveloped it. It filled my chest up to the throat; I almost choked from its fullness. Heat spread through the cavity of my body, my heart was aflame, and all the Sacred Names appeared to me in their glory. Anything upon which my eyes fell, on the earth or in the sky; anyone whom I looked at, I saw as I have never seen before, because of the beauty and joy and sweetness [which filled me]. Then a verse in Persian descended upon my heart: 'We have given you one thing!'
>
> "Again I was filled with joy, elation, and great energy."
>
> "The next day," she said, "another verse descended on my heart: 'We have given you three things: Our Glory, Our Might, and Our Beauty.'
>
> "Then," she said, "I saw this glow behind me, and it stayed above my head as if in a dream, and in this glowing light these three things were revealed to me: the knowledge of the Divine Glory, the knowledge of the Divine Might, and the knowledge of the Divine Beauty. Then I saw something shimmering and moving, and it was conveyed to me: 'These things are going to take place; all that moves is from God; the Might and the High Rank are from God, and so is the Beauty and the Merit. This fire that I saw in the sky is from God, and now I see it as sparks of emerald and silver, blown and kindled.' "
>
> On the third day these words descended on her heart: "We have given you the knowledge of Past and Future."
>
> She remained in this state for some time, and then the knowledge of the names of God was revealed to her. Each day new names were opened up to her, and the glowing light was upon her heart, and the inward meaning of the names was revealed to her. This lasted for ten days. On the tenth day she came to me and said that the [Divine] name "The Gracious" (*al-laṭīf*; this name means also: the Kind, the Gentle, the Subtle) was revealed to her.

From the care with which these, as well as the rest of the dreams contained in the document, were recorded, it is clear how seriously dreams were taken as heralds of destinies by the early Muslim mystics. At-Tirmidhī's record of his and his wife's dreams allows us an insight into the importance assigned to dreams as instruments of spiritual teaching. And this is how Abū ʿAbdallāh's own account ends, this account of the mystical union of two souls connected by love, faith, and vision.

The Unfolding Universe

Within the mystical world of Islam, a shift began to occur; the original impulse guided by the Qur'an and the example of Muhammad began to unfold and spread more and more widely. The early Sufis acted autonomously, flowing freely in communication and worship, gathering to share spiritual conversation or listen to a particularly illuminated individual, yet each following more or less an individual path. By the end of the twelfth century, clusters of Sufi adepts were beginning to more closely follow a particular exemplar. Around these Sufi lights of inspiration, *tariqahs* (literally, "Ways" to union with God)—brother/sisterhoods based upon the example of a Pir, or primary saint, developed, though each *tariqah* was always firmly rooted back through the spiritual lineage and example of the Prophet Muhammad and the revelation of the Qur'an.

All of the resulting Sufi *tariqahs* were founded upon the example of outstanding saintly men, and their *silsilahs*, or traditional lineages, generally mention only male transmitters of the line. However, though sometimes hidden, there continued also to be many luminous women within these Sufi communities who assisted in the conveyance of the practices and manners of their order. As the more structured brother/sisterhoods evolved, rather than taking a public teaching role, women tended to share their light as sisters, mothers, wives, daughters, cohorts, and students, only occasionally acting as formal teachers, or *shaykhas*. There were however, in many of the orders, coordinated women's circles that were led and continue to be led by women. Occasionally a woman might also be appointed to stand as teacher and exemplar for both women and men within a particular community. A number of Sufi biographers do include documentation of these radiant women. Shaykh 'Abd al-Haqq Muhaddis Dihlawi (one of the important early biographers) included a chapter on women saints in his book *Akhbaru'l-akhyar* (Stories of the Chosen Ones). In *Rawdat al-nazirin wa khulasat manaqib al-salihin* (The Garden of the Guardians and the Extract of the Deeds of the Upright), Abu Muhammad al-Witri (d. 1512) also recorded the lives of some of the Sufi women of later centuries. Many of the later Sufi luminaries, like Ibn al-'Arabi in his *Sufis of Andalusia*, refer to radiant women who had a strong influence on their development and the continuation of the Sufi teaching. Among others, Ibn al-'Arabi speaks of Zaynab al-Qal'iyyah from the fortress of the Banu Jamad:

> She was of those devoted to the Book of God, the foremost ascetic of her day. Although she possessed both great beauty and considerable wealth she freely abandoned the world and went to live in the region of Mecca, a woman ennobled by God. I had contact with her both in Seville and at Mecca. She was the companion of many eminent men of the Folk, among them, Ibn Qassum, al-Subarbuli, Maimun al-Qirmizi, Abu al-Sabr Ayyub al-Qahri, and others.
>
> When she sat down to practice Invocation [of the Name of God] she would rise into the air from the ground to a height of thirty cubits; when she had finished she would descend again.[1] I accompanied her from Mecca to Jerusalem and I have never seen anyone more strict in observing the times of prayer than she. She was one of the most intelligent people of her time.[2]

As the principles of Sufism were polished and implemented more widely, Sufism developed not only as an intensified path for devoted mystics but also as what might be called "popular Islam." This was because *tariqahs*, rather than "official" Islam, were the most frequent vehicle for the spread of the faith in most areas of the Muslim world. Accompanying many trading caravans, in search of knowledge and the exchange of ideas with other wise ones of far-flung communities, Sufis spread the *tariqah* culture of generosity and hospitality and the thirst for knowledge and depth of Spirit, characteristics at the core of Islam, northward through Central Asia and up the Volga River, east through Southeast Asia and into China and Indonesia, westward through northern Africa into Europe, and northwestward through the region now known as Turkey into the Balkans and beyond.[3] Compared with the more orthodox clerics of Islam, Sufis tended

1. Levitation is one of the more familiar phenomena of mystical experience. Cf. Evelyn Underhill, *Mysticism*, pp. 376f.

2. Ibn 'Arabi, *Sufis of Andalusia*, pp. 154–55.

to be more tolerant of local customs and were generally more egalitarian. Status in the *tariqahs* was based more on personal sanctity than on textual, legalistic learning. The resulting social integration of essential Islamic principles occurred as Sufism not only spread to farther lands but also repenetrated the heartland of Islam, enabling the "heart's blood" to flow more freely throughout the whole body of Islam.[4]

In many areas, the Sufi centers—known variously as *dergahs, tekkes, khaneqas*, and *zawiyahs*—became similar to colleges or universities, where in addition to study of the Qur'an and *hadith*, and the intensified practice of prayer, language and the arts of music, calligraphy, and many handcrafts, as well as sciences, were also explored and studied. Great libraries of hand-copied manuscripts were established. It was in these centers that *sohbet* (spiritual conversation), prayer, and *zhikr,* as well as the everyday duties of the community transpired. *Zhikr*,[5] a continuous repetition of various words and phrases in praise of God, is the main ritual of the brother/sisterhoods and is usually performed individually on a daily basis, as well as collectively one or more times a week.

> The Sufi shaikh, or guide, inculcates the traveler[6] in divine unity, informing the traveler that he [or she] lacks being and that God, may He be exalted, exists in all being, and teaches him the meditation of the heart (*zikr-i qalbi*). That is, he [or she] [instructs] the traveler to continually remember God, may He be exalted. However, the traveler should be warned that if, after being occupied with remembrance of God in the heart for some time, he forgets the meditation, he must continue as soon as it occurs to him or her. If this forgetting should occur a hundred times during the course of one day, it will occur one time less the next day, and one more time less the following day, decreasing until a day will come when the heart, just as it once forgot God, the Truth, will forget everything but God. In the heart where once all other than God resided, now remembrance of God will reside.

3. Among those who have documented the spread of Sufism is Ibn Battuta, who mentions encounters with numerous Sufis in the journals of his travels in the mid-fourteenth century.

4. See Martin Lings, *What Is Sufism?,* p. 116.

5. In the Qur'an (Surah 'Ankabut 29:45), we are told to *Recite what is sent of the Book by inspiration to you and establish regular prayer: for prayer restrains from shameful and unjust deeds, and remembrance of God* (*dhikrullahi*) *is surely the greatest* [of all things in life]. *And God knows that which you do.* And we are commanded to remember God often (Surah Ahzab 33:41), and God says, *Remember Me, and I will remember you* (Surah al-Baqarah 2:152).

6. Traveler: *salik.*

> Once the heart is familiar with the remembrance of God, remembrance of others cannot abide. With time the eye will see in another way, the ear will hear in another way.[7] In sum, as remembrance changes, thought will change. As time goes by the traveler will not be able to see any being in the self that he or she should be able to do anything with that being.[8]

One's personal will becomes merged with the Divine Will. As one's acts become unified in the Divine intention, one's qualities gradually become also more irradiated by the Divine qualities, leading to the possibility of the unity of essential Being, or *tawhid.*

The first full-blown *tariqah,* or brother/sisterhood established upon the example of one who made this journey was organized by the followers of Sayyid 'Abd al-Qadir Jilani (d. 1166)[9] and became known as the Qadiriyya. 'Abd al-Qadir Jilani's aunt, Umm Muhammad, and his mother, Umm al-Khayre, were both women of great spiritual significance. His mother in particular had a strong influence upon him. She raised him carefully until the age of eighteen, when he determined to set out from Baghdad. His mother gave him forty gold coins, his share of his inheritance, before he left and advised him to always be truthful and honest. He promised that he would be. Not long after, his caravan was intercepted by thieves. One of them approached him and asked if he had any valuables. He replied, "Yes, I have forty gold coins hidden in my cloak." The thief questioned him again and he replied in the same way. A third time the thief questioned him, cautioning him that he was not playing games, but again 'Abd al-Qadir responded in the same way, showing him that it was the truth. The thief was astounded that he would reveal his treasure without hesitation when he might have easily kept it hidden and intact. He asked 'Abd al-Qadir why, and the young man responded that his mother had given him these forty coins as his inheritance and in parting had advised him always to tell the truth. If he were to be true to all she had imparted to him, he could not so quickly go against her advice as to lie to a thief. The thief was

7. This phrase refers to the Hadith Qudsi: "When my faithful servant draws near to me with voluntary acts of devotion, then I will love him or her, and I will become the ears with which he or she hears, the eyes with which he or she sees, the hand with which he or she touches, the foot with which he or she walks."

8. Victoria Rowe Holbrook, "Ibn Arabi and Ottoman Dervish Traditions: The Melami Supra-Order," *Journal of Muhyiddin Ibn 'Arabi Society* 9 (1991).

9. This was a branch of the somewhat older Junaydi line, named after Junayd of Baghdad. See Martin Lings, *What Is Sufism?,* pp. 111, 112.

so impressed by this response that he repented of his wayward life and became a companion of 'Abd al-Qadir and a follower of the Sufi Way. 'Abd al-Qadir counted the real inheritance of his mother's example as more precious than the worldly inheritance of forty gold coins. And so his mother's influence and efforts toward the spiritual education of her son continued to bear fruit.

It seems that throughout the history of the Qadiri order, women have been respected and included in the activities of the order. As Beverly Mack and Jean Boyd mention in their biography of Nana Asma'u, a luminous nineteenth-century Qadiri woman of Nigeria, "it seems that the education of women was a prominent feature of Qadiriyya communities, particularly as they later spread through northern Africa. The most prominent *shaikhs* of the order were sometimes written about in the context of the learned women who were close to them. For example, Sidi Ahmad al-Bakka'i of Mauritania (d. 1552) came from a Qadiri community where it was noted that seventy young girls knew the book called *Mudawwana* by heart, and the famous Sufi master Sidi al-Mukhtar (d. 1811) [is mentioned as] readily acknowledging the great gifts of his wife, Aisha."[10]

In Africa, "it was not exceptional to see women in important informal roles as scholars teaching ritual and Islamic sciences and the actual running of the brotherhood; but it was less common to see them acting as formal teachers of men and women."[11] However, another outstanding African Sufi woman of recent years is Mtumwa bint 'Ali of Malawi (d. 1958), "a well known former slave who, living in Zanzibar in her youth, there took the Qadiriyya and carried it to the Nkhotakhota region of Malawi, where she became the dominant scholar. She initiated both men and women into the order."[12] The Qadiri order was the first order established and continues to be one of the most widespread, with its many branches extending throughout the world.

Another of the early *tariqahs* that developed was the Rifa'i, which developed around the example of Ahmad Rifa'i and his family. The wife of Ahmad Rifa'i, Rabi'a bint abi Bakr, was well known for her sanctity. Abu Muhammad al-Witri (d. 1512) describes her in his *Garden of the Guardians and the Extract of the Deeds of the Upright*:

10. See Beverly B. Mack and Jean Boyd, *One Woman's Jihad*, p. 19. For further details of the life of Nana Asma'u, see pages 137–40 below.

11. Knut V. Vikor, "Sufi Brotherhoods in Africa," in *The History of Islam in Africa*, ed. Nehemia Levitzion and Randall L. Powell (Athens: Ohio University Press, 2000).

12. Nehemia Levitzion and Randall L. Powells, *The History of Islam in Africa*, pp. 463–64.

> Among the saints is the woman master (*shaykha*), the long-lived knower of God, Rabi'a [d. 1216], the daughter of the illustrious shaykh Abu Bakr al-Najari al-Wasitit. It is said in *The Clarification* that the noble lady, the perfect knower of God, the wife of Sayyid Ahmad [al-Rifa'i], the mother of Sayyid Salih, the lady of the *faqirs*,[13] Rabi'a was sound of heart[14] and pure of mind. She experienced divine attractions and constant sorrow. No one could blame her for anything before God. She had a beautiful life and admirable qualities. Sayyid Ahmad called her the "lady of the *faqirs*" and he also nicknamed her "the mother of the *faqirs*."[15]

Both she and her daughter are noted as quite remarkable women. Al-Witri continues to describe her daughter, Zaynab:

> It is said in *The Clarification* that among the saints was the patient, humble lady, the one who recollected God, the perfect woman saint, the pure knower of God, the pious God-fearing one, the hopeful luminous one, the one who took precedence over saintly men, through her lofty qualities and her illustrious spiritual states, the mistress of sublime degrees, the mother of men, my lady Zaynab [d. 1232]—I mean the daughter of the supreme savior, Imam al-Rifa'i (may God be pleased with her and him, and may He illuminate her tomb and whiten her page with His excellence). She wore rough clothing and gave up fine food and drink. She wore out her veil, and inclined to the service of God, the generous King. She was content with simplicity despite her power, and she served the needs of her father and followed his example. Her spiritual path was humility and contrition, and her habit was peace and poverty.[16]

Her father, Ahmad Rifa'i, said that "God promised me that He would give life to the tradition through the lady Zaynab and that He would make

13. *Faqir, faqira*: a poor one. The Prophet Muhammad was known to have said, "Poverty is my pride." Not only material poverty is referred to, but also nonattachment to this world of existence and reliance only on God. (C.A.H.)

14. It is said in the Qur'an that on the Day of Reckoning, what will be of use is to *bring to God a sound heart* (Surah ash-Sh'ara 26:89). (C.A.H.)

15. Carl W. Ernst (trans.), *Teachings of Sufism*, p. 190.

16. Ibid., pp. 191–92.

17. Ibid., p. 192.

the lands flourish through her."[17] The Rifa'i branch has indeed flourished. There continue to be many luminous women in the Rifa'i order in many parts of the world. Included in this volume are contributions by a Rifa'i *shaykha* of Istanbul, Samiha Ayverdi,[18] and also her compatriot Nezihe Araz.[19]

As Sufism spread eastward into India, the Chishtiyya brother/sisterhood was one of those with the strongest influence. Mu'in ad-Din Chishti, (d. 1233), originally of Chisht in Afghanistan, was the founder of this branch that soon became the most widespread Sufi order in India. Since the early days of the Chishti order, women have been accepted as students. In early centuries the initiation took place in a special manner for women: "Following the directive of a passage in the Qur'an [60:12] women could take initiation with a male Sufi *shaykh* just as women had taken the oath of allegiance to Muhammad. The procedure, derived from a *hadith* from 'Umar, was for a woman to place her hand into a cup of water, after which the *shaykh* (again following the example of the Prophet) would also put his hand in the water, and then the oath of initiation would be administered."[20]

Over the centuries there have been many devoted Sufi women in the Chishti line. The main successor of Mu'in al-Din Chishti, Nizam ad-Din Awliya', was carefully raised by his saintly mother, who "supported him in his spiritual exercises. It is said that, as soon as the new moon became visible, thus inaugurating a new month, Nizamuddin used to lay his head on his mother's feet to obtain her blessings for the new month."[21] After her death, during times of difficulty he would go to her tomb to pray and await spiritual nourishment.

Bibi 'A'isha, the daughter of the second main successor, Farid ad-Din Ganj-i Shakkar (d. 1265), was also known for her sanctity, as was his adopted sister, Bibi Fatima Sam, who was known to have said, "The saints will cast away both worldly and religious blessings to give a piece of bread or a drink of water to someone in need. This state is something one cannot obtain by one hundred thousand fasts and prayers."[22]

18. See pages 299–300.

19. See page 285.

20. Carl W. Ernst, *Eternal Garden*, pp. 128–29. This was after the example of the Prophet at the Battle of Badr, where women also pledged their allegiance to him and the Muslim effort.

21. Annemarie Schimmel, *My Soul Is a Woman*, p. 91.

22. Ernst, *Teachings of Sufism*, p. 187. See also Saiyid Athar Abbas Rizvi, *A History of Sufism in India*, pp. 402–3.

When a woman demonstrated intense strength in her spiritual endeavors, she was often referred to as "a man."[23] This was true of Bibi Fatima Sam and also of Mawlana Khwan Bibi (Sahiba), the adopted daughter of the famous Sufi master Zayn ad-Din Shirazi (d. 1369). Because of her spiritual strength, she was referred to as "Mawlana" (our master), a title usually reserved for male spiritual guides.

> From childhood she was benevolently nurtured in the shade of Mawlana Zayn al-Din. The Mawlana too had great affection for her, and for that reason she is known as "the adopted daughter" (*mutabanna sahib-zadi*). She was a great devotee and ascetic. Having mastered the external and internal sciences with the Mawlana, she attained the rank of unveiling (*mukashafa*). The story is well known that once the Bibi was in a state of spiritual intoxication when it came time to eat. When the table was laid out, she was summoned. Because of this state, she came but could not begin to eat. The Bibi lifted up some bread from the table and stretched out her hand, saying, "Take it!" The Master asked, "To whom are you giving the bread?" She replied, "You cannot see that [name in original is illegible] in blessed Mecca is asking for it; I have given it to him."[24]

When one visits the tomb of Khwan Bibi, one sees countless talismans, bracelets left as pledges by the many female visitors to her tomb. An anniversary festival of her death takes place there on the twenty-first of the Islamic month of Shaban.[25]

Another saintly Sufi woman of India who was referred to as a man, and strongly preferred that form of address, was Gulrukh (Rose-faced), known as Hazrat Babajan, originally from Afghanistan, who resided bare-headed beneath a neem tree in Poona (now Pune), India, and held *sohbet* there in the open air for many years until her passing in 1931.

> The act of eating was described by Babajan as *jodna*, meaning "patchwork" to the body. Her *mujawar* (attendant) would use the same word when bringing food to her. This description reflects her attitude to the physical organism: it is necessary to maintain it as a vehicle for the pursuit of an intrinsic evolutionary development and not for

23. See Sachiko Murata's *The Tao of Islam*, and the chapter "The Way of the Soul" on page 177 below. Also note that according to Islamic tradition, when God invites the elect into paradise with the words "*Yā rijāl* (O men!), the first to enter will be Mary, mother of Jesus.

24. Ernst, *Eternal Garden*, p. 144.

25. Ibid., p. 237.

indulgence. Her own meals were small and irregular, though accompanied by frequent servings of strong Indian tea, . . . [though] this combination would be enough to shatter any robust constitution. But this diet was evidently suited to Babajan's requirements of longevity.

. . . Many have testified that the love emanating from Babajan was so intense that visitors felt pained at leaving her presence, departure involving the sensation of a powerful healing current being suddenly switched off. There were numerous incidents in which her compassion for humanity was made strikingly apparent, a transmuting influence which positively affected even the most crude mentalities.

She maintained a habit of sharing her meals with the needy. Devotees would frequently gift her with clothing and other items, but these she would share with the poor and eventually (if not outrightly) give away. Not content with this charity, however, some would even dare to steal such gifts from her, feeling convinced that she would not protest. A characteristic expression of her attitude towards such happenings occurred on the occasion when a man tried to steal a costly shawl recently presented to her. This shawl covered her apparently sleeping form, and one portion of it was held underneath her body, causing the thief considerable difficulty in attempting to remove it, since he tried not to rouse her. Her response was to raise herself a little without opening her eyes, to help him achieve his purpose.

. . . She addressed everyone, young and old, male or female, as *bacha* or "child.". . . Though she was fully conversant with Arabic, Persian, Pushtu, and Urdu, Babajan's speech was largely cryptic. In no way did she conform to logical expectancy in most of her verbal interchanges, instead representing the developed (as distinct from undeveloped) intuition which operates in a much wider context and demands a much higher degree of response. Her sentence structure was packed with allusion to abstruse processes, and her words were often unintelligible to those who could not think outside plain everyday contexts and associations. She did not give any set "teaching"; any verbal instruction came in asides or what seemed to be chance utterances. The verbal level was extraneous to her function; the qualities that she radiated were palpably felt by visitors in a different and more crucial area of their being than the formal intellect—which is not to deny the value of the developed intellect in assessing such phenomena.[26]

26. Kevin Shepherd, *Hazrat Babajan* (Cambridge: Anthropographia Publications, 1985), pp. 52–54.

Hazrat Babajan, like the mother of 'Abd al-Qadir al-Jilani, also advised one to "always tell the Truth."

As Annemarie Schimmel has highlighted, further study of the role of mothers in the development of Sufism could prove quite enlightening.

> Many stories are told about pious sons who carried their aged mothers on their shoulders to enable them to partake in the pilgrimage to Mecca. It would be worthwhile to study the role of the mothers in the biographies of the Sufis. Although the energetic mother of Majduddin Baghdadi, herself an accomplished physician, is certainly an exception, many religious leaders admitted that they received not only their first religious instruction but also their preliminary training in the mystical path from their mothers. Did not the Prophet say: "Paradise lies at the feet of the mothers"? . . . Whether it be Farid Ganj-i Shakar's mother in India or 'Abdu'l Qadir Gilani's[27] mother and aunt, there is no doubt that many elderly women in the families contributed to the spiritual formation of some of the great Sufi leaders.[28]

Nor should one forget "the role assigned by Sufi legends to the 'old woman' who suddenly appears and warns or instructs the adepts in some mystical problems"[29] "Her prayer can stop armies, her complaint can change a ruler's mind, and her appeals to the religious law are always heard, since the Koran teaches respect and affection for widows and orphans. The 'faith of the old women of the Muslim community' is often favorably contrasted with the hairsplitting discussions of intellectual theologians. Many a simple soul among them found salvation through sheer love and faith. How touching is the legend of Lalla Mimunah in the Maghreb! She was a poor negro woman who asked the captain of a boat to teach her the ritual prayer, but she could not remember the formula correctly. To learn it once more, she ran behind the departing boat, walking on the water. Her only prayer was: 'Mimunah knows God, and God knows Mimunah.' She became a saint, greatly venerated in North Africa."[30]

In Africa, the Sufi orders, especially the Qadiriyya, Kubrawiyya, Suhrawardiyya, Naqshbandiyya, Shadhiliyya, and Tijanniyya, were the main influence in the spread of Islam. In the process, they contributed greatly to African Islam's developing independently from Middle Eastern

27. This is an alternate spelling for al-Jilani.

28. Annemarie Schimmel, *Mystical Dimensions of Islam,* pp. 429–30.

29. Ibid., pp. 430.

30. Ibid.

or Arab Islam because "the mystic orders within the African milieu were dominated by native Africans rather than Arabs."[31] "Not until the arrival of *tariqas* did Africans assume leadership posts in the Sunni community. . . . In the *tariqa*, it was possible to become a *shaykh* because of one's piety rather than one's textual learning. . . . Virtually every *shaykh* who was involved in disseminating orders, especially in the hinterland and far interior, was an African."[32] Ahmad al-Tijani of Fez, Morroco, the Pir of the Tijanniyya order, authorized those who followed him as representatives to give instruction to "whoever asks for it among the Muslims, young or old, obedient or rebellious, man or woman, slave or free."[33]

"In traditional African culture as opposed to what occurred [over the centuries] in Arab culture, women participated more equally in religious activities."[34] It was a Qadiri leader in east Africa who championed the admittance of women to the local mosque when men in the community were discouraging their participation.[35] Along with twice-a-week *zhikr* ritual, the Qadiri *murids* [devoted students] there hold a number of annual celebrations, including commemoration of the birth of their founder and the birthday of the Prophet Muhammad.[36] These celebrations, which thousands attend, include the collective *zhikr*, which usually lasts all night for these occasions, as well as musical accompaniment and the serving of food. "The female Qadiri *murids* there meet on Friday mornings at one of the residences of the *shaikh*; at this meeting, . . . they perform the *zhikr* ritual under the *shaikh's* leadership. The women also take part in the annual celebrations, although their participation is carried out in separate quarters from the men."[37]

Until recently, the gathering of women separately from men was the usual mode of meetings for many *tariqahs* in many areas of the world, with the particular exception of the Bektashi order, and to some extent the Mevlevi order, both of which originated in what is now Turkey. The

31. August H. Nimtz, Jr., *Islam and Politics in East Africa*, p. 56.

32. B. G. Martin, *Muslim Brotherhoods in Nineteenth-Century Africa*, p. 73.

33. Ibid., p. 71.

34. Nimtz, *Islam and Politics in East Africa*, p. 79.

35. Ibid., p. 80.

36. The birth dates *(mawlids)* of venerated saints—often the founders of an order—are the most important annual celebrations. These entail visits to the tombs of the saints in which the blessing *(baraka)* of the deceased is invoked. The bond between *shaykh* (or *murshid*) and *murid* takes precedence over any particular doctrines of the orders.

37. Nimtz, *Islam and Politics in East Africa*, p. 127.

Bektashi community, from the beginning, was a vessel that held men and women equally; Bektashis have always allowed equal participation of men and women together in sacred ceremony just as in daily endeavors. There continue to be many strong women, such as Avidye Ana (see pages 280–84), involved in both of these orders. The Mevlevi order has spread worldwide and recently has attracted many female as well as male participants in Europe and the United States with the increasing popularity of the mystic heartfelt words of Mevlana Jelaluddin Rumi and the sacred ritual of the "whirling dervishes" of the order that was established upon his example (see pages 125–127).

In many places, "after Qur'an school, which was usually attended before puberty, a woman's participation in organized religious activities was restricted because she either could not or was not expected to pray at the mosques, [and so] the solidarity incentives of the *tariqa* were even more attractive for women."[38] Though a few orders, like the Ahamadiyya *tariqah* in East Africa, actually prohibited female membership, many, like the Qadiriyya and Shadhiliyya,[39] welcomed them, so sometimes a husband might join the Ahamadiyya while the wife might join the Qadiriyya. Sokhna Magat Diop is the daughter of one of Ahmad Bamba's *muqaddamas* (leaders and caretakers of the shrines of saints) who took formal leadership of her father's branch of the Muridiyya when he died in 1943. She functions as a *marabout* (formal leader) like the others, with full recognized authority over the branch, although she normally stays out of the public eye, leaving speechmaking to her son.[40]

It was also through Sufism that Islam spread in Indonesia, brought to the region by Muslim traders from Persia and the Hijaz (the desert region now known as Saudi Arabia that includes Mecca and Medina). From still extant tombstones and also Chinese documentation we witness the first waves of Islam arriving in northern Sumatra and Java as early as the late seventh century C.E. Indonesians, who seem to have a natural tendency toward mysticism, readily welcomed the Sufi understanding of Islam. The Hindu and Buddhist rulers of that era seemed tolerant to the Sufi teachings of love and asceticism that had penetrated the mystic-minded royal courts, while the Sufi teaching of equality of all human beings before Allah had absorbed the commoners who were placed low in the caste-system of

38. Ibid., p. 130.

39. The Shadhiliyya, founded upon the example of Abu Hasan ash-Shadhili (d. 1258), is one of the largest of the Sufi orders, especially in northern Africa.

40. See Vikor, "Sufi Brotherhoods in Africa," in *The History of Islam in Africa*, p. 73.

the Hindu kingdoms. The Sufis in turn were tolerant of the Indonesian reverence for Krishna and Buddha, whom the Sufis regarded as "prophets." This tolerance was a logical outgrowth of the Sufi teaching of the Oneness of Being (*wahdah al-wujud*).[41]

Through the arts of literature, music, and hand crafts, Sufism was further introduced to the Javanese, who had a highly developed appreciation of artistic creativity. The Sufi saints of Java of the late fifteenth century, known as the nine *walis* (saints)—Walisanga or Walisongo[42]—were very much aware of that and made use of the already popular Hindu epics, the *Ramayana* and the *Mahabharata*, to teach Islam through the shadow-puppet play and *gamelan* (traditional orchestra of xylophone-like instruments) music. It was also through children's games and songs that Sufi ideas were taught, and it was not long before the spread of Sufism enabled Islam to become the predominant faith of Java. The foremost teacher and leader of the Walisongo was Sunan Ampel. The "nonaggressivenness" of his teachings facilitated better communication among scholars of different *mazhabs* (schools of Islamic law) and also attracted new converts to the faith. Integral to this unfolding was the presence of the noble wives of these saints, Nyi Ageng Manila (or Dewi Condrowati), daughter of a high-ranking officer in Majapahit kingdom and the wife of Sunan Ampel; the daughter of Prabu Menak Sembuyu, king of Blambangan who was married to Syekh Maulana Ishak; and the daughters of Arya Baribin, ruler of Madura, who married Kalifah Husayn and Ali Murtadho. It was Sunan Ampel's aunt, Darwati, who persuaded her husband, Sri Kertawijaya, the king of Majahapit, to embrace Islam before she died in 1448, and it was the marriage of Sunan Ampel's daughters to two of his strongest leaders—Dewi Murthosiyah was married to Raden Fatah and Raden Paku was married to Dewi Murthosimah—that enabled a peaceful deepening and further spreading of the faith.

The spread of Islam, the peace that comes with surrender before the Ultimate Reality and the heartfelt expression of its practice that is Sufism, northward from the Hijaz into the "Land of Mothers" that is now called Turkey and further into the Balkans and the Caucasus, has been docu-

41. See Mark R. Woodward, *Islam in Java: Normative Piety and Mysticism in the Sultanate of Yogyakarta*, p. 234.

42. Walisongo is actually a council of Sufi masters that always consists of nine members. If one member died or moved abroad, he would be replaced with a new one, elected by the remaining members. So Sufi masters who became members of Walisongo were more than nine. The council of Walisongo was first formed by Sunan Ampel (Raden Rahmat) around 1474. See www.walisongo.com.

mented by many. One finds practitioners of many *tariqahs* in these areas, notably the Mevlevi, Qadiri, Naqshbandi, and Bektashi. In recent years, under political duress, much of the practice in these areas moved from active community centers into private homes. Stories and writings of women in all of these *tariqahs*, as well as others that have been mentioned, are included in the following pages, from many countries and unfolding eras.

Sometimes the way and the understanding of Sufism have been conveyed by words, sometimes by example. As said in the Qur'an, the "faithful" are those who remember God *standing and sitting and lying down* (Surah 'Imran 3:191, Surah an-Nisaa 4:103) and *whom neither business nor possessions can divert from the remembrance of God, nor from constancy in prayer, nor from the practice of regular charity, and who remain ever vigilant regarding that day when hearts and eyes will be transformed* (Surah an-Nur 24:37). In addition to verbal forms of expression, the handmade masterpieces of Spirit woven with the dedication of hearts in textile design, calligraphy, *ebru* (paper marbling), and ceramics relate women's stories, as do the unfolding of the lives of the children whom they raised in security of Faith. The garden of paradise and the symbolism of the seven stages of development of the soul and the seven heavens as well as other Sufi imagery have carefully been woven by Sufi women into carpets for prayer and general household usage for centuries. Remembrance was brought beneath one's feet and also surrounded one in the embroidery on pillows and wall hangings that shone with the calligraphy of the Qur'anic verses or sayings of the Prophet entwined with flowers or stylistic arabesques.[43] In the Mevlevi tradition, everything is worthy of our respect, including the carpet upon which we stand. These would have been rendered with loving hands by women who learned their art from their mothers, sisters, and aunts. While listening to Qur'an recitation, or themselves reciting, in the midst of *zhikr*, in the mosque or at home, women have often occupied their hands in prayer as well, edging scarves for prayer with delicate lace or beaded berries and flowers whose forms were full of meaning, or continuing the flow of internal prayer while bearing children, nursing those children, cooking, cleaning, being a companion to their husbands, or while pursuing any endeavor they may have been given to practice in the realm of business or trade.

Though after the early centuries of Islam until recent times, women were seldom educated to write or to analyze religious or philosophical

43. These embroidered and woven imageries became the inspiration for the calligraphic illuminative borders of manuscripts. See Marie-Rose Seguy, *The Miraculous Journey of Mahomet*, commentary on plate 1, p. 32.

works, occasionally women of well-to-do families gained the education to be able to read and write, and of these we have some written record, such as the Princess Jahanara. Shuhda bint al-'Ibari (d. 1178 C.E.) of Baghdad was also one of the most well-educated people of her time. She was a famous calligrapher and scholar of *hadith* and was a teacher of Ibn al-Jawzi, who had developed a strong interest in women's spirituality under the tutelage of his mother and aunt. 'Aisha of Damascus (d. 1516 C.E.), a lady of "cultivated virtue, the daughter of Yusof,"[44] was one of the renowned gnostics of the fifteenth century C.E. She was the author of a celebrated commentary on Khwaja 'Abdullah Ansari's *Manazal as-sa-irin* (The Stations of the Wayfarer), entitled *Al-asharat al-khafiya fi'l-manazal al-awliya*'s (Concealed Allusions in the Sublime Station).

Fortunately, in recent times women are receiving the education necessary to be able to share their experience and knowledge by the written word. Yet, still, despite the difficulties, for those who search, a record of Sufi sisters of the past will emerge. Their sacred songs and poetry, their dreams and visions, the stories of their efforts in many realms, and their witnessing of the Truth was in some cases recorded by the men who were able to tell the tales in written form. Occasionally their own voice is heard, pouring forth from a heart full of love for their Most Gracious Sustainer. As Zeynep Hatun, one of the strong women of Sufism around whom people have gathered for light and guidance in the Ankara region of Turkey for many years, expresses:[45]

I am a fountain, You are my water.
I flow from You to You.

I am an eye, You are my light,
I look from You to You.

You are neither my right nor my left.
You are my foot and my arm as well.

I am a traveler, You are my road.
I go from You to You.

44. Nurbakhsh, *Sufi Women*, p. 147 (*Rayhanat al-adab*, vol. 6, p. 367).

45. The translation of Zeynep Hatun's poem/song is courtesy of Murat Yagan.

TOWARD THE HEART

Eva de Vitray-Meyerovitch (1909–1999) was a French scholar trained in law and philosophy who came to accept the Islamic faith as her own through the process of her writing about and study of Sufism. She authored over forty books, including *Prayer in Islam* and *Towards the Heart of Islam: A Woman's Approach.*[1] In *Towards the Heart of Islam* she orients us to the core of all true religion—the personal internal reflection and the universal connection, imbued with love, that mysticism represents. In this autobiographical account, she describes her own journey, beginning with a very proper education in Roman Catholic schools appropriate to her aristocratic lineage. She speaks with warmth of the total sincerity of her Protestant Scottish grandmother and describes her own growing discomfort with dogmatic religion. She relates how, after her marriage to a Frenchman of Russian Jewish origin, she escaped from Nazi-occupied Paris in the company of the son of Pierre and Marie Curie. Following the war, her life as a director of research was abruptly changed by the gift from a former classmate of a book by Muhammad Iqbal, the brilliant twentieth-century Islamic philosopher and poet. Suddenly the external form of religion paled before the internal quest.

Eva was then drawn to learn Persian and to translate into French Iqbal's works as well as those of the thirteenth-century mystic Jalaluddin Rumi, who became her spiritual guide. Her love for Rumi and his work led her to translate into French the whole of his masterwork, the *Mathnawi*, a six-volume masterwork of over 26,000 couplets. This affirming internal connection continued to sustain her throughout her life including her pilgrimage journey to Mecca and her time spent teaching at al-Azhar University in Cairo. She joins her intention in writing with that of Rumi's with his words:

1. Currently being translated from the French by Cathryn Goddard and forthcoming from Fons Vitae. The biographical information presented here is courtesy of Cathryn Goddard.

> I did not write these lines for people to wear them or repeat them, but to put them under their feet and fly with them.

The Path of Sufism

The living heart of Islam (the actualization of the revelation), added to the faithful observance of the ritual practice, the *tariqa* is designated by the word *Tassawuf,* or Sufism. It is the esoteric dimension of the Islamic message, which, like the Shari'a, the religious Law, has its origin in the Koran and the prophetic tradition. That Sufism is fundamentally Islamic, whatever the more or less arbitrary affiliations attributed to it by the western orientalists may be—Vedanta, Christianity, Neo-Platonism—can in no way be doubted, for the spiritual realization is founded on the teachings of the Sacred Book, and Muhammad's practices.

The circle, as a geometric symbol, has been used sometimes to clearly show the link between the fundamental dimensions of Islam. The circumference represents the religious law which encompasses the whole Moslem community, the radius symbolizes the roads (*tariqas*) which lead to the center where the Supreme Truth (*Haqiqa*) is found. This truth, being everywhere and nowhere, symbolically creates the *tariqa* and the *shari'a*, as a point creates the radius and the circumference at the same time. The Law and the Path, both brought into existence by God, who is Truth, reflect the Center, each in its own way.

> If you ask me, oh my brother [or sister], which are the signs of the Path, I would answer you very clearly and without ambiguity. The Path is to look at the truth and break with the falsity, it is to turn your face to the living universe, to despise the earthly dignities, to free your mind from any ambition of glory and fame, to stoop to His service, to purify your soul from evil and strengthen it with reason, to leave the house of those who talk too much and to go to the one where people are silent and to travel from God's manifestations to God's Attributes and from there to His Knowledge. Then, God will extract Poverty from your heart, and when Poverty is gone from there, God will stay in your heart. (Sana'i, *Hadiqa*, pp. 112–113)

This selection is excerpted from *Rumi and Sufism* by Eva de Vitray-Meyerovitch (Sausalito, Calif.: Post-Apollo Press, 1977), pp. 77–79, 83–89, translated from the French by Simone Fattal (Sausalito, Calif.: Post-Apollo Press, 1987). Reprinted by permission of Post-Apollo Press.

For Sufism, the notion of *Tawhid*, that is, the Divine Oneness which is the essence of Islam, is not a different reality from the revealed religious Law. They are both complemental aspects of that ultimate reality which constitutes the basis of the mystery of Being. As we read in the Koran, God is the External (*as-Zahir*) and the Internal (*al-Batin*) at the same time. They manifest simultaneously "on the horizons and in the soul" (*afaq wa anfus*). Therefore there is no real Sufism unless it is approached by two paths, obedience to the Law and the search for inner meanings (*al-ma'na'l-batini*). This is explained in an old classical treatise, the *Risalat* of Al-Qushari [al-Qushayri]:

> The *shari'a* deals with the observance of the rites and devotional acts, whereas the Truth (*Haqiqa*) is involved with the inner vision of the Divine Glory. Any devotion not filled with the spirit of Truth is worthless, and the spirit of Truth not structured by the Law is incomplete. The Law exists to govern humanity, and Truth makes us know the dispositions of God. The Law exists for the service of God, the Truth, for His contemplation. The Law exists for us to obey His prescriptions, whereas Truth makes us understand His commandments. One is external, the other is internal. . . . Know that the Law is Truth because God has commanded it and Truth is also the Law because it is the knowing of God, which He has ordered as well. (*Ar-Risalat al-qushairiya*, p. 43)

In the preface to the *Mathnawi*'s fifth book , Rumi insisted on the close links which join the Sacred Law (*shari'a*), the Path that the Sufis should follow, (*tariqa*) and the Ultimate Reality (*Haqiqa*), which is the goal of one's search.

> The revealed law is like a candle lighting the way—as long as you don't hold the candle, you cannot travel. When you get on the road, your journey is the Path and when you have reached the goal, you have reached the Ultimate Reality (Truth). That is why it has been said: "If the truths were manifest, the religious laws would be useless." Thus, when copper becomes gold, or when it is gold already, it does not need alchemy (i.e., the Law). It does not need to be rubbed against the alchemical stone, which is the Path, for one should not ask for a guide if one has reached his goal, and it is a shame to send the guide back before reaching it. To recapitulate, the Law is like learning the theory of alchemy from a professor or a book, the Path is like using chemical products or rubbing the copper on the alchemical stone, and the

> Truth is like actually transmuting copper into gold. Those who know alchemy are happy with their knowledge, they say: "We know the theory of that science." Those who practice it are happy with their practice, they say: "We accomplish these deeds." Those who have experienced Truth enjoy this reality and they say: "We have become gold and are delivered from the theory and practice of alchemy, we are the freed men of God. . . ."

Etymologically, the word *Shari'a* comes from a root meaning "road." We have already seen that *tariqa* means the "Path." It is, therefore, a symbolism based on the notion of passage, itinerary, pilgrimage. The one who takes up that road is called a pilgrim, *salik*. The *Shari'a* represents the wider road, made for all people, while the *tariqa* is a narrow road, destined for a smaller number of those who want to accomplish *hic et nunc* [here and now] the realization of their full stature as Universal Human Being, or Perfect Human (*Al-insan ul-kamil*).

Given the diversity of character and the different spiritual capacities in people, the Sufis say that there are as many individual paths as there are people seeking God. Every time one reads the Qur'an, one reads it as if it has been revealed at that moment.

Who are these Sufis, who practice *tassawuf* and whose name is derived from wool, *suf*, which they wear for humility? They always refused to give a rational explanation of the Path, as the knowledge *(ma'rifa)* they seek is the opposite of science *('ilm)* and is obtained only with the help of grace and spiritual teaching.

The Arabic and Persian treatises nevertheless try to give some definitions of the term. One of the oldest is found in Al-Hujwiri's works. He tells us that the real meaning of the word "has been discussed at length and numerous books have been written on that subject. Some say that the Sufi is called thus because of the wool mantle that he always wears (*jama'i suf*), others, because he stands on the first row (*saff-il-awwal*), still others say that the word comes from their claim to belong to *Ashab-i Suffa* (Disciples of the Prophet),[2] may God be pleased with them! Others declare that the etymology of the word is *safa* (purity). All these explanations of the real meaning of Sufism are far from satisfactory, although each is based on very subtle explanations. . . ."

The treatise concludes: "Sufi is a name one gives and that has been given in earlier times to saints and spiritual disciples. One of the Masters has

2. See note 6 of "Fatima," page 10.

said, "The one who is purified with love is pure and the one who is absorbed in the Beloved and has renounced everything else, is a Sufi."

Entering the Path

To enter the Path demands a *metanoia*, a change in perception.

My goal is to know through the eye and the vision . . .
the desire of the vision tells me: Rise up and move . . .
In the same way that the child washes his tablet
before inscribing his letters on it,
God transforms the heart with blood and pitiful tears
before engraving His mysteries on it. (*Mathnawi* I, 1821)
Come acknowledge that your imagination, your thinking,
your sensorial perceptions and your understanding
are like a reed stick on which the children ride.
(*Mathnawi* I, 3445)

Therefore we have to look for what Rumi calls a second knowledge. The "conversion" of the mind implies that one goes beyond the plane of common psychology and that "turning around" will lead to the understanding of the reverse side, the mystery of all things. The seeker must "sell the intellect and buy the marvel of God." Thus, "the result of the religion is nothing but the rapture" (*Mathnawi* I, 312).

Everything started with the cry of the craving soul:
Nourish me for I am hungry and hurry for time is a sword.
(*Mathnawi* I, 132)

That search is, itself, an answer to God's call, for to look for the Friend is to have found Him already.

Look for the answer in the same place that you found
the question.
(*Mathnawi* III, 1120)

That hunger, that thirst, the *shawq* of the Sufis, that burning desire, irrepressible, is the internal echo of the primordial Question which establishes forever the alliance between the Lord and the soul which has accepted its vassality. "Am I not your Lord?" and they answered: "Yes" [Qur'an 7: 172]. Likewise, the *sama'*, dear to the Sufis, is a means of awakening, of getting to the knowledge that illuminates, because it is the reminiscence of eternal musics. Again, this need to go beyond is an answer springing from the depths (*sirr*) of the being, for it is there that the treasure one is looking for lies.

The reality of knowledge consists, according to all the Sufis, in admitting that the human being is unable to comprehend God in His Supreme Wisdom. Abu-Bakr, the first caliph and the Prophet's dearest companion, declared: "Not to be able to comprehend understanding is already to understand!" The soul which awakens to the truth at the call of divine grace, which steps out of the sleep of forgetfulness, indifference and carelessness (*ghaflah*), is comparable to the mother taken by the pains of birthgiving:

The pain will be born from that look cast inside yourself,
And this pain will make you go beyond the veil.
(*Mathnawi* II, 2517)

From then on, it has to pursue its way, without respite.

By God, don't remain in any spiritual station you have gained,
but desire more,
The one who suffers from dropsy can never have enough water.
The Divine Court is the infinite plane:
leave behind you the place of honor.
It is the path itself which is the place of honor.
(*Mathnawi* III, 1960, 1961)

When Plato talks about the "sciences that awaken the thought," he reminds us that the ascension toward contemplation, the *theoria*, can only be done by stages or degrees. (See *The Banquet*, 211, c.) The symbol of the ladder that we find in Egypt's *Book of the Dead*, in the Bible and in the Christian mystics, is often used by the Sufis in general and Rumi in particular, for depicting the ascent. It works on two levels, cosmic and psychological. Commenting on the notion of *Mi'raj*,[3] the Assumption of the Prophet, Rumi explains that this ladder is the very being of man [or woman]. "He ascends toward himself, from the exterior, which is darkness, to the interior, which is the universe of light, and from the interior to the Creator" (Sultan Walad, *Ma'arif*, Persian text, p. 121). The ultimate goal of the Sufi's search is this spiritual experience, for which the "Nocturnal Journey" of the Prophet is the ultimate example, "Crossing the skies, or the multiple

3. *Mi'raj* (ladder) is the miraculous ascension of the Prophet Muhammad, in which he was transported through the seven heavens to the Divine Throne, to within "two bow lengths or closer" of the Presence of God. Just prior to this ascension, he was miraculously transported from Mecca to Jerusalem (whence he ascended), in the night journey known as *al-isra'*. (C.A.H.)

layers of being which symbolize the concentric skies of traditional astronomy, he ascended to the Divine Presence."[4]

Likewise, the pilgrim on the Path, following this example, will try to clamber up the ladder of the universal hierarchy of Being. For Rumi writes:

At the moment you entered this world,
A ladder was placed in front of you to allow you to escape.
First you were a mineral, then you became a plant,
Then you became an animal: how could you ignore it?
Then you were made into a human being
  gifted with knowledge, reason and faith;
  Observe this body, drawn from dust: what perfection it has
  acquired!
When you have transcended the condition of humanhood,
  no doubt you will become an angel.
  Then you will have done with this earth, your dwelling will be
  in heaven.
Go beyond the angelic condition, dive into this ocean,
So that the drop of water that is you can become a sea.
  (*Mystic Odes*, 11)

. . . The notion of *fitra*, i.e., of the original nature of the human being, participating in the divine and created according to God's image, is essential. It is to restore this image that all his efforts should lead, and the "purifying path" has no other aim. Then he can say:

My image dwells in the heart of the King,
the heart of the King would be in pain without my image.
When the King commands me to fly in His Path,
  I take to the skies
  reaching the zenith of the heart like His Rays.
I fly like a moon and a sun,
  I tear open the veils of heaven.
The light of intelligence comes from my thinking;
  the sky has been created
  because of my original nature . . .
I hold the spiritual realm . . .
  I'm not the equal of the King . . .
But I receive from Him the light of His Theophany.
  (*Mathnawi* II, 1157)

4. S. H. Nasr, *Islam: Perspectives and Realities*, p. 194.

This supreme mission conferred on the human being is a *mandate*; he is free to accept or not, but it is the reason for his eminent dignity.

Rumi wrote: "The human being is in this world to accomplish a mission. This mission is his true goal, if he does not accomplish it, he has done nothing. 'We had proposed this mandate (*amana*) to the skies, to the earth and to the mountains; they refused to take it up for they feared it. Only the human being assumed it, but he is unfair and ignorant' (Qur'an, 33: 72). This mandate was proposed to the universe but it was unable to accept it. Consider how many feats are done by the universe, they are so great that the reason is dismayed. It transforms the stones into rubies and coral, the mountains into mines of gold and silver, it makes the plants to bud and gives them life . . . It is capable of all these mysteries, but is unable to accomplish this one thing. Only the human being can do it. God has said: 'We have ennobled the descendants of Adam' (Qur'an 17:70). He did not say: We have ennobled the sky or the earth. The human being, therefore, accomplishes things that the sky, the earth and the mountains are unable to do. When he does accomplish them, then he is free from ignorance and perversity.

"God the Almighty has given you a true bargain. He has said: 'God has bought, from the faithful, their riches and their lives in exchange for Paradise.' (Qur'an, 9:3) The Almighty God has said: 'From you I bought yourselves, your riches and your time. If you consecrate them to Me, your price will be Eternal Paradise. That is your worth in My eyes' " (*The Book of Inner Knowledge*, pp. 40–41).

The ascent on the ladder of Being, prompted by the Divine Love, makes the parts of the whole, dispersed in the multiplicity, reintegrate into the One, as colors, when refracted through a prism, result in whiteness. [See the story of the painters in Rumi's *Mathnawi* I, 3467.] The steps one has to climb are numerous passages which allow one to escape what is perishable. Now everything is ephemeral except God's Face, says the Qur'an. "His Face is always present, actual, uninterrupted and eternal." It is therefore the return to the center which makes the soul find the heavens inside it. "The ultimate state for a human being," said a famous Sufi, "is to go back to his [or her] first state" (Sarradj, *Kitab-al-Luma'*). Rumi also speaks of this *self* which, in the end, is conscious of escaping the world of illusion: "Your first *self* goes back to your real *self*" (*Mathnawi* VI, 3769).

A similar vision is expressed by Amiel, in terms that could be those of the Master of Konya. "Disciple of life, chrysalis of angels, work toward your future opening, for the divine odyssey is but a series of metamorphoses more and more ethereal, where each form is the result of those preceding it and is the condition of those which follow. The divine life is a succession of deaths in which the spirit rejects its imperfections and its symbols and yields to the ineffable attraction of the center of the sun of intelligence and love."[5]

5. Eva de Vitray-Meyerovitch, *Mysticism and Poetry*.

MY SOUL IS A WOMAN

ANNEMARIE SCHIMMEL is perhaps one of the most prolific writers in the field of Sufism today, having authored more than eighty books and innumerable essays and lectures. Her knowledge of languages in the field, which began with the study of Arabic at age fifteen, and her academic expertise, which has earned her two doctorates and seven honorary degrees, are legendary. Doctor of Philosophy, Doctor of Science of Religion, Professor of Indo-Muslim Culture at Harvard University for many years, she has now retired to Germany, her birthplace. Perhaps even busier in retirement than while formally teaching full time, she continues to lecture and to write prolifically.

Dr. Schimmel studied Arabic, Persian, Turkish, and Islamic Art at Berlin University and held teaching appointments at the universities of Marburg, Ankara (Turkey), and Bonn, as well as Harvard. She is the author of numerous books in German and English, among them *Mystical Dimensions of Islam* (one of the most important current reference books in the field of Islamic Sufism, 1975), *Islamic Calligraphy* (1970), *The Triumphal Sun* (a study of Maulana Rumi, 1978), *Gabriel's Wing* (a study of the religious ideas of Sir Muhammad Iqbal, 1963), *As Through a Veil: Mystical Poetry in Islam* (1982), and *Islam in the Indian Subcontinent* (1980). Awards she has received include the Sitare-yi Quaid-i Azam (Pakistan); honorary degrees from the universities of Sind, Islamabad, and Peshawar; the Friedrich-Rueckert prize for outstanding translations, the Golden Hammer-Purgstall medal; and the Voss-Prize of the German Academy for Language and Literature. She is also a foreign member of the Royal Dutch Academy of Sciences.

Among her recent books is *My Soul Is a Woman: The Feminine in Islam.* In several of her works she has pointed to the great influence of mothers in the transmission of spiritual principles. And in her *Mystical Dimensions of Islam*, she acknowledges the help and encouragement of her own mother, who, in her unfailing support, demonstrated the "virtues of patience and love, which are so typical of the true Sufi."[1]

Dr. Schimmel says in the foreword to *Mystical Dimensions of Islam*:

> To write about Sufism, or Islamic mysticism, is an almost impossible task. At the first step, a wide mountain range appears before the eye—and the longer the seeker pursues the path, the more difficult it seems to reach any goal at all. He (or she) may dwell in the rose gardens of Persian mystical poetry or try to reach the icy peaks of theosophic speculations; he (or she) may dwell in the lowlands of popular saint worship or drive his (or her) camel through the endless deserts of theoretical discourses about the nature of Sufism, of God, and of the world; or he (or she) may be content to have an all-round glimpse of the landscape, enjoying the beauty of some of the highest peaks bathed in the sunlight of early morning, or colored by the violet haze of a cool evening. In any case, only the elect few will reach the farthest mountain on which the mythical bird, Simurgh, lives—to understand that they have reached only what was already in themselves.[2]

Women in Mystical Islam

Synopsis: Women played a positive role in Sufism. Even though the early ascetics were rather negative in their statements about women, it was a woman who introduced the concept of pure love into Islamic mysticism, and has been venerated for this reason throughout the centuries. One meets women in almost every avenue of Sufism. They act as patrons of Sufi *khanqahs* and as *shaykhas* of certain convents. They have been venerated as saints and accepted as spiritual guides. The symbol of the woman-soul who embodies the highest ambition of the God-seeking human being, has been popular in the Sufi tradition of Indo-Pakistan. As mothers, many mystically inclined women have deeply influenced their sons who in turn became leading masters of the Path thanks to their early education. The role of women for the expansion of mystically tinged Islamic thought in the countryside and down to the lowest levels of population cannot be overrated;

❧ Reprinted from *Women's Studies International Forum* 5, no. 2, "Women in Mystical Islam," by Annemarie Schimmel, pp. 145–51, ©1982, with permission from Elsevier Science.

1. Annemarie Schimmel, *Mystical Dimensions of Islam*, p. xviii.

2. Ibid., p. xvii.

they were the most important depositories of mystical lore and the simple, unassuming faith in God and the Prophet.

In the early 1950s, a Turkish student came to the University of Marburg where I was teaching, and knowing my interest in Sufism, he began to talk frequently about his "mystical aunt" and urged me to see his family during my next stay in Turkey. I promised him that I would do so and, in fact, found in Ankara his elderly aunt deeply steeped in mystical Islam and constantly engaged in prayer and meditation; but even more, I met through his family a number of young and middle-aged Turks, mainly women, who carried on the tradition of the Rifa'i order. Their center was in Istanbul where Samiha Ayverdi, then in her later forties, acted as the *khalifa,* the official successor, of Kenan Rifa'i, a master to whose memory she and three of her friends—ladies from upper class families—had devoted an important book (*Kenan Rifa'i*, 1951).[3] That one of the authors was a Christian made the situation even more interesting.

Samiha Ayverdi excelled as a writer of novels, short stories, and autobiographical books about the past glory of the Ottoman Empire and particularly her hometown Istanbul; her sketches called *Istanbul Geceleri,* "Nights of Istanbul," are a delightful tapestry of memories and lyrical descriptions of the various quarters of Istanbul at the beginning of our century. This book, like her other works, is highly charged with emotion and mystical thought, and I loved to listen to her when she spoke in long, musical sentences about the great Turkish Islamic mystical tradition which she and her followers tried to preserve.

It seemed not surprising to me that a Turkish lady of noble background should be a practicing mystic; for one knows that women had played a certain role in the Turkish dervish tradition. Was not the Bektashi order, founded in the late thirteenth century in Anatolia, known for the free social intercourse between men and women, women participating in all parts of the ritual? This fact has of course given rise to accusations against the order whose members were considered immoral and prone to obscene behaviour. Incidentally, the relation between the mystical leader, the *shaykh* or *pir*, and his female *murids* (disciples) was often regarded with severe mistrust by sober critics who tended to interpret the spiritual relationship between master and disciple as something not exactly spiritual—perhaps not always without justification. Yakup Kadri's novel *Nur Baba* (1922) depicts

3. See also Annemarie Schimmel, "Samiha Ayverdi: Eine Istanbuler Schriftstellerin," in Wilhelm Hoenerbach, ed., *Festschrift fur Otto Spies* (Wiesbaden, 1967).

with the interest of a psychologist and critic the case of a young woman from Istanbul society who falls prey to an attractive Bektashi shaykh, and it may well be that this novel was instrumental (among other things) in persuading Ataturk[4] of the necessity of closing the dervish lodges. Later on, other novels took up the same topic in less sophisticated form. But whatever the accusations of alleged libertinism of the Bektashis and other Sufi orders in Turkey may claim, it was and is a fact that women played a certain role in the mystical life of Islam. Indeed, it was Sufism which opened more avenues of life to women than "orthodox" Islam.

To be sure, early Islamic asceticism and the mystical writings based on these ascetic ideals were as inimical to women as is any ascetic movement in the world of religion, be it medieval Christianity or early Buddhism. It was easy for the Muslim ascetics of the eighth and ninth centuries to equate woman and *nafs*, the "lower self that incites to evil" (see Surah 12:59 in the Qur'an), since the word *nafs* is feminine in Arabic.

Furthermore, as they saw in woman, as it were, the *nafs* principle personified, they also represented (like their Christian colleagues) the world as a hideous ghastly old hag who tends to seduce man and then devours the stupid creatures who followed her invitation to indulgence in sensual pleasures. However, the Sufis, in spite of all their theoretical aversion to the *nafs*—woman in general—rarely used such crude expressions about women as are found in Christian medieval monastic literature. For, the concept of original sin being absent from Islamic dogmatics, they could not blame Eve for being responsible for the all-pervading original sin as did the Christians. Thus, their blame of women is merely ascetic, not metaphysical.

Furthermore, according to the Prophet's example there should be no celibacy in Islam. Marriage was the *sunna*[5] of the Messenger, and even though some Sufis interpreted their married life as a kind of spiritual education in patience and forbearing, or as a kind of substitute for hellfire, they still accepted it because they would not like to act against the Prophet's example. Also, they had to acknowledge, though grudgingly,

4. Ataturk, the dynamic leader of the newly formed republic of Turkey, closed all the Sufi *tekkes* (centers of mystical study) in 1925. Many of the members of the orders agreed with his action, as they, too, felt it was time to usher in a new era. Some of the *tekkes* were later reopened as museums. The teaching of mysticism then found its way through gatherings of families and friends and became more subtle in practice. Sufism is still passing through a stage of transition in Turkey, where its practice continues to be technically illegal. (C.A.H.)

5. *Sunna* is a basis of Islamic Law. It consists of a group of directives originating from the Prophet. Following them is commendable; however, ignoring them is not punishable.

that some exceptional women were able to reach the lofty stage of a "Man of God." Not only was Rabi'a al-'Adawiyya considered to be equal to or even to surpass men, but as late as the eighteenth century the mystical folk poet Shah 'Abdul Latif of Bhit in the Indus Valley applied the old Indian Sufi saying *talib al-maula mudhakkar* ("He who seeks the Lord is male") to his heroine. She represented the longing soul which braved all the difficulties on the path toward the Divine Beloved.[6] For, the true seeker transcends the limits of sex. Similar descriptions are still used in our day when a particularly outstanding woman is to be honored.

At a time when the ascetic outlook was prevalent among the pious Muslim seekers of the late Omayyad and early Abbasid period it was a woman, Rabi'a, who was credited with introducing the concept of pure love into the gloomy worldview of "those who constantly weep," as some of the ascetics were called. We now know that the ideal of the absolute love of God was in the air long before Rabi'a introduced it. It was probably first formulated by Ja'far as-Sadiq (d. 765), whose ideas she may have known. Rabi'a al-'Adawiyya or al-Basriyya (d. 801), a freed slave girl in Basra to whom Margaret Smith has devoted a fine study (1928), was the first to sing of her Divine Love in short, unassuming poems. Her love of God was absolute and did not allow room even for love of the Prophet—something that would become unthinkable a few centuries later. The story of her carrying a torch and a ewer through the streets of Basra in order to burn down Paradise and extinguish Hellfire has been repeated time and again not only in the Islamic world but also in Europe.[7] It was Rabi'a who stressed the importance of the Qur'anic saying *He loves them and they love Him* (The Qur'an, Surah 5:59) as the cornerstone of all manifestations of love between God and man.

6. The saying is ascribed to the Chishti saint Jamaluddin Hanswi (d. 1260); its full text is *talib ad-dunyd mu'annath, talib al-akhira mukhannath, tdlib al-mauld mudhakkar*, "Who seeks this world is a female: who seeks the Otherworld, is a catamite; who seeks the Lord, is a Man." The last part has several times been applied to pious women in the Indian environment.

7. The story goes that she was seen one day in the streets of Basra, carrying a torch and a ewer, and upon being asked what that meant she answered: I am going to pour water into Hell and set fire to Paradise so that these two veils disappear from the eyes of the believers, and they worship God not out of fear of Hell or hope for Paradise but solely for His eternal Beauty. This story was known all over the Middle East and came to France after the crusade of Louis IX; it appeared in a French treatise on Quietisme, called *Caritée ou la vraie Charité*, by Camus, printed in 1640, where even a picture is found, showing an Oriental woman with a torch and a ewer, over whose head a sun is shining with the engraved Hebrew word *Yahveh*. The story then appears in various guises in European countries, usually shorn of its original context: the last version known to me is by the Austrian writer Max Mell, and is called *Die schoenen Haende* (The beautiful hands). We published an Arabic translation of this story in our magazine *Fikrun wa Fann*, vol. 10 (1969).

Thus, her name has become a coterminus for Divine Love at its loftiest, for a love that gladly gives up everything but God and wants nothing but God's eternal beauty.

Rabi'a set an example for the generations to come, who elaborated her basic statements into the multifaceted love theories of Sufism. Her little verses have been repeated up to our day. However, she was not the only woman saint in early Islam, as Margaret Smith has shown in her study, and is becoming more evident in the light of recent research. We may particularly mention the name of Fatima of Nishapur, the wife of a well-known Sufi. Apparently she was a much stronger personality than her husband whom she guided in spiritual and worldly affairs. She was a woman who, as legend has it, disputed without veil with the great Sufi masters of her time. She deserves an in-depth study both as a historical figure and as a paradigm.

The celibate Rabi'a and the married Fatima stand side by side. They were followed by innumerable other women who took to the mystical path. These women apparently participated in the gatherings of the mystics—a Sufi's daughter in Baghdad died about the year 900 in a gathering where the noted preacher an-Nuri spoke about mystical love (three men, too, died at that occasion from excitement). They may have taken their places, as they do today, in a special section of the hall, or on the balcony, but they were certainly not excluded from the performances. History indicates that some women were known as benefactors of Sufi *khanqahs* which they endowed with money or regular food rations. In fact, throughout the centuries we find the names of noblewomen—even family members of rulers such as the daughters of the Moghul emperor Aurangzeb—who enjoyed building houses, mosques, and schools for renowned mystics of their time and received, in return, their blessings. A careful investigation into inscriptions on religious buildings as well as legal deeds which mention women's names would probably bring much more information than is presently available about the activities of women in this field.[8] These activities were not restricted to a particular country: we find woman patrons of Sufis in India and Iran, in Turkey and North Africa. In medieval Egypt (and possibly in other areas, too) even special *khanqahs* for women were erected where they could spend either their whole life or a span of time. For instance, divorced women would retire to such a *khanqah* until they remarried. We know the names of some *shaykhas* in such places in medieval Egypt. We also know of

8. Some fine examples about the role of women in the environment of the famous Persian Sufi Abu Sa'id-i Abul i-Khair (d. 1049), and in medieval Sufism in general, are given in Fritz Meier's *Abu Sa'id-i Abul i-Khayr*, Leiden (1976).

an Anatolian woman who lived in the late fourteenth century and who was a descendant of Maulana Jalaluddin Rumi (d. 1273). This woman was head of a dervish *tekke* and guided the men. It is worth mentioning that female members of Rumi's family worked to spread his ideas in central Anatolia, and that women from various walks of life were among his most faithful disciples.[9] Some of them arranged mystical concerts for him in their homes. Furthermore, even though the great mystical poet rarely indulged in the traditional ascetic language when speaking of women, he devoted some beautiful verse to women as mothers and even claimed that a woman could almost be called "a creator, not a creature" *(Mathnawi-yi ma'nawi,* Book 1, verses 2433–2437).

Women also gained a sanctity of their own, as Rabi'a did. Nezihe Araz, a writer from the circle of Samiha Ayverdi, devoted a fine book to the *Anadolu Evliyalari,* the Saints of Anatolia. Among these one can find many girls and women whose very names *(Pisili Sultan,* "princess with the pussy cat," *Karyagdi Sultan*, "Princess Snow-has-fallen," etc.) suggest romantic stories. But again, Anatolia, though particularly fertile in women Sufis, was not the only place where one could find venerated women. In the Maghrib, a considerable number of women saints is known. Indeed, no one less than Ibn 'Arabi, the *magister magnus* of Islamic theosophical mysticism (d. 1240), studied under two women saints in Spain, among whom Fatima of Cordova must have been a person of extraordinary power. Though more than ninety years old, she still looked like a young girl, and was served by heavenly powers such as the *sakina.* It seems highly probable that Ibn 'Arabi developed some salient features of his mystical thought under the influence of Fatima as well as of that of a young Persian lady whom he met in Mecca during the pilgrimage and who inspired him to write delicate mystical love poetry.[10] The female element plays an important role in Ibn 'Arabi's system so that he even sees in woman the highest manifestation of the Divine. He devoted the final chapter of his book on Prophetology, *Fusus al-hikam* (Bezels of Wisdom), to the Prophet Muhammad's saying: "God has made dear to me from your world perfume and women, and my consolation is in prayer."[11]

9. For more details see Annemarie Schimmel, *The Triumphal Sun: A Study of the Work of Jalaluddin Rumi.* London & The Hague (1978).

10. One may find these poems in *Tarjuman al-ashwaq: A Collection of Mystical Odes* by Ibn al-'Arabi (London: Theosophical Publishing House, 1978). The young woman was Nizam, daughter of the imam of Maqam Ibrahim near the Kaaba. While Ibn 'Arabi was circumambulating the Kaaba and reciting mystical verse, she overheard him and responded with interpretation, and he was entranced. (C.A.H.)

11. For an excellent discussion of the meaning and indications of this *hadith*, see Sachiko Murata, *The Tao of Islam.* (C.A.H.)

That led him to an elaboration of the role of women for the spiritual life of mankind. As the early ascetics had enjoyed playing with the feminine character of the *nafs*, Ibn 'Arabi discovered that the word *dhat*, "essence," is feminine and thus gained a feminine aspect for the inner life of the deity.[12] He also did not exclude the possibility that women might be among the most high-ranking saints in the mystical hierarchy. It would be surprising if Ibn 'Arabi's early spiritual education at the hands of a woman Sufi did not play a role in the formation of such speculations.

As in Morocco and Spain, we find women saints in Egypt[13] and particularly in Muslim India. In India, the lower Indus Valley and the Punjab are dotted with minor sanctuaries of women saints, either single individuals or whole groups (preferably "Seven Chaste Ladies" or so) who are said to have performed some acts of unusual piety. Some are venerated for their chastity, some were blessed with performing miracles and others are noted for their healing properties (thus Mai Suparan in Balochistan cures those bitten by mad dogs). Numerous legends surround them and still today women go to their tombs to hang bunches of bangles at their doors in the hope of having a wish fulfilled. Furthermore, while women are usually excluded from the innermost part of the shrine of a male saint, men are not allowed inside the sanctuaries of a woman saint. Among the more famous women in Indo-Muslim hagiography we may single out Bibi Jamal Khatun (d. 1639), the sister of Mian Mir, to whom the Moghul heir apparent Dara Shikoh (executed 1659) devoted a chapter in his hagiographic work *Sakinat al-Auliya*. One may also think of Dara Shikoh's elder sister, Princess Jahanara (d. 1689), who attained such a perfection in mystical experience that her spiritual master, Molla Shah Badakhshi, would have made her his successor if that had been possible in the Qadiriyya order. Princess Jahanara never married—not for religious reasons, but because no worthy husband could be found for the princess. After her mother's death, she remained the active and influential First Lady of the Moghul Empire; but many of

12. Ibn 'Arabi, as quoted by Reynold A. Nicholson in his commentary on the previously mentioned passage in the *Mathnawi* (Vol. 8, pp. 155 ff.), thinks: "God cannot be seen apart from matter, and He is seen more perfectly in the human *materia* than in any other, and more perfectly in woman than in man. For He is seen either in the aspect of *agens* [active] or in that of *patiens* [receptive] or as both simultaneously. . . . God manifested in the form of woman is *agens* in virtue of exercising complete sway over man's soul and causing man to become submissive and devoted to Himself, and He is also *patiens* because inasmuch as He appears in the form of women He is under the man's control and subject to his orders: hence to see God in woman is to see Him in all the forms in which he manifests Himself." It is understandable that orthodox Islam has accused Ibn 'Arabi of the illicit use of "parasexual symbolism."

13. See the analysis of contemporary Arabic novels dealing with this topic by Muhammad Mustafa Badawi, "Islam in Modern Egyptian Literature," *J. Arabic Literature* 2 (1971).

the women saints were married and were again mothers of far more famous Sufis. The female visitor to Burhanuddin Gharib's tomb in Khuldabad (Deccan) will not leave the place before offering *Fatiha* at the shrine of the saint's mother.[14]

Here we touch an important aspect of Sufi life: the biographies of many of the leading mystics throughout the centuries mention that their interest in the spiritual path was kindled by their pious mothers, and sometimes by a "mystical aunt." Typical of this tradition is the touching story of the saint of Shiraz, Ibn-Khafif (d. 982 at the age of 104 years). He spent months and months in mortifications in the hope of seeing the Divine light during *lailat al-qadr* in Ramadan, but all his striving, fasting and his vigils were of no avail."[15] His simple, pious mother was blessed with the vision of this light. One could easily collect numerous tales about the influence of a pious mother upon her son who then turned into a great saint. We need think only of 'Abdul Qadir Gilani, the founder of the widespread Qadiriyya order, or of Chishti saints Fariduddin Ganj-i Shakar (d. 1265) and Nizamuddin Auliya (d. 1325) in India or of Khwaja Mir Dard (d. 1785) in Delhi—again a fascinating topic for someone who carefully studies biographies of medieval and modern Sufis. (There he or she will also find interesting accounts of servant girls who, in the presence of a spiritual guide, matured into fully-fledged mystics.)

It might be difficult to find many unmarried women who pursued the Path. For, contrary to the Christian ideal of the virgin saint, the nun or recluse who experienced the highest ecstasies in her lonely cell far away from the bonds of husband and children, most of the Islamic women saints were married and usually had a family. It was thanks to them that their children grew up in an atmosphere of perfect trust in God and piety as we can still observe in the villages of Anatolia and Pakistan.

As far as we can see there are not many women who excelled as authors of theoretical mystical works, and I do not know of any counterpart of a woman like Hildegard of Bingen in the medieval Islamic world. When they belonged to the upper classes they were able to sing and even compose mystical verse in the classical languages such as Persian and Ottoman

14. The *Fatiha* is the opening chapter of the Qur'an. It begins the recitation of each of the prayer cycles of the traditional Islamic prayer, *salah*, and also is recited at the beginning of any endeavor. When one visits the grave of someone, one offers a recitation of the *Fatiha* as a blessing for that person. (C.A.H.)

15. *Laylat al-Qadr* (the "Night of Power") is a special blessed night during which angels descend to earth and grant any witness of this event his or her wish. It is said that only very pious people witness this event. Others are made to fall asleep.

Turkish. Also, we know that the classics of mystical education in these languages (in India, later also in Urdu translations) were read and taught in the women's quarters of pious families. But the women were also the addressees of mystical folk poets who were able, particularly in the Subcontinent, to explain the mystical path in simple, easy verses which the women could sing while spinning or grinding grain so that their household chores were transformed into symbols of spiritual activities. Just as by unceasing spinning the thread becomes fine and so precious that it can be sold at a high price, thus the heart becomes refined by the constant repetition of religious formulas or the names of God so that God will "buy" it at Doomsday for a high price. (The relation between the constant murmuring of the sacred words and the humming sound of the spinning wheel makes this image particularly fitting.) Besides, while the ascetics of olden times tended to equate simply the *nafs* and woman in general, later Sufis in the Subcontinent used the image of the woman-soul who undertakes the difficult journey to the Divine Beloved by spiritualizing the folk tales of Sind and the Punjab so that the loving, daring heroines of these tales stand out as glowing examples of true mystical pursuit, faithful to the Primordial Covenant (The Qur'an, Surah 7:171) in which they promised eternal love and obedience to the Divine Beloved. Thus in the folk poetry of the Western part of Indo-Pakistan as well as in Bengal and partly in the songs of the Ismaili community, women appear as the true depositories of mystical love and yearning. This idea was taken over from Hindu literature but elaborated in a perfect way by the Muslim mystical poets who finally identified themselves with the suffering heroines of their songs.

The wisdom which the illiterate women thus learned and memorized thanks to the activities of the folk poets constituted a major source of inspiration for the population of the rural areas and brought the ideas of mystical Islam to the masses, women being generally the most devout representatives of this current.[16] Rabi'a stands out as an early heroine of mystical love, but she has had many successors on a smaller scale. What has been remarked about her can be said of all of these: "When a woman walks in the path of God she cannot be called a 'woman.'" One should not be

16. Further details and sources are to be found in Annemarie Schimmel, *Mystical Dimensions of Islam*, Appendix II, Chapel Hill (1975). I should also like to draw the attention of scholars to the book by Wiebke Walther, *Die Frau im Islam* [Woman in Islam], published simultaneously in 1980 in Leipzig (East Germany) and Stuttgart (West Germany). It gives an excellent survey of the various aspects of women's life from early Islamic days to their representation in modern novels and activities in various cultural fields. It has a great number of illustrations taken from every sphere of Islamic art, and is the first comprehensive, well written, and informative book on the topic by a woman trained in Arabic and Islamic studies.

misled by the constant use of the word "man" in the mystical literature of the Islamic languages: it merely points to the ideal human being who has reached proximity to God where there is no distinction of sexes;[17] and Rabiʿa is the prime model of this proximity.

17. For further exposition of this idea, see Murata, *The Tao of Islam*.

WOMEN IN THE LIFE OF IBN AL-'ARABI

CLAUDE ADDAS, like her father, Michel Chodkiewicz, has been a major contributor to the understanding of the life and experience of one of the foremost mystics of Sufism, Ibn al-'Arabi (thirteenth century), referred to as the "Pole of Knowledge,"[1] or the "Shaykh al-Akbar." Her book, *Quest for the Red Sulphur,* derives its title from a passage from Ibn 'Arabi:

> Tell me, friend, which place you want me to take you to. . . .
> —I want to go to the city of the Messenger, in search of the Station of Radiance and the Red Sulphur.[2]

She indicates that her aim in writing *Quest for the Red Sulphur* is essentially biographical: "In the first instance it consists of retracing Ibn 'Arabi's spiritual journey while, wherever possible, situating this journey firmly in the religious and historical context of the time."[3] In her work, she documents the profound influence several women had on the spiritual development of Ibn 'Arabi. The strong incorporation of the feminine within his understanding is evidenced by the lyrical poems of his *Tarjuman al-ashwaq* (Book of Theophanies), which were inspired by the beautiful being of a devout young woman in Mecca.

Claude Addas has also written *Ibn 'Arabi: The Voyage of No Return*, an excellent short biography that is a good introduction to Ibn 'Arabi's metaphysical vision as well. Conveying the story of his life and the structure and

1. Pole (*qutb*) is a term used for one who is the axis, the spiritual center. Due to Ibn al-'Arabi's depth and breadth of illuminative spiritual knowledge, he is referred to as the Pole of Knowledge, just as Mevlana Jalaluddin Rumi is often referred to as the Pole of Love. In the Sufi hierarchy of saints, it is understood that there is a *qutb* for each era, the "pole" or "owner of the time." (C.A.H.)

2. Ibn al-'Arabi, *Kitab al-isra* (The Book of the Journey by Night).

3. Claude Addas, *Quest for the Red Sulphur*, p. 9.

inspiration of his vision has been a long and adventurous journey for her. As she says in her introduction to *Quest for the Red Sulphur*:

> . . . I would not have set out at all unless I had been certain at the time that I would find help and comfort in the company of other pilgrims. . . . I am indebted to the lineage—still very much alive—of Ibn 'Arabi's disciples for helping me bring this work to completion. Whether famous or unknown, they have ensured the transmission and preservation of the legacy of Ibn 'Arabi over a period of eight centuries. I trust I am not unworthy to inscribe my name in turn in their *silsila*. . . .
>
> . . . To the best of my ability I have followed Ibn 'Arabi down those strange trails that are not always contained within the four points of the compass. During the course of this journey one can sometimes feel one has lost one's way; sometimes one can feel a prisoner in a labyrinth from which there is no way out. But the Shaikh al-Akbar asserts that "all paths are circular,"[4] which among other things means that the journey which the reader is about to embark on will lead him back to himself.[5]

Sublime Companions

> The Messenger of God has said: "Demand accounts of yourself before they are demanded of you." With regard to this matter God revealed to me a sublime spectacle (*mashhad 'azim*), at Seville in 586.[6]

Ibn 'Arabi (d. 1240 C.E.) says no more; but clearly he is referring to a vision relating to the Last Judgment. Now it so happens that several autobiographical accounts survive in which he mentions the various supernatural perceptions he was granted by way of anticipation of the Resurrection and Last Judgment. The analogies between these accounts are not justification for mixing them up; each of the visions describes one

❧ This selection is excerpted from *Quest for the Red Sulphur: The Life of Ibn 'Arabi* by Claude Addas (Cambridge: Islamic Texts Society, 1993), pp. 84–88.

4. *Futuhat*, III, p. 65; *Risalat al-anwar*, p. 12.

5. *Quest for the Red Sulphur*, pp. 9–10.

6. *Futuhat*, Bulaq edition, 1329H, IV, p. 476.

particular aspect either of the universal Resurrection or of Ibn 'Arabi's own resurrection. In any case two of these texts cannot possibly bear any relation to the "sublime spectacle" of 586 [A.H.], because they refer to visions which he experienced in one case in Fez in 593 and in another case in 599 in Mecca. However, we also possess two other accounts by Ibn 'Arabi which mention neither dates nor place-names but which quite possibly correspond to the vision of 586.

The first of these accounts is to be found in chapter 71 of the *Futuhat*—a chapter devoted to the "secrets of fasting." After explaining that on the Day of Judgment the saints will first of all intercede on behalf of those who have done them harm (he notes that in the case of those who show kindness to the saints, their benevolence will itself be their safe-conduct), Ibn 'Arabi describes the vision he was granted of his own intercession. "God has promised me that on the Day of Resurrection I will be able to intercede on behalf of everyone who falls within my gaze—*those whom I know and those whom I do not know*. He showed me this in a scene (*mashhad*) in such a way that I saw it and experienced it with certainty."[7]

In the *Kitab al-mubashirat* or *Book of Visions* Ibn 'Arabi gives a complete and detailed report of the event. "I saw in a vision that the Resurrection had taken place. People were rushing forward: some were clothed, others naked; some were walking on their legs, others on their faces.

"Then God came, 'in the darkness of thick clouds, accompanied by angels' (Qur'an 2:210), seated on His Throne which was being carried by angels. They placed the throne to my right. While all this was happening I experienced no fear or anxiety or fright.

"Then God placed His palm upon me to make me know what my situation had been [in this low world]; thanks to the authentic *hadith (al-hadith al sahih)* I understood his intention[8] and I said to Him: 'Lord, kings demand accounts of their subjects because they are poor and need what they take from them for their treasury. But You are rich. Tell me then what You will add to Your purse by demanding accounts of created beings.' He smiled and replied: 'What do you want?' I answered: 'Authorize me to go to Paradise [i.e., directly and without rendering accounts].' He gave me His authorization.

"Then I saw my sister Umm Sa'd. I said to Him: 'And my sister Umm Sa'd!' He replied: 'Take her with you.' Then I saw my sister Umm 'Ala. I

7. *Futuhat*, I, p. 617

8. No doubt the allusion here is to the incident of the Prophet's *mi'raj* or "spiritual ascent" when he felt the "fingers of God" on his shoulder. Cf. Ibn Hanbal, V, p. 243.

said to Him: 'And her as well?' He replied: 'Her as well!' I said to Him: 'And my wife Umm 'Abd al-Rahman!' He replied 'And your wife Umm 'Abd al-Rahman.' I said to Him: 'And Khatun Umm Junan!' He replied: 'And Khatun Umm Junan!' I said to him: 'This is taking too much time: let me take all my companions and relatives whom I know, as well as everyone else whom You wish.' He answered: 'Even if you were to ask me if you could take all the people of the Station (*ahl al-mawqif*), I would let you.'[9]

"I then remembered the intercession of the angels and prophets and, out of respect for them, I [only] took with me everyone who fell within my gaze (God alone can count them)*: those whom I knew and those whom I did not know*. I made them go in front of me, keeping behind them so as to prevent them from becoming lost on the way."[10]

The two accounts coincide: in both cases it is a question of Ibn 'Arabi interceding on behalf of "everyone who fell within his gaze, those whom he knew and those whom he did not know." But are we to identify the description contained in these two texts with the vision of the "sublime spectacle" that he experienced in Seville in 586 [A.H.]? One small detail in the names referred to—the name of Umm Junan—would seem to suggest we must answer this question in the negative. We know absolutely nothing about this woman apart from the fact that she was so close to Ibn 'Arabi that he specifically interceded on her behalf. But her name and aristocratic title, *Khatun*, which was a title applied chiefly to the wives of Seljuq and Ayyubid rulers, suggest she was Turkish or Kurdish in origin, and this makes it unlikely that Ibn 'Arabi could have known her in Andalusia.

But there is one particular feature of this account that merits closer consideration. This is the fact that the first four individuals whom the Shaikh al-Akbar asked to be able to take with him to Paradise are all women. The *Kitab al-kutub* contains a long letter written by Ibn 'Arabi to Umm Sa'd to console her over the death of Umm 'Ala,[11] and from this document it emerges that he was very attached to his two sisters (it will be remembered that he had no brothers), whom he took with him to Fez after his father's death with the aim of finding husbands for them.[12] The other

9. This is a reference to a hadith which does not seem to be included in any of the canonical collections but which Ibn 'Arabi cites at length, together with its *isnad*, in *Futuhat*, I, p. 309 and in *Muhadarat*, II, pp. 186ff. According to it, at the Last Judgement man will have to travel the length of fifty *mawaqif* ("halts").

10. *Kitab al-mubashshirat*, MS. Fatih 5322, fo 93a; MS. Bayazid 1686, fo 62b.

11. *Kitab al-kutub*, pp. 35–50, in Rasa'il, *Hyderabad*, 1948.

12. *Durra* 3, in *Sufis of Andalusia*, p. 75.

two women referred to in the passage remain an enigma. Of Umm Junan we know absolutely nothing—not even the nature of her relationship to Ibn 'Arabi. As we have seen, Umm 'Abd al-Rahman was the name of his wife—but which one? Various references in the *Futuhat* indicate that he had two wives. It would appear that his first wife was Maryam bint Muhammad b. 'Abdun al-bija'i; he possibly married her in Seville, and her spiritual aspirations were very much in harmony with his own—as the following passage shows. "My saintly wife Maryam bint M. b. 'Abdun al-Bija'i said to me: 'In my sleep I saw someone who often comes to visit me in my visions, but whom I have never met in the world of sense-perception. He asked me: "Do you aspire to the Way?" I replied: "Most certainly yes, but I don't know how to reach it!" He said: "Through five things, namely trust (*al-tawakkul*), certainty (*al-yaqin*), patience (*al-sabr*), resolution (*al-'azima*) and sincerity (*al-sidq*)" ' "[13]

... Whatever the bonds of kinship and affection which linked Ibn 'Arabi with these four people, one fact is particularly striking—namely that the first beneficiaries of his intercession with God were all women. Indeed, here, too, he distinguishes himself from some of his co-religionists, because for him there was no level of spiritual realization which women are incapable of attaining. "Men and women have their share in every level, including the function of Pole (*qutb*)."[14]

Furthermore, several of Ibn 'Arabi's spiritual teachers were women; they include two whose company he used to frequent in Seville when still a youth—Fatima bint Ibn al-Multhanna and Shams Umm al-Fuqara'.

Fatima bint Ibn al-Multhanna used to tell her young disciple: "I am your spiritual mother and the light of your bodily mother."[15] Although this lady of Seville was over ninety years old, her face was so pink and fresh that Ibn 'Arabi would blush whenever he saw her. She lived in extreme poverty, feeding herself from the refuse that the other people of Seville left outside their doors. She appears not to have had any home of her own until the day when Ibn 'Arabi and two other disciples of hers built her a hut out of reeds. In his *Ruh al-quds* he has no hesitation in stating that "she was a mercy for the worlds," and he states that she had at her

13. *Futuhat* I, p. 278; cf also *Futuhat* III, p. 235. Thanks to a *sama'* dated to A.H. 630 in Aleppo, we happen to know that she was still alive and by her husband's side in that year. The *sama'* in question is to be found at the end of the *Kitab nazm al-futuh al makki*, in MS. Ahmadiyya, Aleppo, 774; Riyad al-Malih was kind enough to provide me with information about this manuscript.

14. *Futuhat* III, p. 89.

15. *Futuhat* II, p. 348.

command an extremely unusual but totally devoted servant: the surah *al-Fatiha*, who—just like Aladdin's genie of the lamp—fulfilled even the smallest of her wishes.[16]

It was apparently in 586/1190,[17] at Marchena of the Olives which was a citadel not far from Seville, that Ibn 'Arabi met Shams Umm al-Fuqara'. As he himself writes in the *Ruh al-quds*, "She had a stout heart, noble spiritual energy and great discrimination. She concealed her spiritual state, but sometimes she would reveal an aspect of it to me in secret because she had been granted a revelation about me, and this would give me great joy."[18]

16. For Fatima bint Ibn al-Muthanna cf. *Futuhat*, 274; II, pp. 135, 347, 621; *Ruh* 55, p. 126; *Sufis of Andalusia*, pp. 143–47.

17. O. Yahia, *Histoire et classification*, p. 94.

18. *Ruh* 54, p. 126; *Sufis of Andalusia*, pp. 142–43.

WHEREVER YOU TURN, THERE IS THE FACE OF GOD

Camille Adams Helminski was born in Florida of an Episcopalian mother and a Baptist father and was raised with a deep awareness of spirit by both her parents. Her father, a botanical watercolor artist by profession, taught Camille and her two sisters to love the mysterious and beautiful creation of this universe. At an early age she began to long to know the One who created it.

Drawn to study comparative religion in college, but instead encouraged by her father to major in fine art, she completed her degree in studio art at Smith College after spending her junior year abroad, at the Beaux Arts in Paris. During her junior year, both parents died suddenly. It was then, in an effort to reconstruct the reality that had been shattered, that she deepened her search.

The journey had already begun to unfold further when in her freshman year she was introduced by a friend to the writings in Persian of Mevlana Jalaluddin Rumi. The way of Sufism began to call to her, but it was some years before real contacts in the family of Sufism developed. Married in 1974 to Kabir Edmund Helminski, she continued her search with her husband, soon accompanied by their stalwart sons, Matthew (born in 1975) and Shams (born in 1978); they were also gifted with a spirited daughter, Cara, in 1985. Through various friends along the way they were introduced in 1979 to Shaykh Suleyman Hayati Dede of the Mevlevi order in Turkey. They felt they had found a true family connection of deep spirit. This led them to journey to Turkey many times, as well as other countries, where they have met and developed friendships with many lovers of God. For more than twenty-five years now they have worked and taught within the Mevlevi path of Sufism.

Camille Helminski is particularly grateful for the brotherhood and support of Dr. Refik Algan, with whom she has translated several Sufi texts.

With her husband, Kabir, she has translated a number of books of Sufi poetry, in particular of Mevlana Jalaluddin Rumi. As publishers of Threshold Books, she and her husband brought into English many classic Sufi texts. Soon after the founding of Threshold Books, they also founded, and continue to direct, the Threshold Society, a nonprofit organization that aims to support spiritual education and direct personal experience of the Divine. She was the first woman to translate into English a substantial portion of the Qur'an, *The Light of Dawn: Daily Readings of the Holy Qur'an,* and has also helped to translate into English the *Mevlevi Wird*, the litany of prayers particular to the Mevlevi order.

At the close of the *Wird* is a prayer that was beloved by Mevlana, a prayer of the Prophet Muhammad's, which has been recited daily by Mevlevi dervishes, both men and women for centuries:

> O God! Grant me Light in my heart, Light in my grave,
> Light in front of me, Light behind me,
> Light to my right, Light to my left,
> Light above me, Light below me,
> Light in my ears, Light in my eyes,
> Light on my skin, Light in my hair,
> Light within my flesh, Light in my blood, Light in my bones.
> O God! Increase my Light everywhere.
> O God! Grant me Light in my heart,
> Light on my tongue, Light in my eyes, Light in my ears,
> Light to my right, Light to my left,
> Light above me, Light below me,
> Light in front of me, Light behind me,
> and Light within my self; increase my Light.

As she indicates in the preface to the *Wird*:

> With the recitation of the *Mevlevi Wird*, we begin in the name of God which is Peace; and our ultimate return is to our Sustainer who is Peace. Upon entering the holy city of Mecca, the holy sanctuary surrounding the *Kaaba*, one enters best by the Gate of Peace, *Bab As-Salaam*. As one enters during the *Hajj*, one recites words of prayer similar to those that begin the *Wird*, invoking the Peace of our Lord. The Holy Precinct is a safe haven, free of the turmoil of the outer worlds. As we enter the *Mevlevi Wird*, we begin in the same manner, recognizing the One who enlivens us with Peace and to whom all praise is due. "Allow us to enter Your Garden, the Abode of Peace."

Now, in this moment, allow us to enter, following the water of this *Wird* back to its Source, into the Garden of Presence. May we continuously open to, nurture, and cultivate *rabitah* (our bond) with God . . . *and keep your connection that you may attain felicity* [Qur'an 3:200].

Mevlevi Women

In the family of Mevlana Jalaluddin Rumi[1] (1207–1273) there had long been a tradition of the recognition of the spiritual beauty, yearning, and wisdom of women. It was his grandmother, the princess of Khorasan, who first lit the spark of inquiry in Rumi's father, Bahaeddin Weled. It was under her care (Bahaeddin's father died when he was two years old) that he grew to be the "Sultan of the Learned" and a great spiritual light for his world. Mevlana's mother, Mu'mine Khatun, a devout and saintly lady, was very dear to him. Mu'mine Khatun was the beautiful daughter of Rukhneddin, the governor of Balkh in what is now Afghanistan.

As the threat of the Mongol hordes approached, when Mevlana was about seven years old, his mother and father and he and his older brother together with loyal students of his father's and extended households all set out together to emigrate from Balkh. His sister, Fatima Khatun, having already married, chose instead to settle with her husband in her native country. She came to be known as one of the wisest women of her time and was often consulted on legal matters.

The caravan of family and friends journeyed to Mecca and Damascus and then, after some years passed, heading north, came to rest in the town of Larende (also known as Karaman), where they remained for almost seven years. Just as Bahaeddin Weled was about to move his family to

1. The Mevlevi order was formed around the example and being of Mevlana Jalaluddin Rumi by his son, Sultan Weled, in the late 1200s C.E. Though many people, both men and women, have been referred to as "Mevlana," our Master—and out of great respect and reverence, one might still today address one's spiritual teacher with this term—yet when "Mevlana" is mentioned in conversation, most people understand that it is Mevlana Jalaluddin Rumi to whom the person is referring; hence the name Mevlevi or Maulawi for the order itself. Among the Sufi orders, Mevlana Jalaluddin Rumi is looked to as the "Pole of Love," and his words are studied and beloved by Sufis of most orders as well as by most Persian-speaking people, no matter what their religious affiliation. His masterwork, the *Mathnawi,* is often referred to as the "Qur'an in the Persian language."

Konya, the city in which he spent most of his life and where he is buried, is located in Central Anatolia in what is now Turkey. The reader may notice that the spelling of names within this chapter is influenced by the Turkish conventions of transliteration, which (among other characteristics) often replaces an *a* with an *e*, hence "Mevlevi" rather than "Maulawi," and so on.

Konya, where he had been invited to teach by Sultan Alaeddin Kaykobad, Mu'mine Khatun passed away. Her tomb remains in Karaman as a place of pilgrimage for many of the women of Anatolia. Nezihe Araz, in her book *Anadolu evliyalari* (Saints of Anatolia), describes her meeting with Mu'mine:

> [Mu'mine Khatun] was one of the faithful, and her countenance and her morality were both beautiful. Mirrors would say as she looked into them: We wish she had a fault that we could show her, but she has none!
>
> . . . Mu'mine Sultan's tomb is now visited by many. There is almost no woman in Anatolia who has not visited her. Most of her visitors are women who arrive in her presence, lower their heads, and ask for her assistance. . . .
>
> I also arrived in her presence and had a great deal I wanted to say. I had gone over in my mind many things I wanted to say to her, and with which I wished to ask her assistance. But as soon as I entered her tomb, my mind went blank!! I could neither speak nor extend my hand; I was overwhelmed by the encompassing presence of this sacred mother, a mother who had given such love to the world![2]

Mu'mine Khatun was laid to rest shortly after Mevlana's marriage to Gevher Khatun, the daughter of one of Bahaeddin Weled's closest disciples, Shefereddin Lala. Gevher Khatun had grown up beside Mevlana Jalaluddin, listening to his father's discourses. This beautiful woman, who was known to have the heart of an angel, became the mother of Sultan Weled, to whom Shams of Tabriz[3] conveyed many mysteries. Shams himself, in his *Conversations* (*Maqalat* of Shams-i Tabriz) also reminded those who might forget of the equal capacity of women for intimacy with the Ineffable and the ability to "die before death."[4]

When his dear wife, Gevher Khatun, passed away, Mevlana married the widowed daughter of Izzeddin 'Ali, Kerra Khatun, who also was quite spiritually gifted and well trained in mysticism. She became known for the

2. Nezihe Araz, *Anadolu Evliyalari*, pp. 409–11. Translation by Nuket Kardam.

3. Shams of Tabriz (Shams od-Din Tabrizi or Shams-i Tabriz) was the wandering mystic whose fiery friendship with Mevlana Jalaluddin Rumi catalyzed such a profound transformation in this already advanced mystic master that he became an endless fountain of divine love.

4. The Prophet Muhammad is known to have said, "Die before you die"—that is, make the effort to so purify and transform the "self" (*nafs*) that it may become transparent to the Presence of the Divine.

many miracles that occurred around her, and many notables and ladies of the city of Konya became her students. Kerra Khatun and Mevlana together had a son and a daughter, Melike Khatun, who also became known for her pure spirit:

> One day a group of women passed by Kamil of Tabriz who cried: "A bright light burns in the midst of these women. Such clarity must come from our Master's mine of lights."[5]

In the *Menaqib al-arifin*, Shams ad-Din Aflaki describes the young woman, Fatima Khatun, whom Sultan Weled married:

> The friends told us that when Sultan Weled reached puberty, our Master arranged a marriage with Shaikh Calaheddin's daughter, Fatima Khatun. [Mevlana himself] taught the young girl to read and write, and spent a great deal of time with her since he held her in high regard.
>
> One day he said: "Fatima Khatun (May God be pleased with her and with her father) is my right eye and her sister, Hediyye Khatun is my left. All those honorable women who visit me, come partially veiled, with the exception of Fatima and her sister who come unveiled."
>
> Concerning Latife Khatun who was their mother, he said: "Latife Khatun is the embodiment of God's grace; she is the namesake of the Shaikh's mother. (May God sanctify their sweet souls!)"
>
> One day, our Master [Mevlana] said to his companions, "When Fatima Khatun married our Behaeddin (Sultan Weled) all the archangels and *houris* in Paradise rejoiced and beat their drums congratulating each other and lifting their voices in a chorus of praise." And on their wedding night, [Mevlana] composed this elegy of love:
>
> Blessed be those weddings and festivities of this world
> ordained by God for us;
> Our hearts have opened, and kindred souls are joined.
> Care has flown away thanks to the kindness of our Lord.
>
> . . . Fatima performed many miracles both in the inner and in the manifest world. She constantly fasted during the day and stayed awake at night. When she did eat, it was but once a day. She gave food to the

5. Shams ad-Din Aflaki, *Menaqib al-arifin*, #578, p. 206. Translated from the French edition by Susan Blaylock (d. 1998), may peace be with her, and gratitude for her efforts. Here Kamil (the perfected one) of Tabriz (i.e., Shams-i Tabriz) is referring to Melike Khatun.

> poor, to orphans and to widows, and distributed clothes and gifts to the needy. She made a rule of speaking and eating as little as possible.
>
> Fatima could see very clearly the mysterious forms that are the spiritual beings of heaven and she showed them to those of her friends who were capable of such an experience, to Gurdji Khatun, to Koumadj Khatun, and to the daughter of the Perwana of Toqat. She could also read people's thoughts very clearly. In her youth, she was like the pure milk of paradise [Qur'an 47:16]. She could not bear to be separated from our Master for a moment and learned marvelous secrets of illumination from his blessed discourse. In order to achieve sanctity, inner discipline, and a pure, chaste soul, she studied with this supreme teacher and became an accomplished student.[6]

One of Mevlana's closest disciples and friends who rests in her own *maqam*[7] on the outskirts of old Konya is Fahrunnissa. Her tomb stands watch on Chai-baci Caddesi (Tea-garden Street) near the cemetery where Suleyman Hayati Dede, the former Mevlevi *shaykh* of Konya, was laid to rest. A small *camii* (mosque) built in her name invites passersby to pause and pray there.

Aflaki relates the following story about her:

> Our Friends and dervish brothers told us about Fahrunnisa (Fakr-en-Nisa), a saintly and perfect being, who was known as the "Glory of Women" (May God be Pleased with her). She lived in Konya in the time of our beloved Mevlana and was known as the Rabi'a of her day. Philosophers, Masters of Wisdom, mystics and the leaders of the community alike loved and revered her. She was pious, devoted and sincere, and could perform extraordinary miracles. Fahrunnisa loved to be in the presence of our Master and he, as well, liked to be in her company.
>
> At a certain point, her disciples encouraged her to make the pilgrimage to Mecca. This corresponded with inner guidance that she had been receiving concerning this pillar of Islam.
>
> "Let me consult our Master first because I can't possibly go without his permission. I'll do whatever he wishes."

6. Aflaki, *Menaqib al-arifin*, book 2, #578, p. 206.

7. *Maqam* (station) refers to a spiritual station, the predominant quality or "resting place" of a soul. It is also used to refer to a tomb area.

She went to visit Mevlana, who immediately said, "It's a very good intention; may your journey be blessed. I hope we will be in each other's company."

Fahrunnisa only bowed her head and didn't say a word in reply. Her friends and followers, puzzled at her reaction, wondered what had taken place during the meeting. That night, Fahrunnisa remained in conversation with Mevlana at his home, until quite late. Shortly after midnight, Mevlana went up on the terraced roof to pray. After he had completed his nightly devotions, he began to shout excitedly, signaling to Fahrunnisa and calling her to join him on the roof.

"Look!" he said, pointing at the sky. "There is your destination." And to her amazement, Fahrunnisa saw the Kaaba spinning around our Master's head like a dervish in his sacred dance. It was clearly visible and Fahrunnisa gasped as she plunged deep into ecstatic bewilderment.

After a while, she bowed her head again and told Mevlana that it no longer seemed a good idea to go on the pilgrimage and that she would like to relinquish the journey. Mevlana's reply was this beautiful *ghazal*:[8]

The Kaaba spins like a dervish
    around the abode of only one idol.
O Lord, who could this possibly be,
    so distraught and so full of longing?
Compared to her, the full moon is a broken plate
    and her sweetness puts the flowers to shame.
All the Masters of the Way, all the faithful angels, bow to her,
    crying, "O Adored One, for the love of God, have mercy on us."
The creatures of a thousand foam-covered seas
    are the shells which contain this pearl of Love;
    her elevated thoughts reveal Honour and Glory . . .
She is his paradise, his dancing girls, his infinite pleasure.
In her overflowing light, one sigh of worship
    is like an entire verse of the Qu'ran.
Listen to this short tale and be aware
    that one of the sun's tiny atoms has befriended an idol.

8. A *ghazal* is a poem with a particular rhyme scheme that was used by many of the Sufi poets.

O you, who are the Shams of Tabriz of Mercy
and Compassion, a sun bestowing a thousand blessings;
Your words have become like a jug full of wine—
let's drink of it forever.[9]

In the 1980s when the city of Konya needed to conduct some road renovations that required the moving of Fahrunissa's tomb, Suleyman Dede was asked to attend the repositioning. He related to us how after seven hundred years, when her grave was opened, her body was still intact and the fragrance of roses filled the air.

Another woman of the time of Mevlana who has long been beloved by many was Tavus Hatun (Khatun), or "Peacock Lady." Nezihe Araz tells the following story about this beautiful woman who had heard of Mevlana and journeyed like many others from Bukhara and Samarkand, Shiraz, and many areas of Central Asia to Konya to be in his proximity, though as Mevlana said to those near him, "Since our fame has increased, and so many people have begun visiting us, I am no longer comfortable; no wonder Muhammad, peace be upon him, has said, 'Fame is hardship, comfort comes from lack of fame!' But if the divine order is such, what can be done? Because I was told to show my qualities to the people, 'so that whoever sees you, would see Me (God).' " This beautiful lady whom no one knew arrived by caravan like the countless others who came to meet Mevlana. Like many of them, she also remained in Konya.

> She picked a small hill called Gullu (Rose) Hill in the Meram vineyards around Konya and had a house built on it. This hill resembled a paradise with its beautiful fire-colored roses, and hyacinths.
>
> The lovers of Mevlana, as they were returning from a *sema* ceremony in the Meram vineyards early one morning, heard a sweet sounding *rebab*.[10] This sound invited all souls to awaken. The ensuing ecstasy of the lovers erased their weariness, and they cried out for the Friend.[11] The *sema* ceremony continued as long as the wailing of the *rebab* lasted up on the hill.

9. Aflaki, #240.The metaphor of wine drinking occurs frequently in Sufi poetry and literature. It is understood that the wine is the metaphorical wine of love of the Beloved (God). (The drinking of tangible wine is forbidden by the Qur'an.) Drunkenness is then intoxication with God's love, and annihilation in God, the moment when the wine, the cup, and the cupbearer all become one. Shams-i Tabriz in his *Maqalat* speaks of the limitations of mere intoxication, explaining that the greater attainment is the sobriety that can contain intoxication.

10. A *rebab* is a stringed instrument made from a coconut shell sound-bowl, with a rounded long neck with three pegged strings. It is played with a bow and has a very throaty, emotive voice. Mevlana himself played the *rebab*, and for centuries now it has been one of the traditional Mevlevi instruments.

From that morning on, the lovers of Mevlana always passed by that small hill. Every morning as the sun rose and their souls awoke with the sound of that beautiful woman's *rebab*, the *sema* ceremony would begin and Mevlana and his friends would bathe their souls in the sweet sounds flowing through Konya's renowned roses and hyacinths.

Konya was drunk with love but sometimes still found time for gossip and envy. Some prying people started asking whether this lady was veiling her beauty from Mevlana, too.

Early one morning, as the lovers of Mevlana waited by the foot of the Gullu Hill and watched life awaken, they could not hear the sound of the *rebab* for which they were waiting. They became worried and their hearts were in a quandary as to what to do. They all looked at Mevlana, while he waited in silence. Once the sun had risen in the sky, Mevlana asked one of his young students to go and check the house on the hill. Those who went to the house saw nothing but a few peacock feathers in the middle of the house, still warm from having just left a live body.

When they recounted this to Mevlana, he ordered that a tomb (*turbe*) be built for her. To this day, the people of Konya bring their relatives who are sick with tuberculosis at early dawn to the small brick building (the *turbe*) and pray to Tavus Khatun (Peacock Lady) for assistance with their health. These days there are no roses or hyacinths around the *turbe*. A few years ago, some people claimed that the person lying there was not a woman but, in fact, a man called Tavus Baba and that he was not a Mevlevi but a Hudai.[12] The nameplate was changed from *Tavus Khatun* to *Tavus Baba* because it was considered by some that the name "Khatun " should not be spoken. However, whomever I have asked among Konya's people, they have not forgotten and have all recounted to me this story of Tavus Khatun as they knew it; they so love the Peacock Lady.[13]

Over the centuries, many women have followed the path of Sufism opened by Mevlana Jalaluddin Rumi. His granddaughters (the daughters

11. "Friend" (*Dost*) refers to God and also has the meaning of "Beloved."

12. The date on the plaque was also changed from the 1200s to the 1400s. When in Konya recently we visited "Tavus Baba's" tomb with some Turkish friends, one of whom was the son of a local Qadiri shaikh. At first this dear friend made reference to the "man" who was buried there who had been a disciple of Mevlana's. When I questioned him further, saying that I had understood that the person buried there was actually a woman saint, he called his father to verify. Indeed, his elderly father confirmed that yes, it was a woman, but that some people had caused the nameplate to be changed in recent times.

13. Nezihe Araz, *Anadolu Evliyalari*, pp. 26–28. Translation by Nuket Kardam.

of Sultan Weled), Mutahhara and Sheref Khatun, both were women of great spiritual depth who had numerous *murids*[14] throughout Asia Minor.[15] Mevlana endearingly called them Abide (adoring one) and Arife (the mystic knower). Devret Khatun, daughter of Divan-i Çelebi, wife of Sultan Beyazit I and mother of the next sultan, Mehmet Çelebi, was also an important Sufi student and teacher of her time; her tomb is in Bursa, Turkey. Divani Mehmet Çelebi's great-granddaughter, Destina Khatun (Shah Mehmet Çelebi's daughter), was appointed the *shaykha* of the Kara Hisar Mevlevi Tekke. She wore the traditional *khirka* and *sikke* (a tall felt hat with turban wrapping for a *shaykh*) and made *sema* together with men, standing as the representative of the order in the Mevlevi *mukabele* (*sema,* or whirling ceremony, the "meeting face to face"). When she "translated,"[16] Kutchuk Mehmet Çelebi took on the leadership, but after his passing, instead of the leadership passing to his son, his daughter, Gunesh Khatun, who was regarded as having the greater spiritual attainment, assumed the post.[17] She was known for her abundant love and consideration for everyone regardless of sex, race, or religion. Each of these women took responsibility for teaching both men and women on the Sufi path, as did Arife-Hashnika Hanim of Konya, who held the position of *shaykha* for the men and women of Tokat.[18]

The Mevlevi *tariqah* is known for its emphasis on beauty and the refinement of the arts, as well as the art of living the life of a true human being. "Many of the more influential Ottoman musicians, composers, musical theorists, calligraphers, and other visual artists traced their artistic genealogy through the Mevlevi Order,"[19] and a substantial number of these were women. The hundred most important composers in Turkey have been followers of the Mevlevi *tariqah*, according to the former Çelebi, Dr. Celaladdin Çelebi, who passed away in 1996. Dilhayat Khalifa was a female

14. A *murid* (or *mureed*) is a devoted student, accepted by a particular teacher.

15. See Aflaki, *Menaqib al-arifin,* book 2, chap. 10.

16. In the Mevlevi way, rather than saying that someone has died, one refers to their "translation," as it is considered that the person has changed abode, returning to their true "home country" where, as Shams of Tabriz relates in his *Maqalat*, after being confined in a cramped house they are now able to stretch, unfold, and walk around at ease.

17. Mention of some of these women is found in the *Menaqib al-arifin*. These details are also documented by Golpinarli, in the chapter from his history of the Mevlevi order, "The Place of Women in the Mevlevi Order."

18. Celaleddin (Jalaluddin) Çelebi, "The Place of Women in the Mevlevi Way," unpublished manuscript, 1990.

19. Victoria Rowe Holbrook, "Diverse Tastes in the Spiritual Life," p. 100.

Mevlevi *tanbur*[20] player of the early 1700s who wrote numerous *ilahiler* (sacred songs). Layla Saz, who lived in the late 1800s, was another brilliant female Mevlevi composer and musician; she rests in the *hamushan* ("the place of the silent ones," the cemetery) of the Galata Mevlevihanesi.[21]

Women have also always performed the *sema*, the mystical whirling ceremony of the Mevlevi Way. In the early days of the Mevlevi order, women and men were known to pray, share *sohbet* (spiritual conversation), and whirl within each other's company, though more often as the centuries unfolded, women held their own *semas* and men also whirled in *zhikr* separately from women. However, in the time of Mevlana, spontaneous *semas* would occur including both women and men. There was an intimate friend of Fahrunnisa's, Nizham-Khatun, whose love for God had been deeply inspired by Mevlana. A yearning arose in her to host a *sema* gathering. She had little with which to provide for the guests, so she determined to sell the only thing of any value that she owned, a piece of cloth from Bursa she had been saving for her shroud. However, the next morning, Mevlana and the friends appeared at her door. He told her to keep her shroud, that he and the friends had arrived for the *sema*. That *sema* continued for three days and nights.

In the summer of 1991, during a visit to Turkey, we discussed with the Çelebi, the then-presiding head of the Mevlevi order, Celaleddin Bakir Çelebi, the issue of men and women turning in *sema* together in our time. No formal permission had yet been given by the order to hold such mixed ceremonies. The Çelebi recognized the need to seriously consider the appropriateness of mixed ceremonies that might be held in our current era, and especially the public sharing of a mixed *sema*. He requested that all those whom we had trained as *semazens*, both men and women, might write to him of their experience. Many did so. After deep reflection, in October of 1991, he responded (in his own English):

> I don't think anybody has the right to differentiate between women and men, as God gives this right for the existence and the continuation of being of human beings. We are obliged to give the same rights to both of them as creatures of God.
>
> . . . we are all under a great responsibility regarding women in a mixed *sema*, because it will be a rule once this permission is given. Any person wishing to become *semazen* must have certain perimeters of

20. The *tanbur* is a long-necked stringed instrument played with a long pick; it is one of the foremost classical instruments of Turkey.

21. The Galata *tekke* in old Istanbul, also known as *Kutuphanesi*.

behaviour or code of ethics. How do you mean to practice if we do not lay down rules so that in the future this may be carried out? Please can you guarantee the same maturity for all the groups existing in the world or which will be formed in the future? It is for this reason that we need to clarify certain outlines at the outset so that in the future all the essence and the beauty of the *sema* will be preserved and seen by all, just as it was in the beginning—pure love.

Some weeks later, we at last received the following faxed letter from Dr. Çelebi (again in his own English):

The 11-11-991

Dear Helminski,

I receive the holy message that I was waiting from Hz.Mevlâna :

... *Till when will continue the patience of these clean and pure hearts in the soil ?*
Go all together jump, blow up, exit from the tombs. A favour of forces comes to you as help" ...

You can do a mixed ceremony every 30 September and 17 December in public !

Whish always the best to everybody.
The servant of Mevlâna and his followers .
The Çelebi Celâleddin
Çelebi Celâleddin

Note : The permission of guiding given to you by Suleyman Dede was with my approuval. I am and will be always morally responsable of everything concerning you and your followers... To day I fill my self obliged to remember you that there is a rule who was followed respectively by all dervishes in the tekkes : The reunion was beginning by **conversation and discussion**... followed by a **prayer**... by a **zikr** (only the name of God)... then **the semâ** and immediatly after the semâ, staying alone in a cell or a room, as long as the social obligation of the participant person permit: "**meditation**".

God willing, a new time is opening for the greater sharing of spirituality among men and women, in purity, patience, and mutual support, as we turn in steadfast and trustworthy devotion to the One who turns us all. As the *shaykh* or *shaykha* prays in one moment of the whirling ceremony:

May Allah grant you total soundness,
O travelers on the Way of Love.
May the Beloved remove the veils from your eyes
that you may see the secrets of your time and of the true center.

. . . and may it be for each of us that Wherever you turn, there is the Face of God.[22]

22. Surah al-Baqarah 2:115.

A PRINCESS OF PIETY

JAHANARA (1614–1681) was a daughter of Mughal emperor Shah Jahan [(1592–1666) and his beloved wife, Mumtaz Mahal, in memory of whom he built the wondrous Taj Mahal]. Like her brother, Dara Shikoh . . . ,[1] she was drawn to Sufism, and like him she is the author of biographical works on contemporary and historical Sufi saints. She was also responsible for the creation of a number of stately Mughal gardens and other architectural projects. [Her niece, Zebunnisa, was also a renowned scholar of the Qur'an, a philanthropist, and a poet whose verses were gathered posthumously into a volume entitled *Diwan-i makhfi* (Book of the Hidden One.)]

Although relatively few non-elite Muslim women left well-attested literary legacies, among upper-class women there was much freer access to education as well as the possibility of acting as a patron for religious and cultural activities. [Jahanara (or Fatima, as she was also called) wrote a book on Sufism that included an account of her initiation, entitled *Risala-i sahibiyya* (Message of a Companion). She also wrote a biography of her Sufi teacher Mulla Shah of the Qadiriyya line.[2] The selection that follows is drawn from her biography of the famous Indian saint of the founder of the Indian branch of the Chishti order, Mu'in ad-Din Chishti (d. 1236) and his disciples, *Munisu'l-arwah*.]

1. The spread of Islam in certain places—in India for example—has been partly due to the exaltation of its mysticism. Prince Dara Shikoh (d. 1619), the sufi son of the Mogul emperor Shah Jahan, was able to affirm that Sufism and Advaita Vedantism are essentially the same, with a surface difference of terminology. "The Chishti tariqah founded by 'Abd al Qadir's younger contemporary Mu'in ad-Din Chishti (d. 1236) has become one of the most widespread Sufi orders in India." From Martin Lings, *What is Sufism?*, p. 112. (C.A.H.)

2. Bibi Jamal Khatun, the sister of Mian Mir, who was Mulla Shah's teacher and also the first to inspire Jahanara and her brother Dara Shikoh, was also "one of the outstanding saints of the Qadiriyya order during its formative period in the Punjab." See Annemarie Schimmel, *Mystical Dimensions of Islam*, p. 433, and *My Soul Is a Woman*, p. 50. (C.A.H.)

Jahanara is buried in a small white marble tomb, open to the elements and devoid of any dome, outside the shrine of the Chishti saint Nizam ad-Din Awliya' in Delhi. The inscription reads as follows:

> He is the Living, the Sustaining.
> Let no one cover my grave except with greenery,
> For this very grass suffices as a tomb cover for the poor.
> The annihilated *faqir* Lady Jahanara,
> Disciple of the Lords of Chisht,
> Daughter of Shahjahan the Warrior
> (may God illuminate his proof).

Jahanara's biography of the Indian founder of the Chishti Sufi order, though compiled from existing works on Sufi saints, is highly regarded for its judgment and literary quality. The conclusion and an appendix, which describes the author's pilgrimage to Mu'in al-Din's tomb at Ajmer in 1643, convey the author's personal engagement with Sufi practice. There she uses the word *faqira*—the feminine form of *faqir*—to signify her own spiritual vocation as a Sufi woman. She clearly regarded Mu'in al-Din Chishti as the supreme Sufi saint of India and as the master who initiated her, over four centuries after his death (initiation is referred to by the expression "taking the hand," which is the ritual gesture that seals this relationship). At the same time she also remembers her living Sufi master, Mulla Shah. Her pilgrimage was timed to coincide with the death anniversary of the saint, and at his tomb she performed the customary rituals that are still carried out at Sufi shrines around the world, including the recitation of prayers and sections of the Qur'an, with the dedication of their benefit to the inhabitants of the tomb.

Confidant of Spirits

Know that, after the performance of religious duties, requirements, and the recitation of the Holy Qur'an, this weak woman who hopes for salvation regards no action as nobler than the remembrance of the spiritual states and stations of the revered saints (may God sanctify their spirits).

❧ "Confidant of Spirits" is excerpted from pp. 194–95 and 196–99 of *Teachings of Sufism*, selected and translated by Carl W. Ernst, Ph.D. © 1999 by Carl W. Ernst. Reprinted by arrangement with Shambhala Publications, Inc., Boston, www.shambhala.com. Text in brackets was written by the editor.

Therefore, I have spent a portion of my time in reading books and treatises that contain the felicitous accounts of the great ones of religion and the mighty ones of certainty. This *faqira* had such perfect sincerity and devotion that I wrote a summary of the career of the revered master who took my hand in discipleship, as well as the chief successors of that revered one (may God inspire their spirits).

Praise and favor be to God, for by the assistance of God the Knower, the Powerful, and with the helping grace of the revered master who took my hand, I attained this desire of mine, and this treatise *The Confidant of Spirits* was edited and put on the robe of completion on the 27th of the blessed month of Ramadan, 1049 (January 21, 1640).

The lives of these great ones, who are the close ones of the court of Eternity, having been extracted with great care from well-known books and treatises, have been committed to writing. In the belief of this weak woman, whatever is affirmed in this text is completely correct. I hope that readers will have the full blessing and benefit of it . . .

After praising the one God—and He is all eternal, great is His majesty—and following the adoration of His messenger Muhammad the chosen one (may God bless him and grant him peace)—this lowly *faqira* Jahanara, with the aid of fortune and ascendant victory, went from the capital Agra in the company of my great father toward the pure region of incomparable Ajmer. From the 17th of Sha'ban 1053 to Friday the 7th of the blessed month of Ramadan [October 31 to November 19, 1643], when I entered the building on the shore of the Anasagar tank, I was committed to this idea, that every day in every station I would perform two cycles of optional prayer. Then, having recited the Book of [Ya Sin, Surah 36] and the Opening [Fatiha, Surah 1] with perfect sincerity and devotion, I bestowed the reward for that on the generous, pure, illuminated spirit of the revered master Lord Mu'in al-Din Chishti (may God be pleased with him).

For the several days when I stopped in the above mentioned buildings, from extreme courtesy I did not sleep on a leopard skin that night, I did not extend my feet in the direction of the blessed sanctuary of the revered saving master, and I did not turn my back toward him. I passed the days beneath the trees.

By the blessing of that revered one, and the gracious influence of this Heavenly land, I experienced concentration and mystical experiences. One night I performed a wonderful birthday and lamp festival for the saint. I did not stint in adorning and serving the blessed sanctuary with what I had and will have, nor will I ever do so.

Praise and favor be to God, and a hundred million thanks, for on

Thursday, the fourth of the blessed month of Ramadan, I attained the happiness of pilgrimage to the illuminated and perfumed tomb of the revered saving master (may God be pleased with him). With an hour of daylight remaining, I went to the holy sanctuary and rubbed my pale face on the dust of that threshold. From the doorway to the blessed tomb I went barefoot, kissing the ground. Having entered the dome, I went around the light-filled tomb of my master seven times, sweeping it with my eyelashes, and making the sweet-smelling dust of that place the mascara of my eyes.

At that moment, a marvelous spiritual state and mystical experience befell this annihilated one, which cannot rightly be written. From extreme longing I became astonished, and I do not know what I said or did.

Finally with my own hand I put the highest quality of attar on the perfumed tomb of that revered one, and having taken off the rose scarf that I had on my head, I placed it on top of the blessed tomb. Having gone to the marble mosque erected by the great and God-knowing father of this lowly woman, I performed ritual prayer, and then, sitting in the blessed dome, I recited the Book of [Ya Sin, Surah 36] and the Opening [Fatiha, Surah 1] for the generous spirit of the master. I was in that place until sunset prayer, and I lit a candle to the spirit of that revered one. I broke my fast with spring water. It was a marvelous night I saw there, which was better than the dawn.

If the sincerity, love, and spiritual concentration of this annihilated one demanded that I should not go back home after having gone all the way to that blessed and gracious place, the corner of security—what can be done?

> The Beloved has placed a noose on my neck,
> And He pulls me wherever He wishes.

If I had the choice, I would always have stayed in the sanctuary of that revered one, which is the marvelous corner of security—and I am a lover of the corner of security. I would also have had the honor and happiness of walking around it continuously.

Unwillingly, weeping and with burning heart, with a hundred thousand cries, I was excused from the court of that revered one and came home. All night long a wonderful restlessness was in me. That Friday morning, my great father ordered that we head toward Agra.

I have presented this elegant, noble, and sublime book, which this lowly woman compiled from well known books and treatises according to their value, having collected it and entitled it *The Confidant of Spirits,* as the perfect and felicitous life of that revered saving master (may God be pleased with him), so that it may always be in the illuminated and blessed sanctuary.

It is hoped that, from the complete grace and great generosity of that revered one, he will confer special acceptance on this treatise by this least of his devoted disciples, that he will be happy, and that be will turn his attention upon this woman disciple.

Our Mu'in al-Din is annihilated in God,
And after that he subsists in the absolute essence.

This lowly one is a *faqira* who is in the reality of realities, by the blessing of the saving master, the revered lord Mu'in al-Din Chishti, and from the external and internal attention of the real master, the revered Mulla Shah (may God lengthen his shadow and preserve him). Fictitious existence has gone, and that endless existence remains by itself.

THE WINE OF LOVE

Bibi Hayati [Kermani, early nineteenth century] was born into a family with a long tradition of Sufism, in the town of Bam, in the Kerman province of Iran. She was raised under the supervision of her brother Rawnaq 'Ali Shah, a Shaikh of Nur 'Ali Shah (one of the masters of the Nimatullahi Order). Perhaps it was due to his guidance that her contemplative life later acquired such brilliance.

In the early years of her maturity, she was taken by her brother to attend one of the Sufi gatherings of Nur 'Ali. The spiritual light of his presence apparently caused a change of state in her and awakened an intense ardor for spirituality within her. Shortly thereafter, she was initiated into the Nimatullahi order. Progressing gradually but steadily in both the esoteric development (*sayr*) and exoteric ethics (*soluk*) of the Sufi path, Hayati succeeded in acquiring virtues of both a spiritual and secular nature.

Eventually, the relationship between master and disciple exerted a further attraction over Hayati, and she fell under the sway of the lightning flash of human love. Soon afterwards, she married Nur 'Ali Shah, then master of the Nimatullahi Order. In her own eloquent words:

> The arrow of my supplication reached the target of Nur 'Ali Shah's acceptance. An aurorial breeze wafted to my soul where the whiteness of the sun of the true dawn broke. The sun of his loveliness, in whose atmosphere the bird of my soul soared like a moth of dancing light, suddenly shone forth. My outcast eye opened to the light of his world-adorning countenance.

Hayati's Sufi life, in conjunction with the wife/husband relationship, only served to further perfect her poetic and spiritual nature. She became a rhapsodist in the orchard of love and affection.

Knowing his wife's poetic inclination, Nur 'Ali Shah finally requested that she try her hand at verse. As Hayati writes in the introduction to her *Divan,* "One day that king in the climes of gnosticism, that guide in the lands of heart and soul, parted his pearl-strewing lips while in the midst of conversation and declared:

> If you must adorn yourself, you should become a diver in the profound ocean of rhetoric, breaking open the pearl-laden oysters of verses, till you gird about yourself an ode of decorative jewels.

In an attempt to excuse herself, Hayati insisted that she was neither a man of letters nor of the pen.

"But being a lover," replied Nur 'Ali Shah, "is the work of men, since the seeker of the Lord is male. In the realm of love, sincerity, and Sufism, you too are a man. True manhood is courage. The real man is one who never retreats, who remains constant once he has put down his feet in search of perfection."[1]

Following her master's command, Hayati set her hand to compose a *Divan* of poems, which eventually came to constitute a remarkable collection of profound and beautiful verses. Reviewing her collected poems, it appears that Hayati was perfectly acquainted with both the exoteric and esoteric (or mystic) sciences. She adhered both to the external principles of her religion and to the fundamentals of Sufi gnosticism. In addition, she possessed a highly practical nature and a talent for domestic organization. She was accomplished not only in the ways of Love, but often demonstrated her capacity as a warm-hearted caretaker and cook for her Sufi brothers and sisters.

... Insofar as can be gathered from her poems (in particular her "Ode to the Cupbearer" (*Saqi nama*), Hayati was perfectly acquainted with the conduct of Sama', as well as the different varieties of Persian musical scales.

Hayati bore Nur 'Ali Shah a daughter by the name of Tuti, and it is said that she, like her mother, possessed a command of literature and was given to the expression of mystical subtleties. Tuti eventually married Sorkh 'Ali Shah, one of Nur 'Ali Shah's disciples from Hamadan. Tuti's youngest son was Sayyed Redha, one of the renowned Shaikhs of the Nimatullahi Order. At age sixty-five, God bestowed on him a son by the name of Mohammad Said Khushcheshm, also a renowned Shaikh of the Nimatullahi Order.

1. An Arabic proverb (J.N.). For a discussion of women being referred to as "men," see the selections by Annemarie Schimmel, pages 98-108, and Sachiko Murata, pages 177-85. (C.A.H.)

Our Intoxicating Beloved

Ghazal 56[2]

How ever again will one behold
The moon's glory
If, over the heart his visage beams blazing, like the sun?
Through the soul, the Turks of his eyes
Ravage, charge, while, those curls of blasphemy,
Tresses of infidelity, subvert our faith.

But once were he to lift the veil
from his face the world would be nullified,
the universe stupefied.
He struts, brandishing his upright grace,
His stature, elegant, dandy
Through the garden, mocking the cypresses.

He charges in a cavalcade
Riding a gnostic steed,
In the hallowed space of Divinity,
Sphere of Sanctity . . .

Tonight the Saki, lips stained red
Like rubies, pours forth wine
To every drunkard's pleasure
To each ecstatic's taste.

Since Hayati has imbibed his ecstasy—
Soul-sated by his pure-hearted wine,
To what fountain of life could she incline?

The Night of Power

Ghazal 96

Is this then the Night of Power[3]
Or merely—your hair,
Is this the dawnbreak, or your own face?

2. In translation the original order of lines of this *ghazal* has been rearranged to give what seems to be more logical cohesion to the metaphors of the poem. (J.N.) A *ghazal* is a poem with a particular rhyme scheme that was used by many of the Sufi poets. (C.A.H.)

3. The "Night of Power" (Laylat al-Qadr) was the night when the Qur'an was revealed to the Prophet Muhammad, a night of immense blessing (see Qur'an 97), traditionally celebrated on the 27th night of Ramadan but watched for every night by mystics who await the blessing of Divine inspiration. (C.A.H.)

In the divan of Beauty
Is it an immortal first distich?
Or a mere couplet,
Inscribed from your eyebrow?

Boxwood from the orchard,
Or cypress from the rose garden . . . ?
Is it the tuba tree, date-bearing in paradise
Or your own stature—elegant, empathic . . . ?
Is it that odor of musk carried by Chinese deer,
Or rosewater's delicate scent?
Is it the rose's wafted breath,
Or the qualities of your perfume?

Is this a scorching lightning bolt;
Or fire radiant from Mt. Sana'i?[4]
Or my burning sigh,
Or your innate character?

Is this Mongolian musk,
Or unadulterated ambergris?
Is it your hyacinth curl
Or your braided tress?

Is this a chalice of the red wine of dawntide
Or White Magic?
Your narcissus-like eye, in a drunken stupor
Or your sorcery?

Is it the garden of Eden
Or an earthly paradise?
Is it a Ka'ba of the heart's masters
Or your back street?

Everyone faces to pray
A *qibla*[5] of adobe and mud,
The *qibla* of Hayati's soul
Is turned towards your face.

4. Mount Sana'i (Sinai) was the location where Moses received the Ten Commandments. As Mevlana Jalaluddin Rumi declares in the opening lines of his *Mathnawi*, "With love this earthly body could soar in the air; the mountain could arise and nimbly dance. Love gave life to Mount Sinai, O lover. Sinai was drunk; Moses lost consciousness" *The Rumi Collection*, edited by Kabir Helminski. (C.A.H.)

5. The *qibla* is the direction Muslims face when performing the ritual prayer (*salah*), toward the Kaaba in Mecca. It is often marked in a mosque with a tiled or stuccoed prayer niche, or *mihrab*. (C.A.H.)

FROM A QADIRI HEART OF NIGERIA

NANA ASMA'U (1793–1864) was a Qadiri Sufi woman who helped to guide an entire community in what is now Nigeria. Born in the small village of Degel in the dry sandy plains of Hausaland at a time when the French Revolution was at its height, she played an important part in an Islamic revolution that affected an area the size of Western Europe.

Nana was raised under the careful eye of her father, who was the spiritual and tribal leader of the Shehu people, as well as her mother and a number of other scholarly women. She was a pearl on a string of women's scholarship that originated long before her, stretching from the Middle East to West Africa. At an early age Nana had memorized the entire Qur'an, and she soon spoke and wrote in the local languages of Hausa, Fulfulde, and Tamachek, as well as Arabic.

When she was quite young, her family and their expanding community of Qadiri Muslims began their journey of emigration to settle in a place where their community might be free to practice with appropriate care the *sunnah* of the Prophet Muhammad. As they moved from one place to another during a time of intense civil war (1804–1830) when strong efforts were being made to reform and purify the practice of Islam in the region, one of the few things they carried with them was the family library consisting of hundreds of carefully copied loose-leaf manuscripts. These books were continually passing through a process of renewal, as in that climate, even though the hand-copied tomes were enclosed in sturdy goatskin bags, it was not long before the parchment pages would begin to disintegrate. Books were of such importance that wherever the family journeyed, a room was always set aside for the copying of texts so that the library of important Islamic and Sufi texts might be preserved.

Nana Asma'u became an enthusiastic teacher of both men and women and one who was well loved by her students and her whole community. At the same time that she was both a wife and a mother, devoted daughter and sister, she was also an educator, an author, and "a respected scholar of international repute who was in communication with scholars throughout the Sub-Saharan African Muslim world," as Beverly Mack and Jean Boyd report.[1] "Her efforts to promote reconciliation, education, and justice helped change forever the Muslim culture in which she lived. This was her personal '*jihad*'[2] and it took three aspects: First was the preservation and propagation of all that the Shehu stood for (the rightful following of the *sunnah* of the Prophet and justice for all). Second was the education of women, who were the primary mentors of future generations. . . . Thirdly, she devoted her life to reconciliation and peaceful coexistence, using her wit, her imagination, and her immense prestige to find pragmatic solutions to the problems that faced her."[3] Asma'u was "as comfortable in intellectual debate as she was in domestic endeavors, understanding both to be of equal importance to life in this world."[4] For her, daily life was imbued with Islamic devotion.

"Asma'u never patronized her students, but she provided in her works access to multiple layers of meaning at every level. Her works were replete with a wide variety of meanings hidden among features from the simplest to the most erudite, including clever vernacular wordplay, chapter and line citations from the Qur'an, and paraphrases from the classics. Through these techniques, Asma'u's students enjoyed a rich experience in reciting her poetry. For those unprepared for such techniques, her works provided the most basic of satisfactions by establishing for them mantras in the simple repetition of the rhymes. Asma'u recognized that in truly pious endeavors there is no room for intellectual elitism: she met each individual at his or her own level, in keeping with the Sufi tenets of humility and patient piety.

"Asma'u's Sufism, piety, and good deeds made her an admirable person, but her literary skills and her ability to compose effectively in several languages spread her fame among the educated and illiterate alike. She was not only famous among the Muslim scholars in her community and beyond, but she was also loved by ordinary unschooled villagers because

1. Beverly B. Mack and Jean Boyd, *One Woman's Jihad*, p. 1.

2. *Jihad* means struggle or effort. Though occasionally it may be used to refer to an external struggle, it is understood that the "greater *jihad*" is the struggle within one's own self, grappling with the forces of the ego to unify one's self with the Divine, in alignment with the Divine Will, in *tawhid* (complete Oneness).

3. Mack and Boyd, *One Woman's Jihad*, p. 6.

4. Ibid., p. 10.

she offered them, in languages they could understand, a place in Paradise with the Shehu through the works she composed. . . . In addition to religious instruction and enlightenment, Asma'u's poetic works offered views on recent history, with which they were familiar, and practical tools for their participation in a community newly unified under Islam.

"Her poetry demonstrates that she was a strong-willed woman, engaged in her cause, the unification of a Muslim state, in addition to being a poet sensitive to matters of grief and loss. She never wrote in isolation, but always was an activist, whose writings were merely instruments in bringing her fellow citizens to a higher good."[5]

As mother, wife, sister, statesperson, poet, scholar, healer, and friend, she experienced the whole range of human emotions and human duties. Upon the death of her brother, Muhammad Bello, who had succeeded their father as caliph of the infant Islamic state, she was grief-stricken. An outpouring of this grief found its expression in her book *Tabshir al-ikhwan,* relating Qur'anic remedies "for specific emotional, mental, and physical maladies. 'When light enters the heart,' she wrote, 'darkness departs from it and it is rightly guided. No matter how difficult to attain a desire may be, you must frequently bless him (the Prophet Muhammad) for he is the mediator between us and our Lord, the Exalted.' Following her own injunction, she wrote a long poem, in Hausa, in praise of the Prophet, in the same year as *Tabshir*, 1839. 'God has enjoined us all to praise Him . . . that we might obtain light and radiance of heart so that we might be cleansed.'[6]

Asma'u was "an innovator and an organizer; it was her reputation (she was described by her kinsman Sheikh Sa'ad as 'the tireless lady who excels in everything she has to do') which persuaded men to allow their womenfolk to trek on foot across country, without male escorts, for educational purposes. Asma'u had pupils (*'yan-taru* or 'women disciples') from many towns and they included women from several ethnic groups, namely Fulani, Hausa, and Sulubawa."[7] In recent years, her great-granddaughter, the Modibo of Kware (Hajara), has been among those who have continued the tradition of spiritual education of rural women.

Asma'u's teaching songs in Hausa are still well known today and continue to be learned by both young girls and boys. Her people "speak of her as if she were alive and recite the injunctions she taught their great-grandmothers. . . . She herself spoke and wrote about the women of her father's

5. Ibid., pp. 58, 61, 62.

6. Jean Boyd, *The Caliph's Sister*, p. 72.

7. Ibid., p. 76.

generation who had been 'teachers of women, teachers of exegesis of the Qur'an, and women of great presence.' They in turn had been taught by earlier generations of women who included her grandmother and great-grandmother. In her own generation there were six other women writers whose poetry survived: they were her sisters Hadiza, Fatima, Habsatu, Safiya and Maryam—the sixth was her cousin Aisha."[8]

Following here are three of Asma'u's song poems: the first is a *silsilah* of Sufi women in praise of all those who have carried the Light before her as well as some of her dear companions. The second is a eulogy for her beloved friend and sister-in-law, 'Aisha, and the third is a commentary on Surah 94, Inshirah (or ash-Sharh):

Bismillah ar-Rahman ar-Rahim
Have We not expanded your chest,
and removed from you the burden
which weighed down your back,
and increased your remembrance?
Truly, with every difficulty comes ease:
Truly, with every difficulty comes ease!
So, when you have been emptied strive onward,
and to your Sustainer turn with longing.

Surah ash-Sharh, THE OPENING UP OF THE HEART

Sufi Women

Alhamdulillahi, we thank God,
We invoke blessings on God's Messenger.
We invoke blessings on his family and Companions
And those who followed them, thus we gain self-respect.
We invoke blessings on the Companions of the Prophet
Who are now sanctified.
My aim in this poem is to tell you about Sufis
To the great ones I bow in reverence.
I am mindful of them while I am still alive

"Sufi Women" (*Tawassuli Ga Mata Masu Albarka*) is excerpted from pp. 127–31 of *One Woman's Jihad*, by Beverly B. Mack and Jean Boyd (Bloomington, Indiana: Indiana University Press, 2000). Reprinted by permission of Indiana University Press. This poem was written in A.D. 1837 / A.H. 1252–53; language of original: Hausa/Fulfulde; sources of text: Hausa, Bello Sa'id's Thesis, pp. 253–59; Fulfulde, *Waziri Junaidu*.

8. Ibid., pp. 98–99.

So that they will remember me on the Day of Resurrection.
The ascetic women are all sanctified
For their piety they have been exalted.
They prayed ceaselessly to be delivered from the Fires of Hell
Take this to heart, my friends.
I have written this poem to assuage my heart:
I remind you how they yearn for God.
I swear by God that I love them all
In the name of the Prophet, the Messenger of God.
The scent of their yearning engulfs me
Its intensity exceeds the perfume of musk.
To the Prophet's disciples who draw close to God
I bring all Muslims to Aisha
Aisha, the noble daughter of Al-Siddiq
The believer, an honest man, Abubakar the esteemed.
To Muslim women I speak of Zainabu Jahshi
I cherish them, Lord of the World.
You made her to exceed, according to Aisha,
She was held in esteem by the Prophet.
I speak of all the mothers
Who were the wives of the Prophet
And Fadima Zahra'u, or Batulu
Gracious lady, close follower of the Prophet.
She was peerless, she who shunned the world,
The Prophet's daughter, who was better than any other child.
I speak of Aminatu Ramliyya
And Ummu Hassanu, both of Kufa.
As was Ummu Sufyanu of Suriyyi
And the relative of Fudailu, a most kind person.
The mother of the Prophet was pious
A reformer, and upright.
I speak of the wives of the Prophet
For his wives were ascetics.
She was very generous and kind
Daily she gave away gifts: she never ceased.
She gave alms most generously
Undoubtedly she wept day and night.
She used to say, "I have no tongue"
She had no wish to speak.
She bought horses for the Jihad of the Lord
And to follow the Way of the Prophet of God.

I speak of Al'umatus Salliyatu
For her asceticism and also Umayyatu.
Umma Haruna had radiance
And Habibatu Adawiyyatu recited the Divine Names.
I speak of Rabi'atul Adawiyya
Who was more pious than anyone else.
Adawiyyatu Kaisiyyatu of Basra
Exalted, able to see the unseen, radiant.
She had a mastery over learning and exceeded all women
She was the outstandingly pious person of her time.
And so to Ummu Ayyuba of Lansariyyatu
And Umm Darda'u and Mu'azatu.
Her prayer was a thousand prostrations
Rabi was cognizant by day and by night.
In order to please the Prophet's heart.
On the Day of Judgment you will understand her zeal.
Rabi'atu the daughter of Ismailu
Zealously praying to God.
She could see male and female jinns[9]
Because of her sainthood and praying to God.
And Ru'kayyatu of Mausiliyyatu
And Raihanatu Majnunatul the Pious.
And Sha'awanatu, also pious
And Atika Unawiyyatu Hidatu.
Aisha, the daughter of Jaafaru, Ubaidatu
Daughter of Abi Kulaibu, and Ahhiratu.
Umratu was an ascetic and so was Mu'azatu
Of Mausili, and so too Majidatu.
And Maryamu of Basra and Muazatu
Maimunatul Majnu'atul akilatu.
I speak of Maimunatu Sauddu
All pious, and Zahara'u.
Whose intense piety made her appear transformed;
For when they reached this stage of Sufism they gained much.
I speak of Fadimatu Nisaburi
Who was zealous even to those who understand enthusiasm
And so to the daughter of Hassan, Nafisatu
Who prostrated herself on account of her piety.

9. *Jinns* (anglicized as "genies") are elemental spirits whose being is of fire and air. *Jinns* are capable of assuming many different forms and are said to be responsible for much mischief affecting human beings, but like humans they are also subject to final judgment by God.

She recited the Qur'an six thousand times in the grave
Prayed and fasted: note well her devotion.
Born at Mecca she was a descendant of the Prophet
She grew up in Medina where she was honored.
Anyone visiting her grave
And praying there would receive blessings.
The blessings and compassion of God
Fell upon Egypt on account of Nafisatu.
I speak of Fadima, daughter of Abbas Saihatu
Who taught and was a preacher.
She used to mount the steps outside the mosque
    and preach to women
Her sermons caused them to fear and repent.
She made an attempt to stop using the steps
But realized that the Prophet had heard of this decision.
"She is a truly noble person on account of her work"
The Prophet told Tarinu in a dream.
She set aside considerations of family and possessions
Choosing instead God and His religion.
I speak of the ascetic who withdrew from the world
Fakhriyyatu of Basra, mother of Yusufu.
She entered into a Sufi state of holiness
In which she stayed for forty years.
At the end of her life she went to Mecca
Where she died and was buried near Hadiza.
I pray, O God, for their blessings
Give me the grace to repent my sins.
Out of respect for their greatness I dedicate myself
Believing that I will receive what I request.
For their majesty will wipe away my sins
And because of them I will escape the burden
    of my wrong doings.
In this world and the next, where souls await judgment
I will rely on them for my salvation.
I know full well that I have committed many sins
Yet I hope for escape on the Day of Retribution.
The rest is about the women members of the community of
Shehu dan Fodiyo, for whom I pray.
I speak of those who are still alive
And those who have died.
I mention first of all Shehu Degel, our father

Dan Fodiyo, he is our leader.
And Iyya Garka who was exceedingly pious
Giving alms, she completely ignored worldly things.
Then Inna Garka who was very pious
Good-natured and generous to her kinfolk.
I speak of the other wives of the Shehu.
For they were all pious.
The teacher of women, Habiba
She was most revered and had great presence.
I speak of Aisha, a saint
On account of her asceticism and determination.
And Joda Kowuuri, a Qur'anic scholar
Who used her scholarship everywhere.

I speak also of Biada who was diligent
For her attribute was in reclusion.
And 'Yar Hindu, daughter of the Imam
Who was diligent at solving disputes.
There were others who were upright
In the community of the *Shehu*; I have not listed them.
Very many of them had learned the Qur'an by heart
And were exceedingly pious and zealous.
They never tired of preaching the righteous Faith
Those of the *Shehu* reached as many as a hundred.
The song which has listed them is now finished
And you now know of their fine reputations.
May God reunite us with them in the Next World
And through them may we achieve salvation.
Together with my mother and father and all Muslims
May we be delivered, O Lord of Gifts.
For the sake of the glory of him who was exalted
Above all other mortals. My song is finished.
I thank God Almighty
To whom all prayers are addressed.
May He bless Ahmadu and all his family
And all those who followed them.
And his Companions, all of whom were exalted
And the faithful who are enshrined in light.
The chronogram of the year of the Prophet's *hijra* is Nabshiru
It is ended, let us say Nabshiru.

Lamentation for Aisha I

In the name of God the Beneficent the Merciful. God bless the noble Prophet Muhammad. This is the poem of Asma', daughter of the Shaikh, the Renewer of the Faith, the light of the times, Usman dan Fodiyo, in lamentation of her sister Aisha, the daughter of 'Umar Alkammu, may God forgive all their sins and make Heaven their resting place. Amen.

To God I make plaint of the kinds of anxieties that rest in the
gloom of my innermost heart
Because of the loss of shaikhs, leaders of the Faith, masters, and
our brothers, companions of goodness and achievement.
The death of the beloved Aisha reminded me of those who have
passed away from among the wise and pious sisters.
My sorrows, my loneliness, and my melancholy increase the flow
of tears on my cheeks into torrents.
At the loss of the noble Aisha. Oh what a woman! Having all
the virtues
Of the pious women, humble to their Lord; of the women who
have memorized the Qu'ran by heart and who do extra
In prayers, alms-giving, then recitation of the Qu'ran, defending
the unjustly treated, carrying the burdens of many
responsibilities.
She was a guardian of orphans and widows, a pillar of the
community, ensuring harmony.
I am desolate over losing her, for she was my bosom friend, my
confidante from our earliest days.
This is no surprise; the love we had for each other came to us
from our fathers before us; it was not short-lived.
God of Heaven, judge her with pure forgiveness and make room
for a grave in perpetual light.
On the Day of Judgement, preserve her from all that is feared,
from everything terrifying on that day.
And place her in Paradise with our Shaikh, her father and her
husband in the heavenly abodes.

"Lamentation for Aisha I" (Marthiya Asha) is excerpted from pp. 168–69 of *One Woman's Jihad,* by Beverly B. Mack and Jean Boyd (Bloomington, Indiana: Indiana University Press, 2000). Reprinted by permission of Indiana University Press.

This poem was written in A.D. 1855 / A.H. 1272; language of original: Arabic; source of text: *Waziri Junaidu.*

Protect all of her descendants from the evils of their enemies
from every tribe,
From the evil of Satan, from the jinn that fights, and from every
evil thing, secretive and assailing.
I shed tears for them but that is in this earthly world; in matters
of religion our Lord is for them the good protector.
Blessings and protection upon the Best One, Muhammad who
hastened to inform us of all messages from our Lord
And upon his family, his companions, and his followers from our
community, which is thriving with God's permission.
When he announced the sign of the times by the hijra, the
Prophet served as your messenger of good tidings.

Completed with peace in the year 1272.

So Verily . . .

Lord God Almighty, all Powerful, he who asserts there is more
than one god will perish.
One God, Almighty, nothing is perfect except it comes from
Him.
Come to God, receive His generosity: all good things are derived
from Him.
Anyone who says he requires nothing of God is either ignorant or
an unbeliever.
Everyone who seeks God's help will receive it, for God allows
people to make requests.
I pray God will show me the Way of religion and that I will keep
to it until I die.
God is Pure, and forgets nothing: those whom He forgives find
peace.
May He bless us and show us the Path, and may He help us to
remain one people.

❧ "So Verily . . ." (Fa'inna maa al-usriyusra) is excerpted from pp. 132–33 of *One Woman's Jihad,* by Beverly B. Mack and Jean Boyd (Bloomington Indiana: Indiana University Press, 2000). Reprinted by permission of Indiana University Press.

This poem was written in A.D. 1822 / A.H. 1238–39; language of original: Fulfulde; source of text: *Waziri Junaidu.*

We pray for victory and that the rebellion of Ibra may be overcome.
We pray, too, for forgiveness in this world and the next.
Call upon God always, so that things which are too difficult may
be made easy.
Pray to God, do your meditations, praying for forgiveness and
giving thanks.
Look at His generosity! It is unbounded, His munificence is
infinite.
We give thanks to God and pray for our Lord of the Universe.

YASHRUTIS OF PALESTINE

Sayyida Fatima (1883–1978) was for many years the member of the Yashruti family with the greatest influence. It was her father, a shaikh who lived a hundred years ago in the ancient port of Acca, Palestine, who was the founder of this Sufi branch. The following excerpt from Charis Waddy's *The Muslim Mind* reveals a little of her story and that of her family.

Today the Yashruti order is spreading in many countries; in parts of Asia and Africa—Madagascar and Mozambique, for instance—as well as in Syria. Its appeal is widely heeded among Palestinians, a fact which reveals a little-known side of their character, and something of their spiritual roots.

The Yashrutis form a branch of the Shadhili order, founded seven hundred years ago by a North African Shaikh, Abul-Hassan al-Shadhili, who died in A.D. 1258. It has a world-wide following and network.

It was in Kuala Lumpur that an expert on the history of the Shadhilis, Dr Abdul Majeed Mohamed Mackeen from Sri Lanka, gave the writer fresh insight into the ways of those who seek to follow the Sufi path. He and his brother talked of the experience that had come to them through their father. He played a record of a gathering of hundreds of people in Cairo, the sound capturing the rhythm of deepening concentration on the remembrance *(dhikr)* of God. A number of leading university men in Kuala Lumpur, he said, meet regularly for this same purpose of *dhikr*. He told me that I would learn more from Sayyida Fatima al-Yashrutiyya, who lived in Beirut. There I visited her, and her sister and life-long companion, Miryam.

Sayyida Fatima was herself in her nineties. She was eight years old when her father, Shaikh Ali Nureddin al-Yashruti, died at the age of a hundred and eight, in the year 1891. He was born in 1783, and his life and hers between them span all the history of a fast-changing world since the French Revolution. Her brother Ibrahim, who succeeded his father as leader of the Yashruti branch of the order, was seventy years her senior, but they were very good friends. The early years of her life made the deepest impression on her. She had little or no formal education, but has written four books the last of which was finished in 1978, a few days before she died. *Journey to Reality* is the first of these. It is rich in the teachings, the songs, the prayers, of the order, but richer still in the scores of people one meets in its pages: men and women widely differing in character and circumstance, and all on the road to faith.

Acca, on the Palestinian coast, north of the modern city of Haifa, was in Ottoman days a busy port and military centre. There the Shaikh established himself in the 1850s. After his death in 1891, Sayyida Fatima lived there until the 1940s, when she left for Beirut.

In 1948 all the property of the order fell into the hands of the Israelis. She regarded this as unjust, but refused to harbor personal feelings of rancor about it. She said, "I was resentful. I felt bitter for fifteen days. It took me as long as that to hand it all back to God. It is better not to be entangled with possessions."

There are many stages on the "journey to reality," and the study of them can take a lifetime. Something of the spirit of the men and women who through the centuries have led others to make that journey may be glimpsed through Sayyida Fatima and her books. As she says, "Mysticism is hard to explain. It is a wide sea. It is the relationship between the human being and God."

The life she so vividly remembers, in the home of her father and his followers, is described by her from the point of view of the women in his home—a rare source for such an account. The following selection is summarized from her book *Journey to Reality,* and from her conversation.

Asked about the strength of the Yashruti following today, Sayyida Fatima replied:

"Ours is a materialistic age, but there are those who follow the Way. Good people are always in the minority. But that does not matter. Numbers are not what counts.

"One person can be worth more than thousands, and many thousands not worth one good person."[1]

1. Charis Waddy, *The Muslim Mind*, pp. 164–65. Dr. Waddy has herself devoted her life to the building of briges between the Islamic peoples of the Middle East and those of Western culture and upbringing.

Journey to Reality

Shaikh Ali Nureddin al-Yashruti al-Hassani al-Husseini was born in Benzarta, Tunis, in the year A.H. 1208 / A.D. 1783. He died in Acca, Palestine, in A.H. 1316 /A.D. 1891. He was a great shaikh and a very holy man. He was fortieth in spiritual descent from Shaikh Abul Hassan al-Shadhili, founder of the Shadhili order, and he inherited his spirit, even though there were thirty-nine shaikhs between them.

His father was a soldier. His mother, Miryam, was cultured in an age when few women had so much knowledge. She was the only daughter, and her father himself taught her to read and write. She married and had children, four of whom were growing up when suddenly, in one week, they all died of smallpox. Miryam, already middle-aged, was overcome with grief and despair. The family urged her husband to take another wife, so as to have children, but he loved his wife greatly and did not wish to do so. "Then God in His mercy put things right for her, and she bore a son—the great shaikh, my father. God took their grief away and gave them back happiness."

When this son grew up, he became a leader of the Shadhili order in Tunis. When the shaikh who had taught him died, he decided that the time had come to travel eastwards. After many adventures he reached Mecca, where he spent four years. He visited the tomb of his predecessor Al-Shadhili, near the Red Sea, then set his face to visit the holy city of Bait al-Maqdis (Jerusalem). He went by ship from Alexandria intending to land at Jaffa, but the ship was blown northwards along the coast. The passengers were put ashore at a point between Sidon and Beirut, where stands the tomb of the prophet Jonah.

The master of the ship refused to take any payment for carrying the Shaikh and his company. "I would like to reward you," said the Shaikh, and he explained to him his teaching and way of life. So this man was the first in that part of the world to enter into the life of the Sufi order through the Shaikh. He became one of his most faithful disciples.

The Shaikh then settled outside Acca, and soon the crowds of those who came to learn from him grew to such proportions that it became necessary to build a centre (*zawiya*, the word for any regular meeting place of a Sufi order). This was the first of many, in Acca, Jerusalem, Haifa, Damascus, Beirut, Rhodes and elsewhere.

❧ This selection is excerpted from *The Muslim Mind*, by Dr. Charis Waddy (London: Grosvenor Books, 1990), pp. 164–68. Reprinted by permission of Grosvenor Books.

The zawiya in Acca was a big establishment. It was a centre of religion and learning, where everyone worked, and all took part in the common life. Strict attention was paid to health and hygiene. Food was provided for the disciples who came to visit the Shaikh, and there were at least four or five hundred a day. On special days the numbers would rise to one or two thousand.

. . . An important general in the Ottoman army came to Acca. He had been stationed in Yemen, and was an alcoholic. One night he had had a dream, in which a man advised him to stop drinking. "You are my son," he said, "and you do not need to drink like this." A few nights later the dream was repeated. He asked the man in the dream who he was. "I am Ali Nureddin al-Yashruti," was the reply, "and I live in Acca. There is no man who is unable to repent and start to live a useful life."

Six months later, the general was transferred to Acca. He sought out Shaikh Ali Nureddin, took instruction from him, and came to live in a house near the zawiya. As his faith increased, he brought many officers and soldiers under the Shaikh's influence. He lived in Acca for fifteen years, and gathered round him a group of army leaders who all worked in the service of the order.

The Shaikh loved birds and animals. No one could beat an animal in his presence, or put too heavy a load on it. One of the horses in the zawiya lost its sight. The owner of an oil press wanted to buy it, so that it could turn the wheel, but the Shaikh forbade this. "The horse has gone blind in our service. It must have its food as long as it lives, as a reward for a life of toil."

My father had a great respect for women, both for their rights and for their duties, and he tried to raise the level of their education. When he married my mother she was illiterate. He brought in a special teacher to instruct her how to read and write, and himself gave her much encouragement, so that she reached a very high level of spiritual life.

Special lessons were given every morning to all the women in the house, not only those of his own family. He himself chose the books and the subjects, and appointed a lady teacher. Often he was with us himself. Everyone came, after which they went to their household tasks.

Young as I was, he began to teach me, explaining things so simply that I could understand. The other children in the house came to his lessons, too. He taught me to treat all equally, whether rich or poor. Though he was a great shaikh and I was but a little girl, he gave me an indelible picture of the Sufi way of life.

My father lived in exactly the same way as his disciples. He never smoked—he was not a man in the grip of habits. We were a household of sixty or seventy people, but the house was always quiet.

When I was five, he used to wake me to pray at night. My grandmother protested, but he said, "I want her to have the picture of me praying imprinted on her heart." {We continued with our night prayers} until the night before he died.

THE LIGHT OF WOMANHOOD

NOOR-UN-NISA INAYAT KHAN (1913–1944) was the sensitive daughter of Ora Ray Baker, an American mystic and relative of Mary Baker Eddy (the founder of Christian Science), and Hazrat Inayat Khan, the Indian Sufi teacher who brought the broadening of his branch of the Chishti line to Europe and America in the early 1900s. Noor was raised in a family immersed in Sufism and music. Though she was born in Moscow, it was not long before the family moved to England, where her father founded a new branch of the Chishti order. An accomplished musician, Hazrat Inayat Khan had been trained in the subtleties of music as a vehicle for the remembrance of God, one of the characteristics of the Chishti order. He shared music of the Spirit wherever he traveled, with friends and with family. When at home, he would often sing the children to sleep. And so musical remembrance was part of Noor's everyday experience. She herself played the harp.

Noor also had a strong interest in psychology and most probably learned a great deal in that field at the feet of her father. She earned her degree in the psychobiology of the child at the University of Paris and spent time both playing and teaching music and writing. Together with a friend she gathered a collection of stories of the compassionate deeds of the Buddha, which was published in 1939 as a beautiful and inspiring children's book, *Jataka Tales.*

Jean Overton Fuller, her biographer, writes:

> It was perhaps true . . . that Noor-un-nisa was "as nearly wholly selfless as it is possible for a human being to be." Vilayat[1] was always troubled about this. On leave from Fareham, he remarked, "She thinks all the time about other people. She doesn't ever consider there is such a

1. Pir Vilayat Khan, her brother, who became head of the Sufi Order of the West (leadership has since passed to his son, Pir Zade Zia), a branch of the Chishti order established upon the example of his father, Hazrat Inayat Khan. (C.A.H.)

person as herself. That idea doesn't occur to her." Much later he wrote to me: "Noor-un-nisa was born for sacrifice, like the Iphigenia of our school books. As a child I used to struggle hard at times to repress an obsessive thought that she would not live long. Indeed, she had something of the ethereal fragrance of those angelic adolescents who rarely outlive a score of years. I don't suppose she was ever conscious of herself. This gave her a forthright transparence that would attract friends like a magnet. If, however, a matter of principle were at stake she would defend it so fiercely that the less discerning would despair of seeing her revert to the same meek and carefree person."

Yet, I would have said that Noor was too interested in human development not to watch her own. . . . She wanted to be accepted for what she was, on her own; to discover herself: "I want to find out what I am!" She could only do that amongst people who did not know her background.

I did not doubt that the teachings in which she had been brought up underlay her deeper thinking (even perhaps to a greater extent than she realized) but at this time, she clearly felt that she had been living in a world of images of her father and his family in the minds of the disciples, and felt it as absolutely necessary to herself to make a naked contact with the ordinary world.[2]

Noor did not know how prophetic she was being when she wrote of one of Hazrat Inayat Khan's close students, Mme. De Armas, who had been of great inspiration to her:

> I owe her many things. I owe her that she showed me how to see life in a more profound manner. You can imagine how much I was moved to see in a woman the conception of life I have so much sought and [a being] such as I have so much wanted to be, the living softness which emanates from her, ready to console every heart which comes to her. Her mother, our "grandmamma," told me she had suffered very much. And God be thanked if I, in suffering, could have the same light in me.[3]

When the Second World War broke out, Noor enlisted as a spy for the Allies and worked as an undercover radio operator in Paris; her code name was "Madeleine"; she was also known as Nora Baker. While serving her country and the cause of freedom, both outwardly and inwardly, she was

2. Jean Overton Fuller, *Noor-un-nisa Inayat Khan (Madeleine)*, p. 117.

3. Ibid., p. 68.

captured and executed at the age of thirty-one. Posthumously she was awarded the George Cross and the "Croix de Guerre with Gold Star" for her valor and selflessness. For her courageous, light-filled spirit, and compassionate heart she has long been an inspiration to many Chishti Sufi women in Europe and the United States.

> The key to her being is in her name, which means "light of womanhood." *Noor* is the condition of our being when we have been totally purified of our self, making us transparent to the *Noor-al-Anwar*, the light of lights or divine Intelligence, the light that makes all things clear. This condition arises when there is nothing we wish for and we have no opinions, doubts, fears, inadequacies, or reservations. The real meaning of purity is not washing something away, but returning to one's original condition which is light.[4]

A Woman of Valor

The first political prisoner to be sent to Pforzheimı[5] was Nora Baker. Herr Wilhelm Krauss, the Governor, now retired (he was seventy-two in 1943) says he was not warned of her arrival.[6] He came into his office one day and was told that men from the Karlsruhe Gestapo had come and put a British spy in one of his cells. They had brought papers with instructions concerning her. These said her name was Nora Baker, that she was a "very dangerous prisoner" and had to be kept "under the most severe regime," in chains by day and by night, in solitary confinement, and without the possibility of communication with other prisoners. None of the guards was to speak with her; he was forbidden even to do so himself.

Nevertheless, he went at once to the cell where she had been put. There he found her, sitting on the edge of the bed, her hands in handcuffs, her feet in handcuffs, and a chain from the handcuffs on her hands to the hand-

❧ This selection is excerpted from *Noor-un-Nisa Inayat Khan (Madeleine)* by Jean Overton Fuller (London and the Hague: East-West Publications, 1971), pp. 241–45, 250–51. Printed by permission of East-West Publications.

4. Taj Inayat, *The Crystal Chalice: Spiritual Themes for Women* (Lebanon Springs, N.Y.: Sufi Order Publications, 1980). p. 47.

5. Pforzheim was the small prison of an industrial town of the same name, known for jewelry-making near the Black Forest in Germany. (C.A.H.)

6. Testimony of Krauss to the author [Jean Overton Fuller] in 1950.

cuffs on her feet. He was horrified that he should be required to keep her in this condition night and day—even when she ate, which would mean that she would hardly be able to lift a spoon to her mouth. He ordered that when her food was taken to her the handcuffs should always be removed, and replaced when her feeding-bowls were collected.

In all the fifty years of his service he had never known a prisoner to be kept under such conditions, or heard of one so kept elsewhere. He had had murderers in his prison, but had never been required to keep them in chains. But he did not dare refuse, for fear of the Gestapo. Herr Friedrich Fässer, Hauptwachtmeister at the time when I visited Pforzheim prison, told me that each of the chains was about five feet long.

The only person besides Herr Krauss who was allowed access to her cell was Herr Anton Giller, at that time Hauptwachtmeister. The instructions were that she was to be kept strictly segregated from the other women prisoners; even the woman attendant, who normally served in the women's section of the prison, was not to enter her cell. When she arrived at the prison, Noor was completely dressed by the woman supervisor, but after that the supervisor was not allowed to see or speak with her. She was never to leave her cell, or to see or be seen by any other prisoners. The cells on either side of her were to be kept empty.

. . . It is impossible to tell how long she was kept completely chained, as at first. That the conditions of her detention were gradually eased emerges from the statements of all my informants, though they naturally do not tally in every detail.

Krauss says he thought at first that she would be left with him only for a few days, but time passed and he became troubled. She could not live in chains forever. Eventually he took it upon himself to have the chains taken off, and ordered that once a week she should be brought out from her cell and allowed a few minutes' walk round the courtyard.

A few days after he had taken this step he was telephoned by an official of the Karlsruhe Gestapo, who asked whether he was still following his instructions faithfully, and in particular whether he was still keeping her in chains. He replied, "No, not any longer, she cannot escape from here. If she does escape, I will be responsible." He was anxious about the possible consequences of this defiance; but there were no repercussions.

She seems to have been allowed to walk round the courtyard of the prison under the surveillance of Giller, for about three quarters of an hour on each occasion. Some of this time she spent doing gymnastic exercises. Fässer, the only person still on the staff who knew her personally, speaks of her with an admiration which convinced me as being sincere and deeply felt. "She made a very good impression on me; not only because her conduct gave no cause for complaint, but above all because in spite of her obviously unhappy position she was always frank, open, and friendly. She could speak some German, and as often as the situation allowed we would talk to her. On such occasions she always showed a good spirit and a healthy humor. Her courage made a very strong impression on me. I shall not forget her expressive face, her friendly smile, her athletic figure, and her lively manner. She always had a word of thanks when we stopped for a few moments' conversation with her, or allowed her out for a walk."

Giller remarks how she would sometimes ask him to explain this or that phrase in the German books she read, but he never talked with her about politics or the war. There were two days, he remembers, when she was particularly sad—the birthdays of her mother and her brother.

Krauss came in the end to know her quite well. He used to sit down beside her on the little iron bed. Their conversation was rather laborious, because she did not speak German very fast; nevertheless, she could express most things, and told him something of her history—that she was a spy, and had been captured in France. It was only from her that he learned this, since the papers he had received from the Gestapo revealed nothing of her story and bore no indication that she had been captured in France. She said she had volunteered in London for the Secret Service and had asked to be infiltrated as a spy into German-Occupied France. He was impressed by the courage with which she emphasized that she had chosen this work freely; a less honest type would have said she had been persuaded into it. She said she had been brought to France by aeroplane and had sent back communiqués to England until she was arrested by the Gestapo and taken to their headquarters. She said that after a few weeks she had escaped and had rejoined some people with whom she had worked prior to her capture. . . . She said that if she had not been recaptured she would have resumed her communications with England and former work.

One thing perplexed him for some time. His idea of a spy, if female, was a woman who made love to men and drew their secrets out of them. Miss Baker seemed to him so obviously respectable that he could not imagine her doing this. At last he plucked up the courage to ask her. She assured him that she was not that sort of spy!

She told him that she was half Indian, which surprised him very much since she was so fair-skinned he would never have thought it. She said her father had been a kind of priest, and she had spent some time in his country as a child, and had studied Indian literature and philosophy, about which she told him something. He realized she was a very well-read girl and possessed a developed mind.

She bore the conditions of her detention with a great fortitude. He asked sometimes if she had any complaints, but she always said she had not. She never made any comment upon the chains, even at the beginning when the fettering was complete. She seemed to realize that he was not responsible for their imposition, and did not hold it against him.

When she first arrived it was obvious that she was having a great spiritual struggle with herself. She looked tormented, and sometimes her expression was quite wild. She said she had come from Karlsruhe, and he thought she had perhaps had some bad experiences. As time passed she became calmer, and he thought the tranquility did her good. Her present circumstances, if not comfortable were probably less frightening than the adventures through which she had come. His final impression was that she was a very fine person.

[Noor] had told me, in London, that if ever she found herself with the time to be alone she would try seriously to practice meditation, and I have not a doubt in the world that in Pforzheim, in the solitude of her cell, she meditated . . .

Central Chancery of the Orders of Knighthood
St. James' Palace, S.W. 1.
April 5th, 1949.

The King has been graciously pleased to approve the posthumous award of the George Cross to Assistant Section Officer Nora Inayat Khan (9901), Women's Auxiliary Air Force.

Assistant Section Officer Nora Inayat Khan was the first woman operator to be infiltrated into enemy-occupied France, and was landed by Lysander aircraft on June 16th, 1943. During the weeks immediately following her arrival the Gestapo made mass arrests in the Paris Resistance groups to which she had been detailed. She refused, however, to abandon what had become the principal and most dangerous post in France, although given the opportunity to return to England, because she did not wish to leave her French comrades without communications, and she hoped also to rebuild her group. She remained at her post therefore and did the excellent work which earned her a posthumous Mention in Despatches.

The Gestapo had a full description of her, but knew only her code name 'Madeleine.' They deployed considerable forces in their effort to catch her and so break the last remaining link with London. After three and a half months she was betrayed to the Gestapo and taken to their HQ in the Avenue Foch. The Gestapo had found her codes and messages and were now in a position to work back to London. They asked her to co-operate, but she refused and gave them no information of any kind. She was imprisoned in one of the cells on the fifth floor of the Gestapo HQ, and remained there for several weeks, during which time she made two unsuccessful attempts at escape. She was asked to sign a declaration that she would make no further attempts but she refused, and the Chief of the Gestapo obtained permission from Berlin to send her to Germany for 'safe custody.' She was the first agent to be sent to Germany.

Assistant Section Officer INAYAT KHAN was sent to Karlsruhe in November 1943 and then to Pforzheim, where her cell was apart from the main prison. She was considered to be a particularly dangerous and unco-operative prisoner. The Director of the prison has been interrogated and has confirmed that Assistant Section Officer INAYAT KHAN, when interrogated by the Karlsruhe Gestapo, refused to give any information whatsoever, either as to her work or her colleagues.

She was taken with three others to Dachau Camp on September 12th, 1944. On arrival she was taken to the crematorium and shot.

Assistant Section Officer INAYAT KHAN displayed the most conspicuous courage, both moral and physical, over a period of more than twelve months.

[For her valor and selflessness, a further citation awarded Noor-un-Nisa the "Croix de Guerre with Gold Star."]

SERVING PEACE

RABIA TERRI HARRIS is the founder and coordinator of the Muslim Peace Fellowship, an influential forum for progressive Islamic thought. The Fellowship describes itself as "a gathering of peace and justice-oriented Muslims of all backgrounds dedicated to making the beauty of Islam evident in the world."[1] In her role as coordinator, Rabia Harris edits an international newsletter and regularly addresses congregations, schools, and community organizations on a variety of Islamic issues. Harris also serves as associate editor of *Fellowship* magazine, the bimonthly publication of the Fellowship of Reconciliation, the oldest, largest interfaith peace and justice group in the world. Rabia has been working in this field for years, striving to open dialogue and encourage rightful action toward peace.

An independent scholar, Harris graduated from Princeton University with the departmental prize in Religion in 1978, the same year that she embraced Islam; she received her graduate degree from Columbia University in Middle Eastern Languages and Cultures in 1985, and a Fulbright scholarship to study the work of the Shaykh al-Akbar Ibn al-'Arabi at the world-famous Suleymaniyye Library in Istanbul in 1989. She has published a number of translations of classical Sufi texts, including the famous Islamic encyclopedia, *The Risalah: Principles of Sufism*, by Abul-Qasim 'Abd al-Karim bin Hawazin al-Qushayri and *Journey to the Lord of Power: A Sufi Manual on Retreat* (the *Risalat al-anwar*), by Ibn al-'Arabi. Some of her insights into the history of the retreat process are presented in the following selection.

Rabia Harris currently lives in New York State and is a senior member of the Halveti-Jerrahi (Khalwatiyya-Jarrahiyyah) order, headquartered in Istanbul. The order was founded upon the example of Pir Nur ad-Din al-Jerrahi (d. 1678), a Turkish Sufi master.

1. See www.MPFweb.org.

Reflections on Retreat

> A friend of God went forth on a pilgrimage, and on the road in the middle of the desert came across a little black ant struggling along. "Ant, where are you going?" he asked, in the way some people have of speaking with creatures. "Why, I'm going on a pilgrimage to Mecca, the same as you." The saint objected, "Why, you'll never make it. It's hundreds of miles, and besides you have a broken leg!" "What does it matter" the ant asked him, "as long as I'm on the way?" Ah, but we would like to speed it along sometimes.

Retreat is a provocative topic for me. I once had the honor of translating Hazrat Ibn al-'Arabi's *Risalat al-Anwar,* published as *Journey to the Lord of Power,* which is a manual on the technical practice of retreat. Some passages of that work have remained with me ever since, as do certain questions. In addition, those masters who have taught me pretty much all I understand of the concrete mystical life have been Halveti shayhks. And the tradition they transmit is that of the Halveti Order—*halveti* being the Turkish for *khalwati,* and *khalwah* being the Arabic for retreat. Yet this technical *khalwah* or *chille,* rather to the disappointment of some of us, is no longer prescribed. Well, why not?

About two centuries before the time of the Shaykh al-Akbar, Ibn al-'Arabi, the great Sufi encyclopedist 'Abd al-Karim al-Qushayri differentiated between the advanced practice of *khalwah* and the beginner's version of withdrawal from the world, specified by the term *uzlah. Uzlah* means disengagement from social life in search of God. This tactic is still widely available. But let us think about dramatic inner journeys and the history of *khalwah* first.

Khalwah is an accelerated practical implementation of the great advice of the Prophet, "Die before you die." *Khalwah* is deconstruction of the self, a coming apart that is the necessary prologue to the gradual access and final triumph of the divine light in a given human location. The sign of the

❧ This selection is excerpted from "The Relevance of Retreat," a talk delivered at the University of California, Berkeley, at the annual U.S. symposium of the Muhyiddin Ibn 'Arabi Society in 1994.

2. *Mi'raj*: the Prophet Muhammad, peace and blessings be upon him, underwent a night journey and ascension, passing body and soul from Mecca to Jerusalem, and from Jerusalem up through the Seven Heavens and the unconditioned world, into the very Presence of Allah and then back again, in no more than a blink of an eye.

access of that light is the opening of inner vision, or *basirah*. Through *khalwah*, the friends of Allah dive into the wake left by the Prophet's ascension, the *mi'raj*.[2] Those currents cannot be crossed by just anybody. *Khalwah* is extremely dangerous. Therefore, *khalwah* proper has always been rigorous, but it was once more generally accessible. Perhaps rigor is more easily attainable by some generations than it is by others.

In the age of 'Abd al-Qadir Jilani, who left this world the year after Ibn 'Arabi was born, and who is his spiritual father according to oral tradition, it appears that entering into *khalwah* was a matter of personal choice. In his *Secret of Secrets*, Hazrat 'Abd al-Qadir gave instructions to "whosoever has chosen to withdraw himself or herself from the world in order to come close to God." Such a person must know the appropriate prayers and recitations, and the saint proceeded to specify them at great length. The endeavor involved a very elaborate and precise routine of formal *salah*, readings and invocations. Hazrat 'Abd al-Qadir's *khalwah* sounds to us today like so much empty ritual. Where in the midst of all that activity would we find time for our treasured interior voyage?

Veils are raised and lowered for people as conditions change. And so in *Risalat al-Anwar*, written a generation later, we find a little difference of approach. Perhaps it is the time and perhaps it is the place, the difference between the Islamic East and the Islamic West, but Hazrat Ibn al-'Arabi recommends no elaborate regimen. He applies only the last of Hazrat 'Abd al-Qadir's spiritual tools. "Occupy yourself with *zhikr*, the remembrance of God," he says, "with whatever sort of *zhikr* you choose." "Aha!" pipes up our would-be interior voyager, much encouraged. "I'll bet I could manage that." Let's try twenty minutes of it before volunteering for eighteen or twenty hours at a time. The prescription may be simpler, but it is emphatically not easier.

Al-Shaykh al-Akbar is still writing for the private individual who independently decides to enter *khalwah*. Like his great predecessor, he cites conditions which that individual must fulfill if he or she hopes for any success. But he specifies them carefully. That person must be soundly religiously established in the elements of ablution and prayer, fasting and reverence; must have cultivated all grossness out of his or her character and learned how to be patient and how to remain spiritually awake. That person must be able to work, able to pay close moral attention to the quality of acts, able to avoid attachment, able to place full trust in Allah. You see, we are rather narrowing the field here. That person must definitely not publicize his or her retreat or hold court during its term—instantaneous disaster. And to that select person who meets these conditions the Shaykh gives a very interesting final piece of advice. "Watch your diet. Keep your constitution in balance. For if dryness becomes excessive it leads to corrupt imaginings and long delirious ravings." For imagination is the key to this business, involving as it does a necessary passage through that imaginal world which speaks to our romantic souls. And Hazrat Ibn al-'Arabi is quite worried about it. "For God's sake," he writes, "do not enter retreat until you know what your station is [and how many of us actually know in any objective sense where we stand?], and until you know your strength in respect to the power of imagination. For if your imagination rules you, then there is no road to retreat except by the hand of the Shaykh who is discriminating and aware. If your imagination is under control, then enter retreat without fear." *If* your imagination is under control—again, not an easy matter.

In the late twelfth century, it seems it was still possible, as it had been earlier, for the right people to make an effective *khalwah* simply by closing their doors and taking up some form of unbroken remembrance of God. Perhaps those times supported a more straightforward self-evaluation of readiness and of the state of one's own imagination, at least in certain cases. But Hazrat Ibn al-'Arabi is already becoming doubtful. And within another century or so, as the great river of *tassawuf* began to flow definitively into the channels of the *tariqah*, self-evaluation was no longer deemed safe or therefore acceptable. The Sufi community standardized its modes of training and established a more formal structure of peer review. Under *tariqah* discipline, the ancient process of *khalwah*, like many others, became closely regulated and refined, and sometimes yielded remarkable results.

To give you a sense of this, let me share with you the methods used until very recent times by the Turkish Halvetis, as well as some illustrations provided by a former Grand Shaykh of the Halveti-Jerrahi Order of Istanbul. A dervish who goes into seclusion is technically called a *halvetnishin*. The place that the *halvetnishin* retires to is called a *halvethane*. Although in Ibn al-'Arabi's time, one's home might still serve as a *halvethane*—"The door of your house is between you and your people," he wrote—the *halvethane* became thereafter a much more daunting affair. The site of retreat came to be specified as a windowless cell, more or less the size of a grave ("Die before you die," the Prophet said) that is neither high enough for standing up nor long enough for lying down. As was directed also by Hazrat 'Abd al-Qadir, it must be next to a mosque or other place where the five daily prayers are made in congregation. For the *halvetnishin* may—and sometimes must—pray in congregation, though with a veil-covered face and in complete silence. He or she might come out for that purpose, to answer a call of nature, or to make ablutions; otherwise, not at all. Sometimes a *halvetnishin* might be locked into the *halvethane*.

The *halvetnishin* kept a complete speech fast, and fasted from food between each night prayer and the evening prayer of the following day (about twenty-two hours at a pass). The food assigned at fast break was some water, some olives and dates, and a few slices of barley bread. Within the *halvethane* were exactly three objects. These were a prayer rug to sit on; a *cillekolane,* a belt that loosely tied the *halvetnishin*'s bent neck to his thighs (for leaning back against the walls was not permitted); and a *mawine*, a short staff with a cross-bar on which to rest the forehead or the chin to prevent the head from falling down. So equipped, the *halvetnishin* remained in total darkness for the fixed period of forty days.

This exercise was by invitation only. It could be assigned only by the Shaykh, whose decision about the readiness and the needs of a prospective *halvetnishin* might be influenced by the aspirant's dreams. But considering the size of the staterooms on this voyage, are there any left among us who are anxious to volunteer? It is freely recognized that the first period in *halvet* resembled the tortures of hell. People regularly long to die. Later, however, events might take a very different turn. A *halvetnishin* might not ever want to come out of the cell again. And particular masters didn't. Successful disengagement from the visible world, we learn, bestows certain advantages.

The last person to enter *halvet* in the Jerrahi line was Fahreddin Efendi, master of the order from 1914 to 1966. Interestingly, although there are *halvethanes* at the Jerrahi Dergah in Istanbul, Fahreddin Efendi did not make his own *halvet* there. Instead, sometime before 1914 he was sent by his Shaykh to the Halveti-Shabbani Dergah of Shaykh Ahmed Efendi in Nevrekop, which is now in Bulgaria. It seems that this particular dergah had 250 cells of retreat. And from all over the world, in the nineteenth century, every *tariqah* sent its qualified dervishes to enter *halwah* at that place. I wonder what has become of it today. The intense closed cell *khalwah* that was regulated and maintained by *tariqats* for some seven hundred years is now no longer allowed.

When Safer Efendi, our teacher and Grand Shaykh from 1985 until his recent passing, approached his own teacher to request the practice, Fahreddin Efendi firmly refused. For the feasibility of *halvet* is dependent not only on the spiritual capacity and needs of particular seekers, but also on the capacities and needs of their Age and world. "The time of *halvet* has passed," Fahreddin Efendi told his pupil. "Now is the time of *jalvet*, the time to get out of retreat, go into the world, and keep company with people, though reserving our hearts for God."

In undertaking retreat there are certain crucial variables. The first is preparedness, what Ibn al-'Arabi called *istidad*. "If someone designs a path which is beyond worship without preparedness for it," he comments, "nothing will be revealed, and the design will not profit. On the contrary, such people resemble the diseased. Their strength and capacities are completely nullified, and with them the wish, the design, and the ability to act become seriously damaged. How can they possibly reach what they seek?"

Istidad has two dimensions. One is appropriate training. The second dimension of *istidad* is natural endowment, what Ibn al-'Arabi calls the strength or weakness of one's spiritual nature, *ruhaniyya*. This sort of preparedness varies a great deal. For some people the veil of the unseen is ordinarily filmy, for others it normally resembles a brick wall.

If we as experiencing subjects are to keep tabs on our own propensities for deception, we need the full weight of an external spiritual tradition to assist us. As a Turkish dervish hymn puts it, "You can't travel without a guide, the roads are full of bandits." Or as the great early Sufi Abu Sulayman al-Darrani comments, "Sometimes a subtle observation stays in my mind for days, but I never accept anything unless I find it verified by two trustworthy witnesses, the Qur'an and the Sunnah."

The religion of Islam prohibits the drinking of wine. Yet wine, we read in the Qur'an, forms one of the four great rivers of Paradise. Everybody who gets there can drink it. So what makes the difference? Location. Here is here, and there is there, and the object of religion is to get us safely from here to there, a course that is called *as-sirat al-mustaqim*, the straight path. Those who drink, we know, have a great deal of trouble walking a straight path. They wobble a lot, wander off course, and sometimes fall down in ditches. Once one has made it back home, a little unsteadiness scarcely matters—since in the home we are speaking of, one can never get hurt or lost again, or rather more importantly, injure or misguide another.

Even in the world of imagination that buffers bodies and spirits between this world and the next, it is necessary to be careful. Hazrat Ibn al-'Arabi tells us in *Risalat al-Anwar* that "wine" means the knowledge of states. If in the course of retreat it is offered to us in images, symbolically, we still must carefully consider. His advice is: "Never drink unmixed wine." Even if it is mixed with the waters of rivers and springs, with water that has come through channels in the earth, we should not drink it. Only if it is mixed with "rainwater," with life that has come directly from heaven, ought we to accept this gift. For *khalwah*, we remember, is meant to be an exercise in *mi'raj,* in ascent, and rainwater, like revelation, comes from above.

Revelation, moderns believe, is a product of the religious imagination. It never occurs to us that the religious imagination might be a product of revelation. Yet Hazrat Ibn al-'Arabi repeatedly cites the Qur'anic warning that we ought not to make metaphors for God—that only God can know what metaphors will point us to God's truth. The distinction is crucial. When human beings take revealed images up, unravel them, develop them, embroider them, the roots of their functionality remain in the divine name "the Guide." When we invent metaphors ourselves, their roots are in us. We cannot travel through them any further than their origin. If they are private inventions, they can lead us to meet our own qualities. If they are social inventions, they can lead us to meet the qualities of our culture. Only if they are divine inventions can they lead us to meet the qualities of God.

We need to have some idea of what it means to see. It won't hurt us to think about *basirah*. We should mention first that "seeing" in these terminologies is shorthand for the full range of the faculties of perception. *Basirah*, the faculty of inner vision, is often referred to as the "eye of the heart." And so it is, when it reaches its full maturity and perfection. But in the beginning, before it becomes clarified, *basirah* is merely the "eye of the mind." It is a perfectly everyday human capacity that we all make use of on a regular basis when we dream. Raw *basirah* is a routine and necessary process of a functioning brain. Hazrat Ibn al-'Arabi explains to us that the process of inner vision and the process of ordinary vision are the same. Only their objects of perception differ. Our current intellectual climate encourages us to refer that statement directly to the realm of neuropsychology, which indeed testifies that the dreaming self makes use of the same perceptual hard-wiring that the waking self employs. But while ordinary vision uses the sensory vocabulary to look at bodies, extraordinary vision uses the imaginal vocabulary to look at meaning. And what is not generally understood is that looking, in either realm, is not automatically identical with seeing.

Anyone can look. Only a few can see. In the world of visible reality, many look *with* their eyes. Only a few look *through* them. Those few can see. Whether they are artists or scientists, poets or moralists, they have taken the eye itself seriously, trained it, challenged it, disciplined it until it is able to engage vibrantly with the world that is there to be seen. In the realm of invisible reality, too, many look with the forms of their beliefs: only a few look through them. Those few can see. They are the contemplatives, the ones for whom sleeping *basirah* comes into its own. In them, the imaginal vocabulary and its understructure have been refined, cultivated, and seasoned until they serve as a bridge between the namer and the named, allowing the invisible to be known. These people never look at images—through images they look on something else. They never experience states. Through states, too, they experience something else. And it is meeting this "something else," with whatever eye, which is the whole point of the exercise of vision. Everything else is merely calibration.

Safer Efendi of Istanbul commented that in the old days, *khalwah* might be prescribed for many reasons, but chief among them was the final step in the opening of *basirah*. *Khalwah* could activate cascades of states in full-time imaginal vision. But this is a very dangerous condition, far more so now than it ever was before. These days, for purposes of *basirah*, the world presents a serious tuning problem. Following the coinage of a recent book, we might call this problem "information smog." There are too many coruscating bits of data, too many riveting images, too many claims, too many changes for us to incorporate, to embody, attune to, and they go by too fast. The rush and flow and intimation of power intoxicate with their simple force, but they articulate nothing but themselves—at least, so far.

Whether this imaginal storm will bring us fertilizing rain or devastating destruction remains to be seen. But a storm it is. And it is because the clouds have grown thick enough to obscure rather than adorn the heavens that so many have now decided that the heavens do not exist. Many others of us, of course, remember perfectly well that they do. But this is perhaps weather in which sane people should not attempt to venture out.

The masters have closed the *halvethane*, but *uzlah* is still available. We can, if we wish, decide not to embrace the storm. Imam Qushayri warns us that if we make up our minds to withdraw, it cannot be because we think we are better than other people. It must be because we recognize that we are not fit to interact with them. How can we become so?

Times change. Sometimes *khalwah* has one protocol, and sometimes it has another. Sometimes it works, and sometimes it doesn't. *Khalwah* is technology, not revelation. It is only revelation that reliably sustains passage through the imaginal world. Perhaps we should consider anew the full range of implications of the Prophet's statement that the *mi'raj* of the faithful is in the ritual prayer.

We are lame ants on the road in the midst of a breaking storm. But fortunately this road is not about faith, nor about vision either. Attractive and desirable as those may be, the Divine Presence does not depend on them in any way. It is not our business to seek ecstasy and secret knowledge. It is our business to seek servanthood, what Hazrat Ibn al-'Arabi calls "the station of no station." And to such a quest, time and circumstance neither present any impediment nor bestow any advantage. Wherever it is we find ourselves, it is to that place that we have been taken, and in that place our responsibility may be found.

A WINDOW INTO FORTY DAYS

MICHAELA ÖZELSEL, though born in Germany, was raised mostly in Turkey. She received her B.A. and M.A. in clinical psychology from the University of North Carolina and a Ph.D. from Goethe University in Frankfurt.

In various European and Asian countries, as well as in the United States, she has lectured at numerous conferences and received recognition for her work in training professionals in clinical hypnosis, behavior modification, and systematic family therapy and in linking these modalities to ancient Sufi healing techniques. Currently, she is a lecturer in psychology for the University of Maryland, European Division, and continues her private practice in Germany.

Because of her multicultural background and her Western scientific training, her Sufi master designated and then prepared her to be a "bridge" or "translator"—that is, to provide the service of conveying some of the traditional wisdom of Sufism to the West. It was as part of this endeavor that she undertook the documentation of her first forty-day retreat, which she underwent in Istanbul in 1991. During her retreat she kept a journal and later added a psychological commentary. This work became *Forty Days: A Diary of a Traditional Solitary Sufi Retreat*, which presents us with an unusual combination of the documentation of personal religious experience as well as self-analytical/psychological assessment of that experience; this is especially unusual in modern times when so few are undertaking such traditional retreats.

When Michaela embarked on her forty-day retreat, at the recommendation of her teacher she took with her only books by Ibn al-'Arabi and Mevlana Jalaluddin Rumi, in addition to the Holy Qur'an. As the days of the retreat unfolded, she found her previously dim interest in the Qur'an intensifying as she began to penetrate its layers of meaning. On Day 37 she noted, "Reading the Qur'an isn't something cognitive anymore; it's a direct opening on an intuitive level."[1] She found herself craving the nourishment of the Qur'an, the holy book that has nourished so many in similar circumstances for so many hundreds of years.

Take refuge in the cave:
God will spread His grace over you, and will endow you—
whatever your outward condition—
with all that your soul may need.

SURAH AL-KAHF 18:16

In the Lion's Presence

DAY 14

. . . Outside it's snowing. After evening prayer, soup![2] This time there's lots of rice in it. Although I eat very consciously and with pleasure, when my bowl is empty I think, what is the big deal? Perhaps a hint about the relative unimportance of worldly needs? *Everything is perishing but His face* (Qur'an 28:88). What an austere day!

This time, thinking about Hz. Mevlana makes me cry. I'm sure I haven't cried so much in the last thirty years together as in these last two weeks. But why not? Who could I be disturbing here? I decide to perform, very concretely, one of the old exercises, the "The Way of the Dervish": "When the *nafs ammara*[3] is in a mood to complain, at that point one should work against it, expressing such exaggerated gratitude that you acquire yourself some love. Lying while saying, 'Thank You,' is a way of seeking love from God."[4] Thanking, perhaps, for having already outgrown what in fact I'm still dealing with?

So I start in as fervently as I can, giving thanks that my obsession has already been taken from me. The first thing I notice is that this exercise leads

❧ These selections are excerpted from *Forty Days: A Diary of a Traditional Solitary Sufi Retreat,* by Michaela Özelsel (Brattleboro, Vt.: Threshold Books, 1996), pp. 46–48, 54–56, 146–48.

1. Michaela Özelsel, *Forty Days*, p. 91.

2. Michaela was isolated in a small apartment in Istanbul. She was given olives, dates, and apples enough to last her for the forty days. Occasionally, Yusuf, a man connected with her retreat guide, would leave soup or extra olives for her outside her door in the evening.

3. The *nafs ammara* is the "commanding self" (ego), the first of the seven stages of the development of the *nafs* (self). (C.A.H.)

4. Mevlana Jalaluddin Rumi, *Fihi ma Fihi*, p. 366. Translation by Michaela Özelsel.

to an intense pain of greater and greater severity. I feel Allah's presence near me, feel more veils lifting. How much better the pain of the presence than the indifference of the isolation! I'd want more and more pain, till I'm burned completely and utterly clean, like the *ney* that is passed through the fire till its tone comes forth full and pure.[5] I'd like more and more pain till finally I stay "open." I think of ear-piercing. While the ear heals, you have to keep turning the new earring so that it doesn't become ingrown, to make sure a hole is really formed. This turning hurts as long as the ear is still trying to close itself. Only when the hole stays open voluntarily does the turning not hurt any more, at which point it also isn't needed any more.

I ask for more and more pain. It feels so much more right than the dead indifference that preceded it. I also sense more and more distinctly that the process of transference from Teacher to Allah[6] is going on, realize that the actual goal of my obsession is the presence of Allah. If I could only remember that always. If the veils will just keep from closing again. All at once I also understand Hz. Mevlana's seemingly paradoxical verses: "In pain I breathe easier," "When I'm ruined, I'm healed." (OS, quatrains 1131 and 1115).[7] The normally gentle, pleasant "currents" inside me have become, as they did at the beginning of last summer, a violent trembling of the whole body. Could that be what Hz. Mevlana means when he says:

> So it has become clear that trembling and passionate love are needed on the quest for God. Whoever doesn't tremble must be the

5. The *ney* is a reed flute that is one of the traditional musical instruments of Mevlevi dervishes. To form a good instrument, a good reed must be found that has matured with just enough sunshine and rain so that the sections have formed in a balanced way. Then a red-hot iron is passed through the center of the reed, opening all the sections to the passage of air. One by one, the holes for toning are then opened along the side. Only then can the instrument be played by the breath of the musician. Often it is used as a metaphor for the human being, played by God. In the opening lines of his masterpiece, the *Mathnawi*, Hazrati Mevlana Jalaluddin Rumi says, "Listen to the *ney* and the tale it tells, how it sings of separation . . . and how it longs to return to the state of union." (C.A.H.)

6. Ruzbihan (d. 1209) points out that what the pupil experiences as "transference" is actually a deeper level of the knowledge of love. According to Ruzbihan's teaching, "human and divine love do not stand in opposition to each other as a dichotomy that forces the mystic to choose between them. They are two forms of the same love, the text of one and the same book, but one must learn how to read it (that is, how to read with the 'eyes of light'). The transition from one to the other does not consist in transferring love from one *object* to another, because God is not an *object*. God is the absolute *subject*. The transition from one form of love to the other consists in the *transfomation of the subject,* the lover, the *ashiq*. The whole of Ruzbihan's teaching tends toward precisely this direction" (Corbin, 1989, p. 117, emphasis in original). Henry Corbin, *Die smaragden Vision* (The Emerald Vision). Munich: Diedrichs, 1989. German translation by Annemarie Schimmel.

7. OS = *Open Secret: Quatrains of Rumi*, translated by John Moyne and Coleman Barks (Putney, Vt.: Threshold Books, 1984). (C.A.H.)

servant of those who do. No fruit grows on the trunk of a tree, because trunks don't tremble close to the ground, it's the tips of the branches that tremble (*Fihi ma Fihi*, p. 346).

Would that my trembling could always make me remember. How many are the veils of forgetfulness! There suddenly opens before me a deeper meaning to two other guiding principles of Sufism: "It is not enough to give thanks for the rose or for its thorns, one must give thanks even when there is no rose there at all," and "Hell is sweet for the unbelievers, since it teaches them to be aware of the Presence of Allah. And nothing is sweeter than His presence."

Day 18

The *zhikrs* are becoming even deeper; in the truest sense of the word they are taking on "substance." This is where the inner peace unfolds, the peace described so beautifully by Islam as the tranquility of the heart. My head moves inside a column formed by my air body. Then I get the feeling that every back-and-forth motion of my head is spraying strings of this substance all over the room. Like water spraying from the hide of a wet dog when it shakes itself. Except that these strings have some kind of life of their own that draws them out farther and farther into the universe. Right above the heart region is where you feel it, as if pulling open curtains (veils?) on either side. With the steady, broad-stepping movements of a skater's legs—right, left, right, left. . . . So is this the "polishing of the heart"?

Sometimes it feels as if I'm penetrating directly into the syllables of the holy formulas, into the sound that echoes silently within me. The greater the awareness, the more intense the experience is. The *zhikr* is showing me how to do *zhikrs*! The old precept comes to mind: "At first you act as if you're doing the *zhikr*. Then you do the *zhikr*. Then finally the *zhikr* does you." All at once I perceive this steering process as one of the "signs" of Allah: "*He is closer to you than your jugular vein.*"[8] Where can one perceive the One Who is immanent and transcendent if not in one's deepest insides? The signs of which the Holy Qur'an speaks are "*on the horizons and within yourselves.*"[9] Is that it? "His Heaven and His Earth cannot contain Him," says Islam, "only the [shiny, polished] heart of the believer has room for Him."

8. Surah Qaf 50:16. (C.A.H.)

9. Surah al-Fussilat 41:53. (C.A.H.)

Suddenly it becomes painfully clear to me. There's really only one way: absolute surrender, absolute giving-up of wanting-for-oneself. The voluntary giving-up of "whatever is dearest." In the words of Hz. Mevlana: "to take the step toward the lion *in the lion's presence,*" to "jump into the fire," to "fall into the trap."

The Lion

> So the reports of a lion reached every corner of the world. A man amazed by the rumors made his way to the forest from a faraway place to see the lion. For a whole year he endured the rigors of the journey, traveling from way-station to way-station. When he got to the forest and saw the lion from afar, he stood still and couldn't go a step closer. "What's this?" they said to him. "You came all this way out of love for this lion. This lion has the trait that if a person boldly comes up to him and strokes him lovingly, he will not hurt that person or do anything to him; but if someone is fearful and anxious, then the lion becomes furious at him; indeed he attacks some people meaning to kill them because they have a bad opinion of him. That being so, you've given yourself a year of trouble. Now that you've gotten close to the lion, you stand still. What kind of standing there is that?" No one had the courage to go a single step farther. They said, "All the steps we took up to now were easy. Here we can't take a step farther." Now, what Omar[10] meant by faith was this step, taking a step in the lion's presence toward the lion. This step is extremely rare; it is the part of the elect and God's close friends alone. It is the real step, the rest are only footprints.[11]

The dearest thing I still have is not anything that I possess: it is my despairing wish to see my Teacher again. I make several approaches to sacrifice this. I feel as if I am once again about to die, till I finally succeed in praying never to see him again.

The pain is as burning and fresh as if a whole year had not passed. At some point, much later, the terrible pain ceases all at once just for a second, and I experience the deepest and richest tranquility of the heart that I have ever felt. Hz. Mevlana's "poorhouse of not wanting," this must be it. Now I have given everything, I have nothing left. Will I ever be able to

10. One of the four "Rightly-Guided Caliphs" (ruled 634–644) and companion of Muhammad (Peace be upon him).

11. Mevlana Jalaluddin Rumi, *Fihi ma Fihi,* p. 206. Translation by Michaela Özelsel.

stop crying? Only three weeks more, then they'll come and get me out. I wonder whether I can get myself back together by then.

And yet these few seconds of such a qualitatively utterly different, such an indescribable feeling of the peace of the heart are enough to strengthen me in the assumption that I'm on the right track. So I go on and on, until, between the tears and the exhaustion, I no longer know for sure whether I'm asleep or still praying. Absolutely empty and spent, I pull myself off my mattress sometime toward morning to perform the washings for the night prayer that still remains to be performed.

In front of my door, I find a little sack with some olives. Dear old Yusuf!

Zhikr

> Anyone who has ever experienced such a rhythmic *zhikr* with its accelerating tempo and the shortening of the words till only a kind of intense sighing remains knows that even an outside observer can easily be carried away by the power of the experience.[12]

The practice of *zhikrs* can be understood as the "heart" of Sufism: "heart," because it is the central exercise for reaching the goal on the path, the goal of intuitively perceiving the oneness of all being, and "heart," in the sense of Sufi terminology, as being the "organ of recognition" of God's reality. Furthermore, it is absolutely the core exercise of a traditional *halvet*. This fact is expressed in the title of a commentary by Abdul Karim Jili (fourteenth century) on Ibn 'Arabi's treatment of the *halvet:* "The Unveiling of the Secrets That are Revealed to Those Persons Who are Given to the Practice of the *Zhikr*."

It is also in this light that Sufis understand the Quran verse 29:45: "*Convey unto others what of this divine writ has been revealed unto thee, and be constant in prayer* [salat]*; for, behold, prayer restrains the human being from loathsome deeds and from all that runs counter to reason; and remembrance of God* [zhikr] *is indeed the greatest good. And God knows all that you do.*"

These practices, also characterized in a statement by the Prophet (Peace be upon him) as "keys to the gates of realization," go directly back to the Quran: "*Remember God with unceasing remembrance*" (Quran 33:41). The exhortation to approach the Creator through *zhikrs,* that is, "remem-

12. Annemarie Schimmel, *Mystical Dimensions of Islam*, p. 250.

bering" and "being mindful," runs like a scarlet thread through the holy scriptures of Islam. This word is used in the vocabulary of the Quran when the revelation of higher forms of adoration is concerned.[13] It is also so used, among other instances, in the Quran verse, "*So remember Me, and I will remember you*" (2:152), which, for the Sufis along with the verse, "*He loves them and they love Him*" (5:54), expresses with particular clarity their ardent and intimate relation to Allah, the "Beloved," the "Friend." Both verses express the idea that the original invocation comes from the Creator, not from humanity:

> *Zhikr* is a light whose origin is in the divine and whose purity draws the Sufi heart onward to the Beloved.[14]

Kalabadhi (d. ca. 996) traces the *zhikr* right back to the "primal contract":

> Humanity heard its first *zhikr* when God addressed it with the words: *alastu birabbikum* (Am I not your Lord?). This *zhikr* was locked in their hearts, just as the fact itself was locked in their intellect. As they heard the Sufi *zhikr*, the secret things were shown forth from their hearts again.[15]

The outward execution of this specifically Sufi form of invocation varies from one *tariqat* (Sufi order) to another but is of central importance in all of them. *Zhikr* can be carried out alone or in groups; aloud or internally (*zhikr* of the heart); while sitting, standing or turning around. Always it is a combination of sound (external or internal), concentration, breathing, and movement. As in the ritual prayer, a person surrenders his or her totality to this holy proceeding. And just as in the case of the ritual prayer, the effect unfolds only gradually. An ancient precept says: "At first you pretend to do the *zhikr,* then you do the *zhikr,* finally, the *zhikr* does you." In the process, the "heart is awakened" or—according to a saying by the Prophet (Peace

13. For example, in *surahs* 2:152, 3:41, 4:103, 7:205, 13:28, 18:24, 18:28, 20:14, 23:39, 28:13, 29:45, 33:35, 33:41, 37:75, 53:29, 62:10, 73:8, 76:25.

14. Ruzbihan, d. 1209 in Shiraz.

15. Quoted according to Annemarie Schimmel, *Mystical Dimensions of Islam*, p. 244. [Dr. Schimmel is referring to what is known in the Islamic tradition as the Day of Alast, the moment in pre-eternity when God asked all the souls the question "Am I not your Lord?" and we responded, "Yes, truly." (C.A.H.)]

be upon him) "polished"[16]—which is followed by the "happy state in which all book-learning is no longer useful."[17]

What is recited consists of holy formulas—for example, the first part of the profession of faith, "*La ilaha il Allah*"[19]—or selected "Most Beautiful Names"[18] of Allah. The head (in the standing position, this goes for the whole body) moves rhythmically from right to left, then later back and forth. The combination of sound and movement gives rise to specific breathing patterns, which in some *tariqats* are consciously intensified. For example, the emphasis can be placed on the exhalation. This can lead to hyperventilation, which may be accompanied by convulsive twitching and partial catalepsy. These phenomena are neither sought after nor avoided. If they appear, they are interpreted in some *tariqats* as special signs of grace.

According to Schimmel:

> . . . in performing a *zhikr* based on one of the names of God, the wisdom of the mystic leader must be shown to a particular degree, because it is his responsibility to instruct and carefully watch over the pupil, lest the pupil be exposed to serious mental and psychic dangers. The rules for use of these names of God have been worked out by the Sufis in painstaking detail. The name *Al-Fa'iq*, "the Overwhelming One" [for example], should never be used by a beginner, but only by a high-ranking gnostic. The wrong use of a name of God can have serious consequences for the person affected or those close to him or her, which can even be displayed in the form of physical symptoms, as I know from the personal experience of friends.[20]

16. [It is said in the Sufi tradition that] "There are ways and means of polishing everything. *Zhikrs* are what removes the rust from the heart." 6 A. Moinuddin, Die Heilkunst der Sufis: Grundsätze und Praktiken (Freiburg, 1984).

17. A. Moinuddin, *Die Heilkunst der Sufis: Grundsatze und Praktiken* (Freiburg, 1984).

18. "There is no god but God"; there exists no reality but the One Reality. (C.A.H.)

19. The names or qualities most often remembered in Islamic practice are ninety-nine, comprising both *jalal*, or strong, powerful qualities, and *jamal*, or beautiful qualitites. (C.A.H.)

20. Annemarie Schimmel, *Mystical Dimensions of Islam*, p. 252.

THE WAY OF THE SOUL

SACHIKO MURATA, while studying family law at Chiba University outside Tokyo, became intrigued by what she discovered about Islamic law. With the help of a friend she was enabled to attend the University of Tehran in Iran. After three years of study in Persian, she wrote a doctoral dissertation on the role of women in the *Haft paykar*, a poetical work of Nizami. She then continued with the study of Islamic law in the Faculty of Theology and with the help of Professor Izutsu was able to translate the sixteenth-century classic on principles of jurisprudence, *Ma'alim al-usul*, into Japanese. Forced to leave Iran during the revolution, she came to the United States. In 1983 she was invited to join the faculty of the State University of New York at Stony Brook. Dr. Murata continues to teach comparative religious studies at Stony Brook, including "Feminine Spirituality in World Religions," and has become one of the foremost female scholars of Sufism today.

Her book *The Tao of Islam: A Sourcebook on Gender Relationships in Islamic Thought* was published in 1992. Included in it are her translations of passages from numerous important texts of Sufism that had not previously been available to English-speaking readers. Other books by Dr. Murata include *The Vision of Islam,* which was written together with her husband, Professor William C. Chittick, and *Chinese Gleams of Sufi Light*, a study and translation of two Chinese-language works on Islamic spiritual teachings, which she has translated into English. She continues to research Sufism in China,[1] and the early treatises conveyed there, while she

1. The Prophet Muhammad is known to have said, "Seek knowledge, even unto China." Islam arrived in China during the first generation after Muhammad, during the Tang dynasty (618–907). It was predominantly Sufi traders who brought the Muslim faith into China beginning in the 700s A.D. As much of the tradition was conveyed orally, for centuries, it was not until much later that the first Sufi text was translated into Chinese: *The Path of God's Servant from the Origin to the Return* by Najm al-Din Razi (d. 1256), a Kubrawi master. With the arrival of Islam, a beautiful cross-fertilization took place resulting in numerous Chinese Sufis with a Confucian-Muslim perspective. There are now numerous Chinese Muslims of whom most are Sufi in understanding and practice. (C.A.H.)

lives, writes, teaches, and gardens together with her husband in Stony Brook, New York.

The following selection is excerpted from the transcription of an informal discussion with Dr. Murata on the feminine gender of the word for "soul" in Arabic (*nafs*), followed by a discussion of the soul as Virgin Mother from the *The Tao of Islam*. For further discussion of the feminine grammatical gender of the *nafs*, the "one degree" of difference between male and female, and the illuminative role of human marriage, readers might refer to the chapter "Human Marriage" in the *Tao of Islam*. As Dr. Murata states there:

> From the perspective of incomparability, God is unknown and cannot be experienced. But from the perspective of similarity, God shows Himself in all things and can be experienced through all things. The whole cosmos and everything within it is God's self-disclosure. But the greatest locus of experiencing God's self-disclosure is the sexual act.[2]

> If men and women fall short of each other by a certain degree, yet they find fulfillment in each other precisely for that reason. What separates them gives rise to the desire that brings them back together. In the same way, God's love for the cosmos brings it into existence, "so that the Hidden Treasure might be known."[3] Thereby "other than God," difference, diversity, separation, make their appearance. But just as this love brought the world into existence, so also it brings creatures to the perfections for which they were created. Thereby it reunites them with God. God "loved to be known." Without the original separation demanded by the cosmos, a separation that begins on the human level in ignorance of God, the subsequent knowledge of God by the "other" would not have been possible.[4]

> . . . Human appetite reflects God's attribute of desire and love. Within human beings, it incarnates God's desire for creation and His joy in bringing the world into existence. In order for human beings to develop their appetite in a healthy and wholesome manner, fully in accord with the nature of the Real Itself, they must keep it within the bounds set down by the *Sharia* [the principles of Islamic law]. Then appetite will follow the course of what God desires for mankind. Once

2. Sachiko Murata, *The Tao of Islam*, p. 186.

3. I.e.: "I was a Hidden Treasure and I so loved to be known that I created the two worlds that my treasure of mercy and lovingkindness might be known" (Hadith Qudsi).

4. Sachiko Murata, *The Tao of Islam*, p. 183.

human beings reach the Garden, their appetite is freed from all outside constraint, since at this stage of human perfection appetite coincides with God's desire by its very nature. Like the activity of angels and beasts, the activity of the felicitous in the Garden flows with the Tao.[5]

Yet we each begin with the state of servanthood:

Awareness of one's weakness, incapacity, and yin position in relationship to the Real is the state of servanthood *(ubudiyya)*. . . . Being a servant is the proper human relationship with God, a necessary prerequisite for actualizing the yang qualities that pertain to vicegerency.[6] Hence, Qushayri's "subtle allusion" here suggests that men can be deluded by their natural state of projecting and displaying yang attributes. They tend innately toward claiming authority and vicegerency, but this is a great danger, since they have no valid claim to it without first attaining servanthood. In contrast, women have the advantage of relative weakness and incapacity in the outward domain. Hence they will be less inclined to take unjustified claims. They have the advantage of a kind of natural servanthood.

Attributing yang qualities to oneself is perilous because all yang qualities belong by right to God. As Rumi puts it, alluding, through "king" and "dust," to yang and yin qualities,

If I be a king but without Thee,
then how false are this "I" and "we"!
But if I am dust and with Thee,
how comely is my I-hood![7]

Recognizing one's own yin qualities in face of God is an aid to *tawhid,* since it makes a person ascribe all power, strength, glory, creativity, and so on, to the Real. As the Prophet put it, in a saying that traditional Muslims frequently recite: "There is no strength and no power except in God, the High, the Tremendous."[8]

5. Ibid., p. 187.

6. The true nature of the human being is understood to be both servant in relation to the Real and representative caretaker, vicegerent, in relation to creation. (C.A.H.)

7. Rumi, *Divan* 33594 (SPL 193).

8. Sachiko Murata, *The Tao of Islam*, pp. 177–78.

Soul Bridges

From the standpoint of Islamic cosmology, the human being has an *aql*, (intellect/spirit), a soul, and a body—three things—which of course correspond to universal spirit, universal soul, and universal body—this is our nature. The relationship of the spirit, soul, and body is such that spirit—light/angel/the pen/intellect—is an image of the "masculine," because it is a single reality. The light has nothing to do with any corporeal reality—it is a single disengaged reality—while the human body is dark, a compound reality. And between light and darkness there is no relationship. As a bridge, the *nafs* (soul)[9] was created. And this human *nafs* is, of course, the mixed-up human, psychic domain. The highest part of the *nafs* is almost light. *Nafs* is synonymous with Iblis[10] because it is made of fire. The psychic domain is the domain of fire, and fire needs fuel. Fire as such doesn't exist. Therefore when we have fire, [that means] we have fuel; we have the wood to be burned, and then this fire gives light. Then this light, when it rises, enables us to see. So, the highest part of the human *nafs* is almost light, while the lowest part of the human *nafs* is almost darkness.

And there's a reason that before the creation of Adam, Iblis was allowed to mingle with the angels in paradise. The story is that Iblis was a believer

"Soul Bridges" is excerpted from a transcript of an informal talk by Sachiko Murata at the Threshold Society annual gathering in San Juan Bautista, California, 2001.

9. In the Islamic tradition, it is understood that the *nafs* (self or soul) has the possibility of development and refinement. Classically, this journey of refinement is depicted as passing through seven levels or stages: (1) *nafs al-ammarah*, the "commanding self," the unruly animal self, the coarsest of the stages of the soul; (2) *nafs al-lawwamah*, the "reproachful self," the self of awakening conscience, that begins to turn to God in repentance; (3) *nafs al-mulhamah*, the inspired self through which, by the inspiration of spiritual knowledge, one distinguishes rightful from that which is wrongful and learns discernment; (4) *nafs al-mutma'innah*, the tranquil soul that enjoys relationship with the Divine; (5) *nafs ar-radiyyah*, the satisfied soul in harmony with Reality; (6) *nafs al-mardiyyah*, the self that is not only pleased but is also pleasing to God (Surah al-Fajr 89:27), the self in total submission; (7) *nafs al-zakiyyah* (or *nafs al-kamilah*), the completely purified or perfected soul. (C.A.H.)

10. Iblis ("slanderer") is the personal name of the devil or satan, who is also referred to as *ash-shaytan*. Originally he was one of the angels closest to God, but he refused to bow down before Adam at God's command, thinking himself better and saying, "You made me of fire and him of clay," and so God expelled him from heaven. The Prophet Muhammad is known to have said that *ash-shaytan* circulates in the blood of the human being. We each have this tendency toward pride and arrogance, the unruly, fiery aspects of the *nafs al-ammarah*. The Prophet also said, "My satan has become a *mu'min* (one of the faithful)," pointing to the transformation of the *nafs*. (C.A.H.)

and was so purified that he was almost light. Now, in the human being as a microcosm, this hierarchy of states should be observed. If the spirit is "pen," then soul is "tablet." If the spirit is "male," soul should be "female," because the spirit, the "pen," is something that acts, and the "tablet," the soul, is something that is acted upon. So in the relationship between spirit and soul, soul should be "feminine," gentle, receptive.

Now, one of the problems in the West is that people take "feminine" as passivity, and passivity is considered a very negative quality. But "receptivity"—now, "receptivity" is the highest quality in Taoism. That is, *shunyata,* "emptiness," in Buddhism—in Taoism *wu wei*, "no action," and then "no ultimate." The "workshop of nonexistence"[11] is appropriate for that highest level of emptiness, and that emptiness is being manifested through this receptivity. Now, if the soul in relation to spirit is "feminine," the soul, which has a wide range, in relation to the body should be "masculine," because if one side is active, the other side is receptive. So the soul should be "male" in relation to the body, and then the body is "female." So if the body is governed by the soul, then the soul is governed by the spirit: this is the proper order of the hierarchy of the psychic realm and the spiritual realm.

So, just putting this aside, now let me very quickly explain how things are looked upon in Eastern cosmology in general, and then go back to Islamic cosmology. In the Far East, cosmology regarded both heaven *and* earth. Here in the West we see diverse complaints about the body, as though it is because of this body we have problems. Some say: "I wish we did not have this body, because if we didn't have a body, we would have no problems." But if there is no body, there is no soul. Because soul without body cannot function. We need a donkey so that the rider can be someplace.

In the relationship between heaven and earth, heaven is active, and then earth is the receptive. So earth takes everything, whatever heaven gives. Now the problem is, if you take one heaven, one earth, many women say it's not fair, because the earth is always receptive and never active. But there are so many heavens and so many earths. And many cosmologists say, "Look, when we compare two heavens, whichever is higher we call 'heaven'; the lower we call 'earth.' " In other words, the relation between "heaven" and "earth" alternates the moment we change our point of view.

So we do not have one set of heaven and earth, we do not have one set of male and female, we do not have one set of active and receptive, one yin

11. Mevlana Jalaluddin Rumi refers to the unseen world as the "workshop of nonexistence." As he enjoins us in his masterwork, the *Mathnawi*, "Come into the workshop and see Him clearly." (C.A.H.)

and yang. Once we change our viewpoint, yin and yang change. Yin becomes yang; yang becomes yin. Many of you know the terminology of both from the *I Ching*. In T'ai Chi, the Great Ultimate, we have yin and yang. Yin and yang, the male and female principles, are the only principles through which this whole universe is created. Yang is the shining, the sun and the day, and yin is the shadow, moon, the night, and darkness. So likewise, as activity, movement is yang, and receptivity or tranquillity is yin. So if we say, man is "male," this is yang, and woman is "yin"—so he is yang, and I am yin. But right now I am referred to as "yang," because I am the one speaking, and all of you are "yin"—you are listening to me. But then in the next moment, someone else speaks and they become yang and I, in listening, become yin. So the relationship changes all the time. So woman in relation to man is "yin," but woman in relation to her children is "yang." Again, a woman's relationship to her mother is "yin." But when a man is sleeping and a woman is awake, the woman is "yang."

These relationships between yin and yang are very well adapted to Islamic cosmology also. Try to see in the relationship between spirit, soul, and body if you can observe this relationship of yin and yang. If the spirit, instead of acting toward soul, becomes receptive, then soul becomes active toward the spirit. Then in return, soul becomes receptive toward the body, while the body becomes active toward the soul. So we become no longer "man," no longer "human being," because as al-Ghazali says, the body in human reality is like four things in one sack: a wise man, a devil, a pig, and a dog. The pig represents sensuality, and the dog represents hunger. He says that the difference between philosophers and the Sufis is, that the philosopher says, "Go, kill your pig and dog," and Ghazali says, "No, if you kill your pig, how can you feel love? If you kill your dog, how can you gain strength?" You have to purify, transform your pig into pure love, and your hunger into pure aspiration/power/strength, so that the pig and dog become your two wings to fly toward God.

If the spirit is "yang," or "active" toward the soul, in turn the spirit is in the position of receptivity toward God. So, whoever seeks God is "man." The Virgin Mary is the one of whom God says, "Of men, on the Day of Resurrection, Mary will come first." So Mary is considered "man," in that sense: whoever has spirit dominating his or her soul is called "man" forever. Whoever has the *nafs* dominating over spirit is referred to as "woman." And there is no offense here for women, because we're talking about the inner reality. We are dealing with one set of cosmology of yin and yang, female and male. In the *I Ching* it's very clear with the trigrams, the three lines, and the science of change. With the cosmic family, father and mother, heaven and earth, and six children—three sons and three daughters—all three males are represented by one yang line and two yin lines, and female children are represented by one yin line and two yang lines. So whatever manifests outwardly is actually only one side of the relationship; it is not revealing both sides. That is the human reality. In form we may manifest as man or woman, but inwardly in relation to spirit, [our position] may be totally different.

The Soul as Virgin Mother

The ideal soul receives the infusion of the spirit and gives birth to the heart. This is the soul at peace. Sometimes our authors compare this soul to the Virgin Mary, while Jesus is the heart to whom she gives birth. Rumi, in a slight variation on this theme, depicts the human body as Mary. He is explaining why the pain of love and longing are necessary on the path to God.

> As long as Mary did not feel the pain of childbirth, she did not go toward the tree of good fortune. *And the pangs of childbirth drove her to the trunk of the palm tree* [19:23]. That pain took her to the tree, and the barren tree bore fruit.
>
> The body is like Mary, and each of us has a Jesus within. If the pain appears, our Jesus will be born. But if no pain comes, Jesus will return to his Origin on that same hidden road by which he came. We will be deprived of him and reap no benefit.[12]

Kāshānī interprets Mary in a similar microcosmic sense in commenting on Koran 3:42–45:

> *And when the angels,* the spiritual faculties, *said to Mary,* the purified and pure soul, "*God has chosen you,*" because you have freed yourself of appetites, "*and*" He has "*purified you*" of ugly character traits and blameworthy attributes. "*He has chosen you above all women.*" Women are the appetitive souls[13] that are colored with blameworthy acts and

❧ "The Soul as Virgin Mother" is reprinted by permission from pp. 313–15 of *The Tao of Islam: A Sourcebook on Gender Relationships in Islamic Thought,* by Sachiko Murata, the State University of New York Press © 1992, State University of New York.

12. Rūmī, *Mathnawi, Fihi ma Fihi*, 20–21 (cf. SPL 241).

13. As in Dr. Murata's previous discussion, she is referring here to the *nafs ammarah*, which is the lowest level of soul, the "commanding soul" that relentlessly urges the indiscriminate following of desire. (C.A.H.)

despicable habits. "*Mary, be obedient to your Lord*" through your duties, which are acts of obedience and worship. "*And prostrate*" yourself in the station of brokenness, lowliness, poverty, incapacity, and asking forgiveness. "*And bow yourself*" in the station of humility and fear "*with those who bow*," those who are humble. . . .

The angels said to *Mary*, the soul, "*God gives you good tidings of a Word*," the heart, which is a gift *from Him*." His "*name is 'Messiah*,' " since he will "anoint" [*mash*] you with light.

"*High honored shall he be in this world*" because of his perception of particular things and his governing of the best interests of livelihood. He shall be the best, the purest, and the most correct that can be. Both the "human beings," that is, the outward faculties, and the "jinn," the inward faculties, shall obey him, follow him, attend to him, and glorify him. "*And in the next world*," since he perceives universals and holy sciences and he undertakes to govern the return to God and guidance to the Real. Hence We give to him the Kingdom of the Heaven of the spirit and We honor him. He is one of those "*near stationed to God*," receptive to His self-disclosures and unveilings.[14]

The Perfected Heart

If we suppose that intellect and soul have been perfected and live together in utter harmony, then the heart will have been born. But the soul, this virtuous "woman," is none other than her husband, since her union with the intellect is complete and total. Heaven and earth have achieved such perfect harmony that their properties cannot be distinguished. Their oneness is precisely the heart itself, which is identical with the Tao. And indeed, the essence of the true human being is the heart.

In the midst of the *tawhīd* that has been established, relationships can be discerned in any given situation. Is the perfect soul yin? Yes, since it has submitted itself to the will of heaven. Is it yang? Yes, since it incarnates the will of heaven that rules over the Ten Thousand Things. Is the perfect intellect yin? Yes, since it is receptive to the light of God. Is it yang? Yes, since it irradiates the soul.

One can also express this state of union by saying that the heart has two faces. One looks at God, the other at the cosmos. Inasmuch as the heart looks at God and receives from Him, it is His servant. Inasmuch as it looks toward the cosmos and governs it, it is God's vicegerent. Thus Qūnawī

14. Kāshānī, *Ta'wīlāt I*, 185–86.

writes that a human being considered as an integrated whole—as having actualized the perfections of all the divine attributes—is yin only in respect to the Presence of All-comprehensiveness (*ḥaḍrat al-jamʿ*), which is designated by the all-comprehensive name Allah. And this occurs only after the person achieves total and utter annihilation (*fanaʾ*) of the limiting attributes of the soul:

> When receiving activity [*infiʿāl*] embraces both the outward and inward dimensions of the human being and complete annihilation has been achieved, then the situation pertains to the Presence of All-comprehensiveness. For the human being as a whole does not act as a locus for the reception of activity except in relation to this Presence.[15]

Human beings who attain to this station of perfection function as the heart of the macrocosm, since only within them are all the qualities of heaven and earth, or all the properties of the two hands of God, fully realized. Hence Qūnawī and his followers sometimes refer to the perfect human being as the "heart of all-comprehensiveness and existence." Such a person comprehends the attributes of heaven, earth, and the Ten Thousand Things and has become a totally integrated whole that embraces all reality. As servant and vicegerent, he or she stands at the center of existence, tying all things together. This individual human being is "the point at the center of the ontological circle," a circle which is all of existence, or everything other than God.

The perfect human being is a *barzakh* or "isthmus"[16] in respect of embracing all the qualities of God and all the macrocosm and bringing them together within a single reality that is both yin and yang, servant and vicegerent.

15. Qūnawī, *Miftāḥ al-ghayb* 324.

16. *Barzakh*, isthmus or barrier, is the place where the two worlds meet. (C.A.H.)

MOTHER LOVE

MURSHIDA VERA CORDA (1913–2002), one of the strong women of the North American Chishti line, was a tireless teacher and guide who contributed important work in the field of child development awareness. She was a follower of the teachings of Hazrat Inayat Khan from a young age and was one of the first to meet him when he brought the teachings of his branch of the Chishti lineage to the United States in the early 1900s. Later she was also a student and close associate of Murshid Samuel Lewis, the student of Hazrat Inayat Khan's who initiated his own branch of Sufism, the Sufi Islamia Rahaniat Society. In the 1960s Murshida helped to establish the first alternative Sufi schools for young children, based on the teachings of Hazrat Inayat Khan, who emphasized spiritual principles in the raising and educating of children.

Murshida's whole life was devoted to service. She received her B.A. in primary education, her M.A. in the Education of Exceptional Children, and a Ph.D. in Health and Human Services. While teaching in the public schools she also founded the Sufi Seed schools and developed curricula for children from infancy through elementary school as well as training programs for parents and teachers. She also practiced psychiatric nursing, taught principles of Sufi healing, and was an artist and author. Her book, *Cradle of Heaven: Psychological and Spiritual Dimensions of Conception, Pregnancy, and Birth*, was published by Omega Press in 1987.

It was when Murshida was herself a small child that she first encountered Hazrat Inayat Khan. When she was quite young she would sometimes walk through the tall cornfields near her home. She was struggling to read and pointing to words in one of her father's books, repeating, "Read, read, read!" when suddenly a man appeared to her and said, "That's not the way; this is the way," and taught her how to read. He then told her to call him Hazrat. Some years later when she was a teenager, she was studying dance with Ruth St. Dennis and one day happened to notice a photograph of a music group called the Hindustani Musicians who were coming to play at a hall in San Francisco. As soon as she saw the photo, which included Pir-O-Murshid Hazrat Inayat Khan, Murshida recognized him as the man who had appeared to her in her vision in the cornfield. She did everything she could to arrange to be at that concert, but as soon as Hazrat Inayat Khan appeared on stage, she was overcome with emotion. She yelled, "Hazrat, Hazrat, I'm here; I'm here." Ushers quickly carried her out so she was not able to hear him play that evening, yet the connection only continued to deepen.

For many years Murshida was of great support to parents seeking to nurture the essential spirit of their children. As has been witnessed for millennia, mothers, especially, have a great deal of influence on their children. The early years of development are particularly important and precious. When a child is raised with love, with the awareness of being loved, it is much easier for him or her to then share love and spread love as each grows into maturity.

Someone once asked a Sufi teacher, "Do we ever reach a state when we no longer need love?" The response was, "Yes, when we love."

The First Goal of Sufi Mothers

The selections by Murshida Vera Corda were first published in *Rustle of Wings*, a newsletter for the Sufi Seed Schools of the Sufi Order of the West, and other pamphlets produced by the Sufi Seed Schools, 1977. Reprinted by permission of the Murshida Vera Corda Foundation.

The Sufi mother has the first duty to see that her doctors support her in the bonding of her child to herself in the first forty minutes after birth. This means bare skin to bare skin over her heart with eyes meeting and alone, following clean-up.

The Sufi mother keeps her infant within the closest environment of her home for the first forty days, discouraging visitors generally and getting her intimate family adjusted to its new member. The Sufi mother during this time gets her new act together, concentrating on learning the spirit of her child and the quality of the soul manifesting through the

❧ The selections by Murshida Vera Corda were first published in *Rustle of Wings*, a newsletter for the Sufi Seed Schools of the Sufi Order of the West, and other pamphlets produced by the Sufi Seed Schools, 1977. Reprinted by permission of the Murshida Vera Corda Foundation.

human personality. The mother's diet and emotional security when guided and encouraged will soon have the nursing pattern well established.

The Sufi mother realizes that attitudes are the most important thing to keep clear. Each mother has to learn her care-taking methods by experience with her own child. Awareness of the vibrations with which she surrounds the infant is most important in the early weeks after birth.

Rest, relaxation, and creative outlets make mothering a joy rather than a duty. Communicating her new goals and objectives to the new father is important, too. A close friend or a spiritual guide can help keep these lines of communication open and growing. The Sufi mother takes responsibility for her new relationship to the father of her child, holding the unity of the family together.

Going out into nature with her baby while avoiding large public gatherings is wise. Within nature the new mother can renew her energy field and introduce her child to light, shadow, and brilliant color.

Sufi mothers implant their ideals and philosophy by reflection, mental mirroring, and consistent patterns of care-taking. Respecting and upholding the infant's rights are her important duties also. The right to light, warmth, rest and regular intake of nourishment, bathing, massage, patting the spine, and regularity of sleeping patterns together with the security blanket of love patterns the new infant for emotional security and early learning experience.

First Lessons of Love

The first lesson that love teaches us is: "I am not, thou art." The baby demands constant care and awareness and is indeed the little "king" or "queen" of the household. The mother loses self in serving her child.

Successful care-taking builds and strengthens a mother's self-image and her confidence in her own intuitions. As long as the mother nurses her baby she fills the link of oneness of heart, mind, and body. Weaning, therefore, takes place when the mother is ready emotionally for the separation. She places her child before herself or her own needs, nursing at times that fill the infant's needs even though her own desires may have to be postponed. When there is a second or third child the mother's love must expand to give that special one-to-one time to each child, building each one's self-image by stressing the need of each for the other and her love for all. When the second or third child is prepared and included in the care of the new baby, jealousy and aggression toward younger siblings does not develop. One mother tells us of how her son called himself the knight-king of his new baby sister, helping and protecting her in many ways. Including the first child in the birthing room and sharing with him or her body-closeness in bed with the mother and the new baby helps to assure the first child that his mother's love is all-inclusive and plentiful as the Light within her heart. "When the mother discovers God within herself by diving deeply into herself, she touches the unity of her whole being and her love is unlimited."[1]

Mother love manifests in stages. It begins by recognition of the very special and individual pattern of each child's soul. The mother invites friendship and understanding. She loves the baby's body, its purity, light, and utter dependency. The mother's love is like a river running pure and progressing onward as she relives the developmental stages of infancy with her child. Is there any joy like the first vision of the baby's smile, his or her first toothy grin, his or her first steps, or the first time we are addressed as "mumum?" As the training of her own mothering experiences progresses, mother love becomes Divine love, capable of including all children, understanding their frustrations, partaking of their joys in attaining independence from their mother-love guides. She protects, understands, perfects, expands, and includes all children within her heart. This process begins within her immediate family, expands into the community family, and finally realizes itself in the family of God. No power in the world is stronger than mother love.

Patterning takes place as the child's care-taker introduces and reinforces times for rest and play, eating and potty training or diaper changes, crying and fuss times, group play and enjoying his or her own company. Patterning develops behavioral habits that parents set as their goals for the child. A good schedule of activities, which reflects activity and repose, builds happy, busy toddlers. Whenever the infant is kept in an infant seat or backpack for a period of time, that period should be followed by a like amount of time to play on the floor freely moving about. The need for learning to be alone, to enjoy one's own company, is learned in the first year. [Large packing boxes from a refrigerator or stove], when given a mouse hole to crawl inside, make lovely places for a young child to enjoy his or her own company with a construct toy. A blanket or pad on the floor in a corner of the sleeping room will work with the younger infant. Active times can be moments of being carried in a backpack, swinging in a canvas swing, or using a walker.

1. Hazrat Inayat Khan, vol. X, p. 80.

> Before one comes to the real conception of God,
> the first thing is to build Him in One's heart.
>
> —HAZRAT INAYAT KHAN[2]

The care-taker builds love into his or her heart, falling in love with the purity and utter dependency of the infant. Holding the infant next to one's heart, patting from one end of the spine to the other with open palm method can soothe and comfort an edgy child. Sending the glance of love from your heart to the heart of the child through the eyes builds the pure love of God through "the innocence of the child." Rocking an ailing or cranky child while singing nursery rhymes or humming pacifies and transmits the caretaker's love and builds the child's security. Lying down with a sick child wrapped in a blanket and held close to the heart is very comforting to a sick and restless child. The blanket enables the care-taker to extricate herself or himself without disturbing the sleeping infant. A chamomile herb tea blend given warm in a bottle sweetened to taste with barley malt gives rest to both mother and child on sleepless nights. Heart love can also flow to the infant through the rays of our finger-tips and the repetition of chants or *wasifas*[3] to the glory of God.

The growth of the family demands that the mother stretch the capacities of her heart. She must learn to divide her mothering love. Giving eye contact and full attention, eye to eye, heart to heart, soul to soul, is the real work of the mother, not the mundane tasks she performs. Being entirely interested in the child's emotional need even when you're interrupted in your work happens often.

The father-image is important at bedtime. Take turns reading to the two youngest: this is one way of managing three children. An older child may read to his or her parents. The choice of a song when the night-light goes on is a happy ritual. To sit on the bed and sing the song to the child, who is keyed up, holding his/her hands or stroking the head consoles and bonds.

Etheric Body Massage

The physical body of the infant is never touched during this massage of the energy body except at the heart and lightly on the crown chakra and

2. Hazrat Inayat Khan, vol. VII, p. 218.

3. A *wasifa* is a name of God that is recited regularly as a chant of remembrance and contemplation, for example, *Ya Wadud*, O Loving One. (C.A.H.)

the big toes. The hands make circular motions. When going upwards the circular motions are like the movement of the breast-stroke in swimming. When going downwards the circular motions are reversed.

The mother might first wash her hands with cold water and table salt. Then rub the arms from shoulder to finger-tips to strengthen magnetism. Do this until you feel a tingling in the finger-tips or until the palm and wrist temperature are equal. Another method you can use is rubbing the side of your thumb in your palm, the right thumb in your left palm or the left thumb in your right palm, alternating both thumbs until heat is felt.

The mother first places her fingers, "pointer" and "middle-finger," over the heart of the child, and here recites the Invocation: "Toward the One, the perfection of Love, Harmony, and Beauty, the only Being united with all the illuminated souls who form the embodiment of the Master, the Spirit of Guidance."[4]

Then moving the hands in circular motions (small circles) from the heart upwards to the child's head, move up to the sides of the head, get well around the ears and glands, then move up to the crown center and touch lightly. Reverse the circular motions and go back to the inner eye, go around the eyes, nose, nostrils, out to the ears, behind the ears, under the ears and then back to the throat center and shoulders. Work down the arms towards the fingertips. Work across all joints, because they are very important energy centers.

Then reverse your motions, going back to the center of the chest (chest bone), heart area (do not stop to work at the solar plexus). Move quickly to navel and pubic area and down both legs at once and do not forget to work across all joints. After the knees go down to the ankle bones, then to the toes, then very lightly pinch the big toes.

Reverse the circular motions going upwards and stop at the heart center. Here, repeat again the Invocation to bring the massage to completion.

4. An invocational prayer taught by Hazrat Inayat Khan.

THE FRAGRANCE OF PRAYER

Farzaneh Milani is an assistant professor at the University of Virginia. A poet like her mother before her, she holds a Ph.D. in comparative literature from the University of California, Los Angeles. She immigrated from Iran to the United States in 1967 and found herself "dislocated . . . immersed in discontinuities . . . neither the daughter of my mother, nor the mother of my daughter."[1] As part of her process of grounding in her own being, she began studying Iranian women writers seriously in the mid-1970s. As she says in her preface to *Veils and Words*, her book on Iranian women writers,

> After the loss of a jasmine-like certainty and years of disorientation, I finally found a surrogate home in Iranian literature, a place to return to and to embark from. I put down roots in it and found myself especially drawn to women's writings. I saw reflected in this literature a persistent effort—now overt, now covert—to negotiate the aesthetics of silence, to free women's public voice, to come to terms with the symbols and institution of the veil.[2] In the writings of Iranian women I found the exquisite eloquence of my mother tongue. Through their voices, their richness and diversity, I discovered my own voice. I began to rediscover, not without pride, Iranian women such as I knew them rather than as I read about them in male-authored texts.
>
> . . . Perhaps the subject of veiling, its paradoxes and ambiguities, its multi-layered symbolic significance, would not have preoccupied me

1. Farzaneh Milani, *Veils and Words*, pp. xi–xii.

2. Nowhere in the Qur'an is full veiling enjoined of women. Both men and women are enjoined to lower their glance in modesty and to behave with modesty and chastity. Within the Islamic community, the practice of veiling developed first in emulation of the wives of the Prophet, who covered themselves for safety when moving about in a hostile society in the early days of the community. The practice of veiling had previously been in usage in local societies. Cultural overlays continued and extended the practice. (C.A.H.)

so long and so intensely had it not been for the many connections that I gradually came to see between veiling, women's literature, and literary criticism. My exploration of the visible and invisible topology of the veil, its symptoms and consequences, became a journey of discovery and self-discovery. . . . Perhaps there is always yet another layer of walls and veils to rend.[3]

But as Mevlana Jalaluddin Rumi says:

> This is love: to fly heavenward
> to rend, every instant, a hundred veils.[4]

Farzaneh continues her search for certainty as a personal journey informed by the beauty of Sufi poetry, particularly that of Mevlana Jalaluddin Rumi. The following poem, "Fresh Jasmine," which she wrote about her grandmother, reveals the intimate world of one who stands alone in prayer with her beloved Lord. Jasmine is often used as a metaphor by Sufi poets to evoke the beauty and fragrance of the Divine Presence. A classical Sufi text by Ruzbihan Baqli of Shiraz is entitled *Jasmine of the Lovers*, which he indicates that he wrote "to explain human love and divine love with the help of God and His wonderful assistance, so that it would be the delight of intimacy and the fragrance of the secret enclosure [sanctuary]."[5] The Prophet Muhammad is known to have said: "Three things of this world of yours were made beloved to me: women, fragrance, and the coolness of my eye was placed in the ritual prayer." This poem interweaves all three to bring us into the presence of a quiet certainty.

Fresh Jasmine

Jasmine, too, derived from the Persian word *yasaman*, seems locked forever, like Grandmother, with my childhood memories. There is something about jasmine that captures with special intensity the incandescence and luminosity, the simplicity and innocence of childhood. Is it its starlike whiteness? Is it the trembling delicacy of its blossom hovering over its stem and leaves almost like a dream? Is it its ephemeral beauty, its long-lasting sweet fragrance, its generous yielding of flowers every single day of summer? Whatever it is, there's something about the jasmine that takes me to

3. Farzaneh Milani, *Veils and Words*, pp. xiv–xv.

4. Mevlana Jalaluddin Rumi, quoted ibid., p. 7.

5. Carl W. Ernst, *Teachings of Sufism*, p. 94.

places where I have to leave words behind, to the places where I have left my childhood, places that continue to invade my dreams—in the setting of my earliest memories. In my past. There, there is jasmine; plenty of it; in abundance; in profusion. I grew up with it. The hot summer sun. Dust in the air. And suddenly, the jasmine. Like fresh snow; like a mind untainted by questions. Like certainty.

She always smelled of jasmine
and wore black shoes that shined
crowned with a ribbon on top.
It is Grandmother I'm talking about,
with her jasmine scent
and her world marked and bounded,
as clearly as her prayer rug.
And as she prayed
her arms would rise from the prayer rug
like pillars soaring into the sky
above sadness
above storms
to the height of creativity
to the pinnacle of heaven,
then again to the depths of submission.
She always smelled of jasmine
and never harbored any doubts
as to her choice of perfume.
It is Grandmother I'm talking about.
She knew with astounding confidence
that her life-story was but her destiny
that she held in her own hand
the key to eternity,
she even knew that if she wanted
she could summon the prophet Khezr[6]
to demand of him whatever she desired.
And how generous he was,
Grandmother's green-clothed phantasm,

6. Khezr, or Khidr, is the mysterious and hidden Prophet who may suddenly appear to assist a devoted servant of God. Khidr was the Friend of God whom Moses sought and attempted to accompany in order to learn more deeply the ways of God. (See Surah al-Kahf 18:60–82.) He is sometimes referred to as the "green man," as often he has appeared in green and brings the gift of renewal of life. (C.A.H.)

magnanimous, bearer of plenty
without anger, without guile,
beyond needs, beyond expectations
with his blessings and gifts
flowing free like the waters
of an endless stream.
She always smelled of jasmine
and wore black shoes that shined
crowned with a ribbon on top.
I'm telling you about my grandmother.

AN ESSENTIAL LANGUAGE

ALIAA R. RAFEA AND AISHA RAFEA are among the many sisters who have shared the path of Sufism over the centuries. They are the daughters of Master Rafea Mohammad Rafea, who founded the Spiritual Islamic Society in Egypt. Both are very well educated in the Way of Sufism as well as in traditional academia. Aliaa obtained her doctorate from Ain Shams University [of Cairo], where she is currently a faculty member. In her work in the field of anthropology, she is attempting to impart an understanding of how awareness of our spiritual essence can improve our lives on all levels, both in the realm of the individual and society as a whole.

Aisha received her M.A. in public communication from the University of Cairo and is currently a writer who "focuses on sharing with readers the awareness that human beings need to open to the nurturing of the Divine within in order to be able to discern the teachings written on their own souls, rather than those written merely on paper." As a professional journalist, Aisha has worked for Voice of America among other international media institutions and has prepared documentary film scripts for Egyptian National Television. She and Aliaa are both sincerely devoted to the path of Sufism and its universal perspective. Together with their brother, Ali, whom they strongly support as director of the Spiritual Islamic Society, Aisha and Aliaa continue to share and develop the teachings brought forth by their father.

The selections that follow are some reflections about their father by Aliaa and excerpts from a talk by Aisha, both of which reflect their strong concern for the movement of consciousness beyond the mere acknowledgment of diversity to the recognition of an Eternal Law of Life underlying all faiths and from which all blossom forth and, through the grace of our all-embracing Sustainer, flourish. This eternal law is the law of surrender to the Divine. As Aisha states, "The [Qur'anic] Revelation to the Prophet Muhammad clarifies that this potential for surrender to Allah is embedded in the primordial nature of the soul and stamped on its texture since God breathed of His Spirit into humankind. It is what the Holy Qur'an terms *fitra*, asserting that if human beings communicated with their *fitra*, it would lead them to the fulfillment of their souls' longing, to life according to the Law of creation.... It is an objective to be sought, and a fruit of great spiritual struggle; ... *fitra* is revived through purification of the heart." With reference to numerous verses from the Qur'an, Aisha elucidates how all the prophets of the Abrahamic tradition have sought guidance from within and from a higher source, and have prepared themselves to receive that guidance; "the Supreme responded to their striving and revealed to them a path that made of their whole life a language of spirit." She indicates how longing souls have the possibility of becoming accessible to God's graces if they follow the paths of the prophets, and concludes that this journey is of benefit not just for the individual soul, but for the whole community of which he or she is a part. She proposes that it is the resulting greater spiritual awareness and the dissemination of spiritual knowledge that could lead to increased creativity in solving the problems and challenges of the modern age, and that it is in the development and continued sharing of this essential "Language of Spirit," rather than deified dogmas, that our hope lies.

Real Love Means Surrender

My father, you have not left me for a single second, though I may have left you when life was harsh around me, when I lost my direction and doubts started to fill me about my purpose on earth. I was enveloped with darkened layers. I am sure you were beside me, otherwise I would have never emerged. My insistence on challenging the impossible was inspired by you. My struggle not to let anything destroy me took its power from you. Your words, your faith in our message on earth, enlightened my way. My sight was not that strong, but I have been searching for your light. The more I could see; the more and more I felt that you are within me.

My father, honesty is what we learned from you. Honesty is what I shall follow. While to be honest is not a difficult task if the intention is there, yet how can words bring the right expression about the meaning that I want to convey? How can any words describe the presence of love and light

❧ "Real Love Means Surrender" is excerpted from the essay "My Father" by Aliaa Rafea, © 2000.

in a human being? How can any words depict the flow of your emotions in events? I think this is an impossible task because, never mind how hard one tries, words mislead. . . .

My life itself is a version of yours. I passed through deep moments of loneliness to realize that Allah is the only companion. Out of these experiences I came to the world with new spirit, my heart was full of love, without expecting anything back from anyone. If I have the chance to serve, help, or support someone, I am always aware that it is not from me, it is because of God's support, through you whose spirit is continuously supporting me. When people around support me, I can see your face behind them smiling and encouraging me as you have continually done. Through events, I hear you talking to me, assuring me that you are there.

I am lucky with brothers and sisters with whom I may work together for your message first within ourselves and then to spread its light to the wider and wider circle of the world, with the aim of making the world one big family as you instructed us. . . .

All my expectations were not fulfilled, and I was moving from one place to another and from one closed door to another open window, to find in the end that nothing was haphazard, no coincidence. Everything was meant to be as it was for wisdom. I don't regret anything now; neither do I blame anyone. I would not understand what seemed irrational in your circumstances if I did not pass through similar experiences.

If I spent the rest of my life thanking God for what he gave me, it would not be enough. Out of pain, my heart was contented. Out of despair, hopes sprang. Out of failure, success was revealed. I knew it was all because of you. You have never left me. I am physically part of you, but you are spiritually my real me.

"Nothing in vain," our brother Ali has said; I realized gradually that everything was for a purpose. I have been trying to find the purpose, so I responded to life accordingly. My approach was correct, but my created images were wrong. I had to modify my situations and attempt to know the purpose every time things unfolded against all my expectations. That, I will always do. The lesson I learned after those years is that I should not hold on to any image of my own creation.

I can read that in your life, my father. You never were attached to anything, not even to us. I may understand now a sentence that you said—it stuck in my mind because it was a surprise; I could not then grasp its meaning well. I just let it slip inside without thinking. You said once when we sat around the dinner table that you had nothing to do with us, and that you would surrender (us) to God, who would take care. I did not understand this sentence because it did not describe your behavior; you cared, you gave from your time to teach us, you were concerned about how we performed in schools, you were keen to provide us with a pleasing environment as children. Now, I may have understood what you meant. You would not let your children, regardless of how dear they were to you, take your attention from surrendering to Allah. Real love means surrender.

The Soul's Longing

> To my dearest brother, and spiritual teacher Master Ali Rafea, how can I express my gratitude to God for being caressed day and night by your sublime presence, except by being one of the channels through whom your love and mercy flood to the whole universe? . . . I pray God for forgiveness for any misunderstandings or shortcomings that are due to my own limitations.

The journeys of spiritual teachers of humanity, prophets and messengers of God, towards Truth are eternal sources of inspiration for all souls who long for meaningfulness on all levels. Their experiences enlighten the way of humanity forever. Deep reflections on their journeys could inspire the modern world with so many meanings that our era lacks. Learning from them does not imply going back to the past; it is an invitation to humanity to refresh its memory of how a human being can fulfill his or her humanity with the hope that we might have a better future. Of course we are not to handle the life of great spiritual teachers with the assumption that we would be able to absorb them fully. This is not possible because the part cannot encompass the whole. Even though a drop of the ocean carries its entire characteristics, it can never be the ocean. So, a soul who longs for truth is a glimmer of the Light of great teachers, and with that quality he or she is qualified for deriving some wisdom from his or her journey.

The great teachers longed for a truthful life during times when the majority of people were satisfied by a false one. They longed for knowledge during times when ignorance and superstition were overwhelming. They longed for the spreading of peace during times when conflict was commonplace. They longed for the prevailing of justice during times when

❧ "The Soul's Longing" was a talk delivered by Aisha Rafea at the annual Sufism Symposium held by the International Association of Sufism in Fremont, California, in 2001. © Aisha Rafea.

oppression was legitimized. They longed for spiritual freedom while the majority accepted the constraints of matter.

From that perspective, I share with you some reflections on how the Holy Qur'an presented their stories with the focus that all of them sought surrender to Allah, and thus they are all termed "Muslim." Namely, the word "Islam" is used in the Holy Qur'an with a deeper dimension than a creed to be compared to or with other creeds, or a set of social or cultural customs and traditions of certain societies who carry this label. Rather, Islam in the Holy Qur'an points to a living Truth that transcends names, labels, languages, and/or religious affiliations. It is the Law of full surrender to Allah as existentially experienced and sought, by all souls who search for a truthful life infinitely. The Revelation to the Prophet Muhammad clarifies that this potential for surrender to Allah is embedded in the primordial nature of the soul and stamped on its texture since God breathed of His Spirit into humankind. It is what the Holy Qur'an terms *fitra*, asserting that if human beings communicated with their *fitra*, it would lead them to the fulfillment of their souls' longing, to life according to the Law of creation. The Prophet Muhammad said, "Islam is the Religion of the Primordial nature (*fitra*). Every newborn baby is born according to *fitra*, then parents give him or her a name of a religious affiliation (Christianity, Judaism, Magus, ... etc.).[1]

However, to live according to *fitra* to surrender to Allah fully, is not taken for granted, for the human soul is susceptible to being imprisoned in the "vessel of clay" of the body with all its limitations, and to forgetfulness about his or her primordial nature, *fitra*. So, living according to *fitra* is an expression of the highest degree of spiritual awareness. It is an objective to be sought, and a fruit of great spiritual struggle. That is to say, Islam as revealed to the Prophet Muhammad clarifies that even though each human soul has a potentiality to feel his or her longing for submission to Allah by giving the chance to his or her *fitra* or spiritual origin to be awakened, a human soul needs to be liberated from the constraints of matter to be able to communicate with his or her *fitra*.

The Holy Qur'an reveals that the pure nature (*fitra*) has led great souls to a common Path that has fulfilled their longing. That common Path is a language of a spirit who longs for full surrender to the Eternal Law of Life.

1. *Fitra* is not to be confused with "instinct," since instinct is related to the attributes of the physical body, while *fitra* is the primordial nature of the soul that carries the spiritual awareness and quality.

Primordial Nature (Fitra) Leads to a Common Path

Even though great teachers of humanity were living in different times and places, and confronted different challenges, they had something in common: (1) they had a natural deep inner light that made them feel the existence of the Transcendent Supreme, and pushed them to reject the widespread dogmas and practices of their people; (2) they all sought guidance from within and from a higher source, and they prepared themselves to receive that guidance; (3) the Supreme responded to their striving and revealed to them from within and from the Beyond a path by which to lead a truthful life; a path that made of their whole life a language of spirit. They were guided to present the fruit of their experiences to other searching souls.

Rejection of Dogmas

The Holy Qur'an reveals that Prophets can see that people's projection of physical or mental images towards God reflects a direct deficiency of realization and conceptualization of the Supreme Transcendent. As great souls, they can see that such practices lead human beings to being encased in dense layers of falsity through which they can never reach Truth. Prophets are reluctant to be like those people who commit a fatal mistake by being captured in worshiping images of several kinds, those who put limits to what is limitless, and measure what is eternal, absolute, and perfect with the yardstick of what is transient, relative, or imperfect. These lose their link to the really Divine. To take an idol as Divine is not merely an outward practice; it is also an inner attitude of rigidity and stagnation that blocks the human being's capability to be spiritually free. It is an attitude that captures the soul in illusions created by limited existence. From that perspective, we read in the Holy Qur'an that Noah, Abraham, Moses, Jesus, Muhammad, and most prophets were not satisfied with the dogmas of their time. Abraham, for instance says to his father,

> *Takest thou idols for gods? For I see thee and thy people in manifest error.* (Qur'an 6:74)

> *O my father! Why worship that which heareth not, and seeth not and can profit thee nothing?* (Qur'an 19:42)

False deities that great souls reject, the Holy Qur'an clarifies, are not only stone idols, they are stagnant traditions, labels, and dogmas. Joseph, for instance says, *If not Him, ye worship nothing but names which ye have named—ye and your fathers—for which Allah hath sent down no authority* (Qur'an: 12:40).

The Holy Qur'an quotes prophets criticizing those who stick to blind imitation and bestow divinity on stagnant traditions. Prophets try to direct their attention to that deficiency, but the common response is: *Nay! they say: "We found our fathers following a certain religion, and we do guide ourselves by their footsteps"* (Qur'an 43:22).

Another false deity that prophets never have worshiped is what the Holy Qur'an refers to as *hawa*, which means the lust for something of the material realm that a human is apt to adore or bestow an absolute value to. The Holy Qur'an says to Prophet Muhammad that the one who worships his *hawa* (desire) is not qualified to discern the truth.

> *Then seest thou such a one as takes as his god his own vain desire?*
> *Allah has, knowing (him as such), left him astray, and sealed his hearing*
> *and his heart (and understanding), and put a cover on his sight:*
> *Who, then, will guide him after Allah (has withdrawn guidance)?*
> *Will ye not then receive admonition?*
>
> —Qur'an 45:23

The Holy Qur'an relates parables of people who were not ready to receive guidance because they were fully involved in worshiping their *hawa*. It gives the parable of Qarun, who lived at the time of Moses and had such a great lust for money that he could feel no divine dimension in life. The pharaoh at the time of Moses also lusted for authority so much that he made of himself a god, and consequently could not feel the existence of God. In the time of Muhammad, some people adored physical existence so much that they could not feel any spiritual depth in life. They were so captured within the constraints of matter that the paramount dogma with which they lived in accordance was denial of a coming life: *And they say: "What is there but our life in this world? We shall die and we live, and nothing but Time can destroy us." But of that they have no knowledge; they merely conjecture.* (Qur'an 45:24)

> *No vision can grasp Him. But His grasp is over all vision: He is above all comprehension, yet is acquainted with all things.* (Qur'an 6:103)

. . . whithersoever ye turn, there is Allah's countenance. For Allah is All-Embracing, All-Knowing. (Qur'an 2:115)

Glory to Him! He is high above all that they say! Exalted and Great (beyond measure)! (Qur'an: 17:43)

Praise and glory be to Him! (For He/She is) above what they attribute to Him! (Qur'an 6:100)

Glory to Him, and far is He/She above having the partners they ascribe unto Him! (Qur'an 16:1)

There is nothing whatever like unto Him. (Qur'an 42:11)

The Holy Qur'an also clarifies that it is part of the *fitra* that the soul is liberated from dogmas and false deity when he or she believes in the Unseen, *al-Ghaib*. To believe in the Unseen in the Holy Qur'an is an inner certainty within a human that makes him sure that whatever he or she might come to know, there is always more that is beyond the known and the knowable. When this certainty exists, souls do not become imprisoned in dogmas, nor do they bestow divinity on anything in the transient realm. Rather, they continuously move forward towards greater knowledge and freedom ceaselessly.

But how can a human being be liberated from all dogmas and false deities? This takes us to the second point.

Seeking Guidance from Within and from a Higher Source

Since they were not satisfied with other people's practices and approach to life, the prophets began to search within and beyond. They were guided from within to open to listen to what their hearts would tell them. They naturally wanted to distance themselves from the noise of a corrupt life and the negative energy of the overwhelming darkness. They spent time in seclusion purifying the whole of their existence by controlling the physical body's desires. The vibrant *fitra* guided them to allow the divinity within to come to the surface of consciousness. In the meantime, they would also direct their faces to the Supreme Transcendent, seeking guidance from a higher source. We read in the Holy Qur'an that Abraham said,

I will go to my Lord! He will surely guide me! (Qur'an 37:99)

And I will turn away from you (all) and from those whom ye invoke besides Allah: I will call on my Lord. (Qur'an 19:48)

The Holy Qur'an gives us an example of the search of a soul longing for a source of guidance in the story of the experience of Abraham. The story reveals his longing for his Lord, whom he recognizes first in a star, then in the moon, and then in the sun. The moment Abraham came to be fully certain that Allah transcends any of His manifestations was the very moment he realized that he was receiving guidance and support from his Lord. Namely, Abraham reached a moment of receiving great divine knowledge in which he could realize with no confusion that Allah is both Unseen and also Manifest because all aspects of nature [are signs (*ayats*) of His Presence], and also because He manifests Himself to man from within himself as well as all around him. The guidance was not letters or words; it was a superb power of enlightenment that made Truth in Abraham's heart clearer than the rays of the sun. Abraham could evidently discern his own *fitra*, and God's closeness and guidance.

> *So also did We show Abraham the power and the laws of the heavens and the earth, that he might (with understanding) have certitude. When the night covered him over, he saw a star: he said: "This is my Lord." But when it set, he said: "I love not those that set." When he saw the moon rising in splendor, he said: "This is my Lord." But when the moon set, he said: "Unless my Lord guide me, I shall surely be among those who go astray." When he saw the sun rising in splendor, he said: "This is my Lord; this is the greatest (of all)." But when the sun set, he said: "O my people! I am indeed free from your (guilt) of giving partners to Allah. For me, I have set my face, firmly and truly, towards Him Who created the heavens and the earth, and never shall I give partners to Allah."* (Qur'an 6:75–79)

The Holy Qur'an also points to Moses' search for a higher source of guidance when it quotes Moses as saying: *I do hope that my Lord will show me the smooth and straight Path* (Qur'an 28:22). It is that inner quest that pushed Moses to feel God's guidance symbolized in the burning bush.

> *Behold, he saw a fire: so he said to his family, "Tarry ye; I perceive a fire; perhaps I can bring you some burning brand therefrom, or find some guidance at the fire."* (Qur'an 20:10)

Like Abraham, the very moment Moses realized existentially that God transcends any aspect of physical life, he could also feel Him strongly and devastatingly Manifest in all creation, as symbolized in *the Mount*. The guidance came in the form of a burst of knowledge and light that were delivered promptly into his heart. It was at that moment that Moses said, *I am the first to believe*. It is a statement that reflects an attitude where a soul realizes his or her source of guidance coming from within and around concomitantly and clearly.

> *When Moses came to the place appointed by Us, and his Lord addressed him, he said: "O my Lord! show (Thyself) to me, that I may look upon Thee." Allah said: "By no means canst thou see Me (direct); but look upon the mount; if it abide in its place, then shalt thou see Me." When his Lord manifested His glory on the Mount, He made it as dust, and Moses fell down in a swoon. When he recovered his senses he said: "Glory be to Thee! to Thee I turn in repentance, and I am the first to believe."* (Qur'an 7:143)

The Prophet Muhammad's search for guidance was not an exception. His life reveals that the pure *fitra* was strongly awakened in him from early childhood. He never bowed to any of the 360 idols located around the Kaaba, nor swore by the name of any of them. He rejected all the stagnant traditions of his people and held to a very high standard of morality on all levels. Again in his search for a source of guidance towards a truthful life he was guided from within to stay for regular intervals in seclusion in a cave near Mecca named Hira'. He lived the life of a mystic, fasting and praying to God to lead him to a way of life that would be in harmony with His will and Law.

For the Prophet Muhammad the existence of a higher source of guidance within and beyond took several dimensions. The archangel Gabriel said to the Prophet at the very start of the Revelation,

> *Read! In the name of thy Lord and Cherisher, Who created, created the human being out of a connecting substance: Read! and thy Lord is Most Bountiful, He Who taught (the use of) the Pen, Taught the human being that which he/she knew not.* (Qur'an 96:1–5)

The holy words conveyed to Muhammad, *Read (or recite)! In the name of thy Lord*, clarify that the Divine is within, and when the soul is purified enough, that divinity, or *the name of thy Lord*, becomes manifest enough to discern the Truth. The verses of the very first Revelation to the Prophet Muhammad unveil also that the soul is given the means of gaining knowledge, symbolized in *the Pen*. The Revelation also points to the existence of the Law of creation when mentioning the creation of man *out of a connecting substance*. It is implicitly disclosed that the Divine Law works through cause and effect and a human being is qualified to attain knowledge when he or she lives according to that Law. He or she then will deserve to be taught *that which he* [or she] *knew not*.

On another level, the Revelation to the Prophet Muhammad also disclosed that the knowledge that was revealed to the prophets preceding him had not quit the earth, and so they could be a source of guidance for him. The Divine unveils to Muhammad (in Qur'an 6:83–88) that *Abraham, Isaac, Jacob, Noah, David, Solomon, Job, Joseph, Moses and Aaron, Zakariya, John [the Baptist], Jesus, Elias, Isma'il, Elisha, Jonah, and Lot are all in the ranks of the Righteous*. The Divine tells him to take them as a source of guidance.

> *Those were the (prophets) who received Allah's guidance: follow the guidance they received.* (Qur'an 6:90)

It is because of that, that the Prophet, at one time, was guided to turn his face while praying to the Holy Shrine of Aqsa; the place that was honored by the birth and life of Jesus, the last prophet before him. However, in his search for a source of guidance, another dimension was also revealed to the Prophet. It does not contradict the previous dimensions but perfects them.

> *We see the turning of thy face (for guidance) to the heavens: now shall We turn thee to a Qibla that shall please thee. Turn then thy face in the direction of the Sacred Mosque: wherever ye are, turn your faces in that direction.* (Qur'an 2:144)

It was a revelation to the Prophet Muhammad that there has been but One Source of guidance on earth that has existed since humankind began searching for the truth, and that source will remain forever:

> *The Eternal Holy Home (Bayt) was first made available for men (when symbolized by the Shrine) that is at Bakka. It is ever full of Blessing, and Guidance to all the worlds.* (Qur'an 3:96)

Namely, it was revealed to the Prophet Muhammad that it is part of the Divine's creation that Holy Guidance (symbolized in the Holy Home) has existed on Earth since ancient times and it will remain forever supporting souls who long for guidance. So, when the Divine guided the Prophet Muhammad to *Follow the Way of Abraham the True in Faith* (Qur'an 16:123), it was because *Abraham and Isma'il raised the foundations of the Home* (Qur'an 2:127). It is implicit that the Prophet Abraham unveiled to humanity the one Origin of all guidance that transcends any names, and manifests in multiple ways. The Divine unveiled it once again to the Prophet Muhammad.

To conclude, the Holy Qur'an reveals through the stories of the prophets' search for guidance from within and from Beyond that there is a divine law for guiding humans to a truthful path through following which they can attain spiritual freedom. It is part of the Law that the Divine answers the quest of souls who long for guidance by making knowledge spring from their own spiritual origin, and also sending knowledge to them from Heaven. This law is mentioned in the Holy Qur'an as the Divine Choice.

> *Allah did choose Adam and Noah, the family of Abraham, and the family of Imran above all people.* (Qur'an 3:33)

It is implicit in the Holy Qur'an that people whom Allah chooses are those who are guided by their primordial nature, *fitra*, to prepare their existence well, and thus they become accessible to the Grace of God. Their part was to prepare themselves for receiving the Supreme's guidance. However, it is not what they do alone that decides the response of the Divine to their quest, it is Allah's Mercy that overwhelms them according to His Divine Law that transcends human beings' capacities of perception. About that truth Abraham says, *Unless my Lord guide me, I shall surely be among those who go astray*. The Prophet Muhammad says, *It is not your work per se that would destine you to salvation. (A man said,) "Even you, the Messenger of God?" (He said,) "Even me, unless God bestows His Mercy upon me."*[2]

So, we learn from the stories of the prophets that they became accessible to the working law when they sincerely searched for guidance by purifying their whole existence and by directing their faces to the Supreme, praying for a higher source of guidance. However, when the Holy Qur'an mentions how the prophets are chosen, it explains that the Divine does not confine "choice" to prophets alone, rather the Divine, by revealing the journey of the prophets towards truth, opens the door to all humans to expose themselves to God's graces so that they might be chosen when they are in full harmony with the law of choice. To expose oneself to God's graces implies that one opens one's heart and soul to the power of light on earth; the light that all prophets and messengers of God left visible and that will always remain as a Home for all souls who long for their Lord. That is what the Holy Qur'an clarifies when guiding believers to obey Allah and His Messenger.

> *All who obey Allah and the Messenger are in the Company of those on whom is the Grace of Allah, of the Prophets (who teach), the sincere (lovers of Truth), the witnesses (who testify), and the righteous (who do good): ah! what a beautiful Fellowship!* (Qur'an 4:69)

2. *Musnad* of Ahmad Ibn Hanbal.

To follow the path of the prophets is not to make of their teachings new dogmas and literal forms and images. To obey them is not to make of one's religious affiliation an excuse for showing superiority over others. To follow their paths is essentially to give a chance to the soul to engage in a journey of spiritual transformation through which it expresses itself fully. It is because of that the Prophet Muhammad says, "*Make yourselves accessible to God's graces.*"[3]

However, how can a soul make herself or himself accessible to God's graces?

The Fruit of Spiritual Freedom Is Presented to Searching Souls

The Holy Qur'an reveals that the fruit of spiritual freedom that Teachers of humanity attained, by the support of the Divine, was truthful knowledge. Knowledge was delivered from the beyond to their hearts and minds because they were in full harmony with the Will of the All-Merciful to transfer truthful knowledge to humankind, and make it accessible to whoever wills to seek it. Abraham says, *O my father! to me hath come knowledge which hath not reached thee: so follow me: I will guide thee to a Way that is even and straight* (Qur'an 19:43). About Joseph, the Divine says, *For he was, by Our instruction, full of knowledge (and experience): but most men know not* (Qur'an 12:68). *And to Lot, too, We gave Judgment and Knowledge* (Qur'an 21:74). About Solomon and David the Divine says: *We inspired the (right) understanding of the matter: to each (of them) We gave Judgment and Knowledge* (Qur'an 21:79). Noah said to his people: *Sincere is my advice to you, and I know from Allah something that ye know not*. (Qur'an 7:62). The Prophet Muhammad unveiled that knowledge is to be sought infinitely. He was guided to say, *"O my Lord! advance me in knowledge"* (Qur'an 20:114).

The Holy Qur'an uses the word "Book," pointing to the Deliverance of knowledge to prophets from Heaven to earth.

> *A Book which We have revealed unto thee, in order that thou mightest lead mankind out of the depths of darkness into light—by the leave of their Lord—to the Way of (Him) the Exalted in Power, Worthy of all Praise!*
> (Qur'an 14:1)

3. Narrated by al-Tabarani.

When the word "Book" is mentioned in the Holy Qur'an, it is always associated with guidance, light, and wisdom. More specifically, it points to the Law of life or the Path they received with which to live in accordance, and according to which to guide people to live. The Holy Qur'an unveils the Path on two integrative levels: (1) Truthful knowledge is attained when the primordial nature or *fitra* is purified from the taints of matter. Purification is possible when a soul is attached to the divinity within and to a higher source of guidance. (2) Pure *fitra* expresses itself in righteous deeds, deeds which are free from the stains of the lower self.

Fitra Is Revived through Purification of the Heart

The Holy Qur'an demonstrates that all prophets guided people to a way that supports a soul who longs for a truthful life in fulfilling its longing. They tell people that they need to purify their hearts so that they might be able to receive the guidance from within and from a higher source. The Holy Qur'an explains that when the heart is not pure, a human being cannot listen to, or see, the truth: . . . *they have hearts wherewith they understand not, eyes wherewith they see not, and ears wherewith they hear not. They are like cattle, nay more misguided: for they are heedless (of warning)* (Qur'an 7:179). It also asserts that a "sound heart" leads a person to understanding of the truths of life, and those who do have "blind hearts" cannot understand or respond to the divinity within or around: *Do they not travel through the land, so that their hearts (and minds) may thus learn wisdom and their ears may thus learn to hear? Truly it is not their eyes that are blind, but their hearts which are in their breasts* (Qur'an 22:46).

The Divine teachings to the Prophet Muhammad also reveal that purification of the heart is possible when the soul is attached to a higher source of guidance. The guidance to "perform ritual prayers" on a regular basis is a means to attain attachment to a higher source. The symbol of that higher source is the Holy Home that Muslims direct their faces towards during the performance of ritual prayers. To direct one's face towards the Holy Home transcends the physical dimension; it is a symbol for the Divine Light that was manifested through all prophets, and that sustains any searching soul with Light. The need to purify one's existence of the egoistic inclinations of selfishness, greed, and covetousness is expressed in the guidance towards charity. The need for preparing oneself to listen to the Divinity within is expressed in the guidance towards fasting where one stops all the desires of the physical body in one way or another for a period of time. It is because of the human need for such truths forever that the Holy Qur'an confirms that all prophets guided their followers to "Prayers, fasting, and charity or *zakat*." Many verses in the Holy Qur'an point to that fact. Jesus, for instance says about his Lord, *And He hath made me blessed wheresoever I be, and hath enjoined on me Prayer and Charity as long as I live* (Qur'an 19:31). And about Isma'il the Holy Qur'an says, *He used to enjoin on his people Prayer and Charity, and he was most acceptable in the sight of his Lord* (Qur'an 19:55).

The Holy Qur'an also clarifies that fasting had always been a means of purification for all souls who longed for divine guidance: *O ye who believe! Fasting is prescribed to you as it was prescribed to those before you, that ye may (learn) self-restraint* (Qur'an 2:183). The Prophet Muhammad received from the Divine a whole system for spiritual purification that he practiced, and taught to his followers. However, this is not the place to relate in detail how that system confirms and perfects the systems of prophets previous to him. Suffice it to say that all prophets, as revealed in the Holy Qur'an, existentially lived the truth that a human cannot feel the longing of the soul to lead a truthful life unless he purifies his earthly existence. Purification takes place when the soul is attached to a higher source of guidance, when the physical body's lusts are controlled, and when the divinity within is given the chance to express itself and overwhelm the earthly existence. The means to realize that purification are unveiled by the Revelation to all prophets when they were guided by the Divine to uncover the truthful path for souls who long for submission to Allah.

Pure Hearts Find Expression in Righteous Deeds

Prophets attract people's attention to the fact that the "clear sign" of a spiritually free soul is the expression of a righteous deed. Namely, to worship Allah only is to be completely free from the lusts of the lower self or the ego when doing anything in this world. Here is the example of Shu'aib: He said: *O my people! worship Allah; ye have no other god but Him. Now hath come unto you a Clear (Sign) from your Lord! give just measure and weight, nor withhold from the people the things that are their due; and do no mischief on the earth after it has been set in order: that will be best for you, if ye have Faith* (Qur'an 7:85).

The Holy Qur'an clarifies that people at the time of Shu'aib were not capable of entering the path of spiritual freedom because they gave an absolute value to money, and they thought that they had the right to earn it and use it the way they chose regardless of whether they hurt others and cheated them or not. The prophet wanted to reveal to them how much harm they caused to their souls when they behaved that way.

> *They said: "O Shu'aib! does thy (religion of) prayer command thee that we leave off the worship which our fathers practised, or that we leave off doing what we like with our property? Truly, thou art the one that forbeareth with faults and is right-minded!"* (Qur'an 11:87)

There are several other examples in the Holy Qur'an that express the path that was revealed to prophets. The core guidance is that when humans handle anything in this world from the perspective of pure *fitra* that relates them to the Divine, they will be able to see the Face of Allah in every physical act. Accordingly they would respect all aspects of nature and regard them as graces of God, of which they should take good care. The prophet Saleh is an example that the Holy Qur'an gives in that respect. He called his people to realize that they needed to make good use of what God had given them of beautiful nature and of the capacity to use that nature for a comfortable life. *Gardens and Springs, And corn-fields and date palms with spathes near breaking (with the weight of fruit). And ye carve houses out of (rocky) mountains with great skill* (Qur'an 26:147–149). His guidance to them was to worship God alone by making optimum use of all that He had endowed them with. He tells them to try to contemplate what he says to them out of love and caring for them: *But fear Allah and obey me; And follow not the bidding of those who are extravagant, Who make mischief in the land, and mend not (their ways)* (Qur'an 26:150–152). Again, they did not believe him because they were captured in the lust of matter alone. They tell him: *Thou art only one of those bewitched! Thou art no more than a mortal like us: then bring us a Sign, if thou tellest the truth!* (Qur'an 26:153, 154). Saleh tells them that all aspects of creation point to the Supreme, and to worship Him alone is to take good care of all aspects of physical nature: *He said: Here is a she-camel: she has a right of watering, and ye have a right of watering, (severally) on a day appointed. Touch her not with harm, lest the Penalty of a Great Day seize you* (Qur'an 26:155, 156). But again they could not feel what he was telling them because they handled things from the viewpoint of matter alone that embeds selfishness and cruelty. The she-camel in the story of prophet Saleh is most probably pointing to the physical existence of the soul that has a right of watering by the graces of God. When one is ignorant of how to take good care of all aspects of life, physical and spiritual, one kills the truthful life within. *But they ham-strung her: then did they become full of regrets* (Qur'an 26:157).

The stories of all prophets in the Holy Qur'an demonstrate that the fruit of their spiritual journeys is that they became accessible to the Divine Law of transferring Knowledge from Heaven to earth. That Knowledge is a Grace of Allah to souls who seek to live in full submission to the Eternal Law of Life. The Divine revealed to the prophets the Path to a truthful life. Those revelations are expressions of God's graces on earth directed to whoever would make himself or herself available to that. Longing souls have the possibility of becoming accessible to God's graces if they follow the paths of the prophets. Following the prophets is not blind commitment to their teachings. It is making a spiritual journey so that a soul experiences and understands how to become spiritually transformed. The Holy Qur'an clarifies that a soul is accessible to God's graces when it is purified from devotion to the transient aspects of life. That purification is attained through being attached to the Divinity within and around, rendering a soul spiritually free. The sign of spiritual freedom is that a soul performs any action in this life in a state of being free from the taints of the lower self. That is the state referred to in the Holy Qur'an as *stand straight and steadfast* and *work righteousness*:

> *In the case of those who say, "Our Lord is Allah," and, further, stand straight and steadfast, the angels descend on them (from time to time): "Fear ye not!" (they suggest), Nor grieve! but receive the Glad Tidings of the Garden (of Bliss), that which ye were promised!* (Qur'an 41:30)
>
> *Whoever expects to meet his or her Sustainer, let him or her work righteousness, and, in the worship of his or her Sustainer, admit no one as partner.* (Qur'an 18:110)

The Holy Qur'an asserts that the human soul is created to long to know the Divine and to seek to live according to His Law. That longing is part of its primordial nature that the Holy Qur'an terms as *fitra*. The human soul acquired that quality in the moment Allah breathed into Adam of His Spirit. And it is that quality of nature that qualified the offspring of Adam to long for devotion to the Divine. When the human soul lives in accordance with its own primordial nature or *fitra*, it fulfills its own longing, and a human life becomes a language of spirit. There is no wonder then that humankind, at all times, and in different cultures and civilizations, has witnessed the existence of human souls who have been looking for an ultimate goal of existence and have never been satisfied with the objectives of the physical realm. Their whole life has been a language of spirit.

In summary, the Holy Qur'an tells the stories of Great Teachers of humanity, prophets and messengers of God who had such a vibrant and pure *fitra* that it led them each to reject the dogmas of their times. Such great souls could see clearly that dogmas and stagnant traditions deprive people from communicating with their own *fitra*. The prophets' rejection of such practices led them to seek guidance from within and from the Supreme Transcendent. The Divine responded to their striving and hence revealed to them a truthful path to follow, a path that quenches the thirst of their souls for a truthful life. The path they each revealed to human beings can support a soul who longs for truth in finding her/his way. The Holy Qur'an reveals that the power of Light, Mercy, and Love that existed through the prophets has never left the earth, and that it can inspire all faithful souls. The symbol of that power in the Holy Qur'an is the Holy House. When a soul follows the paths of prophets and starts his spiritual journey, he becomes accessible to that Light, and supported in the fulfillment of his longing. With the power of divine light the soul is spiritually transformed and liberated from devotion to false deities. False deities are not only stones; they are dogmas, stagnant traditions, and material constraints of the lower self that form barriers which make the soul inaccessible to divine light. The means to be accessible to Light within and around are many, and they are encoded in all aspects of worship that were made available for searching souls. When a soul understands and experiences the wisdom in those ways of worship, he or she receives spiritual support. A soul best expresses her or his spiritual freedom by doing a work of righteousness; a work that comes out of love for service and creation. Such a work is also very spiritually rewarding, and it increases the soul's spiritual freedom. The Holy Qur'an seems to be summarizing the knowledge that all prophets carried and transferred to people in one recurrent statement that uncovers how a longing soul would make of his or her life a language of spirit. That statement is *those who have faith and do righteous deeds.*[4]

Stories of great souls are not history; they are eternal lessons for humanity, and we are in dire need of them in this modern age. In our time, just as in any other age, we are not free from turning to false deities and worshiping dogmas. Even now, there are several types of dogmas that block the way towards attaining submission to the Divine Law. Examples of them are:

4. This statement is repeated fifty times in the Holy Qur'an. The same meaning is said with different phrasing repeatedly. (C.A.H.)

1. Many people approach life from the physical perspective alone, and hence deny the effect of the Divine on human existence. Such denial deprives awareness of the spiritual dimension of the human being. Advocates of such dogmas suppress the longing of their souls and do not give themselves a chance to learn the language of spirit.

2. We also have the dogmas of those who think of "religiousness" as a blind commitment to commandments under the assumption that to obey the Divine is just to stick to rituals and forms literally and superficially. They suppress the soul's longing to understand, interact, or transform.

3. We also have the dogmas of those who, under the assumption that Religion has led to many wars throughout history, throw away Religion and start their spiritual journeys from within a vacuum. They deprive themselves of benefiting from the spiritual experiences of great souls.

So the different dogmas of our own age have turned into new idols. We also need the language of Spirit to find liberation. The language of Spirit can increase the well-being of humanity. It would encourage all efforts that aim at adding to the knowledge acquired through science because seeking knowledge infinitely is in itself a part of submission to the Divine Law. However, spirituality would help everyone be more cooperative and just in sharing the fruits of knowledge. And it would lead people to use that knowledge for constructive purposes, not destruction. The language of Spirit could also assist in settling many conflicts and wars on Earth because many of them are the outcome of spiritual ignorance. Lack of spiritual knowledge tends to make humans, individuals and states, think that they cannot be safe and strong unless they destroy others or use them for their own egoistic objectives. With spiritual awareness people would come to realize that when they hurt others for no reason, they hurt their own spirits, and diminish themselves spiritually. With spiritual freedom humans might come to know that the natural resources of the earth can suffice all. Starvation happens not because of lack of resources but because of the selfishness and arrogance of some souls who are heedless of spiritual truths. Spiritual awareness could lead to increased human creativity in solving many problems of the modern age, because a spiritual person considers what is useful to all, not just to her/himself. Dissemination of spiritual knowledge is the hope that might save humanity from many present difficulties and unexpected disasters. We need such a powerful spirituality that it might be capable of transforming our whole planet into a more enlightened one. This is not impossible for those who have faith that it is always from the depths of darkness that light is born.

MOTHER OF COMPASSION

HAGGA ZAKIYYA 'ABD AL-MUTTALIB BADAWI (1899–1982) of Cairo was a Sufi ascetic who combined a life of devotion with a life of hospitality, who taught mainly in an indirect fashion but exerted enormous influence, a miracle worker and "one whose prayers are answered." One of her followers mentions among her virtues *muru'a*, which could mean valor or generosity but which literally means "manliness."[1] Yet the epithet most often bestowed upon her is "mother of compassion." Her compassion is almost always the first quality people mention in describing her. It is difficult to know whether this particular quality was cultivated so carefully, or perceived to be so dominant, because it is valued so highly in women. Surely Ahmad Radwan (another recognized Sufi saint) could be characterized as compassionate in his care for his neighbors during the malaria and typhoid epidemic of 1944, yet he is more apt to be described as noble, generous, and righteous. People saw Hagga Zakiyya as a motherly figure, and it would appear that she also saw herself as a "mother" to many "children." She administered no oaths and gave no formal lessons, but the bonds she had with her spiritual children were often intense, and the transformations she effected in their lives were often profound.

Zakiyya 'Abd al-Muttalib Badawi came from the village of Mt. Muragga' Salsil in the Delta province of Mansura. Descendants of Husayn, her family is said to have been pious and exemplary. She married the son of her maternal aunt, Muhammad al-Mahdi 'Assasa, who, according to those who knew him, was a great scholar of Al-Azhar[2] as well as a Sufi. He followed, as

This selection is excerpted from *Sufism, Mystics, and Saints in Modern Egypt*, by Valerie J. Hoffman (Columbia: University of South Carolina Press, 1995), pp. 291–99. Reprinted by permission of University of South Carolina Press.

1. See Sachiko Murata, *The Tao of Islam*, for a discussion of gender; see also the chapter "The Way of the Soul" starting on page 177 of this text. (C.A.H.)

2. Al-Azhar is the oldest university in the world. Founded in 969 C.E., it remains today the primary center of Islamic learning in the world. (C.A.H.)

his parents had before him, a Shadhili *shaykh* named 'Abd al-Rahim al-Sab' (d. 1947), who lived by the shrine of Husayn in Cairo. Through her husband, Zakiyya also came to follow this shaykh and to assume the life of a devotee of the *ahl al-bayt*.[3] She would come to Cairo and visit all the shrines of the *ahl al-bayt* in a single day, beginning and ending with the shrine of Husayn, and on Friday evenings she would attend the *hadra*[4] of Shaykh 'Abd al-Rahim, the only woman present, doing *dhikr* separately on a balcony overlooking the men.

From her marriage she had only one child, her daughter, Nafisa, who was conceived after a number of childless years. When Nafisa was only four years old, she told her father, "Divorce my mother!" Her father was astonished, because they were very happy together. But he consulted Shaykh 'Abd al-Rahim, who advised him that the counsel was from God. He divorced Zakiyya, and both of them remarried. Zakiyya married another cousin from her village, a merchant who had no strong religious inclinations, but the marriage was not happy, and she eventually left him. One of Hagga Zakiyya's spiritual daughters testifies, "And I saw with my own eyes how much she loved her first husband's second wife." She speculates that perhaps God wanted her to experience life with an irreligious man so she would be able to empathize with the troubled people who were to come to her.

Hagga Zakiyya was, to all appearances, blind—since childhood, according to one follower. "But no one ever felt that she had lost her sight. She could see colors and would comment on them. She would see by the light of God." A young medical doctor, however, said, "People said she was blind, but she wasn't really blind. I was there personally when medical doctors examined her and said there was nothing wrong with her eyes. But she didn't use her eyes, because she moved by inner vision (*basira*), not physical vision (*basar*)." Her spiritual devotions included much *dhikr* and recitations of praise, and a daily litany of prayers for blessings on the Prophet. She spent many nights in devotion and rarely needed to sleep at all. After her move to Cairo, she prayed the dawn prayer every morning in the mosque of Husayn.

3. *Ahl al-bayt*, "the people of the house," refers especially to the family of Muhammad (may peace and blessings be upon them all): the Prophet; his daughter Fatima and her husband, 'Ali; their children, Hasan and Husayn; and their descendants. Husayn and many of his descendants are buried in Cairo. (C.A.H.)

4. *Hadra* (or *hadrah*) is the word for "presence," used to refer to the Divine Presence; it has also come to be used as a title of respect (*hazrat*). In Egypt it is the term often used to refer to zhikr gatherings. (C.A.H.)

According to one of Hagga Zakiyya's spiritual sons, "She was overcome by lights, and the *ahl al-bayt* [in a moment of intense spiritual connection] ordered her to come to Cairo." She took an apartment in the Darrasa district, near the shrine of Husayn, where she began her life's ministry of offering hospitality, kindness, and spiritual guidance to "children of the Way." Her spiritual son continued, "She solved their problems, gave kindness to the needy, and prayed for those in distress. God, may He be exalted, did not disappoint her hopes but met needs at her hands, and she solved the problems of all those who came to her. If a rebellious person came to her, God changed him into something good, both women and men. Many repented at her hands and became saints of God, having shrines and being visited by the pious." Later, when her father died, she used her inheritance to buy a piece of land in the Gamaliyya area even closer to the Husayn mosque, where she built a *saha*[5] complex that includes three buildings with a number of bedrooms, a kitchen, and a mosque, in the words of a follower, "to honor those who love the *ahl al-bayt*."

Her method was spiritual discernment and influence by simple association. "God gave her a light in her heart by which she knew the needs of those who came to her and those who needed her kindness," says one of her followers. She would welcome anyone into her presence, and kept her *saha* open and her kitchen operative twenty-four hours a day. Although she spent a good deal of time in solitary devotion, emerging, according to one follower, only on Fridays to sit with her followers and circulate among all the rooms of the *saha*, anyone could knock on her door at any time. She would become angry if anyone were refused an audience with her. "She welcomed everyone," said one of her spiritual daughters. "Each one felt that she loved him more than anyone else. She would be interested in your problem, and you would feel able to bear it after being with her." She would not correct people openly but would test people secretly to determine their character. She offered her children words of counsel and exhortations to be patient, generous, open-minded, striving for what is good, and obedient to God and His Messenger. Little by little those around her would change for the better. One of her spiritual daughters said this was God's grace to her, that she always obtained the desired moral effect on people without making them feel it.

Other stories tell of dramatic healings from moral defects, mental illness, or spirit possession. One woman who suffered from association with a man whose spiritual power was derived from jinn came to Hagga Zakiyya

5. A *saha* is a center for receiving the friends of the Way. (C.A.H.)

in great fear of the man's power. He had threatened to harm her and her family if she ever left him, and when she realized that his power was derived not from God but from jinn, she did not know where to turn. But Hagga Zakiyya paralyzed him and stripped him of his power shortly after she first came to know her, and soon the man died. Like so many people healed by Hagga Zakiyya, she became a close follower, visiting her several times each week despite the distance of her home from Hagga Zakiyya's *saha*.

One man tells of his attachment to Hagga Zakiyya: "On a Friday after the death of my mother, I went to the mosque of our lord Imam Husayn, where I saw a man who was one of the leading followers of the gnostic, Hagga Zakiyya. He asked me, 'What is wrong?' I told him, 'I am terribly depressed over the death of my mother.' He said, 'I will show you a mother who has kindness, compassion, and mercy.' I went with him to the *saha* of this virtuous lady. When I saw her I began to weep. She motioned to me to sit next to her. I did, and said nothing, but wept. She felt sorry for me and patted me without saying anything. Then she said to me, 'You are thinking of your mother. I have more compassion for you than your mother of whom you are thinking. I belong to you in this world and the next. Any time you are troubled, remember me with the *Fatiha*,[6] and your troubles will vanish.' I have lived my whole life with her since 1952, until she passed to the mercy of God, in compassion and contentment."

His attachment to her became profound, and he developed the habit of visiting her and dining with her every day after work. He says, "I have only had troubles in my life since her death." He accompanied her on the pilgrimage four times. He says, "After the morning prayer in the Prophet's mosque, she would stand for a long time. I became tired, but I said, 'It is better that she is with her grandfather, the Messenger of God,' and I was afraid to talk with her [to tell her of my fatigue]. But she [sensed it and] said, 'Visitation is over, Hagg 'Abduh.'

"When she went to the Meccan sanctuary, I saw that the path in front of her was wide open [despite the density of the crowds during the pilgrimage]. When she entered the Kaaba, people made way for her, and no one touched her. She kissed the Black Stone[7] a long time."

Both Hagga Zakiyya's sensitivity to Hagg 'Abduh's fatigue ("everyone felt that she could feel what they felt," said another follower) and the unobstructed path before her during the pilgrimage are seen as miraculous.

6. *Fatiha*: See note 14 of the selection by Annemarie Schimmel, on page 106. (C.A.H.)

7. The Black Stone is the cornerstone of the Kaaba. See note 7 in the chapter "Those Who Weep," page 42.

Most pilgrims are lucky if they get a chance to touch the Black Stone, but she kissed it a long time, following the example of the Prophet. The fact that no one in the crowd touched her implies not only her spiritual power but the preservation of her female modesty and dignity.

Nonetheless, her female modesty and dignity did not prevent her from embracing men or enjoying emotional intimacy with them. A mother, after all, may do so with her sons. As we have seen, Shaykh 'Izz says she used to have him lay his head in her lap, and called him her daughter, not her son, to indicate that fleshly labels had become meaningless. Shaykh 'Izz at that time was a young man, and she was already an elderly woman with an aura of compassion and holiness. I commented to 'Izz that her appearance in her photographs is formidable, swathed in heavy cloths up to her mouth or even her nose, her eyes covered by sunglasses, her features sharp, her body thin. Such things suggested aloofness to me, not the warmth and openness I heard from those who knew her. 'Izz agreed that her appearance was formidably dignified and that when he first met her he was afraid of her. But gradually he came to see her as the warm, loving person everyone described.

"Hagga" (or "hajja") is a title given to a woman who has performed the pilgrimage (*hajj*) to Mecca, just as "Hagg" (or "hajj") is given to a man. There could scarcely be a woman more deserving of the title than Hagga Zakiyya, who performed the pilgrimage twenty-six times and performed the lesser pilgrimage (*'umra*) more than fifty times. Many of her miracles occurred during the pilgrimage. She invited a woman to accompany her on the pilgrimage at the last minute, although the woman had neither a passport nor a plane ticket. The woman boarded the plane with her, and although the flight crew and authorities in Saudi Arabia were alerted that an unauthorized woman had boarded the plane, the number of passengers was always correct, and the woman was never detected. On one of her pilgrimages with Hagg 'Abduh, Hagga Zakiyya pulled fish out of the sand and told him to cook it for the pilgrims. He fried some of it and made soup with the rest, and though many pilgrims ate, the food did not run out. In fact, it lasted for five days in that hot climate unrefrigerated before the supply was finally exhausted, and it always remained fresh.

On one of her pilgrimages performed with a young woman, Hagga Zakiyya instructed the young woman to go on ahead of her at the Kaaba and find a Hagga Zaynab from Husayn, whom she described as a dark woman wearing a green dress. The young woman did as she was told, confident that despite the crowd the saint's *baraka* [transmission of blessing] would enable her to find Hagga Zaynab. Soon she saw a woman of this description. Furthermore, the woman ran to her immediately and, hearing that Hagga Zakiyya was there, rushed to find her. The two women embraced and talked at length, head to head. But when the woman had gone, Hagga Zakiyya said to her young companion, "It is not her." The young woman was puzzled but went and found another woman of the same description, spoke to her, confirmed that she was indeed Hagga Zaynab from Husayn, and went with her to Hagga Zakiyya. After that woman had gone, the young woman asked Hagga Zakiyya about the first woman. Zakiyya replied, "She doesn't speak Arabic." "And this," exclaimed the young woman who told me the story, "after they had talked with their heads close together for a long time! She didn't openly admit it, but she could understand all the languages. Once when I was talking with an American visitor I misunderstood something he said, and Hagga Zakiyya gently and subtly corrected me, saying, 'He meant such-and-such,' although she allegedly knew no foreign languages at all! Although Hagga Zakiyya didn't perform miracles openly, she could have turned a wall into gold if she'd so desired!"

Her miracles were many: miracles of knowledge and healing and the ability to transcend spatial limitations and appear in more than one place at a time. Shaykh 'Izz said that Ahmad Radwan had said that she was one of the *abdal*, that category of saints who could produce replicas of themselves, and appear and disappear at will. A woman said that one time she placed her hand on top of Hagga Zakiyya's, and found there was nothing there at all.

She also visited the tomb of Sidi Abu 'l-Hasan al-Shadhili, in the remote mountainous region of Humaythira, near the Red Sea, three or four times a year toward the end of her life. According to one of her followers, Hagga Zaynab, she was the first woman to visit the tomb, in the early 1920s, before she was even married. At that time the way to Sidi Shadhili was a dangerous desert journey without any proper road to a place that had no electricity or water and was inhabited only by poverty-stricken Bedouins who were ignored by the government and who in turn shunned the rest of society. Later, when Shaykh 'Abd al-Halim Mahmud was head of the Islamic University of al-Azhar in the 1970s, he had a beautiful white shrine and mosque complex built in honor of Sidi Shadhili. Hagga Zakiyya returned, bringing with her a group of women. A woman who was among the group says, "We found that by merely visiting the shrine, everything changed for us: colors changed, we were able to keep from anger, from passions, our spiritual senses were heightened."

When Hagga Zakiyya saw the poverty of the Bedouins of the region around Sidi Shadhili, she decided to build a *saha* to serve them. This *saha* was completed only in the last year of her life, but her generous hospitality became well-known among the local people long before that. Says one of her followers, "The government itself showed no interest in them until after the 1967 war. They had no social services whatsoever, and no conscription. She is the one who brought electricity there and arranged for trucks to bring in water and food every day. The governor went and visited her because he heard there was a seventy-year-old woman in that harsh climate who had no education and was blind. . . . The Bedouin women never used to let any strange person see them at all. They would go to Hagga Zakiyya, where she sat on her bed, and they would call her 'Mama.' She would give them sweet things and money."

Today, the *saha* built by Hagga Zakiyya is one of several in the area around Sidi Shadhili, which, thanks to paved roads and daily public buses, is visited by pilgrims year-round. Among the *sahas* in the area, however, only that of Hagga Zakiyya is constantly open and serving meals to visitors, who also sleep in one of the bedrooms of the *saha* or on the benches on its veranda. Her spiritual children who service the *saha* continue to pay special attention to any of the Bedouin who come for a meal. Indeed, the more ragged and poverty-stricken the visitor, the more he is treated with honor, because these were the ones Hagga Zakiyya especially loved.

It is said that Sidi Shadhili informed Hagga Zakiyya that she would die near him, and indeed this transpired. Hagga Zakiyya was aware of the date of her death seven months before it occurred. Ibrahim Ramadan 'Ali, the "Shaykh Faris" who wrote a book on the virtues of the *ahl al-bayt*, tells in this book that he visited her at the Shadhili shrine during the feast of the great sacrifice (*'Id al-Adha*) shortly before she died, and she requested that he remain twenty days after the feast. He asked why, and she said, "So you can wish me farewell, for I am traveling soon." He excused himself because of prior commitments, and they tearfully embraced before his departure. True to her word, she died twenty days after the feast, on December 24 1982. She is buried in a shrine adjacent to her *saha* in Humaythira.

SONGS OF PRAISE AND SUPPLICATION

The Munshidin of Egypt

In many traditions, singing and chanting have long been ways in which human beings have joined together to share their spirituality and sister/brotherhood. This is certainly also true within the Sufi tradition. Of note are the *ilahi* singers of Turkey, the *munshidin* (singular, *munshid*) of Egypt, the *qawwals* of Pakistan, and the *haddarat* singers of Morocco. All of these evolved as an expression of the sharing of praise and remembrance of the example of the Prophet and the saints of Islam.

One of the most beloved of the early songs that is still sung today by many in the worldwide Islamic community was spontaneously composed by the women of the first Muslim community, "Tala' al-badru alayna" (When the full moon has arisen). "Tala' al-badru alayna" was first sung shortly after the arrival of Muhammad in Medina in 634 C.E. After a long, almost ten-year period of persecution of the budding Muslim community in Mecca, Muhammad had at last received revelation permitting the Muslims to emigrate to Medina, a mixed Jewish and Arab settlement, 234 kilometers to the north. He remained behind in Mecca until most of his community had departed. Then finally he received indication that it was time for him to leave as well. Together with his faithful friend, Abu Bakr, the father of 'A'isha, Muhammad began the journey north. Many in Medina were watching for him. At last he was spotted coming over the dunes. The women of the community gathered on their rooftops and began to sing, keeping rhythm with their tambourines, joyously welcoming their Prophet, their "resplendent full moon."

Love is a key theme of the songs of Spirit that then continued to develop; often this love is associated with *fana'* (union with transcendent reality, the Divine). Ibn al-'Arabi, the great Sufi mystic of the twelfth century who grew up in Andalusia, composed many verses that were then set to music. These and the love lyrics of other mystic poets set the tone for further emerging chants and songs. The musical tradition of the troubadours of Spain and southern France evolved out of this musical tradition, which had reached Andalusia through the Moorish settlers and also through Crusaders returning from the Holy Land, many of whom returned with Muslim wives who raised their children singing to them songs of love they had learned from their own mothers.[1] Songs of the Beloved, which referred to God and the Prophet, were adapted into love songs sung to a divinely perfected human beloved with overlays of romantic love. These troubadour songs were an influential element in the development of the culture of chivalry in Europe in the late Middle Ages, of which the core ethics of the Sufi tradition (based on the example of the Prophet Muhammad and his companions and family) were also an influential part.

Throughout the widespread Islamic world, across the centuries, there have been many who have felt compelled to "render the ineffable into images. This has inspired some of the richest poetry in Islam."[2] . . . "Such verses, sung in a *zhikr*, specifically draw attention to the transcendent dimensions of the saints and confirm the superiority of the mystic vision of reality."[3] Al-Ghazali, one of the early Sufi masters, acknowledged the permissibility of music and song in awakening and stirring religious inspiration. As Al-Ghazali encouraged, "There is no line of verse which cannot be related to various meanings according to the abundance of the hearer's knowledge and the purity of his heart."[4]

"[The *munshid*] often speaks of being driven, of singing out of deep longing, of expressing the abandonment of his desires to God. It is as if the adoption of poetry is the shouldering of a burden, whose implications lead into untold heartaches. At the same time there is a sense of freedom to it, because he believes it will lead him into a closer relationship with God. To sing is to appropriate the poetic character with its inspirational basis as one's own. To sing is to command the vocabulary of spirit as one's own."[5]

1. See Linda Fish Compton, *Andalusian Lyrical Poetry and the Old Spanish Love Songs: Muwashshah and Its Kharja* (New York, 1976), and *Hispano-Arabic Poetry and Its Relations with the Old Provençal Troubadours* (Geneva: Alois R. Nykl, 1974).

2. Earle H. Waugh, *The Munshidin of Egypt*, p. 21.

3. Ibid., p. 143.

4. Ibid., p. 23.

5. Ibid., p. 22.

A poet may use words and phrases that are traditional yet present them in fresh ways, but within the context of both "the literary *adab* [appropriate behavior] and that adab's spiritual potential within the Sufi context; when a *munshid* is accomplished, he will blend these two kinds of *adab* in a powerful and even brilliant manner."[6]

Musical education for centuries was provided by the Sufi orders. Though not all orders in Egypt or elsewhere make use of music, there are many that do. In Egypt, the Shadhiliya, the Ahmadiya, and the Khalwatiya are particularly active in music instruction and sharing. The *shaykh* or *shaykha* would be the main instructor and the one who would generally compose the lyrics and the rhythm of the chants or songs to be sung. "In Sufi performance, the beat is musically essential, since it provides the base upon which *dhikrees* [the Sufis who are chanting] gyrate. But this very beat may be totally out of rhythm with the meter of the poem, and hence it requires ingenuity to lengthen or to shorten the words in order to bring the whole to proper termination."[7] After singing or Qur'an reciting, the *shaykh* would speak about "the *adab* of listening to singing or about the types of tunes and harmonies from which the music of *muwashshahat* (postclassical poetic form) and *qasa'id* had been made."[8] As a *munshid* became more accomplished, he or she might develop his or her own lyrics and appropriate rhythms and scales. It was in the homes of Sufi *shaykhs* or in Sufi gatherings in the mosques that even great Egyptian singers of recent years, like the "first lady of song of Egypt," Umm Kulthum, gained their training.

There are three different occasions when a *munshid* might sing: during a *hadra* (*dhikr* ritual), for a *mawlid* (anniversary celebration of a saint's birthday or death-day), and the more informal *dhikr laylah*, a night of *dhikr* and song, hosted by an individual or a family at their home or some local gathering place as a gesture of gratitude for abundance or blessing they may have received. The *hadras* are usually specific to a single order. Though *mawlids* are usually led by a single *shaykh*, the participants are often of many different orders. The *laylahs* are generally open to the community and thus often welcome both Muslims and Christians and other non-Muslim people, opening across class boundaries as well. Sometimes the Sufi *munshidin* are invited to sing for Christian-sponsored *laylahs*, which spreads the Sufi influence through further realms of the society.

6. Ibid., p. 23.

7. Ibid., p. 24.

8. Ibid., p. 32.

"Much of the discipline imposed on the *munshid*, and indeed on all members of the *tariqah*, derives from the *awrad*.[9] The *awrad* . . . differs from *shaykh* to *shaykh* and from *tariqah* to *tariqah*; as Sahhikh Sitouhy puts it, 'Each *tariqa* has its own way of teaching the mind how to worship God in a special way. The whole thing is worship and the seeking of refuge in God.' Accordingly, Shaikh Ghazouli notes: 'We prefer our songs because they are put in a pedagogical form. Instead of stating them in a plain, ordinary way, we put them in the form of a song, so the *mureed* (student/disciple) can memorize them faster. They apply the teaching. The *munshid* does not come from the outside. We school him within the group, and there he can learn quickly how to sing and to pray.' "[10]

"The *munshid* lives and works in a world in which several spiritual spheres overlap. He/she must relate to the spheres associated with the local sheikh, then the *sheikh* of the *tariqa*, then the saint to whom all Sufis owe allegiance, then the Prophet and finally, God."[11] As his or her own spiritual understanding and experience deepens, the *munshid's* repertoire also shifts and changes. "The *munshid* not only delivers a message from transcendence, but also uses his insights to bring about changes in his listeners."[12]

One of the well-known *munshidin* of Egypt is a woman named Sabra. Although she is unsure of her age, in 1988 Sabra thought she was over thirty. "She was born in Lower Egypt, not far from the Mansoura in the Delta, and lives in a small town called Kafr al-Lam. [Sabra] did not begin singing until in her twenties, but she has been a member of the tariqa al-Desouqi since she was ten; she goes only to *mawalid* and only sings at them."[13] As she cannot read, she composes her songs from oral memory of traditional images and patterns of meaning, woven in a style of her own. Following here is one of her compositions in which she calls for aid from members of the Prophet's family (several of whom have *makams* in Egypt).

> Love for the *ahl al-bayt* [the family of the Prophet] has tremendous spiritual benefits for those who would travel the Sufi path, say many

9. For more specific information on *awrad* (plural of *wird*, a litany of particular prayers), see Aisha Gouverneur's selection, page 257, and also "Wherever You Turn, There Is the Face of God," pages 115–27.

10. Earle H. Waugh, *The Munshidun of Egypt*, p. 73.

11. Ibid., p. 92.

12. Ibid., p. 93.

13. Ibid., p. 143

Sufis, not only because of the high stature of the *ahl al-bayt* but also because of the foundational quality of love as the basis of the Sufi path. Writes one author, "Loving them is the foundation and basis of the way to God. All the spiritual states (*ahwal*) and stations (*maqamat*) are degrees of love."[14]

O Allah!

My dependence, my support, my well-being
rest on the One who is generous and giving.
No one ever cried, "O Allah," and He closed the door in his face.
I beg you, Muhammad, to open the doors for us.
You are our happiness and our longing, you are our basis for acceptance.
You are our knowledge and learning—O, O physician to the unfortunate.
O our beloved Husain, provide me with medicine.
How could you possess the medicine and yet leave me sick like that?
He said, "Don't dwell on it, just ask for *madad*[15] and that will take care of you";
Politeness is the condition for this way, so no one said a thing.
O family of the prophet's house, I said that out of respect.
O men! Am I a stranger here at your place?
O Husain, how could I be humiliated so?
Give me your instruction, to whoever accepts your judgement, to whoever is patient in crisis!
Ah, patient, it's as if you enter a washroom to wash away your sins, and you will feel secure and sleep.
Since acceptance is necessary, we all guard it.
O yes, a physician opened his clinic, with a different kind of medicine—

This selection is excerpted from *The Munshidin of Egypt: Their World and Their Song*, by Earle H. Waugh (Columbia: University of South Carolina Press, 1989), pp. 143–46. Reprinted by permission of University of South Carolina Press.

14. Valerie J. Hoffman, *Sufism, Mystics, and Saints in Modern Egypt*, p. 80.

15. *Madad*: assistance, help, support.

Medicine for crises, medicine for problem-solving, medicine just
for my uncle's family.
It is not medicine like shots and pills.
It is medicine from Gabriel and his brother Michael.
My beloved—the one who is loved and appreciated—
Every day, in the tariqa, lovers are burned and drowned in seas.
Beside the road, show some concern—be a friend to those with
whom you come in contact—
Since the Prophet's way doesn't differentiate between people.
This hour is the hour of acceptance; the question slowly arrived.
The way is the Prophet's way and learning is favored.
On the beach of the sea of love, all (people) are standing.
A hundred would come forward [to stand] beside those who have
already reached their goal.
Mother of Hashim,[16] (you) men were deeply in love.
You whose name is your title, Zain al-'Abdin[17]
You whose title is Ali and who is known as Zain al-'Abdin,
Ask your aunt[18] to light our candles.
O, O Khan al-Khalili;[19] Khan al-Khalili opened the door.
Love is not lightheartedness, my soul, love is founded on torture.
If the house is content, O worshippers of Allah, happiness shows
at the door.
Why are you leading me to misery, and why did I have to drink
from the cup twice?
Why should I be humiliated in my youth, and, when I was young,
become an orphan?
When I didn't know what was going on?
Everyone stayed with their families except me, and I was on
my own.
O, O Husain, father of Ali, I come and I am scared.
You, who accuse people, get up and accuse as you wish if the
world is yours [i.e., if you own the world!]

16. Hashim was the clan to which the Prophet Muhammad belonged. (C.A.H.)

17. Zain (or Zayn) al-'Abidin ("ornament of the worshipers") is a nickname given to 'Ali, the son of Husayn (son of the first caliph 'Ali and Fatima). He is referred to as the fourth Imam and was known for his piety and devotional poetry. His tomb also is in Cairo. (C.A.H.)

18. Zaynab or Zeinab, see note 20. (C.A.H.)

19. "The King of the Beloved Friend," a famous bazaar near the Husain mosque and the location where the *zhikr* took place. (Moses is referred to as the Khalil [beloved friend] of God.) (C.A.H.)

You Hajj Abd-l-Hameed—get up
and arrange it the way you like—
I didn't know this was a tricky road!
You girl, who is filling people's hearts,
You are torturing me, O Zeinab![20]
I didn't know, O Slave of God, that this is a sensitive road, and suspicious money. The uncle says it's forbidden.
O my heart, he who has the medicine is making it very expensive
And he who has my heart should cure it.
O Allah, O Allah, my respect in remembering You!
You people should say that Allah is One!
Ahmad,[21] tell Him of my respect, to He who gives.
I am from you and you are from me.
Zain al-'Abdin who is occupying me,
Love, Love, Love, if you are in love.
Oh, kindness is pleasant, be kind to me, Mama.
Ah, Zain al-'Abdin, take care of him who has beautiful eyes.
Our beloved Husain!
Call the father of Faraj, Ah Bedawi, Ah Bedawi![22]
O soul of, soul of Bedawi, take care of us, O Bedawi!
Call on the beautiful ones—*madad ya Husain*
Call on Nafisa;[23] O my mama!
O papa, your love is burning me!

20. The sister of Husayn and Hasan, daughter of Fatima and 'Ali, who has a tomb dedicated to her in Cairo (as well as in Damascus). (C.A.H.)

21. Another name for Muhammad, "the praised," as well as the name of the Bedawi Pir. (C.A.H.)

22. The Badawi Sufi Pir, Ahmad al-Badawi (d. 1276), whose tomb is in Fez. (C.A.H.)

23. The great-granddaughter of Muhammad. (See the selection on pages 56–59.)

MUSICAL REMEMBRANCE

Sufi Women of Fez

MUSIC, SINGING, AND MOVEMENT are included in the *hadra*,[1] a ritual of mystical Islam which invokes and praises God, the Prophet, and the Saints. It is a supererogatory liturgy that is practiced by a number of Moroccan Sufi groups, including the Aissawa, the Hammadcha, and the Touhama.

Haddarat is the name for women who practice the *hadra*, and who follow the spiritual and musical guidance of a woman leader, known as the *ma'alema*. A well-known group directed by Hassaniya Rahali is composed of residents of Fez who originally came from the south of Morocco (Tafilalet and Hawz of Marrakesh); one of the seven women is of Iraqi origin. [Another well-known group], directed by Lalla Mottlati, is composed of women from Fez, as is the group led by Lalla Batul Lyoubi, although the latter is herself of Saudi Arabian origin.

In traditional Moroccan musical culture, gender differences are reflected in the way musical instruments are used. Like most women's groups, the *haddarat* of Fez accompany themselves only with percussion

This selection is excerpted from the liner notes to the CD *Chants sacres des femmes de Fez* (Al Sur/Media 7 ALCD 243/ M7 853, 1998), written by Antonio Baldassarre and translated by Joseph Rowe.

1. *Hadra* (*hadhrah*); verb *hadara* (*hadhara*), "to be; to be present; to be in the presence of"; noun *hadir* (*hadhir*), "witness, someone who is present; compound verb: *istihdhar* (*istihdhar*), "to evoke, to recall." Another possible etymology: *hadr* (*hadhr*), "incite and inciting." In the Moroccan dialect of Arabic (*darija*) the phoneme / *dh* / (interdental fricative), corresponding to the fifteenth letter (*dha*) of the alphabet, and the phoneme / *d* / (occlusive-dental), corresponding to the eighth letter of the alphabet (*dal*), are not distinct phonemes, but allophones. Hence there is another possible origin of *hadara* (*hadara*, "to bring down or descend."

instruments, involving both skin and metal vibrating surfaces. The general name for percussion instruments is *duzan*. These include: the *bendir*, a circular frame drum with one skin-covered surface; the *thilat*, a pair of small skins stretched over a body made of wood or pottery; the *tarr* or *triyar*, a small tambourine with cymbals on a circular frame; the *derabuka*, the classical Arab pottery drum shaped like a chalice; the *ta'arija*, a tambourine with a tapered goblet shape; the *gwal*, similar to the *derabuka*, but with snares of gut under the skin; and the *hanqa*, or finger cymbals.

[There are several musical forms that are used.] The *Tahdira*[2] *Soussiya*, is an ancient court music form of the *Dar el Makhzen*, influenced by Berber and Saharan rhythms of the Souss region, and by the *Hadra* of the Sidi Rahal brotherhood of the Marrakesh area. The metric form of the verse is known as *'Aroubi*, a dialect version of the classical name *Roub'ai*, for couplets of four verses. These quatrains are sung by two choirs which alternate in call and response. The *Tahdira* is usually dedicated to the woman who is the focal point of the festival, the *'arousa* (wife) or the *nafiysa* (mother who has given birth). . . . The *qasida,* a form from classical Arab music which is derived from the single-rhymed poetry of camel drivers of pre-Islamic Arabia [is here sung in 4/4 time alternating or superimposed on measures of 6/8]. The Moroccan *Qasida* (*Qsida*)[3] is not as rigorously constructed as the classical *Qasid*a, and has become a form of popular song through the intermediary of the *Malhun* . . . .[4]

The *hadra* of the women of Fez is the principal practice of their Sufi sorority, performed for occasions of powerful moments in the lives of women, both as mothers and as wives. Both a religious practice and a path of learning, the musical knowledge of the *haddarat* is expressed through a special attitude of mind and heart (*niya*), which enables them to sing of both sacred and worldly love as means of attaining the Divine. The role played by women of sororities such as the *haddarat* shows their ability to hold their own and to fulfill themselves, beyond the [interpretive] limitations of Islamic scripturalist dogma, and the stereotyped image Westerners have of Arab women. Such a woman may become a spiritual leader (*shaykha*) who is able to bring her disciple (*murid*) into knowledge and wisdom through mystical love. . . .

2. *Tahdhir*, "preparation, confection"; verb: *haddhara*, "to prepare, to make confections," whence the more plausible etymology of the word *Haddarat* "Women who prepare" (the *Hadra*).

3. *Qasida*, derived from *qasas*, story.

4. Concerning the "lineage" relationship which links "feminine" song (religious song in the ritual of Hadra, ceremonial song in rites of passage such as birth and marriage, entertainment songs of the Sheikhat to the recent phenomenon of Rai music, cf. Marie Virolic, "Le chant Rai," Karthala, Paris, 1997.

In Praise of the Prophet (Qasida an-Nabi)

I am rising up to the Messenger of God,
impossible to separate me from him,
I am between snow and sky, my heart full of love.
The son of the sky on earth, God understands him,
The breath of spirit and matter (bone)
cause intelligence and understanding to turn.
A sickness which no doctor can treat,
Sudden death brings the remedy,
The birds in the sky become tired if they have no refuge,
Give me wings so that I may fly to Taha.[5]
Heal me, Mohammed, Taha,
I beg you, help me, Mokhtar[6]
O Lord, heal me, Mohammed.
My mind is troubled, Lord, my mind is troubled
The eye of compassion comes down from the Master
and goes back up to him.
He dwells in the heavenly heights, O Lord.
I see in my life your portrait, where love comes from;
Celebration, the feeling of familiarity, joy,
My felicity I send to you, Lord, my spirit is jubilant.
Light up my heart with the light of your Love.
The strength of the bone, Mohammed Taha.
I see all the people asleep.
I salute you, you of the Beautiful Name,
I go to practice the pilgrimage,
As prescribed by our Prophet and Protector.
He told us to leave and make a tour,
Just as the men of God did.
I'll tie my heart to the Hajar Soad[7]
And then I'll drink from the Bir Zem Zem[8]

❧ This song by Hassania Rahali is excerpted from the liner notes of the CD *Chants sacres des femmes de Fez* (Al Sur/Media 7 ALCD 243/ M7 853, 1998).

5. "The Pure," one of the Beautiful Names of the Prophet. (C.A.H.)

6. "Winged Spirit," another of the Beautiful Names of the Prophet. (C.A.H.)

7. *Al-hajar al-aswad*: the Black Stone, the cornerstone of the Kaaba. (C.A.H.)

8. "The well of paradise" in the Ryad of Mecca.

Between Safa and Marwa'[9] my spirit fills with love.
I pray to God and climb the Jebel 'Arafat.[10]
Heal me, I beseech you, Mohammed Taha,
You of strength and great intelligence, Messenger of God.
I climb the Jebel 'Arafat, I sit down and take the Support,
A lofty station, a high level.
In this place I perform my practices and I become Hajj.[11]
After sunset we go towards Minan,[12]
Each of us full of love.[13]
There we find the joy of being together and patience.
The next day we visit Medina,
The city which gave refuge to the Messenger of God.
There are nobles and disciples there,
There is where I find Mohammed, Peace be upon him,
Let us go, Hajjaj,[14] let us go to Mohammed's, the lord
Messenger.

9. The two hills between which pilgrims run during a stage of the *hajj* (*safa* = purity and *marwah* = virtue).

10. The holy hill where it is said that Adam and Eve were reunited after their long exile from Paradise. Standing in prayer on the plain of 'Arafat for the afternoon of the tenth day of the month of Hajj is one of the obligations of the pilgrimage without which one's *hajj* is incomplete. It is the moment of union. (C.A.H.)

11. One who has performed the pilgrimage (*hajj*) to the Holy Lands of Islam and followed the prescribed rites of pilgrimage.

12. Mina: the place of encampment during the completion of the rites of *hajj*. (C.A.H.)

13, Another ritual stage of the *hajj*, where the "born again" meet together, those who have renewed themselves through the outer and inner practices of the *hajj*.

14. Plural of *hajj*.

INNER VISION

NUHA AND SUHA AL-ABED are two sisters living in Damascus who also, like Aisha and Aliaa Rafea, share an intense love for the Divine. Nuha was inclined toward the mystic life from an early age, while Suha has been drawn to the Sufi path more recently. Nuha's sensitivity to Spirit has sometimes manifested in the form of visions that then open further her comprehension of Spirit. She and Suha live not far from the tomb of Ibn al-'Arabi and also Sayyida Zaynab, the granddaughter of the Prophet, as well as many other saints and companions of the Prophet. Like them, they breathe the air of the numinous.

The following selection opens with the inspiration of the "full moon," reminding us of "Tala' al-badru alayna" (see page 222), in a prefatory letter to Nuha's spiritual father. The original Arabic of Nuha's writing has been translated into English by her sister, Suha, in order that her visionary experience might be shared. Many of the Sufi mystics have received instruction through dreams, like Umm 'Abdallah at-Tirmidhi, and visions, like the great Ibn al-'Arabi. Often it may be through a dream or vision that one is guided to connect with one's spiritual teacher or once connected, may receive further guidance on the path from him or her. In opening to the meaning of these subtler realms, we can be opened further to the Presence of the Divine until the full power of the Divine is evident.

> The vision of the servant is only evidence of the vision of the One who loves and is subject and object of His own love, so that the vision of the beloved (servant) is annihilated, pervaded (overpowered) by the love of Him who is eternally seeing. Thus the vision of the servant is only a reflection.[1]

1. G. W. J. Drewes, *The Admonitions of Seh Bari* (The Hague: Martinus Nijhoff, 1969), p. 23.

Vision of the Truth by Meeting of the Sun and Moon

Devotion kept turning around me, melting my being and my body, until the day when the shadow of the Merciful God manifested in front of me and gave me the power which enables me to see the brightness of God's Attributes without perishing.

The rising of the full moon always meant to me the shining of the eternal divine light on my heart. One day I was reading in a literature book when a sentence attracted me: "The full moon rose from Thaniat al-Wada'a."[2] I closed my eyes, and I saw a vision of the Hajj. The vision was that we are at the edge of the world, on top of a mountain, praying and watching. We are standing there in enormous circles and suddenly we feel the sun of the Attributes of God rising; it covers the sky and becomes clear in our world. Each ray sends the scent of its meaning to this world. I feel my body burning with the fire of this sun as I am exposed directly to its rays.

If this is a manifestation of the Sun of God's Attributes,
How merciful is God
How merciful is the One God
He is The Merciful.

All of a sudden, while the flames are purifying us, the moon rises behind the mountain and goes across the horizon until it faces the sun and blocks the sun's flames by its bright burning body. It shines over all the world, hiding the burning sun behind him. Muhammad, the Full Moon, becomes the veil behind which God's Attributes are hidden. This is a manifestation of the Merciful God.

Then I hear a voice communicating to the waiting world, "We sent you to be a mercy to the worlds."[3] I see Muhammad standing between me and the sun, touching my right arm. At this moment I apprehend what praying is meant to be.

"Vision of the Truth" is excerpted from letters of Nuha al-Abed relating her visionary experience to her spiritual father, Dr. Assad Ali. Translated from the Arabic by Suha al-Abed.

2. The hills outside Medina. When the Prophet Muhammad emigrated from Mecca to Medina, he arrived from this direction. The women of Medina went up to their rooftops and began singing and drumming to welcome him as "the full moon rising over Thaniat al-Wada'a." This song, "Tala' al-badru alayna," is still sung with much love today. (C.A.H.)

3. This is a verse in the Qur'an (Surah al-Anbiyaa' 21:107) and also is part of the lyrics of "Tala' al-badru alayna." (C.A.H.)

When Muhammad, the son of Abdullah, the great prophet, touches my right arm, I smell the scent of his meaning on my right hand. I apprehend that the Muhammad Truth is the moon that hides the sun of the Attributes behind him. So the sun shines on him but does not burn him, and through him all the Manifestation of God passes and then appears from the Source (The Merciful, *ar-Rahman*) and the Branch (The Bestower of Grace, *ar-Rahim*).

This is the rank of completed human reason, which is one of the classifications of human existence. The Muhammad Truth is the completed human reason because it hides the sun of God's manifestations behind it while passing them through the light of the Attributes in accordance with the will of its Master. So it becomes the passage of the Manifestations.

O you, who have faith, celebrate the praises of Allah and do so often
and glorify Him morning and evening.
He it is who sends blessing on you as do His angels
that He may bring you out of Darkness into Light
and He is full of mercy to the faithful.
Their salutation on the day they meet Him will be peace,
and He has prepared for them a generous reward.
O prophet! truly We have sent thee as a witness,
a bearer of glad tidings and a warner.
and as one who invites to Allah's Grace by His permission,
and as a lamp spreading light.
[Surah Luqman 31:41–46]

The Manifestation of God's blessing upon Muhammad is revealing itself. Muhammad is the linkage point between the Manifestations of the Sun of the Attributes on one side and our world, which is covered by the Black Muhammad Truth, on the other side. I apprehend that the Muhammad Truth is black because it absorbs the clear light inside itself so that the light becomes clear in his heart. This is the reason why the Manifestation of Truth is through the moon, which hides the sun behind him, making the day a self-lighted night.

The first revelation is: Reason (mind) is one of the names of Truth.

The second revelation is: Its Truth in the world and the human being.

The third revelation is: Its role which is indicated in "The Confederates," [Surah 3 :56]:

Allah and His angels send blessings on the Prophet.
O you, who have faith,
send ye blessing on him and salute him with all respect.

So the Muhammad Truth is a linkage point between the two sides. From One side it is exposed to the Manifestation of God's Attributes: "God sends His blessing and His angels do also," and from the other side, people are trying to gain God's acceptance by asking Him to bless Muhammad. So the Muhammad Truth is receiving from both sides, and that makes it a linkage point.

At this point, the touch of luminosity is occurring.

Light upon Light.
[Surah an-Nur 24:35]

Through this passage the "burning" becomes "nectar" (*harik—rahik*) and it runs through the veins of the worshipper. For this reason God says to His last prophet, *And pray on their behalf, truly your prayers are a source of security for them* [Surah at-Tauba 9:103]. When this linkage reaches the Reason it goes forth from it and spreads throughout the whole being (the heart) which is the place of Truth.

Through this light I hear "The Sun" Surah [91] echoing in a prayer. This happens only when I apprehend the meaning of the brightness of the Sun inside myself, my self whose way to the brightness of the Sun is through asking God to bless Muhammad, who is conveying the evidences of the Sun; through him pass the Manifestations of the Attributes.

O Lord, heavens and earth hymn your praise
You give all Your creatures
Fine ways to address you.
O Lord, the Only God of day and night.
The Sun of Your Attributes is the brightness
  of my enlightened soul.
The moon of prayer tells me secrets of the Attributes.
Oh Lord, Heavens and Earth hymn your praise.

Just now, when You revealed Your brightness to my days, I comprehended that You reveal Your Manifestations equally in the darkness and in light, in the shade and in heat.

I apprehend now, when my self becomes an extension to the Ray of the Attributes, that You make me free by Your kindness.

When my self aligns within the shade of Your moon, I become the passage of Your Meaning and Manifestations. When I feel that my home is the recourse of Your Mercy, the image of a dream about my grandmother (Su'da) flashes into my mind (I saw this vision a few days before her death).

The Vision

I was standing somewhere, hearing a voice telling me: you will meet now the messenger of Fatima Al-Zahra'a.[4] Suddenly I found myself in front of my grandmother (on my father's side) whose name is Bushra Al-Abed (her name means: "worshipper's good omen," and they call her by her son's name as "mother of Hassan"). I rushed to her, asking her to tell me about my future. She said: "I will tell you one thing only: the Full Power is gifted to you." Then she left me alone perplexed and was carried to the Heavens.

In the beginning I did not expect that this vision was related to the Muhammad Truth. But when I felt my mind becoming familiar with the Muhammad Truth, a question occurred to my mind: why was the divine message revealed on the Night of Power?[5]

I am thinking of your words, father, and I discover that I was too weak to bear being a passage of manifestations. But God trains His worshipper and strengthens him in order to bear Full Power. This Power will connect the worshipper with the inner part of the human being and with the world of manifestations. When the worshipper gains this Power, the Sun of the Attributes will not burn him because he has the Full Power. The worshipper's prayers pass through Muhammad, the messenger of God. The worshipper will have the power of influence only when he has the Full Power.

SO THE FULL POWER IS THE MUHAMMAD TRUTH ITSELF.

The Full Power was completed by the representative of the Muhammad Truth. So the Holy Qur'an was revealed in the Night of Power, i.e., in the Night when the Muhammadan Truth representative became able to bear being a passage of manifestation without getting burned.

4. The daughter of the Prophet Muhammad (see the selection on Fatima, page 47).

5. The Night of Power (*laylat al-qadr*) see note 15 on page 106.

On that night—God Blessed Muhammad

This means that God shows his Manifestations through the Truth of Muhammad and the Muhammad Truth reflects these Manifestations to the heart of the worshipper.

God trains the worshipper until he receives the Full Power; when the worshipper gains the Full Power, God blesses Muhammad, so the worshipper becomes connected with the Sun of Attributes without being burned. This connection happens through the Black Truth of Muhammad towards the heart of the worshipper.

Today, father, I enter a new world.

When I enter the prayer sanctuary (*mihrab*), I realize that I am in the shadow of the Most High God. I hear the angels of the sanctuary saying:

> Glory be to Allah, the Most High, the Only One.
> Glory be to Allah, the Supreme One in Heavens and Earth.
> He is the Most High, He shades His worshipper
> with His providence.
> So, you people, come to His shades.

I feel the shadowing gives shade to the windows of my heart.

He is the Most High God, who cannot be reached within the shades of His High Meanings. I become the worshipper of His Attribute, the Most High.

My being in His shade becomes the meeting point of the shadows, and my heart finds itself in His shade.

So, He isolated me, so that I can see nothing but Him. When I ask about that, I receive the answer that this is happening in order to teach me that I can ask for something only through the Muhammad Truth (the screen).

What is this screen between the worshipper and the Sun of the Attributes? It is the Truth of Muhammad that is established between the human being and his heart so he can see the Manifestations through the screen of the Merciful, the Bestower of Grace. The Merciful God intervenes between the worshipper and the Attributes through one of His Manifestations which is the Muhammad Truth.

Everyone praying says: *Bismillah*, "By the Name of Allah," then she or he blesses the Muhammad Truth, i.e., he starts with the farthest point (Allah) and ends up with the nearest manifestation (The Merciful). So if the one who prays blesses Muhammad (the last Manifestation), then he becomes inspired God Light which spreads the Irresistible Manifestation through the passage of the Muhammad Truth.

At this stage the Light opens the paradise of the heart and its Heavens and palm trees and grapes. So the key of the dawn is "By the Name of Allah the Merciful, the Bestower of Grace" and "Blessings be upon Muhammad and his family."

The circle of the Mercy Truth teaches the prayers: *Praise be to Allah, Lord of all worlds, the Most Merciful, the Bestower of Grace* [Surah al-Fatiha 1:1–2]. So if the Most Merciful, Most Gracious God is not the passage through which the Manifestations pass, then the worshipper would not exist. *Praise be to Allah, Lord of all worlds!*

From that I come to a conclusion that the Muhammad Truth takes its name from its meaning ("Muhammad" means "praise"). This indicates the truth that God is praised for giving him to us, and through him we can worship Him. So Muhammad is the screen behind which the Attributes are hidden.

Blessings be upon him and his family.

I think that Muhammad and his family members are manifestations of the reality of the Merciful God. The cycling of this fact is the Black

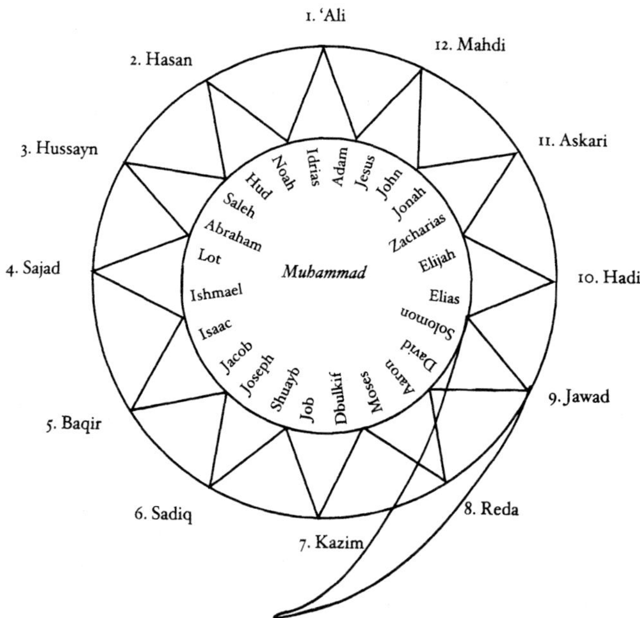

Muhammad Truth. The Muhammad Truth becomes as a kernel planted in my heart. It has two circles: the inner one goes around in the cycles of the Truth, and the outer one goes around also, precisely like the concept of the atom.

The inner circle = the Prophecy circle
The outer circle = the Entrusted Defenders circle

Each circle has its cycle. The inner one goes around and spreads its light on the outer circle, which in turn spreads its light on the world and engenders endless circles. [See illustration on page 239.]

The observer can notice that the Muhammad kernel yields two ideas:

1. The inner circle is concluded at a stage just a little bit before it is totally completed, so it is an incomplete circle and it is concluded at the Christ stage.

This inner circle represents the circle of the Prophets who were sent before Muhammad. This means that the inner circle is open to our world through the expected Christ. And so is the outer circle; it is also concluded at an open stage which is al-Mahdi,[6] i.e., the outer circle is open to our world through al-Mahdi who is expected. So through these two open places both circles can move.

2. When Christ comes down to our world from the inner circle (the Prophecy circle), he draws a descending line from the circle. This line performs a shape like the figure nine (9). The observer of both circles sees the figure (9) doubled which reads: (99),[7] precisely as:

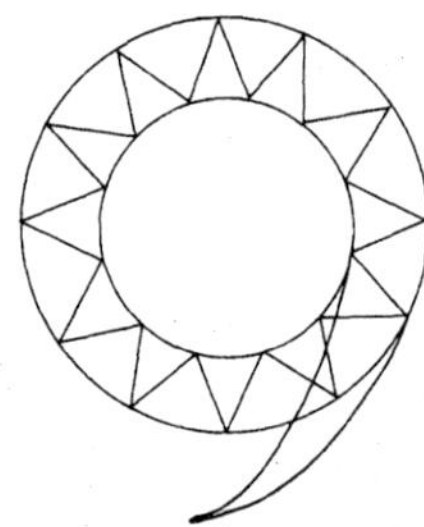

It can clearly be seen that the Muhammad Truth is the passage of Divine Manifestations, and that it is the Full Power through which the Manifestations of God can be seen and it is in itself Manifestations of the Merciful Gracious God.

6. Al-Mahdi (the guided one) is the hidden one who will appear at the end of time to restore righteousness before the world ends with the Day of Reckoning.

7. Ninety-nine is the traditional number of the Divine Attributes or "Names of God" in the Islamic tradition.

Yet who can deliver the unfaithful from a grievous penalty?
Say: He is Allah, the Most Gracious;
we have believed in Him and in Him we have put our trust.
[Surah al-Mulk 67:28–29]

The only thing that might deliver the unfaithful is the screen of the Merciful, Gracious God. Our world is the Manifestation of the Attributes through the Merciful God. So the human being can see this screen through which he/she can see the Attributes and receive inspiration from God, or he or she can be deprived of this screen so that one says to the Prophet:

Our hearts are under veils (concealed) from that to which thou do invite us
and between us and thee is a screen.
[Surah al-Fussilat 41:5]

People who see this screen see it as an eternal light which gathers the sun and the moon, so that the sun does not burn them because it sends its rays through the Merciful God, who holds its burning (fire) nature. These are all symbols or some kinds of Manifestation. But God the Most High is beyond the external (*al-Zahir*) and the internal (*al-Batin*).

A question occurs to me: Where is the soul in relation to all of that? God gives it the proportion and order when he gives the soul its enlightenments.

This rank, father, is the righteousness rank, as I found out later. The righteous awe of God that keeps the worshipper from burning is the Merciful God's screen through which the Manifestations are passing, to which Mary had recourse when the angel greeted her.

She said: I seek refuge from thee to Allah Most Gracious.
He said: Nay, I am only a messenger from your Lord
to announce to you the gift of a holy son.
[Surah Maryam 19:18–19]

This angel Mary had seen is a messenger from her God; he is one aspect of the Manifestations of the Merciful God through whom the other Attributes (the Irresistible, etc. . . .) are passing.

When Mary prayed, she sought refuge in the Most Merciful Gracious God, who had sent her His messenger and whom she asked to save her from the labor pain that she was preparing herself for before she received the good omen. But a voice cried to her from beneath her:

Grieve not, and shake towards thyself the trunk of the palm tree.
[Surah Maryam 19:25]

So we in fact see the manifestations of the other Attributes only through the screen of the Merciful Gracious God.

Allah Most Gracious is firmly established on the throne.[8]

Awe of God is to turn to the screen of the Muhammad Truth, which is the Manifestation of the Merciful, Gracious God. We see through the Merciful God the Merciful Manifestations.

He holds the heavens from falling[9]
and holds the birds praising His Glory[10]
and firstly It is He Who has taught the Qur'an, then has created man.[11]

The Muhammad Truth came into being before God created Adam.[12] Through the Muhammad Truth the material creation took place. So the Merciful God first was established on the throne, then he created man and inspired him with awe. So if the heart is blind and cannot see the Merciful God, it would be wrong. And if the heart is enlightened with the Muhammad Truth it would be rightful. The Merciful God enlightens the soul with the Muhammad Truth and it awakens, so the earth shakes and its stars scatter and its graves turn upside down, so the sight is dazed and the sun and moon meet together.[13]

The observer of this vision, sees everything through the Merciful God, eats from His vessel and drinks from His spring, i.e., reaches the revealing screen. . . .

I apprehend now what it means that each worshipper is one of these columns that holds the Heavens. I apprehend now what it means that each human being is a part of all other human beings, a part that lightens the hearts of the others and overwhelms their senses. Now I comprehend the

8. See Surah ar-Rad 13:2 and see also Surah Ta-Ha 20:5 and Surah al-Hadid 57:4. (C.A.H.)

9. See Surah ar-Rad 13:2. (C.A.H.)

10. See Surah an-Nahl 16:79 and also Surah al-Mulk. 67:19. (C.A.H.)

11. See Surah ar-Rahman 55:2–3. (C.A.H.)

12. It is understood in Islamic theology that the Light of Muhammad, the Nuri Muhammadi, was created first, though his actual expression as a human being in full human life did not occur until the completion of the cycle of Prophethood. Muhammad is also understood to be the seal of the prophets. It is he who brought together both the law of Moses and the Love of Jesus and lived a fully human life. In so doing, he left us with many examples of the way to enact our humanity to its fullest divinely inspired potential. (C.A.H.)

13. See Surah Infitar 82:1–5. (C.A.H.)

secret of the eclipse of the sun that occurred on the new Hijra[14] year. The sun was hidden behind the moon and the secret was revealed. I enter the circling atom in which sun and moon meet; I see the Merciful God's throne manifesting through the Muhammad Truth. So I see the Heavens split and the stars scatter and the balance of justice being established.[15] The worshipper sees that the merciful God created everything perfectly, the worshipper feels that he or she lives in the much frequented *fana'* in which the divine miracles are revealed through the Merciful God.

How wondrous is this human being in whom all prophets meet, and to whom the Qur'an is revealed. Although he or she is very small, he or she can contain the galaxies in his or her heart. Heavens are the heavens of his heart and earth is the earth of his soul, the stars are her ideals, his mind is the passage of Manifestations, his soul is his changing being. I realize that through myself, I feel my being changing to become at one time the Rod of Moses and at another time Jesus's table of the Lord's Supper, and at another time Saleh's Camel, which was killed by whims of the wayward people but which God re-created again,[16] and at another time the Ship of Noah, which was carried by the holy irresistible flood to arrive safely upon Judi mountain,[17] and at another time the Bell of Christ or His Cross or His Church, or Bilal's Minaret[18] or the Garden of al-Zahra's or the Carpet of al-Sajjad or the Cradle of al-Mahdi or anything else, even a stone that praises the Glory of God, or a bird or a beast or a tree or desert. Whatever my soul is it will be the shadow of Manifestations; it is the Qur'an taught to humans by the Merciful God.

Whatever my soul is, the key of existence is His words, one of which is my self. His words move from His Intention to His Will and in this way, His intention becomes creatures.

14. *Hijra*: see note 5 of "Khadija." (C.A.H.)

15. See Surah al-Infitar 82.

16. See Surah al-A'raf 7:73–79, Surah Hud 11:64–67, and Surah ash-Shu'ara 26:142–59.

17. See Surah Hud 11:25–48.

18. Bilal was the first muezzin (the one who calls to prayer from the minaret) of the early Muslim community. (C.A.H.)

PRINCIPLES OF SUFISM

Sayedeh Nahid Angha[1] is an author and translator of many books and articles on the subjects of Sufism, philosophy, and psychology. She has taught Sufism and philosophy for over twenty-five years and, together with her husband, Sayeed Ali Kianfar, was cofounder and continues to be codirector of the International Association of Sufism (IAS). She also helped to establish a Sufi Women Organization, as a department of IAS, which was created to "introduce, disseminate, honor and acknowledge, with Divine Guidance, the contribution and service of Sufi women to the world civilization."

Dr. Angha was raised within a Sufi family in Iran; her father was Moulana Shah Maghsoud,[2] an Oveysi Sufi master, and her mother, Mah Talat Eternad Moghadad, a noblewoman also devoted to the Sufi path. As a young woman, under her father's direction, she meditated for hours at a time, studied spiritual literature and philosophy of many traditions, and also under her father's direction passed through numerous *chilles* (forty-day retreats). It was her father who gave her permission to teach at the age of twenty, and in his presence she did so for many years until his death in 1980.

Nahid then went on to complete university studies in both Iran and the United States, earning her doctorate in psychology. She has continued to study and to teach in the continuation of the Oveysi school initiated by her father.

1. "Sayedeh" indicates one of those who trace their lineage back to the family of the Prophet Muhammad.

2. He himself was the student of his father, Moulana Mir Ghotbeddin, a prominent Oveysi Sufi Master of his time. Oveys, or Uways, was a saint who lived at the time of the Prophet Muhammad and knew and trusted in Muhammad's divine mission, though he lived in remote Yemen and never met the Prophet. Uways was known to receive inspiration directly from God without the intermediary of a teacher in physical form. Since his time, those who have been so inspired often adopt the name Oveysi.

She mentions that her father always emphasized that guidance is in the hands of Allah. "And Allah, the Eternal, the Compassionate, will not leave anyone's guidance in the hands of another. . . . whoever purifies him/herself does so for the benefit of her/his own soul; and all destination is to God" [Qur'an 35:18].[3]

As she writes in her introduction to *Principles of Sufism*:

> It is narrated from Amir al-Moumenin Ali[4] (as well as Imam Sadiq, his grandson), who said that *Tasawouf* is an acronym of four letters. (*Tasawouf* is a four-letter word: TSVF and pronounced Tasawouf in its original language.) Each letter holds a secret representing one stage or quality of a Sufi. Together the word TSVF makes the twelve Principles; one who perfects these principles is a Sufi.[5]
>
> *T*, the first letter stands for three practices of Tark (abandonment); *Tubeh* (repentance);[6] and *Tugba* (virtue).
>
> *S*, the second letter of the word, stands for another three qualities

3. Sufi Women Organization, *Sufi Women: The Journey towards the Beloved*, p. 17.

4. Imam Ali, was the cousin and the son-in-law of the Prophet Mohammad. Amir al-Moumenin Ali was the first man who believed in Islam. He was the heir of the heritage of the prophecy whose guidance throughout the fifteen cetnuries of the life of Sufism has been the greatest inspiration for many. It has been narrated from the Prophet who said, "I am the City of Knowledge and Ali is the Gate."

5. For further elucidation of the essential principles of Sufism, see *Principles of Sufism* by al-Qushayri (986–1072 C.E.), translated from the Arabic by B. R. von Schlegell. Dr. von Schlegell has rendered an excellent translation of this classic Sufi text by one of the early Sufi masters that is the prototype of such discourses. In the introduction to that work, she also informs us about some of the women in the family of al-Qushyri, see page 22. (C.A.H.)

6. Repentance (*tawba*): According to al-Qushayri, this is the first step on the path. In his *Risala*, expertly rendered by Dr. B. von Schlegell in her translation, *Principles of Sufism*, pp. 1–2, he states:

> God says, "Turn all together toward God [in repentance], O Believers, that you may attain bliss" [24:31]. It is reported on the authority of Anas b. Malik that the Messenger of God (may God's blessing and peace be upon him and his family) said, "The one who repents from sin is like one without sin, and if God loves a servant, sin does not adhere to him." Then he recited, "Verily God loves those who turn unto Him [in repentance], and He loves those who purify themselves" (2:222). It was asked, "O Messenger of God, what is the sign of repentance?" He replied, "Remorse."
>
> On the authority of Anas b. Malik, the Messenger of God (may God's blessing and peace be upon him and his family) is reported to have said, "There is nothing more loved by God than the youth who repents."
>
> Therefore repentance is the first degree among the degrees of the wayfarers and the first station among the stations of the seekers. The inner meaning of repentance in Arabic is "return." It is said, "He repented," meaning, "He returned." So repentance is to return from what is blameworthy in the law of Islam to what is praiseworthy in it.

to be perfected by a *salek* [a traveler on the spiritual journey]; *Sabr* (patience); *Sedgh* (truthfulness and honesty); and *Safa* (purity).

V, the third letter stands for *Vud* (love); *Verd* [*wird*] (*Zekr* and remembrance); and *Vafaa* (faithfulness).

F, the final letter, represents another three qualifications: *Fard* (solitude); *Faghr* [*faqr*] (poverty); and *Fana* (annihilation).

During a life of learning, practicing, and teaching Sufism under the guidance and instruction of . . . my physical and spiritual father, I came to the realization that the door toward knowledge may open to afford a glimpse or two of reality to a seeker, but without mastering these twelve principles, such understanding will not remain clear for long.[7]

Patience is one of the doorways from the human level to the Divine. It is one of the Attributes of God. As Mevlana Jalaluddin Rumi, among others, often indicates to us, the practice of patience, along with gratitude, is one of the two main keys to felicity.

Patience (Sabr)

True lovers ponder not upon the bright array of others;
They are measured with the scales of patience.

—NIRVAN

Sabr may be understood as endurance and fortitude through the abandonment of impatience and complaint. In the language of Sufism patience represents the proper manner of awaiting the opening of the Divine. But this patient waiting is no simple matter.

Sabr has been divided into three categories: the patience of the common people in disciplining their *nafs*, the patience of the pious in working

The Prophet (may God's blessing and peace be upon him) said, "Remorse is an act of repentance." Therefore, those well-versed in the fundamentals of religion among the people of the Sunna have said, "There are three conditions of repentance [which must be present] in order that it be sound: remorse for the violations that have been committed, immediate abandonment of the lapse, and firm resolve not to return to similar acts of disobedience." One must apply these principles to make repentance effective.

❧ "Patience (Sabr)" is excerpted from pp. 43–51 of *Principles of Sufism*, by Dr. Nahid Angha. Printed with permission from Jain Publishing Company, Fremont, Calif. (www.jainpub.com).

7. Nahid Angha, *Principles of Sufism*, pp. 9–10.

to benefit future generations, and the patience of the Sufis in avoiding the desires of the world. Some Sufis have said that one who is patient is grateful even in times of misfortune through perseverance in God.[8]

The disciplining of one's nafs is indispensable to the practice of patience, and this discipline is achieved through lessening the grip on the self of the chains of desires, while at the same time setting praiseworthy goals for one's life. Working to achieve those goals assists in striving to avoid low qualities and base manners, while advancing one's knowledge and skill so that one can become a valuable and peaceful member of the society. Such practices demand patience and inward dedication, but the rewards are rich: becoming an outstanding individual is helpful to one's own life as well to the betterment of other members of the human race. But it is not an easy task to be accomplished through good intentions alone. To the contrary, only through patience can the obstacles on the path of enlightenment be overcome.

A second category of patience is the patience of the pious. A pious individual is one who has already advanced himself above the rank of the common people. He has disciplined himself and already achieved praiseworthy goals. He has taken it upon himself to contribute to future generations, to think in advance of his times, and to educate himself accordingly. Preparing a suitable ground for the advancement of future generations demands patience as well as dedication and selflessness.

The third category of patience is the patience of the Sufis. A Sufi is one who is searching for unlimited understanding; remaining attracted to the desires of the world will prevent one from even appreciating the importance of the path of the Sufi. Thus to become a Sufi one necessary preparation is the freeing of the inner self from the imprisonment of the desires of the world, with the awareness [that] such freedom does not lie in mortification, but only true inner freedom. Such freedom clears the ground for better thinking, living, and the attainment of a peaceful manner.

The author of the authoritative *Resaleh Ghosheiri* evokes the nuances of the patience of worshippers and the patience of lovers of the Divine. As he relates, the worshippers' patience is better kept and the lovers' patience better left.[9] One who is pious waits for God through his patience and worship, and so must be persistent. The lover is attracted toward God and cannot remain patient in his love since the heat of love so easily may dwindle into coldness.

8. Abul Ghasem Ghosheiri, *Resaleh Ghosheiri*, edited and translated into Farsi by Badeizaman Furozanfar (Teheran, 1346), p. 280.

9. Abul Ghasem Ghosheiri, p, 287.

The human being lives in the world of nature, and nature is filled with all the different colors, tastes, and dimensions. Pain and suffering, grief and sadness, comfort and good fortune do not spring like flowers from the soil; rather, they are all part of human life, and everyone will taste of them. Should we consider these events to be destiny, then it is a destiny that follows its course without consulting anyone! The individual should not fail and lose hope when misfortune knocks, nor should he forget the bounds of moderation when fortune blesses him. To remain firm on one's own path necessitates patience in conserving one's strength and will.[10] Indeed, it may be fairly said that it is the believer who meets the armada of destiny secure in the armor of patience. The [Qur'an 25:75] provides us with the most succinct wisdom: it reads, "Those are the ones who will be rewarded with the highest place in heaven because of their patient constancy: Therein shall they be met with salvation and peace." Elsewhere: "Ye who believe, seek help with patient perseverance and prayer: for God is with those who patiently wait" (Qu'ran 2:153).

The individual who is impatient in enduring suffering and hardship is not well suited for the path of Sufism. Sufis are the lovers of the truth of Being and are indifferent to the prospect of reward in achieving it. Whether or not they are given good fortune, as Sufis they seek knowledge and understanding of the rules of existence; they know that patience is a part of the achievement of such an understanding. Patience is the state of contentment with the destiny of Being. A Sufi knows that the world of existence is the domain of rules, and that no single particle acts unless in accordance with the rules of the eternal essence. A Sufi is aware in his understanding of the destination of Being. One who discovers the destination and the rules of this infinitely designed system that we call [the] world remains steadfast at all times. He will not lose hope when misfortune occurs, and will not fall into smug self-satisfaction when fortune knocks.

Discovery and success come only through patience, but are not to be thought of as rewards for patience. Sufis live patiently for the Divine; they do not love God because He rewards them with the benefits of life, but because He is to be loved. Since He is the source of that eternal knowledge, those who are attracted toward knowledge will embrace the Beloved within their whole being. Whether or not the road toward the beloved is filled with hardship or paved with ease, such incidentals will not alter their intention and dedication: quite simply, they know that they must achieve their goal.

10. Ghotbeddin Abul Muzaffer Ebadi, *Sufi Nameh* (Teheran, 1347), p. 72.

11. Abul Ghasem Ghosheiri, p. 284.

It is told that once a group of people came to Shebli, an ancient Sufi, and assured him that they were his devotees. Shebli picked up a rock and threw it at them—in consternation they all ran away. Shebli shouted, "If you are my friends, why are you running away from my hardship?"[11] This wise and wry gesture represents a discipline among Sufis. They do not run away from hardship; as the lovers of truth they accept and trust whatever comes from truth, instead of arguing, rejecting, and denying truth.

The world is not all comfort and wealth: pain follows ease, poverty descends from wealth, and richness is bought with hardship. Since the world is a house of change, pain and suffering have the upper hand in the fear of insecurity and doubt, while comfort and ease presuppose a stability that is not to be found within the confines of the world.[12]

The author of *Sufi Nameh* suggests several modalities of patience. One is to keep oneself away from desires and through patient learning master the discipline of life. This is proper patience for beginners and for followers, who must of necessity first close the doors of passion and persist in patience until their heart reaches the light of guidance. Qu'ran 2:155 reads . . . , "Be sure, We shall test you with something of fear and hunger." Next is to endure those pains and hardships that arise out of the faults of others; here we have the model of saints who were patient with all.

The life stories of the prophets and Sufis evoke the value of patience. Noah, Zakarra [Zachariah], Abraham, Moses, and Jesus all were put to test and were told to "persevere in patience and constancy." Prophet Mohammad suffered much hardship from his enemies yet he was instructed to "await in patience the command of thy Lord" (Qu'ran 52:48).[13] The rules and laws of Being suggest that everything must undergo the test of hardship if anything is to develop and progress toward perfection. Indeed, the very history of civilization shows that it is only through endurance that the fittest survive. Whoever shall endure hardship becomes strong: as Nietzsche sagely wrote, "What does not kill me makes me stronger."

Comfort and pain are reflections of each other; patience is the key in understanding both. A Sufi takes patience with him as a friend to assist him in leaving behind the cares of the world. Since it cannot be denied that everything comes from the Divine, thus He is the source of all knowledge for Sufis (and indeed for all knowledge of any kind), whether in times of fortune or misfortune. Such events that we may call ill or fortunate are only words that we apply to the ephemeral; the Sufi patiently seeks the permanent. "Is not God enough for His servant?" (Qu'ran 39:36). Truly, an

12. Ghotbeddin Abul Muzaffar Ebadi, p. 71.

13. Ghotbeddin Abul Muzaffar Ebadi, p. 73.

individual who is ripe for the path of understanding must ask himself if it is not the Divine alone who has brought him forth from the eternity of infinity into worldly existence, and yet again that same God who beckons him forth once more toward eternity and infinity in such a way that not a single fiber of his body could resist. Thus, just as pain is a condition of life, patience is a cure for that condition through its very essence.

Constant change is the rule of the world of nature; in it fortune and misfortune are like the seasons of the year, transient in their course as one replaces another, ephemeral in their effects, like the snows of winter that melt beneath the warmth of spring. Primitive peoples govern their lives and worship their gods according to the seasons; with wisdom the mind may learn to remain patient in times of hardship, since like the winter snow the face of pain will finally disappear, revealing beneath it the profile of patience that will remain.

Like piety, patience as it is practiced in Sufism possesses both an outwardly apparent and inwardly essential aspect. A *salek* always thinks before he speaks, awaiting the opportune moment, so as not to say what he may well later regret; likewise, he constantly attends to the care of his body and mind so as not to fall into distress and helplessness; most important of all, he keeps his heart from falling into rejection and denial: perhaps the most difficult of tests. Weakness in patience reflects uncertainty of belief, since patience is one of the reasons and methods that keeps belief intact.[14] It has been narrated from Amir-al-Moumenin Ali that the relationship between patience and belief is like . . . that of mind and body: a body without mind will not live; belief without patience will not endure.

A believer strives to become learned, familiar with the rules of reality and the laws of the Divine. For a believer, God is all mercy and kindness: and so any event follows through His logic. To understand Divine logic, the believer waits and remains in patience and avoids hasty and imbalanced reactions. Prophet Mohammad said in the *Hadith* that there is that which you like but which is not to your benefit, but that there is also that which you dislike but which benefits you. Here the Prophet offers us an invitation to the understanding of the wisdom that lies behind events, either fortunate or unfortunate in their outward and immediate manifestation. Patience is a quality which comes after the quality of *faghr* (poverty) and it arises from belief. A Sufi must be a person of knowledge; he is aware that all the events of the world of matter arise as events out of the operation of meaningful laws and rules. And so he may remain patient in his suffering

14. Ghotbeddin Abul Muzaffar Ebadi, pp. 75–76.

and thankful in his joy until he learns the rules of Divinity, and then there shall remain no impermanence within him to lie under the shadow of fear, of greed, or of ignorance.

There remains another way of usefully categorizing patience, in terms of its relation to the different elements of the being of the individual. Here it is possible to speak of the patience of the *nafs*; the patience of the heart; and the patience of the soul."[15] The patience of *nafs* consists in perseverance in performing religious duties, and remaining steadfast in times of pain as well as in those of comfort. The patience of the heart lies in persistence in the purifying of one's intentions, and a like persistence in meditation and remembering the Almighty Lord. The patience of the soul consists in persistence in witnessing the Eternal beauty with the help of insight. Among the highest of the unities that underlie the different varieties of patience is patience with and through God, since such patience comes after the annihilation.

As well, patience may be divided into three levels. There is patience at the time of temptation, when one tries to keep away from the forbidden no matter how delightfully alluring it might appear. Above that is patience at the time of worship, which has the sense of grateful worship of God without expectation of reward; this is the best type of worship that may be expected from a person of limited mind. Finally, there is patience during misfortune that consists in waiting until the misfortune passes, since nothing on the face of nature can last forever.[16]

It is said that patience walks hand in hand with intellect, each supporting the other. The more intellect one possesses, the more one may understand the meaning of patience and the essential logic behind it. Knowledge is the soul and patience the body; the foundation of both is intellect.

Moses asked Almighty God to let him know the way to gain His approbation. He heard in response, "You, the son of Omran, My pleasure with you is when you remain satisfied with My Destiny."[17] Moulana Shah Maghsoud has stated that for those who obey the powers of their intellect, destiny is nothing but the will of their being. Those powers of intellect consist in the understanding of the logic of the universe, and the Divine wisdom that underlies it. If there is such wisdom, the human being has definitely his own proper share of it, however imperfectly he might make use of it.

15. Ezeddin Mohammad Kashani, *Mesbahul Hedaye va Meftahol Kefaeh* (Teheran, 1325), p. 370.

16. Ezeddin Mohammad Kashani, pp. 380–81.

17. Abul Ghasem Ghoseiri, p. 297.

Imam Ali says, "You think of yourself as a small body, nay, a greater world is folded in you. You are the Clear Book in which every word sheds light upon a new secret." One who knows remains satisfied, and one who knows not keeps a counterfeit in the place of the original truth, and searches for the truth outside of his being.

Satisfaction with His destiny is the highest rank of reliance upon Him, since satisfaction comes from the heart, the center of life, the House of the Divine, the origin of cognition. Satisfaction is the peace of heart in knowing the wisdom of Being and the agreement of heart with whatever He approves of and chooses.[18] Zunnun [Dhu an-Nun], one of the great Sufis, says a true servant is one who remains the servant of God at all times, as God remains always one's God.

The Prophet Mohammad said, "If you do not see Him, yet you know that He sees you." That is the knowledge of the believer who is aware of God's intimate closeness. Conversely, one may not know the rules of Being, yet one has no choice but to measure one's gait according to them. The maker, the rule, the follower, and the enforcer are all the same: the eternal Being that is the Divine. The more advanced a being is in his understanding, the broader are the bounds of what he can learn and know. That is what reliance on God means. The heart of the abstinent is fortified because of reliance; the heart of the reliant is enriched through approval, and the heart of a Sufi flourishes because of contentment. Thus a Sufi does not look to hardship and comfort, but rather searches for the Giver of all as is his quest.

Rumi says:

> Job was patient for seven years,
> For all the misfortunes he had received.
> During all that time of suffering,
> He prayed and was thankful to God.
> One day he heard in a revelation:
> "I have given patience to every part of you.
> Do not look proudly at your patience.
> You see but your patience,
> See instead the Giver of patience." [19]

Hardship and ease, misfortune and good fortune are all the reflections of one another; they pass across the stage of life but for a while. They play

18. Abul Ghasem Ghoseiri, p. 298.

19. Jalaluddin Mohammad Molavi Rumi, *Masnavi*.

their requisite parts and then disappear. One who has the whole picture and knows the whole story remains steadfast in his intentions and manner. Transient reflections will not become the source of his being, and thus do not play the essential part in his life. He is patient in his quest for knowledge and remains strong until he achieves his goal.

A heart, as Hazrat Mir Ghotbeddin says, which is amused, busied, and impatient with notions of "more" and "less," is not a heart but a stomach.[20] In our impatience, how often should we reflect upon this truth?

20. Hazrat Mir Ghotbeddin Mohammad Angha, *Destination: Eternity*, trans. Nahid Angha (California: International Association of Sufism, 1987).

A CHILD OF THE MOMENT

AISHA GOUVERNEUR is a seventh-generation Kentuckian who from an early age sought to comprehend "the eternal verities, the principles that are behind all." She became interested in Vedanta and Hindu metaphysics as expounded by Shankara and Sri Ramana Maharshi. Enrolled at Sarah Lawrence College, she studied art history and world religions (with the exception of Islam, which was not then taught) under the tutelage of Joseph Campbell. After graduation, she went to New York to study filmmaking and then taught film at Dalton and Fordham University. In New York she met the Venezuelan film director Fyodor Gouverneur, and, as many did at the time, they and their friends plunged into various versions of Eastern philosophy and practice. Soon however, Fyodor found he had reached a dead end. A sudden epiphany led him to the study of Islam. Out of respect, Aisha also began to read, in particular, al-Ghazali, and she discovered with surprise that "Islam is true, too." As the two had from an early age both been deeply attracted to the sanctified state, and continue to be, most of their reading had focused on the exemplary lives and writings of the world's great saints.

Fyodor wrote a letter to Al-Azhar University in Cairo, offering to teach film in exchange for instruction in Islamic studies. Al-Azhar responded with the offer of a scholarship, which he accepted. He and Aisha married and immediately journeyed across the Atlantic on a Yugoslavian freighter. After visiting Morroco and its beautiful people and culture—even living with a Bedouin family in their tents who had come in from the desert to gather dates along the route to Timbuctou—they set out driving across the

❧ The selections by Aisha Gouverneur and the information in her biography are adapted from a talk she gave to university students in 1999. Printed by permission of Aisha Gouverneur.

Sahara and North Africa toward Cairo, "searching for spiritual guidance."

For a year Aisha and Faarid (Fyodor's Islamic name) journeyed across North Africa. Aisha tells how in Algeria she started seeing a "reflex generosity" that she didn't know existed in humankind. Repeatedly, people would quite naturally share with them the best that they had, even moving out of their own bedrooms and sleeping outside so that the then-pregnant Aisha and her husband might have the best room. In countless mosques, and in the faces of so many elderly people as well as the young, they discovered a pure wisdom and a gracious humanity—a truly civilized world they had had no way of anticipating.

Because Cairo was still being bombed during the final throes of the 1967 war, the couple paused in Libya, near the Egyptian border. Here in Beida, Aisha began Arabic "first grade," attempting to gain some familiarity with the language. Muslims from all parts of the world—from the Philippines to Nigeria—were studying there (the majority of Muslims are not of Arabic descent—only seventeen percent are of Arabic ethnicity). She and her husband became close friends with a Yugoslavian, Haris Silajdzic, who twenty-five years later would become prime minister of Bosnia. During the time of the Bosnian crisis, Aisha went to assist her old friend and his people. In 1993 she worked in Bosnian refugee camps. She finally saw that the place she could help most was in the educational realm. School supplies and textbooks were desperately needed, so she contacted school supply companies and raised funds to publish and ship quantities of needed books.

While still in Libya, during the reign of King Idris, their child was born and they named her Haajar—from the root word meaning "to emigrate." According to a saying of the Prophet Muhammad, "Whoever makes his or her emigration for God and his Prophets, his or her life is the getting of that. Whoever makes his going out in this world for the things of this world, that is what he or she gets and that is what colors his or her journey." As Aisha says, "We were *muhajjireen*, people emigrating from the world to the spirit."

Finally, they arrived in Cairo, and soon met several people of strong spiritual presence who became guiding lights for them during their stay there: Dr. Abdul Halim Mahmoud, the saintly director at the university, a Shadhili Sufi; the Sudanese Imam of the Azhar Mosque, Sheikh Salih al-Jafari, who at 110 years of age demonstrated to them what the essence of "kingship" really is, in the realm of the spirit; and the blind Shaikh Hafiz al-Tijani, who was the head of the Tijaniyya order, a very refined human "computer" with vast knowledge of the Qur'an and the sayings of the

Prophet Muhammad. Aisha notes that their dear friend Eva de Vitray-Meyerovitch[1] asked to be Sheikh Hafiz's disciple. Though he gave her his cloak in respect, he did not accept her as a student for fear he would give her more practices than she could manage and would hence feel anxiety; she later connected with an Algerian *shaikh*.

In Cairo, Aisha taught art at a girls' school, living quite simply on their meager budget while attending the university herself. During the next ten years spent in Cairo, their second child, Mustafa, was born, their knowledge of Arabic increased, they made the pilgrimage to Mecca twice, and deepened in their practice and faith. Aisha describes how amazing it was to live in a place with such a strong awareness of faith: "The Name of God is on everyone's tongue and mentioned in every other sentence, and all of life is organized around the times of prayer."

With unfolding work opportunities, after working with NBC, her husband was called to Saudi Arabia. At this time, Aisha and Faarid both placed themselves under the guidance of the Shadhili tradition. She describes this line of Sufism as more gnostic, concentrated directly on realization of the Name within one's own self, rather than devotional, following the path of *muhabbat*, or "love of the master." Aisha and Faarid then moved to Cambridge, England, where they then lived from 1979 to 1991. Together they founded and directed the Islamic Texts Society. Aisha is currently one of the codirectors of the newly established Book Foundation, which is working to create a new Qur'an-based curriculum for high school students, and she is also founder and director of Fons Vitae in the United States, which publishes English translations of many pivotal texts of Islam and Sufism, including the classical collection of biographies by as-Sulami, *Early Sufi Women*, recently translated by Rkia Cornell.[2] Aisha has a lifelong dedication to the spiritual dimension of life and imparting this through teaching and publishing. She says she would never refer to herself as a "Sufi," but as a *mutassawuf*, one who is "attempting" this state of being in the sense of aiming at true humility. *Bow down and draw near* is one of Aisha's favorite verses from the Qur'an, and this *ayat* has been inscribed on her gravestone, already prepared for that moment before us all, that comes all too soon—when we will regret not having become or been more who we truly are. . . .

1. See the Chapter "Toward the Heart," beginning on page 89.

2. See the "Early Sufi Women" section for some of these biographies.

Purifying the Heart

> The saint has no fear, because fear is the expectation either of some future calamity or of the eventual loss of some object of desire; whereas the saint is the "son of his time" (resides in the Eternal Present): he has no future from which he should fear anything and, as he has no fear, so he has no hope since hope is the expectation either of gaining an object of desire or of being relieved from a misfortune, and this belongs to the future; nor does he grieve, because grief arises from the rigor of time, and how should he feel grief who dwells in the Radiance of Satisfaction and the Garden of Concord?
>
> –AL-JUNAYD

In Sufism, as al-Junayd (ninth century) expresses it, the saint is he or she who has no anxiety for the future and no regrets for the past and dwells in the Divine Presence, *ibn waqt*, the "child of the moment." There is the possibility that one's ego might recede; that one might be so humble or be so empty that there is no time, there is only the eternal now. It is truly beautiful, a relief of infinite magnitude, when "you" are not there, but It is.

I had an experience which I feel was a great gift from God to me: I was paralyzed for a year . . . the kind of dependence which that sets up shows us (though we may think ourselves independent) how really dependent we are on God. Some years ago, mysteriously, I came down with what was later diagnosed as Guillane-Barré syndrome, and within the space of a few weeks suddenly found myself paralyzed and completely unable to move. When after some weeks of illness, I suddenly felt my body completely stiffen and solidify, I seemed to separate from my body and lift a distance above it. As I related in a *Parabola* article about that experience, I glanced down and saw my head on the pillow and thought, "This is remarkable—I've read about this kind of thing . . . 'I' am thinking and my brain is down there in my head! I must be dead." I considered what to do. At the moment of death in Islam, the person repeats the *shahada*,[3] "There is no divinity except God," in order to exit this life united with the Source and not caught in some peripheral thought. As I thought the phrase, *la ilaha il Allah*

3. *La ilaha il Allah*: there is no god but God, there is no reality but The Reality. This is the Muslim attestation of faith and the foundation of the Sufi principle of *Tawhid*, the Unity of all that is. For Muslims the completion of the statement is *Muhamamadan Rasulullah* (Muhammad is the Prophet of God.) (C.A.H.)

[There is no divinity except God], I noticed that I seemed to be pulled back into my body, towards my heart—as if by a thread of light. But then there I was, quite all right, but utterly rigid and still. The light of the moon comforted me as it passed through the leafless November branches, making patterns on the blankets. I thought, "Even at night the sun is there, even in darkness and death the Light and Life are present."[4]

As I lay there I thought about how much of a doer I had been; now things were different. I had always been known for my inexhaustible energy and activities. I could always, somehow, get to my feet and do one more thing; but now I would no longer be able to do anything. I thought about the people I most admired, people like Mother Teresa, and I realized that rather than what they did, what was important for me was what they were; the state of being which determined their movement was what actually inspires others. And so I set upon a plan of inward action: the best thing I could do for others would be to sanctify my soul.[5]

I came to accept my condition and to bear it patiently and with equanimity, but I did not love it; that was the key. Some months passed, and then while in Saudi Arabia, where my husband had taken me, hoping that the drier weather might be of benefit, I was invited to deliver an annual talk to a ladies' group. I was still paralyzed and couldn't imagine how I could prepare, but my friends said, "Just give us a topic, we'll do the research for you." I told them, "All right; what does Islam say about why *this* happens to someone, the 'Job story'?" And they came back with all the relative *hadith* and Qur'anic passages in Arabic, translated into English. These all said the same thing: "Illness is a great blessing, because it is an opportunity, if not complained about, to purify one's Being."

And they gave an example where the Prophet Muhammad, peace be upon him, was with a Bedouin, and the Bedouin had a terrible fever. And he said to the Bedouin, "This is a great blessing; it's given to purify." The Bedouin replied, "Oh no it's not; I'm just an old man. It's just a fever. It will probably kill me." And then Muhammad said, "Well, then that's what it is. It's as you see it."

And I realized, as I was giving this lecture, why Muslims always say, "All praise is due to God" whenever they are asked how they are and especially in adversity. I, too, realized that I was overwhelmedly blessed to be given "this," not a broken finger, but the full trial. And suddenly I loved

4. The latter half of this paragraph and the next are excerpted from "Even at Night the Sun Is There," *Parabola* 18, no. 1 ("Healing"), p. 61.

5. Ibid., p. 62.

my illness; I thought, "God thought I was up to this!" And when I loved it, it was like flowing with the Divine Will—my fingers started to move, and then, bit by bit, [the paralysis] came undone. So it showed me very clearly: love your trials, welcome them, really say *Alhamdulillah* [Praise be to God], Hallelujah, for every trial you are offered, because in them is the greatest benefit.

The spiritual guidance I received at this time was: "God doesn't give us what we deserve. None of us deserve the goodness we have received in this life. Do any of us deserve the blessings we have been given? Do any of us deserve the kinds of trials we have been provided? God doesn't give us what we deserve; God gives us exactly what our souls need to return to the Divine Presence with hearts purified." And suddenly I really understood for the first time how trials and blessings are the same thing. We have all been taught this; we all know that our heart should be equal in its reactions to what seems to be good or bad news. You know it, you've read it; but finally I "saw" it—that it is true. At heart, all religious guidance teaches us to trust the Lord, and when either joy or suffering arises, we should in both cases remain centered and steadfast, residing in our hearts unmoved, bearing silent witness—at one with and loving God's Will for us—and looking for the ways each event is a blessed opportunity for the practice of the true nobility we—without our distracted egos—are. Little by little we really can become increasingly equal of heart in both trials and joys; we can become "the child of the moment."

Essential Zhikr for a New Murid

One begins with the recitation of the *shahada*: *La ilaha il Allah*, "there is no divinity except the Divinity"—to be repeated in the morning, in the middle of the day, and at night. As one begins, one recites:

> And what you send ahead for your souls from the good—
> you will find that with God after death and that is the greatest of rewards.
> [See Surah al-Baqara 2:110.]

First one humbly repeats *Astaughfirullah* (May God forgive me) ninety-nine times. This is the emptying of your "self"—the dying to self. This is done sincerely in the spirit of true *tawba*, the turning around again towards God, real repentance.

Then one repeats *Alahumma Salli ala Sayyidina Muhammad* (prayers for Muhammad). When once one is emptied, one can be filled with the "logos" and can regain one's primordial nature, aiming to become the perfected or completed soul [*insan al-kamil*].

This is followed by the repetition of *La ilaha il Allah*. Having been purified, you then return to the One—you are as a drop of light returning to the ocean of light, the Oneness of Being.

This is followed by a recitation of the Surah, or chapter, of Unity:

Say that God is One . . .
Qul Huwallahu Ahad . . .

—Surah Ihklas 112

This whole process is really practicing for your own death in your own life. What you are hoping is that throughout your life, you do empty, you do reform, and you are acceptable directly at the end for Divine Union without being caught in "Oh, I wish I hadn't . . ." or whatever the recriminations of the hellish conscience must be. It is only later, after much work with this *wird*[6]—reciting it in the morning and the evening and during the day—that one might also begin to recite the name Allah. The name Allah is very powerful. It encompasses all the other ninety-nine names or "attributes." The ninety-nine names combine in particular proportions to create all of the manifestations of the created universe. "Allah" includes them all, so when one says "Allah," one literally "says" the manifested world.

It is as if your consciousness is a pool with little waves on it which are all your thoughts and all the phenomena of your mind. And, for example, should that pool reflect a tree, that tree image would be all broken up: when I look out the window, looking through myself, I'm not really seeing clearly that tree; I'm seeing it through all the things that are my particularized ego. By the rhythmic repetition of a Divine Name—it's not like saying "chair," the name contains something of the Named—by placing that into your heart, the heart finally cannot resist the rhythmic pounding of something containing some aspects of the Divinity. In the end, the pool has to still and can then perfectly reflect the Divine. And what is really going on in the repetition of a Name is the hope of that stillness—Being.

6. A particular pattern or litany of prayer. Each Sufi lineage may have its own specific pattern of prayer, though the pattern mentioned here is a general pattern that is in common usgage. (C.A.H.)

Bead by bead one recites, fingering the rosary with each recitation. The word "bead" derives from the Anglo-Saxon verb ***bidden***, meaning "to pray" or "to count," and from the Sanskrit ***buddh***—to realize that one's true nature is already enlightened. The word *wird* comes from the root word *warada*, meaning "to remember." It also has root resonance with the word *ward*, which means "rose"—hence the "rosary,"[7] prayer beads, (or *tesbih*), which are an assistance to remembrance. Even the businessmen you see fingering beads while at work are using this tool for remembrance, to assist them in waking up from the little daydreams of their ephemeral lives. When the mind strays, prayer beads help to bring one back.

Then one also must take days of regular retreat, and if you can, meet regularly with others on the path, other *fuqara*. *Faqir* comes from the root *fqr*; meaning "empty"; it can mean "a poor person," too. *Fuqara* are the collective group. The reason *faqr* is what you want—that inner emptiness—is because you cannot receive anything if you are already full of "yourself." I think the verse in the Bible, "Only the poor, the meek, shall inherit the earth," doesn't refer to material poverty but to inner emptiness, to the capacity for receiving that state of being. So you get together with others regularly, and you may share a small meal together, and you pray and recite the *wird* together.

In the actual meditations that you do on your own every day, you take different divine qualities, or names, to "wear." A saying of the Prophet recommends, "Clothe yourself with the excellent qualities of God most High. . . . God has nine and ninety virtues: whosoever puts on one of them will surely enter the Garden (Paradise)." The great Sufi Master al-Ghazzali (d. 1111) said, "The creature's (human being's) portion respecting this Name ought to be *al-ta' allah* [becoming Godlike, deification, divinization, 'putting on God']." One of the major things we have to do is change our habits; we have poor reflex habits. For example when you are in the Middle East, and you come to someone's home, they immediately give you their best to eat. It doesn't occur to them to think, "Shall I give them the chocolate chip cookies I have just made, or save those for myself later?" To give whatever is their best is their first thought, whereas we may think for a while and get around to that. How do you get to "reflex generosity," "reflex detachment," in your life? Well, one way is to practice it, so in these meditations each day, you take, let's say, "detachment," let's say on Monday. And you

7. The pearl necklace is really the rosary of the emperor desacralized into use as an ornamental necklace. Aisha Gouverneur has produced a beautiful video documentary, *Beads of Faith* (published by Fons Vitae), about the use of prayer beads in many spiritual traditions. (C.A.H.)

practice remembrance, assuming the attitude of detachment, and then as you go out in the day, every bad thing that happens to you, you can see is the opposite of that: "Oh, it's because I really cared; it's because I hung on to this." Then you can take the correct action.

You know how many times in our life we know what we have to do, but we just don't have the will to do it—like get up and say a prayer—but then when you realize that the ego has won over the conscience, you have to just step over it and do it anyway. It's practicing: "Doing it anyway." Then there is inner contentment—which is the practicing of contentment with what you have been given, loving your trials, everything like that. That's very centripetal. It's like light pouring back in, and then you have to practice the attitude of complete generosity, which is like light going back out. You have to practice discernment, union, . . . those come later on in the Way. So that by practicing those concentratedly, assuming that attitude, and then seeing how its opposite is what breaks it during the day, slowly over a period of time, things start to become more "reflex." This is the idea behind all religions—practice or imitate the virtues initially by following commandments—then one day you discover more and more these qualities of Being have become second nature, or "reflex"—i.e., who you are.

What is Beauty? Beauty is present when we wake up to what's really there—the personal God—the All-Merciful, the All-Beautiful. . . . When I look back over the past twenty, thirty years, it's like a snap of the fingers. You think you have a whole life, but in mind-time, you have a couple of seconds. And it's going faster as we move towards death; it's just moments. So we are wasting our time if we don't suddenly decide right this second to be *bodhisattvas*.[8] From this moment, act from the higher self: be utterly compassionate, be utterly generous, be "right Here." We are all wasting our precious human state on just "waste of time" distractions. You can't desire this state, because that is the grasping of the ego. The only thing to do is to recede and be humble or be "empty" and be awake in the Eternal Now. There is no "time," there is only the Eternal Now. Although it was Sufism that brought me to Islam (for my soul from early teenage years yearned for a way to abide in the Deathless state of Peace-Union with God), it is not as though a person cannot reach the Blessed state through normative religion. Many Muslims are clearly illumined by their submission, trust, and love of God. I have met a Muslim woman saint who never heard of Sufism but served selflessly her family and community. But grow-

8. In Buddhism, *bodhisattvas* are those who have vowed to help others to attain enlightenment before seeking it for themselves. (C.A.H.)

ing up in the West, there was no real support and example of community imbued with faith and by prayer. My heart sought specific guidance and a method. When I read al-Ghazali's spiritual autobiography, I found my deepest concerns articulated and a way made clear.

The state which one most naturally seeks is that emptiness where there is no god but God—that emptiness is none other than humility. In order for the ocean to pour in, one must go below sea level. And this universal virtue of true humility would come about gradually were a person to follow what his or her faith prescribes regarding prayer, fasting, pilgrimage, and so on, which are all designed to lead one "home." And that "home" is a place we never leave, but forget and neglect. One need only be one's essential theomorphic essence, which has been variously described as "made in the image and likeness of God" (in Judaism and Christianity), the *fitra* or pure primordial nature (in Islam), the Atman and the Buddha nature (in Hinduism and Buddhism, respectively). And I find that what I love in others is that emptiness becomes God-filled—I don't care about what they do—but what they are as presences. That is all that one can really love—that pure luminous being. The supreme Mercy on the part of each one of us is to increase in emptiness for the sake of those around us—for that generosity of spirit improves the world and those around us are nourished. I find that I am really nothing. The peace of presence that I am beneath my personal package of ego and its agenda is what I am and where true joy and happiness dwell. All else is separative, distancing one from the Good, the True, and the Beautiful. We must polish the mirrors of our souls of the rust that hinders our shining and the reflection of the Divine. As the eleventh-century Sufi saint Ibn Ata'allah al Iskandari said, "Both striving and remissness are signs of the blurring of the intellect." May we each become a "child of this moment."

A DAUGHTER OF FIRE

IRINA TWEEDIE (1907–1999) was born in Russia and educated in Vienna and Paris. Following World War II, after the death of her first husband, she married an English naval officer, whose death in 1954 led her to embark on a spiritual quest. After studying the teachings of Theosophy, she was drawn to travel to India, where she met Bhai Sahib, a Naqshbandi[1] Sufi master. He told her to keep a diary of her experiences as his student. This diary became the book *Daughter of Fire* (which was first published in an abridged version as *Chasm of Fire*). After her teacher's death in 1966, she returned to England and began the transmission of the teachings of his lineage to Westerners. For many years she lectured throughout Europe and the United States. The following selection is a transcript of a conversation with Mrs. Tweedie in London in 1983.

Mrs. Tweedie's teacher, Bhai Sahib, focused on the teaching means of *sohbet* (spiritual conversation),[2] as well as silent meditation and zhikr. Mrs. Tweedie refers to her "Guru's" method of training as an ancient yogic tradition—in his language, spiritual vocabulary, and context, her teacher provided a bridge between his Naqshbandi Sufi lineage and Hindu culture.[3] In addition, she also included the Naqshbandi method of spiritual dreamwork in her teaching.

1. Baha' ad-Din Naqshband, the founder of the Naqshbandi order, was born near Bukhara in 1318 C.E. Many Naqshbandi branches of Sufism stem from the main Naqshbandi line, which formed around the inspiration of his being and teaching in Central Asia. Naqshbandi Sufis are known for the practice of silent rather than audible zhikr. As Baha' al-Din Naqshband stated, "A special awareness arose in me when I began to practice silent zhikr. That was the secret I sought." Hasan Shushud, *Masters of Wisdom of Central Asia* (Ellingstring, England: Coombe Springs Press, 1983), p. 38. This practice of silent zhikr is known to have derived from the practice of the Prophet Muhammad together with Abu Bakr when they were seeking refuge in a cave outside Mecca at the time of the Hijra.

2. For further exploration of the subject of *sohbet*, see Frances Trix, *Spiritual Discourse: Learning with an Islamic Master* (Philadelphia: University of Pennsylvania Press, 1993).

3. See the chapter on Jahanara, beginning on page 128.

Mrs. Tweedie retired from teaching publicly in 1992. Her work is being continued through the Golden Sufi Center in Inverness, California, and the work of her successor, Llewellyn Vaughan-Lee. Irina Tweedie died in London in August of 1999.

Yearning for Truth

IRINA TWEEDIE: It is difficult to begin without a question.

STUDENT: Yes, there is one question I would like to ask. Last time when I came here for the first time I did not know anything about you, and I didn't know anything about the group and I hardly knew anything about Sufism. So since I left you last week and came back today, I had the chance to read your book, *The Chasm of Fire*. Of course when reading your book many, many questions are answered. But for the people who have not had the chance to read your book, I would just like to ask some questions. You were Russian born and were brought up in different countries. You went to school in Vienna, and then you lived in England. You had been in England for quite some while, and married an Englishman. How did it happen that you traveled to India, and how did you meet your teacher? And what happened afterwards, how did you raise up this group?

MRS. TWEEDIE: You see, usually in life you start to think about spiritual things when something very dramatic and very tremendous has happened to you. My husband died. It was my second husband. Four years after the death of my first husband, I married my second husband, Charles, who was in the navy. It was a very happy marriage. When he died, I wanted to die. I didn't want to live—not to commit suicide, that would be nonsense—just to sit on a stone and die. I remember it was thirteen days after he died, after his funeral; I had been sitting at home not knowing what to do, thinking, "in this chair he was sitting the last time," and at the table, "it was the last place where he was sitting." Then I thought, "Who doesn't know that Charles is dead?" My friends knew; most of them had come to the funeral. Then I thought, "Cecile." I picked up the phone and called Cecile. It was a Saturday. Cecile is never at home on a Saturday. But that Saturday she picked up the phone and answered.

❧ This selection is excerpted from the transcript of an interview with Irina Tweedie, with permission from the Golden Sufi Center, Inverness, California.

I said, "Cecile, Charles died." She said, "I'm coming."

I was not washed. The flat was in disorder. I panicked. I said, "Please, don't come!"

I didn't know whether to take a bath first or clean the flat, I was in such a state, in a psychologically absolutely terrible state. But she lived very near, so I decided to quickly have a bath, it would be the best thing. So, she came in; she looked around, and she said, "I am taking you to a library." And she took me to a private library. It was actually the library of the Theosophical Society. She had to exchange a book. I saw those books, thousands of books. I was brought up in academic circles, so I thought, "Perhaps if I read I will be able to live again. Perhaps I can study, do something." And she gave me a book, *Life after Death*. And that's how it all began.

I did not know anything about reincarnation, or karma, or about the spiritual things which are very important to us now and which we all believe. I began to read. I became a member of the Theosophical Society. Then I decided to go to India because one branch of the Theosophical Society was in India. But somehow that didn't satisfy me. You see, there was this beautiful Theosophical compound—there were Americans and New Zealanders and English people and Germans, all Europeans, but it was not India. I wanted to see India. Because outside the compound I saw children with tummies swollen from hunger. I saw mangy dogs dying in the streets. I saw a calf gasping for breath. And I asked, "What is that?" And they said, "He is dying a natural death." I asked, "Why is no one looking after him?" They said, "Well, we need milk, so the calf is taken away from the cow and left there to die; it's quite a natural death—it's all right." Because human beings need milk—this was the explanation given to me.

Well, I felt this wasn't good enough. So I began to travel. I had money—my husband left me enough to live quite comfortably—it would have been uncomfortable now due to inflation. I asked a friend, "Where can I spend the rainy season where I can be quiet, where I can meditate, and I want to be near the mountains." I wanted to go to the Himalayas. So a friend gave me an address of a certain Abadmand. It was five miles as the crow flies from Nepal. There I stayed for several months with Indian friends. I lived actually with them—first I had a villa, but then everything was robbed, and those Indian friends decided it would be much better if I came and stayed with them, which I did. And this Indian friend told me about a certain Miss Lillian—a very interesting person. She sleeps in ancient temples, she loves rats; all her underwear was stolen by the Arabs—so, it was this sort of life. And I was interested in meeting this Lillian, but she wasn't there. After staying with this Indian family, I decided to travel to Kashmir.

While I was in Kashmir I received a letter, from the lady where I had stayed, saying, "Lillian is now in Kashmir." And she gave me her address.

I wrote to her, but there was no answer. I wanted to go to Amernath Yatra, which is the pilgrimage to Amernat. It's a Shiva temple at 14,000 feet, and there is a natural phenomenon there. There is a stalagmite which increases and decreases with the moon. So I went on this Amernath Yatra pilgrimage—it is the full moon in August. Of course I didn't have time for anybody else, so I just went there.

And while we were traveling on horses, Lillian was telling me about her guru. Lillian was with me at that time. One day we were caught in a snowstorm. She was riding in front of me and I was in the back. "Please don't speak to me," she said, "I am going into *samadhi* and will contact my guru, and if we are in danger we will be led to safety." Well, I was very much impressed by that. But it wasn't necessary; the snowstorm abated and everything was all right. This Lillian gave me the address of my teacher.

I remained another summer in Kashmir, she went back to Srinagar, the capital. I traveled in the forest, went to see the glaciers, traveled by horseback; in other words, I had a wonderful time. And then she gave me the address of the teacher. In the tent—I had actually a very elegant tent with a table, and I was sitting, I remember, and she was standing near me—she said, "I have to remain in Kashmir because I have to go to a religious congress. But I will give you the address of my teacher." I did not know he was going to be my teacher, as well, later on. Then she began to write it down. And you know, when she was writing it down, I became terrified. I said, "Listen. I don't want to know his name." It was like a kind of terror in my heart. I felt he must be without a name and without a face. Now you see, there must have been something in me which knew unconsciously, because the ancient tradition is that the teacher must be without name and without face. She smiled and she said, "Why don't you want to know his name?" "Well, I just don't want to, I am terrified." She smiled and said, "That is a sign." Actually, this was a sign that he was going to be my guru, but I did not know that at the time. That was it. So she wrote only, "Mahatma," the town of Kanpur, the street, the house number and that was all. And then after that I went to Amritsar to see the Golden Temple.

Ah, a very interesting incident happened, which again is a point on the road. A young tourist guide, whom the tourist office assigned, said, "I showed you the Golden Temple, now tomorrow I am going to show you a temple dedicated to the twelve martyrs of the Sikh religion. We will go there in the morning;" which we did. People sit on a *tari*, a *tari* is a carpet like here, and people just sit cross-legged on the *tari*, and the one who was acting as a priest was reading from a great book called *Granth Sahib*. And the last paragraph would be written on the blackboard in Punjabi to meditate upon for the believers during the day. And the sentence that day went like this: "To thee to whom I am going, I am going to touch thy feet, and I am going to kiss thy hands, for thou wilt take me to God." You, know there are moments in life when one feels the finger of destiny touching you. I became terrified. I said to myself, "I don't want to know God, good heavens, no."

I decided to go to Ceylon, and then go back to England, and go to work in the library. I was a librarian by profession. But, of course, I did not go; I ran. The very same day I said to the tourist guide, "It is far too hot," which was true. I took the first train to Delhi in the morning. I arrived in Delhi, and asked, "When is the next train to Kanpur?" "In five minutes; quickly." And I just boarded, and the train started.

When I arrived in Kanpur, it was like coming home. I don't know if we left it in the book [*Chasm of Fire*], but certainly it was in the manuscript. I remember the rickshaw going through the street and my heart was singing, and I was saying to myself, "You are crazy! It's just an ordinary Indian town, and here you are so happy, you are coming home." My heart was beating "You are coming home, you are coming home." I did not know why.

Then I went to the place Lillian had said was reserved for me by a certain Mrs. Ghose. Mrs. Ghose said she had never received the letter, and that's how she took me to Pushpa, and that's how the book begins. Passing the street, she said, "Would you like to meet Miss Lillian's guru?" I said, "No, no!" I was hot and sweaty. All I wanted was a cup of tea and a cold bath. It was terribly hot. The last thing I wanted was to meet an important person like a guru. But she was already going inside the villa, a low bungalow, and three men came out. One was very tall, looking like a prophet. It was Munshiji. Then another one slightly less tall—but Bhai Sahib, the guru, was still quite tall, over six feet tall—and then someone much smaller—that was Pandaji, as I knew later. I came down from the rickshaw and something in me stood to attention. It wasn't I. Something in me just stood to attention. I was in the presence of a very great being. And that's how the book begins.

Then things began to happen—I don't need to speak about it, people could read it; I don't like to bore anybody or be repetitious. But what is not in the book is that after his death I had to be alone. Actually, after his death something tremendous happened. It was like—it is impossible to express in words—but every leaf of the tree was an open book. Every child, every dog—the stone-throwing children, the yapping dogs, the fleas and the flies and the sky—all was one. And I was a part of That, being just at the right moment at the right time to be, in the right place, just there. (And everything was luminous and everything was magnificent. And I couldn't bear it, because I thought I was going crazy. A friend of Guruji Bhai Sahib who is now dead, Professor Batnagar, told me to go to a place called Kausani in Almora district. It was a Gandhi ashram. And I stayed in the room opposite the room where Gandhiji had written his Anashakti Yoga, the yoga of selfless action. It was a magnificent place—240 miles of the Himalayas, the whole horizon full of mountains. I remember a Canadian who came there and said, "Gee, I never imagined there could be so many mountains and they could be so big!" (every one over 24,000 feet, by the way).

So there I stayed. And you know when Bhai Sahib—he liked to be called "Bhai Sahib," which means elder brother; he didn't like to be called "guru"—so when Bhai Sahib died I thought he'd betrayed me. I had to give up everything I had. I didn't have even a hundred pounds in the bank. And he would do it in that way: he would say, "Oh, Pandaji has to repair his roof. His wife is in the Delhi hospital, she has TB, and before the rainy period he needs 300 rupees. So, make a postal order and send the money!"

And all my money, thousands of pounds, went like that. So nothing remained. You know, it is difficult to believe, but I was so fascinated that I was not even afraid. I was afraid a little, because those were my savings for my old age, and of my husband. As I said, my husband left me very well off. And nothing was left. It all flowed through his slender fingers. It was too fascinating for words. Thousands and thousands of [pounds]! Given away to so and so whose children have died, etc., just like that.

And I remember when Hanka came with me, she's H. in the book, he did the same with her. He said, "Send so much to Delhi, to this person, or so much to Jaipur." So he took everything away, and I had nothing. So when he died, I thought, "To return to the West—at my age! (I was nearly sixty then). I can't find a job at this age; what will I do?" He had just died away, leaving me nothing.

But the interesting part was that just three weeks before he died, speaking of spiritual life, he said: "Spiritual training? Nonsense! That was only a preparation!" You see, before the ego goes completely, we cannot even begin to look towards the spiritual path. I didn't know that. I remembered this sentence; I was terribly angry. He didn't "begin," my goodness me; I went through all this, but apparently, he says, it wasn't even spiritual life begun!

But in the Himalayas, I don't remember, it must have been an entry in September or October, where I mentioned in my journal very discreetly, with one sentence only, the fact that I could contact my teacher in meditation. That was an experience never to be forgotten. He had no human shape any more; he was an energy, a power. But there was duality. I knew there was a teacher and me. And the whole of me was just like that. It was too tremendous for words. And from then on the training began. Only now I know it after twenty-three years. But at the beginning there was duality, there was the teacher and there was me. It was a wonderfully comfortable situation, like a daddy whom you can ask, and the answer is given. Mind you, I could never ask for myself. This is the law. But I could ask for others. I paid with my self for it. I paid the price, not the money. He said, "To give up possessions is easy; to give up your self, in utter surrender, that is something!"

So I paid the price. I have to ask for any one of you; I can ask, and if it is permitted it will be given. Now, why "permitted"? There is such a thing as karma. He said one day, "We can heal everything, but we cannot heal everybody." Karma permitting, you see; the great saint knows it. So, I just needed to ask; I didn't need any wisdom, I just ask. And if karma permitted, things would happen, and everybody present here knows that miracles happen in this group all the time. But, as I just mentioned, there was duality at the beginning. Later on, and I must confess I didn't notice it; gradually, very gradually, and this is very difficult to put in words, there was no duality, it just was. When help was needed, something happened and my mind accepted it without rebellion, knowing very well that it was not my mind, it was not "Tweedie," it was something entirely different, so I cannot be proud of it.

But there was no duality. You see, I can only explain it technically like that, like the way I read it in the Theosophical books. At one time of the training, the *atma*, or the higher self, of the disciple is united with the higher self of the teacher. Only one remains, there is no duality. And this is the access to the teacher. In the Theosophical books it is said that, I think Madame Blavatsky mentioned it, that part of her remained somewhere with her teacher. I knew exactly how it happened—she used the words: "What you see in front of you is only an illusion, only a shell. The best part of me remains with the teacher." I am quoting now Madame Blavatsky. How it happens, in my case I do not know. I don't think it's quite like that. But something always remains there, otherwise the connection is not possible. I think that's how there is no duality. This is the best thing I can say. It is very puzzling, but it is very true. And the presence of our teacher is tremendously evident here. Hanka told me several years ago, "Whatever happens in this group, I will never be astonished." Because miracles constantly happen and happen and happen—miracle city, with the hearts of people.

Another thing, we Sufis, we do not work on the physical plane. We work from the level of the soul. And sometimes the physical body can be a little bit neglected. You see, all the other lines of yoga, they work from the physical body into the inner planes. We work from the inner plane downwards; I say downwards, but it is neither downwards nor upwards, of course, this is nonsense. I say downwards to say "earthly plane," because somehow we are conditioned to think that spirituality is heaven, and this is the earth, but of course everything is absolutely interpenetrating—the Spirit and matter, utterly interpenetrating. It is very beautifully described in the book of Yoga Vashista, one of the great scriptures of Hinduism.

I think you can ask something now. It seems to me I am empty. Ask again.

STUDENT: You say that your Guruji is present here. It is said in the scriptures that the outer guru leads you to the inner guru. So each person who comes here will find a way to the inner guru?

MRS. TWEEDIE: Yes. It's all individual in the path of the soul; we all are disciples of God.

STUDENT: We don't necessarily have to have an outer guru to be put on the spiritual path?

MRS. TWEEDIE: No, but it is useful to have someone who is just one step ahead of you, because as this person goes ahead further, you also proceed. Great gurus are not necessary, only someone who knows a little more than you. It works exactly like on the physical plane. There will be teachers of kindergarten, there will be university teachers. You know, it doesn't work to go to India or anywhere else in search for the guru, because the teacher has to find you. Guruji told me that he dreamt of me many years ago. Not only of me, of course, but everybody else who came to him, but because he was talking to me he mentioned me. He said, "You should have come long ago. I don't understand why you didn't." Well, my destiny was like that. He, of course, understood why I didn't; he only said that for the sake of saying it. I had my karma which I had to pay off, that was all.

STUDENT: He also mentioned to you, which was in the book, that we can make it within one lifetime. What is it he said to you?

MRS. TWEEDIE: Yes. We can realize the Truth in one lifetime. "If one is not too dense and not too stupid," he said, "and not too lazy, you can realize the Truth within ten years. And," he said, "if you don't realize It, I come at the moment of death and I fetch the soul." Now that, I think, is a covenant of a very great being. Now you will say, "How is it possible to realize in one life when Buddha needed several hundred lives to realize it?" Now, there is a very simple explanation. Great Truths can only be expressed in absolute paradoxes. The simplicity in it is that you are attracted to this path if it is your last life. Otherwise you wouldn't be attracted. If you are attracted to this path, it is your last life, and you can achieve it in ten years' time.

STUDENT: We would have to have a certain discipline which would be to meditate regularly and to live in selfless love in the outside world?

MRS. TWEEDIE: Yes, there is a silent meditation; we are called the "Silent Sufis." We meditate silently without any props like dancing or singing or anything—just silent meditation. When I receive instructions, people get *mantras* or *zhikr*, *zhikr* and *mantra* are the same thing, one is Persian, the other is Sanskrit. And really, that's all. If we meditate sincerely and completely, the meditation which we practice is like a yeast: everything which is dark in the human being will come up to the surface. Everybody has trouble the first two years, absolutely everybody. Because all the darkness which is in every human being will come up, and will be scooped up like dirty foam from water—from anything—even when you cook a soup you have to scoop off what comes up. This is a very strange meditation: apparently we are sitting silently and trying to control the mind. But everybody has difficulties. There will be doubts. There will be jealousy, terrible jealousies, terrible doubts. People are very often against me. You have no idea how many things people have told me, how rude people can be to me, but it doesn't matter, I understand. If one reads my book . . . how rude I was to my teacher! With our Western minds there are certain things we just cannot accept. We are brought up on the mental level. Especially if we are brought up in academic circles, it is quite difficult.

STUDENT: It seems we have to forget everything which we've learned. And of course something which I've learned has been that my own reality—I want to keep it, I don't want to give it up.

MRS. TWEEDIE: Very true. How does it go, the Chinese proverb? "Before you begin meditation you must forget what meditation is."

STUDENT: In India when you go to ashrams and when you meet teachers, very often they are talking about the technical process of Realization that is when kundalini is awakened and when kundalini is working through the different chakras,[4] which starts in the lowest chakra moving upwards to the Taj chakra.[5] But now, reading your book, I find that we should concentrate on the heart, the heart chakra is the one from which we can start and each and every other chakra will then be worked upon, will be opened, when the time is ready for it to be worked on.

MRS. TWEEDIE: Yes, this is this method. There are different methods. This is this particular method of yoga. There are other yogas just as effective as this one.

STUDENT: Will the student be initiated?

MRS. TWEEDIE: No.

STUDENT: Or simply come and be?

MRS. TWEEDIE: If you are initiated, how will you be nothing? One day, there was quite an interesting incident. One of the disciples, Jagan Nathji, he was very proud that day; he came to me, "You know, Bhai Sahib initiated me and I became his disciple." I said, "Yes." He said, "I brought a coconut, some *prasad* (offering), and now I became his disciple. Why don't you ask to become his disciple?" I replied, "I don't feel I need it, he treats me like a disciple. I don't see why I should."

So the next time when Guruji spoke to me—this is the Indian tradition, you mustn't address the teacher unless he addresses you first. So one day he talked to me about something, and I told him, "Bhai Sahib, Pandaji told me etc. etc. etc. But I feel like I shouldn't ask to become a disciple because I feel you treat me like a disciple." He said, "Never ask me, my dear. If you become a disciple, how will you learn to be nothing?"

Now there is a great esoteric truth in that. We work entirely with the divine power, that's why Sufis in this line of yoga are exceedingly powerful. There are two ways of working: you can work with yogic power which achieves everything through your own volition. You practice and you become—the result is the same. You can achieve it by yogic power or by divine power. By divine power you do nothing, except you surrender completely. And you must keep yourself surrendered completely and utterly which I can assure you is a full time job, because the little ego is always lurking just behind the next corner. It's very difficult. We have to become nothing before life, before people, above all before the Beloved. We call this Infinite Power, "the Beloved"—neither judge, nor creator, nor friend, but "the Beloved"—the most intimate relationship of our heart. That's

4. The subtle energy centers of the body. (C.A.H.)

5. The subtle energy center at the top (crown) of the head. (C.A.H.)

why I think this particular line of yoga is very powerful and very effective. But we must keep ourselves completely surrendered.

STUDENT: But this again is very, very difficult.

MRS. TWEEDIE: Here again, the terrible paradox. Complete surrender, complete nothingness, "yes" to everything. This is the greatest power. I find this path is especially difficult for men, especially for the Western man because of the education, you know, the competition: "I am better than thou" in sport, in everything. For women somehow it is easier. Guruji explains one place in the book, how a woman can reach Reality just by being a woman. So I'm very glad, and I said, "Oh, really, wonderful!" It's not like that. It is just as difficult for everybody. To men I give many practices, women need only one practice: the detachment from worldly things. Because we by our very nature are attached to comfort, to children; because a woman has to bear children, she needs security. Women are attached to security. If a woman is prepared to give up security . . . because spiritual life is utmost insecurity, no-man's-land, it's like walking on water, walking on air, you have nothing under your feet. It's a chasm of fire. Actually, the title "Chasm of Fire" is from Gregory of Nisa, the Christian mystic, a contemporary of St. Augustine. He said, "The path of love is like a bridge of hair across the chasm of fire." Of hair, you know. You walk on it; it falls, you fall into the fire . . . very insecure indeed.

STUDENT: Especially since we still have the idea of time. We think time is present, time is past, time is future and most of the time when we are in our world we are out of the now, we are either in the past or in the future. This is one of the difficult steps: to renounce the past, to renounce the future in a certain way, to be in the here and now, to really live in the moment, and I think we all have our difficulties with that.

MRS. TWEEDIE: You say it very beautifully. It's exactly like that. We have great difficulty with it.

STUDENT: We overcome these difficulties by calming our mind, by stilling our mind?

MRS. TWEEDIE: Yes. Only by stilling completely, by transcending the thinking faculty of the mind, can we reach into the different space where spiritual experiences are possible. And this is done entirely through meditation. It takes lifetimes.

Someone sent me a telex, "Read your book. Arrive in three days." Well, my publisher forwarded the letter. I answered of course with my full address. She wrote to me in English; I answered in German. I said, "What! Instant illumination? Why was the telex necessary? It is a lifetime's job, my dear. You are welcome to come, but it won't happen tomorrow nor within three days and perhaps not even in thirty years." She didn't come, by the way. Poor darling.

STUDENT: But of course it does help to come here. I personally feel the shakti very strongly, and also the week that I have not been here, when I have been traveling, I felt the instant link between the lineage and myself. Even as I was to prepare for this talk, I found I couldn't write things down because I either fell asleep or my mind went still. To me it is very interesting to find these things happening, because when there is a person who has a name and one thinks, "Oh, I must do this because I want to do something good for other people, give them a good treat in presenting a person like you, and saying, ah, look, she is a beautiful person. I must do it very intellectually, very nicely, just so, to present her," and then I find I can't do it.

MRS. TWEEDIE: And that is what we call the yo-yo syndrome! Which happens on every level. "Wonderful meditation," then a groan, or "tremendous nearness to the Beloved." You see, spiritual life is exactly like everything in nature. It's subject to the law of nature. There is a tide like the tide in the sea, like the day and night. There is tremendous nearness to the Beloved, and the soul is happy, and we are walking on clouds, and then suddenly there is nothing there. You are suspended naked over a chasm or an abyss, you can't pray and God doesn't exist and everything is cold and everything is horrible. This is another aspect of the yo-yo syndrome. And we have it on every level, you know. This is the path of the mystics. And people have wonderful experiences. Great visions. Great moments of oneness. But, we have to work hard for it through meditation. But outwardly it seems there is very little discipline.

STUDENT: I have noticed that in ashrams everyone is comporting him- or herself in the best way—we have instructions to sit with erect spine, that it's good for kundalini going up and down, etc.—whereas here people are just lying around, moving, and sitting; most don't sit in any yogic posture. So it seems that sitting very straight and beautifully is really not needed.

MRS. TWEEDIE: No. Nothing is needed except the desire for truth. If you want the truth as a drowning man wants air, you will realize it in a split second. That's all.

STUDENT: I want to ask you, how do you give instructions for meditation? What do you say? Since you say it's a still meditation, there's no mantra . . .

MRS. TWEEDIE: Yes, it's a good question. We have to sit or lie down or recline or sit cross-legged as we like, provided the physical body is completely comfortable and will not disturb us. After we are completely relaxed, we fill our hearts with love. Best of all is if we can think of the Great Beloved, God. But that is a very abstract concept and for the beginner it is rather difficult. So I say, think of someone whom you deeply and absolutely love. Then concentrate on this person and fill your heart with a rich, warm feeling of love.

While you are doing that, your mind is occupied with doing that and you are all right. But once you just sit there still feeling love in your heart, the mind will begin to work. "Oh, I forgot to buy potatoes! Oh, I have to bring my suit to the dry cleaners," and so forth. Now suppose you get hold of this thought and drown it within the feeling of love in the heart. And there must be nothing here. I usually give people a little help: imagine a blank television screen, just in front of your closed eyes there is an empty white television screen. And imagine every thought appears on the television. Get hold of it, drown it in love, and the television screen is empty. And go on doing it. It's a spiritual exercise and also an exercise in willpower. It is one of the methods of seeing the light. I don't say the method; there is no such thing as the royal road to God. It's just one of the very effective ways to reach Reality. That's all. And it definitely works.

STUDENT: Another question. How can we help other people?

MRS. TWEEDIE: By being ourselves. By sweeping in front of our doorstep. "Improve thyself, and thou wilt improve the world." No good to speak and criticize and try to improve the world that way because we can do nothing that way. But if I am good and you are good, and everybody else, there will be no wars, if we live like Jesus told us to live. He was the greatest guru; Guruji used to quote him all the time. You know, I was a very bad Christian. I hope I am a much better Christian now than I was, after being with a yogi who had nothing to do with Christianity. Just that—Be yourself.

STUDENT: Jesus, he and his disciples, they were always healing. Is that something that happens on this path, too?

MRS. TWEEDIE: Guruji used to say, "We can heal everything, but we cannot heal everybody." Karma comes in there, you see. So, the healing is done in a different way. What is a disease? You are ill at ease. You must be aligned with your inner vehicle, everything must be aligned; then you will be very healthy. This is a fact, one's health improves when you come to this path, incredibly so. But we are not healers as such. I cannot heal you if you are ill. But I can create the situation in which you can heal yourself. That I can do. I can put a spark in your heart that makes such inspiration, such a longing, that you will do it yourself. We had a charming incident which I always repeat, because it was really charming.

An elderly man came to this group. It was, I think, two years ago. One of our girls happened to sit near him. It was on Friday. On Friday, I am very busy because we have about sixty people here, so I have no time. I was spinning like a top. And this man was sitting in the corner and she happened to sit near him. So he said: "Is this old lady teaching?" She said, "No."

"Is she lecturing?"

She said, "No."

"Well, does she give us practices?"

"No, not at all."

He said, "So, what are we supposed to do?" And she said, "You have to do everything yourself."

The poor man never came again.

How to do it yourself—actually a tremendous inner help is given. The human being is guided from within. How that happens—it's very esoteric, it's very long to explain. But it happens.

STUDENT: God works within you as you.

MRS. TWEEDIE: Yes. That is correct. And also you see we are meeting in the night when we are free. Here lies the great secret of this particular path of yoga. You see, just now I didn't want to tell you that. And this very moment I received instructions saying, "Say," so I am telling you that. I hesitated, waiting for instructions. We meet in the night. A Sufi says, the king is not in his palace, the prisoner is not in his cell. When the soul is free, we go where we are attracted. By desiring something we create a vacuum. Look how here again the law of nature works and how incarnation and karma can be explained. When you take out air, air will flow in. When you take out water, water will flow in. When you create a desire, the desire has to be fulfilled somewhere, sometime. We scatter ourselves in millions of desires. From morning till evening we have desires, desires, desires. If we analyze ourselves and know how to control the mind, we constantly are full of desires. Now if we have only one desire for Truth, we are omnipotent. And the time comes when you have to be careful what you think because it becomes.

It's frightening. So when before you go to sleep you desire to be there where the teacher is, you will be there.

STUDENT: Would it be advisable to read some books such as you were studying, Theosophical books?

MRS. TWEEDIE: I quote Bhai Sahib. He said, "Before you Realize, books are useless, because the more the mind is stocked with knowledge, the less it is inclined to surrender." After Realization books are very useful; they make you more articulate. If you wish to read something, well, do. It is a free path. People come here, and they go also to other schools. I know where they are going, but I will never ask and they will never say. And I frankly don't care. They can do what they like, provided they do meditation at least some time. And also, you see, apparently it is very free, but it is not quite. If I see that the human being is not progressing, they are asked to go; and above all if they don't live the ethics of this path—the ethics are tremendous. Do you know that if I have chairs, and I personally do not need chairs, I am stealing. If I am eating more than I need, I am stealing. No use telling me, "Oh, look, if you don't eat it, just throw it away—throw it away!" There are hungry cats, hungry dogs, or worms who need to be fed.

One day a young man, a journalist, came from Radio Delhi. He asked Guruji a few questions. And he asked him about *ahimsa*, which is harmlessness. Guruji said, "*Ahimsa* is not really 'not killing,' not only 'not killing;' not killing is only on the fringe of *ahimsa*. It's not so very important. The real *ahimsa* is not harming yourself." So that young man said to him, "Gurumaharaj, how is that possible? I would not be such an idiot as to harm myself." And he said, "Oh, yes, you do it, constantly, by creating habits. If you create a habit, you are harming yourself because you put yourself in prison."

If you say, "I cannot be without tea," or, "I couldn't go without a cigarette," I could put myself into prison. You are not free any more. That is real *ahimsa*, real harmlessness. Not to return a library book in time—we are stealing. You know, to live the ethics part of this path of yoga is very difficult. So some human beings when they do something which is quite unethical, they are asked to leave. Otherwise, it is all right. We all are human and who is perfect? Who should throw the first stone? There is another thing, though—once you are with a teacher, once one has to face oneself, and realize how much darkness is within, one cannot judge anybody any more. One just cannot. Each time one thinks, "Oh well, I did the same or even a little bit worse than this human being." One just tries to help; that's all.

And then, there is this question of getting rid of the ego. This is again a very interesting point. One cannot get rid of the ego. One can only keep it in check and use it. Because what is the ego? It is the "I," the "me" in the center of the mental body; "me" different from "you." Only in the state of deep meditation does that disappear, but we are not intended to pass our lives in an unconscious state. That's quite impossible. There is universal consciousness, but not individual consciousness. So one doesn't get rid of the ego—one knows it is there, and one uses it according to one's will. It's actually very creative. If you know how to use it, it's a tremendous power. Also the darkness in us, our ego's "shadow," as Carl Jung called it, is tremendously creative. There comes a time when one is never really angry, but you can be terribly angry; you take your ego and sweep it around. But really and truly in your heart there can be no real anger anymore.

STUDENT: Is it because you feel each and every heart, in each and everybody; and each and everything is just the same?

MRS. TWEEDIE: If I hurt you, I hurt myself.

STUDENT: Thank you.

MRS. TWEEDIE: Thank you . . . I think I've talked enough.

BEKTASHI BREATHS

Avidye Koca, or Avidye Ana-Baci,[1] a Bektashi "mother" of Turkey, passed on to the other world in 1997. Centered in Istanbul with her husband, Turgut Baba, Avidye Ana supported the Bektashi method of training and the sharing of the abundant *sofrat* (Bektashi table and generosity) for many years. An amply radiant presence, she taught in public by being and behavior more than by words, and in private was a strong mother figure for her community. A favorite Bektashi expression is *Ashq olsun!* ("May it be love!"); Avidye Ana was a generous expression of this love.

The sharing of the Bektashi *nefes*, sacred hymns (*ilahilers*), which have gained wide popularity was dear to her heart, and she was inspired to compose several *nefes* herself. The word *nefes* also means "breaths"; moment by moment, one breathes, one remembers one's connection to one's Sustainer, and one opens to the influx of Divine Inspiration and Sustenance. The following selections are translations from the Turkish of two of her *nefes*—"Unfolding Light" and "I Rubbed My Face upon Your Feet"—and a third, "Today I Reached My Pir," composed by Emine Beyza, a Bektashi sister of the Topkapi Dergah of the Istanbul Bektashi community.

A principal teaching tool of the Bektashi community, the *nefes* also provide healing for hearts. For further study of this manner of instruction, one might consult an excellent work on the topic by Frances Trix, *Spiritual Discourse: Learning with an Islamic Master*. A student of an Albanian Bektashi Baba in Michigan for over twenty years, Professor Trix carefully describes in linguistic and anthropological terms her experience of the manner in which her Bektashi master taught her through the study of the *nefes*, while sharing the delicacies of *sohbet* (spiritual conversation). She demonstrates how the learning takes place through listening and careful attention to the master-student relationship:

1. In the Bektashi order, elders or "teachers" are referred to as "Baba" and "Ana" ("father" and "mother") rather than *sheikh* or *sheikha*. *Baci* means "sister."

In the Bektashi world of discourse, that is, in parables, and narratives, poetry and prayers, in the rituals and in talk at the tekke, the centrality of the relationship with the *murshid* [master or teacher] is the norm. . . . [The students] are traditionally known as *talib* (a word derived from Arabic meaning "one who seeks, who strives after"). . . . Each *murshid* is a *talib* of his own *murshid.*

Indeed there is an unbroken chain of *talibs* and *murshids* through which Bektashis connect themselves to their Pir, their "patron saint," Hajji Bektash Veli.[2] (This chain continues back from Hajji Bektash Veli to Ali, whose *murshid* was the Prophet Muhammad, whose *murshid* was the angel Gabriel, and thus back to God. One way this understanding is expressed is in *devriye* or "cycle poems." In these poems, the presence of Hajji Bektash is described at the initial creation of the world, with the prophets, with the imams, up into the ritual conducted by a living *murshid* in the private ceremonial room of a Bektashi tekke.

Building on this continuity, Bektashis come into relation with God through devotion and obedience to their personal *murshid.* This is expressed in their characteristic poetic form, the *nefes* or "breath of spirit," of which the cycle poems are only one sort. *Nefes* are most commonly chanted around a meal table after a ritual in the ceremonial room. In *nefes* the feelings and devotion toward one's particular *murshid* are endlessly evoked and elaborated. The *nefes* can thus be seen as a particular Bektashi language of the *murshid-talib* relationship.[3]

2. Hajji Bektash Veli (d. 1337) was born in Nishapur in what is now Iran. His *murshid* (spiritual guide) was Lokman Perende, whose *murshid* was Ahmet Yesevi (d. 1166), one of the renowned "Masters of Wisdom" of Central Asia. Hajji Bektash journeyed from Khorasan across Iran into Anatolia; it was here, in what is now Turkey, that the Bektashi order began. Hajji Bektash's mother, Hatem Hatun, who was the daughter of a spiritual teacher, Sheikh Ahmet, inspired him with her gracious compassion, as did his father with his love for social equality and justice. Both of these qualities blended in the inspiration that Hajji Bektash later shared. From its inception, women were included equally with men in all aspects of the functioning of the order.

Two centuries later, Bektashi leaders accompanied the Ottoman army westward into the Balkans as far as Albania, where many tekkes were subsequently established. In 1954, the Bektashi Baba Rexheb, under political pressure from the communists, was forced to leave his native Albania and along with other Albanian immigrants came to Michigan, where he opened the first American Bektashi tekke. It was here that Frances Trix came to learn from her master. (C.A.H.)

3. Francis Trix, *Spiritual Discourse*, pp. 8–9.

Unfolding Light

Light unfolded; the soul rejoiced;
We've committed ourselves to this spiritual path.
Our dergah[4] is flooded with Light,
and hand in hand we reach for the Truth.

We met with our honeyed Sultan;
with the young mother we conversed face to face.
Like Farhad[5] we crossed rugged mountains—
we are journeying towards Union.[6]

So annihilated have I become,
to "myself" I cannot return;
I recognize none but Muhammad and 'Ali.
I drank from the Source, and swear I'll never die;
the secret of "Die before you die" became our death.

I am a Turkish daughter, Avidye Baji.
The Turkish elders of surrender are my crown.
My heroic race is the strength of my power;
our master is Sultan Haji Bektash Veli.

I Rubbed My Face upon Your Feet

I rubbed (brushed) my face upon your feet
out of love for the Pir Haji Bektash.

The *nefes* are excerpted from pp. 132–133 and 85–86 of *Gul Deste, Nefesler, Ezgiler, Notalar*, edited by Turgut Koca and Zeki Onaran (Ankara, 1987); translated by Fusun Charles and Ayhan Ozer, Nüket Kardam, and Camille Helminski; and published with special permission from Avidye Ana and Turgut Koca, may peace be with them.

Excerpts from *Spiritual Discourse: Learning with an Islamic Master*, by Frances Trix, ©1993 University of Pennsylvania Press, are reprinted by permission.

4. *Dergah*: Sufi center or *tekke*; also has the meaning of "caravan." (C.A.H.)

5. Farhad, the valiant lover of Shirin, is one of the renowned star-crossed lovers of Indo-Pakistani love poetry. Similar to Layla and Majnun, these lovers came to represent the various aspects of love. Farhad is often symbolic of the staunch and bravely persistent soul. (See Annemarie Schimmel, *As Through a Veil*, p. 75.)

6. *Tawhid.*

It opened my soul and my eyes,
for the love of the Light of Haji Bektash.

We've renounced everything but love of God.
We've made our ablutions;[7]
we prayed at my funeral
for the love of marvelous Haji Bektash.

I attained the domain of Truth,
and I held the hand and hem of the Murshid;
wealth and possessions I've renounced
for the love of brave Haji Bektash.

O exalted guardian,
you hold a poor one by the hand.
My sword-belt[8] they tied to my waist
for the love of the light of Haji Bektash.

The circle of friends came together;
love filled our hearts.
The Garden came within my sight
for the love of the secret[9] of Haji Bektash.

Avidye Baji is my banner;
I'm happy being Turkish.
Turkish ethics I follow
for the love of one Haji Bektash.

Today, I Reached My Pir

Today, I reached my Pir;
I received his blessed grace;

7. Ablution is the ritual washing (of the hands, mouth, nose, face, and forearms, followed by the wiping of the head, ears, and back of the neck and the washing of the feet) that precedes prayer. Sometimes a full ablution of the whole body is required. Ablution is broken by a number of things, in particular by bodily eliminations and sleep. Whenever one's ablution is broken, one renews it as soon as possible so that one might always be ready for prayer. Indeed the faithful strive to be continuously in a state of ablution.

8. *Tigbend*, the sword-belt worn by a warrior, is symbolic of the vigilance and bravery required on the journey of return toward God. The same term is used for the rope underbelt that ties the skirt around the waist of a Mevlevi whirling dervish. Sometimes stones were tucked under the rope, pressed against the stomach to assuage the pangs of hunger from fasting, as was the custom of the Prophet Muhammad.

9. Secret: *sir*, the essence of a human being.

in the ocean of love I drowned.
Benevolence is from you, my master 'Ali.
Come, Blessed Sultan Bektash;
the generosity of God is like Kawthar,[10] O 'Ali!

My head is bound to Muhammad;
all my efforts end with 'Ali;
the twelve imams are my companions on the way;
benevolence is from you, my master 'Ali.

Come, Blessed Sultan Bektash.
The generosity of God is like Kawthar, O 'Ali!

Holy Khadija, Fatima,
don't abandon the humble ones.
Don't pay attention to my wretched rebellion;
generosity is from you, my master 'Ali.

Come, Blessed Sultan Bektash!
The generosity of God is like Kawthar, O 'Ali!

From the hand of the Pir I quenched my thirst;
willingly, I let go of life.
I set out on the journey
following those who attained Divine Truth.
Benevolence is from you, my master 'Ali.

Come, Blessed Sultan Bektash.
The generosity of God is like Kawthar, O 'Ali!

The path of those who attained Truth is one.
A bright saint is my teacher.
Moses climbed Mount Tur;[11]
benevolence is from you, my master, 'Ali.

My master is the greatest of the great;
Emine is one of his servants.
From Kawthar grant us abundance;
benevolence is from you, my master 'Ali.

Come, Blessed Sultan Bektash.
The generosity of God is like Kawthar, O 'Ali.

10. Kawthar is the overflowing spring of Paradise, a symbol of unending abundance.

11. Mount Tur is Mount Sinai, which Moses climbed to meet with God and where he received the Ten Commandments.

A ROSE GARDEN OF LOVE

NEZIHE ARAZ grew up in the Sea of Sufism, learning to swim in that sea at an early age. She was raised in a family with both Mevlevi and Rifa'i bonds and inspiration. She was friends with and frequented the circle of Samiha Ayverdi, the Rifa'i Shaykha (see the final chapter of this book). She was also close friends with the former Çelebi, Celaleddin Bakir Çelebi, of the Mevlevi order and his family. Nezihe has become one of the spiritual and literary elders of Turkey. She is the author of numerous books, including *Bin Bir Gun*, the story of Latife Hanim, the wife of Ataturk, who was the founder of the Turkish Republic, and the well-known *Anadolu Evliyalari* (Saints of Anatolia), in which she tells the stories of many holy ones of that region.

The translator of Nezihe's words, Nüket Kardam, was born in Turkey in 1951 and was educated at Robert College and Istanbul University's Department of Philosophy. She has been living in the United States since 1980, continuing higher education in international relations and political science. Professor Kardam has written and taught courses on gender equality and women's rights in developing countries. She currently teaches at the Monterey Institute of International Studies in California, and consults with international organizations on gender-related issues. She is a follower of the Melamati spiritual path.

You Have to Love People

There is a beautiful small garden shaded by roses in the grounds of the Altay Dergah in Istanbul. In this garden rests Hatice Cenan Sultan.[1] This

❧ This selection is excerpted from *Anadolu Evliyalari,* by Nezihe Araz (Istanbul: Atlas Kitabevi, 1978), pp. 451–77. Translation by Nüket Kardam, printed with permission of Nezihe Araz and Nüket Kardam.

1. Hatice is the Turkish spelling for Khadija, wife of the Prophet Muhammad. Hatice Cenan Sultan lived in Turkey in the nineteenth century.

garden is like a paradise on earth adorned by many different flowers and aromas. Visitors to this garden are struck by its beauty, and they come in continuous streams to pray and ask for answers to their troubles: sometimes a beautiful crib cover is left, symbolizing prayers for a newborn, sometimes a shirt belonging to a sick man. . . .

I know it will be difficult to tell you about this woman saint (*evliya*); you already know her name, but what meaning is there in that? There are many Hatices who have passed through this world before her, and there will be many more after her. But she was different. The river of time left a woman, silent, full of humility and clarity, sincere and ready to surrender everything, on the shores of the earth. She brought beauty, truth, love, and *iman* (deep faith) to this world; she followed the footsteps of truth, taught all she knew, spoke with patience, and shared her maturity and beauty with all.

We don't know where Hatice Cenan Hanim was born or into what family. But we do know that she was brought from the Caucasus Mountains and was the daughter of a *bey*.[2] She never talked much about her life in the Caucasus, maybe because she knew she would never return to the paradise of her childhood, or maybe because she preferred to keep memories of her childhood with her parents and birthplace to herself. But those who knew her could tell where she was from, by looking at her beautiful face and her tall and thin body and lovely hands, as many girls from that area had similar traits.

We first come to know Hatice Hanim in Filibe, as the bride of a well-known family. She is very young, reflects deeply, but speaks little. Her husband fell in love with her beauty, but he could never uncover her secrets; there was always a distance between them. One day the couple came to know that they were expecting a child. The prospective father rejected the child and did not want to see it born. But for Hatice Hanim this would be a fate worse than death! She knew within her heart that nothing could separate her from the baby growing within her. Thus, she accepted every manner that her husband suggested to abort the child, but no attempt was successful.

One night, her husband dreams that the child is born in the shape of a huge, divine tree which grows branches that extend over all the world. Trembling, he awakens his wife and says: "I give up! Let's have this child: I saw a tree, a divine tree, whose branches were embracing the sky; and this tree had grown out of our child's body!"

2. A *bey* is a nobleman from the Caucasus region.

You Have to Love People

Hatice Cenan Hanim felt her first great love towards her son. She called him "Kenko." From the time Kenko was a baby, Hatice Hanim wanted to convey one important truth to him: "You must love people. You have inside you an unlimited wealth of forgiveness, tolerance, and compassion. You must spend this wealth with generosity. You must share it with people and love them with their strengths and their weaknesses. Your job is to turn people towards a common goal, the goal of sincerity. There are many ways to reach this goal, but the easiest one is the way of love and iman. This has long been the way of salvation for humanity. Taking this road, human beings become divine, and reach Allah!"

It seemed as if Hatice Hanim had an invisible teacher. For her there were no unknowns; the wealth of the Unmanifested filled her heart and resolved her every question. When she was alone in the evenings, she waited for this invisible teacher whose presence she always felt, and thought that she might see him/her at any given moment. Meanwhile, she never revealed her inner world; to her husband she was a woman who spoke little, and she was distant to other people, but loved her child.

There were handwritten books in the living room of her Filibe home. While her son, Kenko, played with his cat, she would open one of these books and lose herself in it. These books were the *divans*[3] of Fuzuli, Yunus, and Niyazi. She read this particular verse many times:

> *Sem-i gor ki yanmandan yandirmadi pervaneyi*
> See how Shemsi Tebrizi[4] had to burn himself first
> in order to let the moth be burnt.

She thought that if she is burning, then there is someone making her burn. One day, she learned who that was.

There was a house across from hers in Filibe, and in it lived a young woman with several children. When she came to visit, Hatice Cenan Hanim was no longer herself! This woman's children were also very different from other children. Hatice Hanim resolved to ask her many questions when she visited the next time, but all they could do was to sit together and smile at each other.

3. A *divan* is a collection of poems with a particular meter and rhyme scheme. Many of the great Sufi mystics composed *divans*; the poets mentioned are a few of them: Fuzuli (sixteenth century, Persian), Yunus Emre (thirteenth century, Turkish), and Niyazi Misri (seventeenth century, Turkish).

4. Shemsi Tebrezi (Shams of Tabriz): see note 3 of "Mevlevi Women," page 118.

One day, the children were playing and the two friends were knitting. Hatice Hanim said: "You and I share the same fate!" Her friend couldn't tell what she meant but smiled, while Hatice Hanim was surprised at her own words. What kind of fate could she be sharing with this woman? There was no visible reason to say such a thing, but still a voice inside her was repeating:

Sem-i gor ki yanmadan yandirmadi pervaneyi.

Hatice Hanim's guest took her leave, saying that her husband was going to be coming home soon.

Seyhimin Seyhi Tutuncu Guzeli[5]

Hatice Cenan Hanim awoke that morning with a different feeling, a different kind of enthusiasm. She didn't yet know what life was going to offer her. As she sat on her sofa and started to knit, she saw that her neighbor's husband had indeed come home. His back was turned towards her as he hugged his children and spoke with his wife. It was a perfectly normal scene, but all of a sudden, Hatice Hanim felt like she was going to faint; her face grew pale, and she felt weak. Kenko cried: "What has happened, mother? What's wrong?" She came to herself as her son grabbed onto her skirt, but her wish was that she might not have awakened.

She found out later that this man was called "Tutuncu Guzeli" and that all Filibe women waited for his return from his trips, and that those who see his face feel like they have drunk the water of life and will never die. Hatice Hanim asked herself: "Did I see him? Who saw him?" But she realized that she, also, kept waiting for his return; when she saw him it seemed as if she were in paradise, and when he disappeared, it was like the darkness of hell!

But Hatice Hanim was no longer able to visit with her friend, the wife of the "Tutuncu Guzeli," and was feeling bewildered°. One day her friend came to Hatice Hanim's home to have a cup of coffee with her, and seemed a bit worried. She invited Hatice Hanim to lunch at her home on the following Thursday. How could Hatice Hanim say no to such an invitation? She began to wait for Thursday to arrive, but her friend had a problem: she had invited Hatice Hanim to lunch, but all she had to offer her

5. The Shaykh of *shaykhs*, the beautiful one. "Tutuncu" was the *shaykh*'s family name; *tutuncu* means the "tobacco-seller." (C.A.H.)

was some dried beans. Etham Efendi, her husband, had instructed her to offer just beans, and he, in fact, was the one telling her to invite Hatice Hanim to lunch. His wife knew there must be a reason in what her husband did, but still she worried about how her guest would respond.

Hatice Hanim arrived and sat at the table and saw the beans and knew that some important dialogue was about to take place. The meal of the two women was eaten in silence. Then they sat by the window. Just at that moment, Ethem Efendi passed by the window. Hatice Hanim again became weak in the same way that she had the first time she saw him; she became lost in a world of beauty. And this time there was no Kenko to bring her back to this world! Much later she recovered and awoke and found the wife waiting with a compassionate smile: "Would you like some water?" It was as if she were saying: "I know and I understand; that is exactly what happened to me."

Hatice Hanim's world changed from that moment on. What she had awaited had arrived, but this also meant that a long, difficult journey had begun.

See So That You Can Know

Zehra Hanim, Ethem Efendi's wife, died; just before her death she asked Hatice Hanim to become her four children's godmother. The latter took the three-year-old Nuriye to live with her and helped Ethem Efendi to remarry. Nuriye became Hatice Hanim's student (*murid*). Hatice Hanim never answered her student's questions directly, and when she met with persistence just answered: "See so that you can know!" Hatice Hanim knew that Nuriye was a student who would grow and give fruit; therefore, she did not hurry or worry.

Hatice Cenan Hanim was now very happy: she had met two of her loved ones—Nuriye and her father; their lives became intertwined and enwrapped with hers. Her love lived within her heart and belonged to her; nothing could cast a shadow on this love. Meanwhile, Ethem Efendi leaves from time to time, but nobody knows where he is or what he is seeking. Even if they asked him, perhaps he would not have an answer. All of the Balkan mountains have seen and loved the beautiful face of this man who brought tidings from eternity. One day, Osman Efendi, a friend and colleague of his, witnesses an amazing incident: Ethem Efendi disappears from his sight while Ethem Efendi is sitting, reading a book right in front of Osman Efendi's eyes. Osman Efendi gets up and walks to the chair, and feels the warmth of the pillow Etham Efendi was just sitting on! But Ethem

Efendi is nowhere to be seen! Some people are clearly beyond the limits of space and time.

Ethem Efendi was the kind of man who was content being alone; he carried Allah's trust[6] within him. Whenever he would come in contact with someone, the trust would be enlivened in its owner, and his or her weight would be lifted. It is impossible not to find a similarity between Etham Efendi and Shemseddin of Tebriz.

Ethem Efendi's daughter Nuriye is yet young, but already she can see the future. One day she awakens shivering, when she is sleeping in her father's room. The moon is illuminating the room where they are sleeping. She sees an apparition jumping through the wall in front of her and cries: "Father, there is a thief in the house!" Ethem Efendi puts his finger to his lips as if to say: "Don't say anything!" While the little girl was shivering, the apparition spoke to Ethem Efendi, and he answered: "Of course, whatever is God's will."

This is the night when Ethem Efendi took his leave from Hatice Cenan Hanim. After that, nobody saw him again. Hatice Hanim knew the day he died as if she had died herself; in the same moment, her son came to her, and spoke with her about the work his teacher had given him, and asked for his mother's prayers so that his work might be accomplished with ease.

A Friendship That Doesn't End with Death

For Hatice Hanim, her teacher's departure from this world was not an end but a beginning. Every day she yearned for him; sometimes she would find him in front of her, and they would talk together for a long time. She had completely dissolved herself in him, so that sometimes she would cry: "You are closer to me than my jugular vein; then why am I looking for you outside and yearning for you so?"

When she was alone with her son, the only topic of conversation was their teacher. Little Kenko, her son, was now grown up and worked as a high-level bureaucrat. Still, the work given to him by his teacher was a very difficult one that few were able to engage in. Nevertheless, he did not give up. He was always the little child next to his mother, and during their conversations, sometimes he would begin relating a joke or a short story about their teacher to lighten the atmosphere. The young student sometimes grew tired of his own indulgences, when he worked with his teacher,

6. Trust: *emanet*. Our souls are entrusted to us for safekeeping. We come from God, and we return to God. Tutuncu Guzeli would awaken his murids to this awareness.

Ethem Efendi. He would ask his teacher: "When am I ever going to mature?" Then his teacher used to say: "Here, take this *ney*[7] and blow a little bit." His *ney* competed with the *ezan* [the call to prayer] and revived the tired group of dervishes across the street in their dergah. After these reminiscences, Hatice Hanim was still left with a yearning that could not be stilled. She thought about her teacher and sang a song:

> When fall comes, mountains sing a song (*ghazel*).
> The heart cannot receive just any beautiful one (*guzel*).
> Her heart was not in love with just any lover!
> Ethem Efendi was a lover of God.

Little Nuriye had now grown up and become a woman and called Cenan Hanim her mother. Sometimes she cried out: "Mother, I just saw my father right here!" Then, the whole place would be beautifully fragrant. On such a day, the two women kept completely silent; they were afraid that someone might hear their secret! But after a while, Nuriye left for another town with her husband, leaving Hatice Hanim alone. Nuriye moved to Arabia, and there she became pregnant. She wrote to Hatice Hanim and said that she still saw her father in her dreams and that he offered her fruits and plums cooled in snow to relieve the heat.

Her child was born, but soon after, Nuriye's husband died. And so, Nuriye returned with her baby to live in Hatice Hanim's home. There were now a lot of changes in the household. Her brother had married and brought a bride home. Ummu Kenan Dergah was open and Hatice Hanim was busy working with her son at the dergah. Nuriye felt very alone amidst all this activity; one day she cried for her father for a long time; he appeared and said: "Nuriye, don't cry; I am here and I am leaving some money under your pillow!"

Nuriye awoke the next morning and found a piece of gold under her pillow; she ran to Hatice Hanim and showed it to her. The latter turned pale and said: "Nuriye, let me give you five pieces of gold in exchange for that one, since his hands touched it!" Nuriye gave her the piece of gold, but there was something that Hatice Hanim wanted to tell her but couldn't: she knew from where this gold had come. This gold piece had been in her own purse the day before! That meant that her teacher was still with her! That meant that death had not ended their togetherness! She knelt down with a great sense of love and iman.

7. A *ney* is a reed flute. The opening lines of the *Mathnawi* of Mevlana Jalaluddin Rumi are: "Listen to the reed and the tale it tells, how it sings of separation. Ever since they tore me from the reedbed, I have longed to return. . . ."

Rabi'a of the Times!

Love, *iman* (faith), and sincerity! Those words defined Hatice Hanim. She was such a lover that she could see everything on this earth as a manifestation of God, and knew that to love God is only possible by loving people. For her, everything is a matter of love. To whomever she extended a hand of friendship, she extended it as if it was to her teacher; she saw in everything she did and in the people she served, a sign of her teacher. Her name had already become a legend while she was still alive.

Meanwhile, one day, Osman Efendi came to the dergah that Cenan Hanim's son had established. He called for Hatice Hanim: "*Ya Rabiatul Adeviye!* [O Rabi'a 'Adawiyya!] I have come to visit you! You are so beautiful!" They brought him inside and he began crying and telling of how he had seen Ethem Efendi, and how the latter told him to find Hatice Cenan Hanim. He asked to become her student. Osman Efendi himself was a Shaikh, and Hatice Hanim at first said no, but Osman Efendi insisted that she give him her hand.[8] Finally, one day Hatice Hanim agrees and gives one condition: that Osman Efendi start from ground zero and enter into her son's group of dervishes. Osman Efendi agrees and brings all his dervish students with him.

The only person that Hatice Hanim could not make happy was her husband. Perhaps he felt the saintliness of his wife, and knew that he could never "own" her, and felt insufficient. Meanwhile, her son was burning with the desire to go to Medina and be in the presence of the Prophet, but he wanted to make the journey with his mother, rather than alone. Yet, Hatice Hanim's husband was not willing to let her go. Cenan Hanim had an idea. She knew she could never serve her husband as he wanted; she could not give him anything. How could she, since she did not find anything in her that belonged to herself! Her whole self and life was dedicated to the way of God. But she knew she could give her husband a new, young wife. Her husband was now happy, and the mother and son set out on the road to Medina.

They remained in Medina for four years; everyone there treated them with love; everyone knew, before long, that the new visitors were the guests of the Prophet.

8. The phrase "to give hand" is the expression used for the formal establishment of a connection and the giving of support to a student. From the student's side the expression, "to take hand" is used. This linking of hands is a formal expression of the opening of a connection for the conveyance of grace (with the grace of God) from the teacher and the teacher's whole lineage. (C.A.H.)

I Left Myself!

It is not easy to relinquish oneself! To let go of one's own ego interests requires giving up a great deal. Just one example from Hatice Hanim's life: after she was offered the simple meal of just beans at her teacher's house, she began a diet that she kept for the rest of her life; she ate but one cup of food, some yogurt or pudding, each day. In her prayers, she never limited herself to the five customary prayers a day, but everyone around her knew that as long as she breathed, she was continually in prayer.

The mother and son lived in Medina in a house which in order to reach, one had to climb a great many stairs. As soon as they moved in, a white-haired old man came to visit them and offered to bring them their water. He climbed each stair naming one of the names of God with each step, and when he reached the top and saw Hatice Hanim's face full of light, he forgot all his pain and suffering and left in peace, happy and innocent as a child.

Another visitor was a man who had not spoken to anyone for thirty years but was in a constant state of contemplation. One day, he rang their bell and said that he had come there to die. He showed his white beard to Hatice Hanim and asked her to wash it. His beard was washed and after a short while, he began to faint and then died. Hatice Hanim and her son were shocked and began to pray and they continued to pray until he reopened his eyes and said: "After seeing you, I no longer want to die." He smiled and from that point on, came to visit them every night.

These visitors are just two of the many that frequented their house. After four years, they returned to Istanbul, where the work at the Altay Dergah awaited them.

The Invitation from Bursa

One day, Hatice Cenan Hanim came to Bursa with her relatives and friends. The real reason for this visit was only known to her and her son. She came to visit Shefkat Hanim, who was the older daughter of her guide, Ethem Efendi. The first place she wanted to visit was Emir Sultan's tomb. And then, they visited Uftade Hazretleri, Somuncu Baba,[9] and Yesil Turbe.[10] One day Cenan Hanim says: let's go to Muradiye today.

When they enter the tomb of Sultan Murat, Cenan Hanim's grandson asks: "Why is there a cover over his turban?" They call the man who takes

9. Somuncu Baba was a baker and one of the originators of the Melami *tariqa*.

10. The "green tomb," famous for its beautiful turquoise green tile work and calligraphy.

care of the tomb and ask him to remove the cover. What they see is many mice under it! Children begin crying, and the man is now filled with fear! Hatice Hanim slowly goes up beside this man and says: "It is a pity that a sultan's turban has become a home for mice, isn't it?" The man apologized and promised to clean up everything.

When they returned to Istanbul, one of Cenan Hanim's students related: "She went to Bursa for a purpose—she saw Sultan Murat in a dream, and he asked her for her help!"

But it wasn't just Sultan Murat who waited for her in Bursa; there is also a story of her encounter with Yunus Emre. Yunus Emre had been her *dost*[11] since her youth, and Cenan Hanim knew that there was a Yunus *makam*[12] in Bursa but no one knew where it was! One day, she said, "Let's go up this road." All of a sudden, they see a woman on the road, which had been empty, and she asks: "Are you looking for Yunus Emre's grave—go to a door at the end of this road and ring the bell."

They ring the bell; it is the door to a *turbe* [tomb] and an old man opens the door and says: "Please come in, we were expecting you!" He treats Cenan Hanim like royalty and shows her around. When she places a gold coin in his hand, he says he will keep it for the rest of his life.

She Never Wanted Anything for Herself

Hatice Cenan Hanim's most important characteristic was that she did not want anything for herself. Her "self" did not exist for her. She did not tolerate unfairness or anyone who lied or was unthankful. She encouraged anyone who did good deeds and said: "If you give a poor person money, before it drops into his or her hand, it falls into God's hands." But she also added: "Doing good deeds is not your choice, it is a favor from God. Therefore do not boast of your good deeds, but thank God for this favor."

She wanted to be in both thought and deed someone who did not harbor any envy, and she wanted to teach this to her students: "To live for God, in the name of God and for the love of God." That's all she wanted. This great love of hers became so strong, that she could give without taking, and she became the "Rabi'a" of her time. She was such a person that God spoke through her. And so people surrounding her always followed her example, listened to her, and knew she could shed light on their troubles and show them the right way.

11. Friend and guide. The ultimate *dost* is God.

12. *Makam*: "station," the resting place of a saint or a place known to be imbued with the saint's grace. (C.A.H.)

For example, one day, she said: "I feel faint, please bring me a piece of bread." They brought her a piece of bread. Hatice Hanim took it, kissed it, and prayed: "O God, please don't show us the day that we will lack this bread." Those around her were surprised. Nobody thought that they might lack this bread. Why this prayer? The answer became known in a short time when a war began and the whole country was in dire need of food.

Now neither Hatice Cenan Hanim nor her son remain in this world. But those who can look with the eye of the heart say: "Nothing has changed, the time is always the same time. Those are the people who can see beyond the seen, who can see the Unseen!" Yes, Hatice Cenan Hanim has left this world, but do *evliyas* really die? They are all among us, and they are not forgotten, and they have not left us!

Let us now go back to the Altay Dergah! One night, Dede Cemal Efendi is lighting the candles. All preparations are completed; everyone is waiting for the sema to begin. All the dervishes are waiting to commune with the Unseen world. There are not just Moslems, but a whole crowd of those of many different religions who are waiting. During such a night, Hatice Cenan Hanim knew when she was going to leave this world. She started waiting, knowing that all this longing and yearning was about to end. What did Kaygusuz[13] say? "The reason for life is to know oneself." Those who know themselves can then find their *evliya*. But neither is knowing finding nor is finding knowing. But the point is to fall in love with the *evliya* and be painted in his or her color.

In summary, Hatice Cenan Hanim was someone who knew herself, found her *evliya*, and was painted in the colors of God's friend. What were her last words? Always, she said: "Love one another!" Then I imagine that she turned her face towards her *murshid* and repeated: it is you I have loved!

13. A famous Turkish poet.

LET US ASK PERMISSION OF THE MATURE ONES

HACI TAHSINE HANIM EFENDI (d. 1990) was a Rifa'i dervish and a renowned *tanbur* player in Turkey who lived in the Ankara area until she passed from this earth. She composed a number of *ilahiler* (sacred songs), the most beloved of which is the *rast*[1] *ilahi*, "*Erler demine destur alalim*." This is one of the sacred songs that has gained such popularity that it is sung not only by Rifa'i dervishes but also by Mevlevis and others; it seems that everyone who hears it is drawn to share it further. The translation is as follows:

> Let us ask permission of the mature ones;
> Let us learn from the moth.
> Let us burn in the fire of love. Friend, Friend.[2]
> Let's enter the circle and journey.[3]
> Before wailing "oh no," let's say Allah.
> There is no god but God.[4]
> Days and nights endlessly are going by
> Your hopes, that are your capital, are ending.
> Look at the nightingales that are crying,
> Oh rose bud, the season is passing. Friend, Friend.
> O traveler, please listen to me:
> The caravan is passing; don't stay behind.

1. *Rast* is one of the many *makams*, or scales, of Turkish classical music. Each *makam* is evocative of different qualities and affects the nervous system in particular subtle ways. (C.A.H.)

2. God is referred to as the greatest Friend, the one Beloved. (C.A.H.)

3. The Sufi path is referred to as *sayr-i suluk*, the journey. (C.A.H.)

4. *La ilaha il Allah*: There is no god but God, there is no reality but The Reality. This is the Muslim attestation of faith and the foundation of the Sufi principle of *tawhid*, the Unity of all that is.

The beauty the world called Yusuf[5]
conquered the traveling hearts today. Friend, Friend.[6]

Erler Demine

Erler demine destur alalim (2x)
Pervaneye bak ibret alalim (2x)
Aşkin ateşine gel bir yanalim (2x) Dost . . . Dost . . . Dost.

> Deyrana girip seyran edelim,
> Eyvah demeden Allah diyelim . . . La ilahe illallah . . .

❧ This selection is the musical transcription of a song in common usage by Haci Tahsine Hanim Efendi.

5. Yusuf is the prophet Joseph, who was the personification of the attribute of God's overwhelming Beauty. (C.A.H.)

6. Translated with the kind assistance of Nüket Kardam. (C.A.H.)

Gunler geçeler durmaz geçiyor (2x)
Sermayen olan umran bitiyor (2x)
Bulbullere bak efgan ediyor (2x)
Ey Gonca açil mevsim geçiyor (2x) Dost . . . Dost . . . Dost.

Ey yolcu biraz sen dinle beni (2x)
Kervan geçiyor sen kalma geri (2x)
Yusuf denilen dunya guzeli (2x)
Fethetti bugun kalbi seferi (2x) Dost . . . Dost . . . Dost.

SHARING THE TREASURE

SAMIHA AYVERDI (1905–1993), one of the major literary figures of twentieth-century Turkey, was born of Meliha Hanim and Ismail Hakki Bey in Istanbul, in 1905. In her early years, she learned much from her grandmother Halet Hanim, who was a strong role model for her, and also spent many hours listening to her father and his friends engaged in *sohbet* (spiritual conversation). After her standard education, at the age of sixteen she began to train herself in history, philosophy, Sufism, and literature, using her family's personal extensive library as a resource. The shaikh of the Altay Dergah, Kenan Rifaʻi, became her teacher and spiritual guide, and it was upon his encouragement that she became a writer.

Celebrated for her skill in using the Turkish language and her deep understanding of the Turkish culture, Samiha Ayverdi was the author of thirty-five books of both spirituality and cultural and literary stories of her beloved country. Among the most well-known are *Kenan Rifaʻi ve Yirminci Asrin Isiginda Muslumanlik* (Kenan Rifaʻi and Understanding Islam in the Twentieth Century), which she coauthored with three female friends, Safiye Erol, Nezihe Araz, and Sofi Huri; *The Friend* (*Dost*),[1] her account of the teachings of Kinan Rifaʻi (1867–1950); and *Istanbul Nights* (*Istanbul Geceleri*).[2] In Istanbul Geceleri, Samiha relates an account of the Rifaʻi ceremony for investiture as *khalifa* (representative), which Annemarie Schimmel summarizes in her book *Mystical Dimensions of Islam*:

1. Published by Kubbealti Akademi Kultur ve San'at Vakfi, Peykhane Sok. No. 3, Cemberlitas, Istanbul, Turkey in 1995. Portions of the above biographical information and the following selections are excerpted from pages 47, 149–50, 162, 163 of *The Friend*. The Kubbealti Foundation was established by Samiha and her brother and sister-in-law in 1972. It was begun to help ensure the continuation of the Turkish language and culture. Also quite active in social reform, Samiha led the establishment of the Turkish Wives Association in 1966.

2. See the article, "Women in Mystical Islam," by Prof. Schimmel, pp. 101–10 of this text.

> All friends of the order were invited, candles were lit according to a prescribed ritual, recitation of the Qur'an and mystical music alternated, and after the candidate had kissed the sheikh's hand four dervishes held a veil over the two persons so that the master might introduce the khalifa into the secrets of the office. The whole night was spent in recitations, music, and prayer.[3]

For Samiha, the very substance of life was spirituality, and she lived it purely. It was not her intention to be a novelist, storywriter, or historian; for her these were simply a means of communication. In her writing and her teaching she unfolded modern interpretations, expressions, and metaphors from the classical Sufi perspective. On issues related to history, the environment, women, ethics, and education, she never hesitated to ply her pen in an attempt to better the relationship of human being with human being, and human being with his or her Creator.

She tells us: "The human being is not, as supposed by many, some mortal being who was arbitrarily tossed on a part of this universe by accident. In the composition of the universe, the human being has a place and a position determined and designed by the Greatest Will. The human being is the creature who in his or her person represents the whole universe and his or her relationship with the Creator is ongoing."

All her life, Samiha tried to convey the principles she learned from her mentor, Kenan Rifa'i, to the students who loved her. She passed away in 1993 and was laid to rest in the Merkez Efendi cemetery. She is survived by one daughter, two grandchildren, and many lively students who all refer to her as Samiha Anne (Mother Samiha). Professor Schimmel refers to Samiha as "one of the leading mystics in our time,"[4] and dedicated her book *My Soul Is a Woman* to Samiha Ayverdi.

Awakening

The human being and the world are in a sense twins. People sometimes fall ill. Why should that not be true also of the world?

❧ This selection is excerpted from *The Friend* (*Dost*), by Samiha Ayverdi, translated by Ismet Turnturk (Istanbul: Kubbealti Nesriyati, 1980). Reprinted by permission of Kubbealti Nesriyati.

3. Annemarie Schimmel, *Mystical Dimensions of Islam*, p. 236.

4. Annemarie Schimmel, "Sufism and Spiritual Life in Turkey," in Seyyed Hossein Nasr (ed.), *Islamic Spirituality Manifestations*, p. 225.

That is what we have been seeing for a long time. The world is sick in thought and in feelings. Therefore the world is suffering from nightmares. And so is the individual human being because each has committed the blunder of driving away wisdom from his/her life. The body of the human being and his/her soul are no longer in harmony. We have a world in discord, and people who are sick in body and soul.

There are those who diagnose correctly the basic cause of all of this. But diagnosis is not enough. There must also be a cure. And people are as yet unaware of the right cure.

Both the human being and the world are now sunk into a nightmare of thoughtlessness. It is urgently necessary that they wake up from this nightmare.

Who is to awaken the human being? Who is to bring body and soul into harmony? The Friend[5] saw clearly that people have embedded their heads deeply in materialism, and yet are unaware of it. All through his life the Friend tried to awaken people and to bring them to the remedy of Islamic ethics.[6]

For people who can think and eyes that can see, the total union of both the Universe and the human soul is the ultimate coming together to which reliance in God inevitably leads everything. What a pity that lack of proper realization of this truth has led humankind to endless conflict and confusion, like the ceaseless jangling of chains.

All the troubles which afflict the world, all the evils, intrigues, hypocrisies and lies which destroy the spiritual peace and happiness of the human being, can be traced back to people failing to see the basic Oneness of life, and to being blindly and obstinately tied up in various illusions of multiplicity.

When one reaches a full realization of Oneness in faith in God, one finds not only peace and happiness for oneself, but also a spiritual treasure in human values that can be freely and inexhaustibly given to all creatures. However, the human being who has not reached truthful self-discovery and self-appraisal has no spiritual treasures either for him/herself or to give to others. Some heroic natures, born with the capacity to sacrifice themselves for others and for sublime goals, have suffered great pains in life, and have been able to endure such pains and sacrifices through the power they received from their faith in God.

5. Samiha's beloved teacher, Kenan Rifa'i. (C.A.H.)

6. Samiha Ayverdi, *The Friend (Dost)*, p. 47.

Fourteen centuries ago, Islam brought to humanity a unity of faith, in common moral values, in a sublime moral order, and in the spiritual elevation which this created. However, many people diverged from that, entangled their skirts in thorns during the long march, and strayed far afield. From time to time some heroic figures have pierced the enveloping darkness and have tried to make people remember and realize what they have lost. These noble natures, architects of souls, have tried to awaken to nobler goals the masses of people who had abandoned their goals to enemies and to petty purposes. These noble natures often have met with great suffering as a result.[7]

The world is like a wheel that keeps on turning.

It is an insatiable wheel; turning on and on forever; stripping off from people what it gave them; grinding down people as grains of wheat are ground; never being satiated; turning on and on.

It turns on insatiably, mercilessly. . . . Whatever it gave, it wants to take back. Of course it shall. That is the law of nature. Let it do so. Let it take everything away. It is the creditor. We are the debtors.

We are glad to give everything away. For we are under the wing of a great blessing. May God never take that wing from over us, till the end of time![8]

Thanks! Many thanks! There lives a munificent, compassionate Friend in our midst. He might be walking on the earth, or he might be buried underneath, always he guides us and remains ever loyal to us.[9]

We are now in the last stage of our passage through the world. Let each do or say as they see fit. But the voice of the Friend, indifferent to praise or blame, keeps calling all to virtue, faith, and love. Tirelessly. Forever.

Why do we not hear? If we hear the sound of the words, why do we not understand? If we understand, why do we not act accordingly?[10]

7. Ibid., pp. 149–50.

8. Ibid., p. 162.

9. Ibid., p. 163.

10. Ibid., p. 162.

Hand in hand may we go with, and into God.

mother/father—daughter/son,
husband—wife,
sister—brother, teacher—student,
friend and friend,
friend and Friend.

And the hand of God is over their hand.

[Surah Fatih 48:10]

Bibliography

Addas, Claude. *Quest for the Red Sulphur*. Cambridge: Islamic Texts Society, 1993.

Aflaki, Shams ad-Din A. *Manaqib al-'arifin*. Translated from the French translation by Susan Blaylock. Unpublished manuscript. Threshold Society, 1998.

Ahmad, Fazl. *Aisha the Truthful*. Lahore, Pakistan: Sh. Muhammad Ashraf, 1976.

Akili, Muhammad M. Al. *Ibn Seerin's Dictionary of Dreams*. Philadelphia: Pearl Publishing House, 1992.

Alim (Islamic software). CD-ROM. Release 6.0. Silver Spring, Md.: ISL Software Corp., 1999.

Amri, Nelly, and Laroussi Amri. *Les Femmes soufies oú la passion de Dieu*. St. Jean-de-Braye, France: Editions Dangles, 1992.

Andrae, Tor. *In the Garden of Myrtles: Studies in Early Islamic Mysticism*. Translated from the Swedish by Birgitta Sharpe. Albany: State University of New York Press, 1987.

Angha, Nahid. *Principles of Sufism*. Fremont, Calif.: Asian Humanities Press, 1991.

Araz, Nezihe´. *Anadolu Evliyalari*. Translated by Nüket Kardam. Istanbul: Atlas Kitabevi, 1978.

Arberry, A. J. *Muslim Saints and Mystics: Episodes from the Tadhkirat al-Auliya (Memorial of the Saints) by Farid al-Din Attar*. New York: Penguin-Arkana, 1990.

Armstrong, Karen. *Mohammad: A Biography of the Prophet*. San Francisco: HarperSanFrancisco, 1993.

Asad, Muhammad. *The Message of the Qur'an*. Gibraltar: Dar al-Andalus Limited, 1980.

Ayverdi, Samiha. *Istanbul geceleri*. Istanbul: Istanbul Enstitu, 1977.

______. *The Friend* (*Dost*). Translated by Ismet Turnturk. Istanbul: Kubbealti Nesriyati, 1980.

______; Nezihe Araz; Safiye Erol; and Sofi Huri. *Kenan Rifa'i Ve Yirminci Asrin Isiginda Muslumanlik*. Istanbul: Kubbealti Nesriyati, 1951.

Badawi, Muhammad Mustafa. "Islam in Modern Egyptian Literature." *Journal of Arabic Literature* 2 (1971).

Beck, Lois, "The Religious Lives of Muslim Women." In *Women in Contemporary Muslim Societies*, edited by Jane I. Smith. Lewisburg, Pa.: Bucknell University Press, 1980.

———, and Nikki Keddie. *Women in the Muslim World.* Cambridge, Mass.: Harvard University Press, 1978.

Behari, Dr. Bankey. *Fariduddin 'Attar's Tadhkaratul-Auliya or Memoirs of Saints*. Lahore, Pakistan: Sh. Muhammad Ashraf, 1975.

Bewley, Aisha. *Islam: The Empowering of Women.* London: Ta-Ha Publishers, 1999.

Birge, John Kingsley. *The Bektashi Order of Dervishes*. London: Luzac and Co., 1965.

Blaylock, Susan. *Stories of the Mevlevis: A Translation of the* Menaqib al-Arifin *of Attar.* Forthcoming: Threshold Society.

Boyd, Jean. *The Caliph's Sister: Nana Asma'u (1793–1865), Teacher, Poet and Islamic Teacher*. Chippenham, Wiltshire: Antony Rowe Ltd., 1995.

Chants sacres des femmes de Fez. Al Sur/Media 7 ALCD 243/ M7 853, 1998.

Chodkiewicz, Michel. "Female Sainthood in Islam." *Sufi* 21 (1994): London: Khaniqahi Nimatullahi Publications.

Corbin, Henry. *Creative Imagination in the Sufism of Ibn 'Arabi*. Princeton, N.J.: Princeton University Press, 1969.

Corda, Murshida Vera. "First Goals of Sufi Mothers." In *Rustle of Wings* 1, no. 2 (1980). San Jose, Calif.: New Age Sufi Schools.

Cornell, Rkia. *Early Sufi Women (Dhikr an-niswa al-muta 'abbidat as sufiyyat* of Abu abd ar-Rahman as-Sulami). Louisville, Ky.: Fons Vitae, 1999.

Cuneen, Sally. *In Search of Mary, the Woman and the Symbol.* New York: Ballantine Books, 1996.

Darwish, Linda. "Images of Muslim Women: 'A'isha, Fatima, and Zaynab bint 'Ali in Contemporary Gender Discourse." *McGill Journal of Middle East Studies* 93–132.

de Vitray-Meyerovitch, Eva. *Rumi and Sufism*. Translated from the French by Simone Fattal. Sausalito, Calif.: Post-Apollo Press, 1977.

Drewes, G. W. J. *The Admonitions of Seh Bari, a Sixteenth-Century Javanese Muslim Text Attributed to the Saint of Bonan*. The Hague: Martinus Nijhoff, 1969.

Dunn, Ross E. *The Adventures of Ibn Battuta, A Muslim Traveler of the Fourteenth Century*. Berkeley: University of California Press, 1989.

Ernst, Carl W. *Eternal Garden: Mysticism, History, and Politics at a South Asian Sufi Center*. Albany: State University of New York Press, 1992.

———, trans. *Teachings of Sufism.* Boston: Shambhala Publications, 1999.

Fuller, Jean Overton. *Noor-un-nisa Inayat Khan (Madeleine)*. London and the Hague: East-West Publications, 1971.

Glasse, Cyril. *The Concise Encyclopedia of Islam*. San Francisco: Harper SanFrancisco, 1991.

Hammarlund, Tord Olsson, and Elisabeth Ozdalga, eds. *Sufism, Music, and Society in Turkey and the Middle East.* Istanbul: Swedish Research Institute in Turkey, 2001.

Helminski, Camille Adams. *The Light of Dawn: Daily Readings from the Holy Qur'an.* Boston: Shambhala Publications, 2000.

Hibri, Azizah al-. "A Study of Islamic Herstory." *Women's Studies International Forum* 5, no. 2 (1982): 207–19.

Hoffman, Valerie J. *Sufism, Mystics, and Saints in Modern Egypt*. Columbia: University of South Carolina Press, 1995.

Holbrook, Victoria Rowe. "Ibn Arabi and Ottoman Dervish Traditions: The Melami Supra-Order." *Journal of Muhyiddin Ibn 'Arabi Society* 9 (1991).

Ibn al-'Arabi. *Sufis of Andalusia*. Translated by R. W. J. Austin. Oxford: Beshara Publications, 1988.

Ibn Sa'd, Muhammad. *The Women of Madina*. Translated by Aisha Bewley. London: Ta-Ha Publishers, 1995.

Iqbal, Mohammad. *The Virtues of Women*. Brattleboro, Vt.: Amana Books, 1989.

Karaosmanoglu, Yakub Kadri. *Nur Baba*. Istanbul, 1922. German translation by Annemarie Schimmel, under the title *Flamme und Falter* (Gummersbach, 1948).

Khan, Qamaruddin. *Status of Women in Islam*. Islamabad: Islamic Book Foundation, 1988.

Kimbal, Michelle, and Barbara R. von Schlegell. *Muslim Women in the World: A Bibliography, with Selected Annotations*. Boulder, Co.: Lynne Rienner Publishers, 1997.

Koca, Turgut, and Zeki Onaran, eds. *Gul Deste, Nefesler, Ezgiler, Notalar*. Ankara, 1987.

Levitzion, Nehemia, and Randall L. Powells. *The History of Islam in Africa*. Athens: Ohio University Press, 2000.

Lings, Martin. *What Is Sufism?* Berkeley: University of California Press, 1977.

Mack, Beverly B., and Jean Boyd. *One Woman's Jihad*. Bloomington: Indiana University Press, 2000.

Martin, B. G. *Muslim Brotherhoods in Nineteenth-Century Africa*. Cambridge: Cambridge University Press, 1976.

Meier, Fritz. *Abil Safid-i Abul I-Khayr*. Leiden, 1976.

Milani, Farzaneh. *Veils and Words: The Emerging Voices of Iranian Women Writers*. Syracuse, N.Y.: Syracuse University Press, 1992.

Murata, Sachiko. *The Tao of Islam: A Sourcebook on Gender Relationships in Islamic Thought*. Albany: State University of New York Press, 1992.

______, and William Chittick. *The Vision of Islam*. St. Paul, Minn.: Paragon House, 1994.

Nasr, Seyyed Hossein, ed. *Islamic Spirituality Manifestations*. New York: Crossroad Publishing Co., 1997.

______. *Three Muslim Sages*. Delmar, N.Y.: Caravan Books, 1964.

Nimtz, August H., Jr. *Islam and Politics in East Africa: The Sufi Order in Tanzania*. Minneapolis: University of Minnesota Press, 1980.

Nizami. *The Story of Layla and Majnun*. New Lebanon, N.Y.: Omega Publications, 1997.

Nurbakhsh, Dr. Javad. *Sufi Women*. New York: Khaniqahi-Nimatullahi Publications, 1990.

Özelsel, Michaela. *Forty Days: A Diary of a Traditional Solitary Sufi Retreat*. Brattleboro, Vt.: Threshold Books, 1996.

Qushayri, Abu'l-Qasim al-. *Principles of Sufism*. Translated by B. R. von Schlegell. Berkeley, Calif.: Mizan Press, 1990.

Rafea, Ali; Aliaa Rafea; and Aisha Rafea. *Beyond Diversities*. Cairo: Sadek Publishing, 2000.

Rizvi, Saiyid Athar Abbas. *A History of Sufism in India*. Vol. 1. New Delhi: Munshiram Manoharlal Publishers, 1978.

Robson, James. *Mishkat al masabih*. Lahore, Pakistan: Sh. Muhammad Ashraf Publishers, 1991.

Rose, H. A., and John P. Brown. *The Darvishes*. London: Oxford University Press, 1927.

Rumi, Mevlana Jalaluddin. *The Mathnawi*. Translated by R. A. Nicholson. London: Luzac and Company, 1982.

Rumi, Jalaluddin. *Mathnawi-yi ma'nawi,* 8 vols. Edited by A. Nicholson, Reynold. London and Leiden, 1925–1940.

Saad, Sheikh Taha Abdul Rauf, and Hasan Muhammad Ali Saad. *Al sayyidd nafisah nafisat al ilm karimat al daariya*. Cairo: Matabat Safa, 2000.

Sakkakini, Widad El. *First among Sufis: The Life and Thought of Rabi'a al-Adawiyya*. Translated by Dr. Nabil Safwat. London: Octagon Press, 1982.

Schimmel, Annemarie. *As Through a Veil: Mystical Poetry in Islam*. New York: Columbia University Press, 1982.

———. *Mystical Dimensions of Islam*. Chapel Hill: University of North Carolina Press, 1975.

———. *My Soul Is a Woman: The Feminine in Islam*. New York: Continuum, 1999.

———. "Samiha Ayverdi": Eine Istanbuller Schriftstellerin." In *Festschrift für Otto Spies,* edited by Wilhelm Hoenerbach. Wiesbaden, 1967.

———. "Women in Mystical Islam." *Women's Studies International Forum* 5 (1982): 145–51.

———. "Sufism and Spiritual Life in Turkey." In *Islamic Spirituality, Manifestations,* edited by Seyyed Hossein Nasr. New York: Crossroad Publishing Co., 1997.

———. *The Triumphal Sun: A Study of the Work of Jalaluddin Rumi*. London and the Hague: East-West Publications, 1978.

Seguy, Marie-Rose. *The Miraculous Journey of Mahomet: Miraj Nameh*. New York: George Braziller, 1977.

Sells, Michael. *Early Islamic Mysticism*. New York: Paulist Press, 1996.

Siddiqi, Muhammad Saeed. *The Blessed Women of Islam*. Lahore, Pakistan: Kazi Publications, 1982.

Smith, Margaret. *Rabi'a the Mystic and Her Fellow-Saints in Islam*. Cambridge: Cambridge University Press, 1928. San Francisco: Rainbow Bridge, 1977.

Stowasser, Barbara Freyer. *Women in the Qur'an: Traditions, and Interpretation*. New York: Oxford University Press, 1994.

Sufi Women Organization. *Sufi Women: The Journey towards the Beloved.* Vol. 1. San Rafael, Calif.: International Association of Sufism, 1998.

Sulami, Ibn al-Husayn al-. *The Book of Sufi Chivalry*. New York: Inner Traditions International, 1983.

Sviri, Sara. *The Taste of Hidden Things: Images on the Sufi Path*. Inverness, Calif.: Golden Sufi Center Publishing, 1997.

Trimingham, J. Spencer. *The Sufi Orders in Islam*. New York: Oxford University Press, 1998.

Trix, Frances. *Spiritual Discourse: Learning with an Islamic Master*. Philadelphia: University of Pennsylvania Press, 1993.

Tweedie, Irina. *Daughter of Fire*. Nevada City, Calif.: Blue Dolphin Press, 1986.

'Umari, Akram Diya' al-. *Madinan Society at the Time of the Prophet*. Translated by Huda Khattab. Herndon, Va.: International Institute of Islamic Thought, 1995.

Upton, Charles. *Doorkeeper of the Heart: Versions of Rabi'a*. Putney, Vt.: Threshold Books, 1988.

Vaswani, T. L. *Friends of God*. Poona, India: Gita Publishing House, 1971.

Vikor, Knut V. "Sufi Brotherhoods in Africa." In *The History of Islam in Africa*, edited by Nehemia Levitzion and Randall L. Powell. Athens: Ohio University Press, 2000.

Waddy, Dr. Charis. *The Muslim Mind*. London: Grosvenor Books, 1990.

Wadud, Amina. *Qur'an and Woman*. New York: Oxford University Press, 1999.

Walther, Wiebke. *Women in Islam*. Princeton, N.J.: Markus Weiner Publishing , 1993.

Waugh, Earle H. *The Munshidin of Egypt: Their World and Their Song*. Columbia: University of South Carolina Press, 1989.

Woodward, Mark R. *Islam in Java: Normative Piety and Mysticism in the Sultanate of Yogyakarta*. Tucson: University of Arizona Press, 1989.

Zein ed-Din, Nazirah. "Removing the Veil and Veiling." *Women's Studies International Forum* 5, no. 2 (1982): 221–26. Oxford: Pergamon Press, 1982.